More Praise for CHIP WAR

"One of the most important books I've read in years—engrossing, beautifully written. Miller shows that, for all its manifest flaws and failures, the American capitalist system has repeatedly outperformed other systems and in the process has done much to bolster the security of democracy."

> —Robert Kagan, senior fellow, The Brookings Institution,
> columnist for *The Washington Post*, and author of
> *The Jungle Grows Back: America and Our Imperiled World*

"If you care about technology, or America's future prosperity, or its continuing security, this is a book you have to read."

> —Lawrence H. Summers, 71st U.S. Secretary of the Treasury and
> Charles W. Eliot University Professor at Harvard University

"Outstanding. Miller's history of the chip covers all angles: technological, financial, and especially political. . . . The go-to reference on one of the most important industries today."

> —Dan Wang, technology analyst at Gavekal Dragonomics

"The battle for supremacy in semiconductors is one of the most important stories in geopolitics, national security, and economic prosperity. But it's also been one of the least well understood. Thankfully, we now have *Chip War* to give us a clear view and sharp read on this essential subject."

> —Andrew McAfee, coauthor of *The Second Machine Age*
> and author of *The Geek Way* and *More from Less*

CHIP WAR

THE FIGHT FOR THE WORLD'S MOST CRITICAL TECHNOLOGY

CHRIS MILLER

SCRIBNER

NEW YORK   LONDON   TORONTO   SYDNEY   NEW DELHI

Scribner
An Imprint of Simon & Schuster, Inc.
1230 Avenue of the Americas
New York, NY 10020

First Scribner hardcover edition October 2022

SCRIBNER and design are registered trademarks of The Gale Group, Inc.,
used under license by Simon & Schuster, Inc., the publisher of this work.

For information about special discounts for bulk purchases,
please contact Simon & Schuster Special Sales at 1-866-506-1949
or business@simonandschuster.com.

The Simon & Schuster Speakers Bureau can bring authors to
your live event. For more information or to book an event,
contact the Simon & Schuster Speakers Bureau at 1-866-248-3049
or visit our website at www.simonspeakers.com.

Interior design by Kyle Kabel

Manufactured in the United States of America

1   3   5   7   9   10   8   6   4   2

Library of Congress Cataloging-in-Publication Data has been applied for.

ISBN 978-1-9821-7200-8
ISBN 978-1-9821-7202-2 (ebook)

To Liya

Contents

PART V INTEGRATED CIRCUITS, INTEGRATED WORLD?

PART VI OFFSHORING INNOVATION?

PART VII CHINA'S CHALLENGE

PART VIII THE CHIP CHOKE

Cast of Characters

Morris Chang: Founder of Taiwan Semiconductor Manufacturing Company (TSMC), the world's most important chipmaker; previously, a senior executive at Texas Instruments.

Andy Grove: Former president and CEO of Intel during the 1980s and 1990s; notorious for his aggressive style and success in reviving Intel; author of *Only the Paranoid Survive*.

Pat Haggerty: Chairman of Texas Instruments; led the company as it specialized in building microelectronics, including for the U.S. military.

Jack Kilby: Co-inventor of the integrated circuit, in 1958; longtime Texas Instruments employee; winner of the Nobel Prize.

Jay Lathrop: Co-inventor of photolithography, the process of patterning transistors using specialized chemicals and light; formerly of Texas Instruments.

Carver Mead: Professor at the California Institute of Technology (Caltech); advisor to Fairchild Semiconductor and Intel; visionary thinker about the future of technology.

Gordon Moore: Cofounder of Fairchild Semiconductor and Intel; creator in 1965 of "Moore's Law," which predicted that the computing power on each chip would double every couple of years.

Akio Morita: Cofounder of Sony; coauthor of *The Japan That Can Say No*; represented Japanese business on the world stage during the 1970s and 1980s.

Robert Noyce: Cofounder of Fairchild Semiconductor and Intel; co-inventor of the integrated circuit in 1959; known as the "Mayor of Silicon Valley"; first leader of Sematech.

William Perry: Pentagon official from 1977–1981 and later Secretary of Defense from 1994 to 1997 who advocated using chips to produce precision-strike weapons.

Jerry Sanders: Founder and CEO of AMD; Silicon Valley's most flamboyant salesman; an aggressive critic of what he saw as unfair Japanese trade practices in the 1980s.

Charlie Sporck: Drove the offshoring of chip assembly while leading manufacturing operations at Fairchild Semiconductor; later CEO of National Semiconductor.

Ren Zhengfei: Founder of Huawei, China's telecom and chip-design giant; his daughter Meng Wanzhou was arrested in Canada in 2018 on charges of violating U.S. law and trying to evade U.S. sanctions.

Glossary

Arm: a UK company that licenses to chip designers use of an instruction set architecture—a set of basic rules governing how a given chip operates. The Arm architecture is dominant in mobile devices and is slowly winning market share in PCs and data centers.

Chip (also "integrated circuit" or "semiconductor"): a small piece of semiconducting material, usually silicon, with millions or billions of microscopic transistors carved into it.

CPU: central processing unit; a type of "general-purpose" chip that is the workhorse of computing in PCs, phones, and data centers.

DRAM: dynamic random access memory; one of two main types of memory chip, which is used to store data temporarily.

EDA: electronic design automation; specialized software used to design how millions or billions of transistors will be arrayed on a chip and to simulate their operation.

FinFET: a new 3D transistor structure first implemented in the early 2010s to better control transistor operation as transistors' size shrank to nanometric-scale.

GPU: graphics processing unit; a chip that is capable of parallel processing, making it useful for graphics and for artificial intelligence applications.

Logic chip: a chip that processes data.

Memory chip: a chip that remembers data.

NAND: also called "flash," the second major type of memory chip, used for longer-term data storage.

Photolithography: also known as "lithography"; the process of shining light or ultraviolet light through patterned masks: the light then interacts with photoresist chemicals to carve patterns on silicon wafers.

RISC-V: an open-source architecture growing in popularity because it is free to use, unlike Arm and x86. The development of RISC-V was partially funded by the U.S. government but now is popular in China because it is not subject to U.S. export controls.

Silicon wafer: a circular piece of ultra-pure silicon, usually eight or twelve inches in diameter, out of which chips are carved.

Transistor: a tiny electric "switch" that turns on (creating a 1) or off (0), producing the 1s and 0s that undergird all digital computing.

x86: an instruction set architecture that is dominant in PCs and data centers. Intel and AMD are the two main firms producing such chips.

Introduction

T he destroyer USS *Mustin* slipped into the northern end of the Taiwan Strait on August 18, 2020, its five-inch gun pointed southward as it began a solo mission to sail through the Strait and reaffirm that these international waters were *not* controlled by China—at least not yet. A stiff southwestern breeze whipped across the deck as it steamed south. High clouds cast shadows on the water that seemed to stretch all the way to the great port cities of Fuzhou, Xiamen, Hong Kong, and the other harbors that dot the South China coast. To the east, the island of Taiwan rose in the distance, a broad, densely settled coastal plain giving way to tall peaks hidden in clouds. Aboard ship, a sailor wearing a navy baseball cap and a surgical mask lifted his binoculars and scanned the horizon. The waters were filled with commercial freighters shipping goods from Asia's factories to consumers around the world.

On board the USS *Mustin*, a row of sailors sat in a dark room in front of an array of brightly colored screens on which were displayed data from planes, drones, ships, and satellites tracking movement across the Indo-Pacific. Atop the *Mustin*'s bridge, a radar array fed into the ship's computers. On deck ninety-six launch cells stood ready, each capable of firing missiles that could precisely strike planes, ships, or submarines dozens or even hundreds of miles away. During the crises of the Cold War, the U.S. military had used threats of brute nuclear force to defend Taiwan. Today, it relies on microelectronics and precision strikes.

As the USS *Mustin* sailed through the Strait, bristling with computerized weaponry, the People's Liberation Army announced a retaliatory series of live-fire exercises around Taiwan, practicing what one Beijing-controlled newspaper called a "reunification-by-force operation." But on this particular day, China's leaders worried less about the U.S. Navy and more about an obscure U.S. Commerce Department regulation called the Entity List, which limits the transfer of American technology abroad. Previously, the Entity List had primarily been used to prevent sales of military systems like missile parts or nuclear materials. Now, though, the U.S. government was dramatically tightening the rules governing computer chips, which had become ubiquitous in both military systems and consumer goods.

The target was Huawei, China's tech giant, which sells smartphones, telecom equipment, cloud computing services, and other advanced technologies. The U.S. feared that Huawei's products were now priced so attractively, partly owing to Chinese government subsidies, that they'd shortly form the backbone of next-generation telecom networks. America's dominance of the world's tech infrastructure would be undermined. China's geopolitical clout would grow. To counter this threat, the U.S. barred Huawei from buying advanced computer chips made with U.S. technology.

Soon, the company's global expansion ground to a halt. Entire product lines became impossible to produce. Revenue slumped. A corporate giant faced technological asphyxiation. Huawei discovered that, like all other Chinese companies, it was fatally dependent on foreigners to make the chips upon which all modern electronics depend.

The United States *still* has a stranglehold on the silicon chips that gave Silicon Valley its name, though its position has weakened dangerously. China now spends more money each year importing chips than it spends on oil. These semiconductors are plugged into all manner of devices, from smartphones to refrigerators, that China consumes at home or exports worldwide. Armchair strategists theorize about China's "Malacca Dilemma"—a reference to the main shipping channel between the Pacific and Indian Oceans—and the country's ability to access supplies of oil and other commodities amid a crisis. Beijing, however, is more worried about a blockade measured in bytes rather than barrels. China is devoting its best minds and billions of dollars to developing its own semiconductor technology in a bid to free itself from America's chip choke.

If Beijing succeeds, it will remake the global economy and reset the balance of military power. World War II was decided by steel and aluminum, and followed shortly thereafter by the Cold War, which was defined by atomic weapons. The rivalry between the United States and China may well be determined by computing power. Strategists in Beijing and Washington now realize that all advanced tech—from machine learning to missile systems, from automated vehicles to armed drones—requires cutting-edge chips, known more formally as semiconductors or integrated circuits. A tiny number of companies control their production.

We rarely think about chips, yet they've created the modern world. The fate of nations has turned on their ability to harness computing power. Globalization as we know it wouldn't exist without the trade in semiconductors and the electronic products they make possible. America's military primacy stems largely from its ability to apply chips to military uses. Asia's tremendous rise over the past half century has been built on a foundation of silicon as its growing economies have come to specialize in fabricating chips and assembling the computers and smartphones that these integrated circuits make possible.

At the core of computing is the need for many millions of 1s and 0s. The entire digital universe consists of these two numbers. Every button on your iPhone, every email, photograph, and YouTube video—all of these are coded, ultimately, in vast strings of 1s and 0s. But these numbers don't actually exist. They're expressions of electrical currents, which are either on (1) or off (0). A chip is a grid of millions or billions of *transistors*, tiny electrical switches that flip on and off to process these digits, to remember them, and to convert real world sensations like images, sound, and radio waves into millions and millions of 1s and 0s.

As the USS *Mustin* sailed southward, factories and assembly facilities on both sides of the Strait were churning out components for the iPhone 12, which was only two months away from its October 2020 launch. Around a quarter of the chip industry's revenue comes from phones; much of the price of a new phone pays for the semiconductors inside. For the past decade, each generation of iPhone has been powered by one of the world's most advanced processor chips. In total, it takes over a dozen semiconductors to make a smartphone work, with different chips managing the battery, Bluetooth, Wi-Fi, cellular network connections, audio, the camera, and more.

Apple makes precisely *none* of these chips. It buys most off-the-shelf: memory chips from Japan's Kioxia, radio frequency chips from California's Skyworks, audio chips from Cirrus Logic, based in Austin, Texas. Apple designs in-house the ultra-complex processors that run an iPhone's operating system. But the Cupertino, California, colossus can't manufacture these chips. Nor can any company in the United States, Europe, Japan, or China. Today, Apple's most advanced processors—which are arguably the world's most advanced semiconductors—can only be produced by a single company in a single building, the most expensive factory in human history, which on the morning of August 18, 2020, was only a couple dozen miles off the USS *Mustin*'s starboard bow.

Fabricating and miniaturizing semiconductors has been the greatest engineering challenge of our time. Today, no firm fabricates chips with more precision than the Taiwan Semiconductor Manufacturing Company, better known as TSMC. In 2020, as the world lurched between lockdowns driven by a virus whose diameter measured around one hundred nanometers—billionths of a meter—TSMC's most advanced facility, Fab 18, was carving microscopic mazes of tiny transistors, etching shapes smaller than half the size of a coronavirus, a hundredth the size of a mitochondria. TSMC replicated this process at a scale previously unparalleled in human history. Apple sold over 100 million iPhone 12s, each powered by an A14 processor chip with 11.8 billion tiny transistors carved into its silicon. In a matter of months, in other words, for just one of the dozen chips in an iPhone, TSMC's Fab 18 fabricated well over 1 quintillion transistors—that is, a number with eighteen zeros behind it. Last year, the chip industry produced more transistors than the combined quantity of all goods produced by all other companies, in all other industries, in all human history. Nothing else comes close.

It was only sixty years ago that the number of transistors on a cutting-edge chip wasn't 11.8 billion, but 4. In 1961, south of San Francisco, a small firm called Fairchild Semiconductor announced a new product called the Micrologic, a silicon chip with four transistors embedded in it. Soon the company devised ways to put a dozen transistors on a chip, then a hundred. Fairchild cofounder Gordon Moore noticed in 1965 that the number of components that could be fit on each chip was doubling annually as engineers learned to fabricate ever smaller transistors. This prediction—that the computing power of chips would grow exponentially—came to be called "Moore's Law" and led Moore to predict the invention of devices that in 1965 seemed impossibly futuristic, like an "electronic wristwatch," "home computers," and even "personal portable communications equipment." Looking forward from 1965, Moore predicted a decade of exponential growth—but this staggering rate of progress has continued for over half a century. In 1970, the second company Moore founded, Intel, unveiled a memory chip that could remember 1,024 pieces of information ("bits"). It cost around $20, roughly two cents per bit. Today, $20 can buy a thumb drive that can remember well over a billion bits.

When we think of Silicon Valley today, our minds conjure social networks and software companies rather than the material after which the valley was named. Yet the internet, the cloud, social media, and the entire digital world only exist because engineers have learned to control the most minute movement of electrons as they race across slabs of silicon. "Big tech" wouldn't exist if the cost of processing and remembering 1s and 0s hadn't fallen by a billionfold in the past half century.

This incredible ascent is partly thanks to brilliant scientists and Nobel Prize–winning physicists. But not every invention creates a successful startup, and not every startup sparks a new industry that transforms the world. Semiconductors spread across society because companies devised new techniques to manufacture them by the millions, because hard-charging managers relentlessly drove down their cost, and because creative entrepreneurs imagined new ways to use them. The making of Moore's Law is as much a story of manufacturing experts, supply chain specialists, and marketing managers as it is about physicists or electrical engineers.

The towns to the south of San Francisco—which weren't called Silicon Valley until the 1970s—were the epicenter of this revolution because they combined scientific expertise, manufacturing know-how, and visionary business thinking. California had plenty of engineers trained in aviation or radio industries who'd graduated from Stanford or Berkeley, each of which was flush with defense dollars as the U.S. military sought to solidify its technological advantage. California's culture mattered just as much as any economic structure, however. The people who left America's East Coast, Europe, and Asia to build the chip industry often cited a sense of boundless opportunity in their decision to move to Silicon Valley. For the world's smartest engineers and most creative entrepreneurs, there was simply no more exciting place to be.

Once the chip industry took shape, it proved impossible to dislodge from Silicon Valley. Today's semiconductor supply chain requires components from many cities and countries, but almost every chip made still has a Silicon Valley connection or is produced with tools designed and built in California. America's vast reserve of scientific expertise, nurtured by government research funding and strengthened by the ability to poach the best scientists from other countries, has provided the core knowledge driving technological advances forward. The country's network of venture capital firms and its stock markets have provided the startup capital new firms need to grow—and have ruthlessly forced out failing companies. Meanwhile, the world's largest consumer market in the U.S. has driven the growth that's funded decades of R&D on new types of chips.

Other countries have found it impossible to keep up on their own but have succeeded when they've deeply integrated themselves into Silicon Valley's supply chains. Europe has isolated islands of semiconductor expertise, notably in producing the machine tools needed to make chips and in designing chip architectures. Asian governments, in Taiwan, South Korea, and Japan, have elbowed their way into the chip industry by subsidizing firms, funding training programs, keeping their exchange rates undervalued, and imposing tariffs on imported chips. This strategy has yielded certain capabilities that no other countries can replicate—but they've achieved what they have in partnership with Silicon Valley, continuing to rely fundamentally on U.S. tools, software, and customers. Meanwhile, America's most successful chip firms have built supply chains that stretch across the world, driving down costs and producing the expertise that has made Moore's Law possible.

Today, thanks to Moore's Law, semiconductors are embedded in every device that requires computing power—and in the age of the Internet of Things, this means pretty much *every* device. Even hundred-year-old products like automobiles now often include a thousand dollars worth of chips. Most of the world's GDP is produced with devices that rely on semiconductors. For a product that didn't exist seventy-five years ago, this is an extraordinary ascent.

As the USS *Mustin* steamed southward in August 2020, the world was just beginning to reckon with our reliance on semiconductors—and our dependence on Taiwan, which fabricates the chips that produce a third of the new computing power we use each year. Taiwan's TSMC builds almost all the world's most advanced processor chips. When COVID slammed into the world in 2020, it disrupted the chip industry, too. Some factories were temporarily shuttered. Purchases of chips for autos slumped. Demand for PC and data center chips spiked higher, as much of the world prepared to work from home. Then, over 2021, a series of accidents—a fire in a Japanese semiconductor facility; ice storms in Texas, a center of U.S. chipmaking; and a new round of COVID lockdowns in Malaysia, where many chips are assembled and tested—intensified these disruptions. Suddenly, many industries far from Silicon Valley faced debilitating chip shortages. Big carmakers from Toyota to General Motors had to shut factories for weeks because they couldn't acquire the semiconductors they needed. Shortages of even the simplest chips caused factory closures on the opposite side of the world. It seemed like a perfect image of globalization gone wrong.

Political leaders in the U.S., Europe, and Japan hadn't thought much about semiconductors in decades. Like the rest of us, they thought "tech" meant search engines or social media, not silicon wafers. When Joe Biden and Angela Merkel asked why their country's car factories were shuttered, the answer was shrouded behind semiconductor supply chains of bewildering complexity. A typical chip might be designed with blueprints from the Japanese-owned, UK-based company called Arm, by a team of engineers in California and Israel, using design software from the United States. When a design is complete, it's sent to a facility in Taiwan, which buys ultra-pure silicon wafers and specialized gases from Japan. The design is carved into silicon using some of the world's most precise machinery, which can etch, deposit, and measure layers of materials a few atoms thick. These tools are produced primarily by five companies, one Dutch, one Japanese, and three Californian, without which advanced chips are basically impossible to make. Then the chip is packaged and tested, often in Southeast Asia, before being sent to China for assembly into a phone or computer.

If any one of the steps in the semiconductor production process is interrupted, the world's supply of new computing power is imperiled. In the age of AI, it's often said that data is the new oil. Yet the real limitation we face isn't the availability of data but of processing power. There's a finite number of semiconductors that can store and process data. Producing them is mind-bogglingly complex and horrendously expensive. Unlike oil, which can be bought from many countries, our production of computing power depends fundamentally on a series of choke points: tools, chemicals, and software that often are produced by a handful of companies—and sometimes only by one. No other facet of the economy is so dependent on so few firms. Chips from Taiwan provide 37 percent of the world's new computing power each year. Two Korean companies produce 44 percent of the world's memory chips. The Dutch company ASML builds 100 percent of the world's extreme ultraviolet lithography machines, without which cutting-edge chips are simply impossible to make. OPEC's 40 percent share of world oil production looks unimpressive by comparison.

The global network of companies that annually produces a trillion chips at nanometer scale is a triumph of efficiency. It's also a staggering vulnerability. The disruptions of the pandemic provide just a glimpse of what a single well-placed earthquake could do to the global economy. Taiwan sits atop a fault line that as recently as 1999 produced an earthquake measuring 7.3 on the Richter scale. Thankfully, this only knocked chip production offline for a couple of days. But it's only a matter of time before a stronger quake strikes Taiwan. A devastating quake could also hit Japan, an earthquake-prone country that produces 17 percent of the world's chips, or Silicon Valley, which today produces few chips but builds crucial chipmaking machinery in facilities sitting atop the San Andreas Fault.

Yet the seismic shift that most imperils semiconductor supply today isn't the crash of tectonic plates but the clash of great powers. As China and the United States struggle for supremacy, both Washington and Beijing are fixated on controlling the future of computing—and, to a frightening degree, that future is dependent on a small island that Beijing considers a renegade province and America has committed to defend by force.

The interconnections between the chip industries in the U.S., China, and Taiwan are dizzyingly complex. There's no better illustration of this than the individual who founded TSMC, a company that until 2020 counted America's Apple and China's Huawei as its two biggest customers. Morris Chang was born in mainland China; grew up in World War II–era Hong Kong; was educated at Harvard, MIT, and Stanford; helped build America's early chip industry while working for Texas Instruments in Dallas; held a top secret U.S. security clearance to develop electronics for the American military; and made Taiwan the epicenter of world semiconductor manufacturing. Some foreign policy strategists in Beijing and Washington dream of decoupling the two countries' tech sectors, but the ultra-efficient international network of chip designers, chemical suppliers, and machine-tool makers that people like Chang helped build can't be easily unwound.

Unless, of course, something explodes. Beijing has pointedly refused to rule out the prospect that it might invade Taiwan to "reunify" it with the mainland. But it wouldn't take anything as dramatic as an amphibious assault to send semiconductor-induced shock waves careening through the global economy. Even a partial blockade by Chinese forces would trigger devastating disruptions. A single missile strike on TSMC's most advanced chip fabrication facility could easily cause hundreds of billions of dollars of damage once delays to the production of phones, data centers, autos, telecom networks, and other technology are added up.

Holding the global economy hostage to one of the world's most dangerous political disputes might seem like an error of historic proportions. However, the concentration of advanced chip manufacturing in Taiwan, South Korea, and elsewhere in East Asia isn't an accident. A series of deliberate decisions by government officials and corporate executives created the far-flung supply chains we rely on today. Asia's vast pool of cheap labor attracted chipmakers looking for low-cost factory workers. The region's governments and corporations used offshored chip assembly facilities to learn about, and eventually domesticate, more advanced technologies. Washington's foreign policy strategists embraced complex semiconductor supply chains as a tool to bind Asia to an American-led world. Capitalism's inexorable demand for economic efficiency drove a constant push for cost cuts and corporate consolidation. The steady tempo of technological innovation that underwrote Moore's Law required ever more complex materials, machinery, and processes that could only be supplied or funded via global markets. And our gargantuan demand for computing power only continues to grow.

Drawing on research in historical archives on three continents, from Taipei to Moscow, and over a hundred interviews with scientists, engineers, CEOs, and government officials, this book contends that semiconductors have defined the world we live in, determining the shape of international politics, the structure of the world economy, and the balance of military power. Yet this most modern of devices has a complex and contested history. Its development has been shaped not only by corporations and consumers but also by ambitious governments and the imperatives of war. To understand how our world came to be defined by quintillions of transistors and a tiny number of irreplaceable companies, we must begin by looking back to the origins of the silicon age.

PART I

COLD WAR CHIPS

CHAPTER 1

From Steel to Silicon

Japanese soldiers described World War II as a "typhoon of steel." It certainly felt that way to Akio Morita, a studious young engineer from a family of prosperous sake merchants. Morita only barely avoided the front lines by getting assigned to a Japanese navy engineering lab. But the typhoon of steel crashed through Morita's homeland, too, as American B-29 Superfortress bombers pummeled Japan's cities, destroying much of Tokyo and other urban centers. Adding to the devastation, an American blockade created widespread hunger and drove the country toward desperate measures. Morita's brothers were being trained as kamikaze pilots when the war ended.

Across the East China Sea, Morris Chang's childhood was punctuated by the sound of gunfire and air-raid sirens warning of imminent attack. Chang spent his teenage years fleeing the Japanese armies that swept across China, moving to Guangzhou; the British colony of Hong Kong; China's wartime capital of Chongqing; and then back to Shanghai after the Japanese were defeated. Even then, the war didn't really end, because Communist guerillas relaunched their struggle against the Chinese government. Soon Mao Zedong's forces were marching on Shanghai. Morris Chang was once again a refugee, forced to flee to Hong Kong for the second time.

Budapest was on the opposite side of the world, but Andy Grove lived through the same typhoon of steel that swept across Asia. Andy (or Andras Grof, as he was then known) survived multiple invasions of Budapest. Hungary's far-right government treated Jews like the Groves as second-class citizens, but when war broke out in Europe, his father was nevertheless drafted and sent to fight alongside Hungary's Nazi allies against the Soviet Union, where he was reported missing in action at Stalingrad. Then, in 1944, the Nazis invaded Hungary, their ostensible ally, sending tank columns rolling through Budapest and announcing plans to ship Jews like Grove to industrial-scale death camps. Still a child, Grove heard the thud of artillery again months later as Red Army troops marched into Hungary's capital, "liberating" the country, raping Grove's mother, and installing a brutal puppet regime in the Nazis' place.

Endless tank columns; waves of airplanes; thousands of tons of bombs dropped from the skies; convoys of ships delivering trucks, combat vehicles, petroleum products, locomotives, rail cars, artillery, ammunition, coal, and steel—World War II was a conflict of industrial attrition. The United States wanted it that way: an industrial war was a struggle America would win. In Washington, the economists at the War Production Board measured success in terms of copper and iron, rubber and oil, aluminum and tin as America converted manufacturing might into military power.

The United States built more tanks than all the Axis powers combined, more ships, more planes, and twice the Axis production of artillery and machine guns. Convoys of industrial goods streamed from American ports across the Atlantic and Pacific Oceans, supplying Britain, the Soviet Union, China, and other allies with key materiel. The war was waged by soldiers at Stalingrad and sailors at Midway. But the fighting power was produced by America's Kaiser shipyards and the assembly lines at River Rouge.

In 1945, radio broadcasts across the world announced that the war was finally over. Outside of Tokyo, Akio Morita, the young engineer, donned his full uniform to hear Emperor Hirohito's surrender address, though he listened to the speech alone rather than in the company of other naval officers, so he wouldn't be pressured to commit ritual suicide. Across the East China Sea, Morris Chang celebrated the war's end and Japan's defeat with a prompt return to a leisurely teenaged life of tennis, movies, and card games with friends. In Hungary, Andy Grove and his mother slowly crept out of their bomb shelter, though they suffered as much during the Soviet occupation as during the war itself.

World War II's outcome was determined by industrial output, but it was clear already that new technologies were transforming military power. The great powers had manufactured planes and tanks by the thousands, but they'd also built research labs that developed new devices like rockets and radars. The two atomic bombs that destroyed Hiroshima and Nagasaki brought forth much speculation that a nascent Atomic Age might replace an era defined by coal and steel.

Morris Chang and Andy Grove were schoolboys in 1945, too young to have thought seriously about technology or politics. Akio Morita, however, was in his early twenties and had spent the final months of the war developing heat-seeking missiles. Japan was far from fielding workable guided missiles, but the project gave Morita a glimpse of the future. It was becoming possible to envision wars won not by riveters on assembly lines but by weapons that could identify targets and maneuver themselves automatically. The idea seemed like science fiction, but Morita was vaguely aware of new developments in electronic computation that might make it possible for machines to "think" by solving math problems like adding, multiplying, or finding a square root.

Of course, the idea of using devices to compute wasn't new. People have flipped their fingers up and down since Homo sapiens first learned to count. The ancient Babylonians invented the abacus to manipulate large numbers, and for centuries people multiplied and divided by moving wooden beads back and forth across these wooden grids. During the late 1800s and early 1900s, the growth of big bureaucracies in government and business required armies of human "computers," office workers armed with pen, paper, and occasionally simple mechanical calculators—gearboxes that could add, subtract, multiply, divide, and calculate basic square roots.

These living, breathing computers could tabulate payrolls, track sales, collect census results, and sift through the data on fires and droughts that were needed to price insurance policies. During the Great Depression, America's Works Progress Administration, looking to employ jobless office workers, set up the Mathematical Tables Project. Several hundred human "computers" sat at rows of desks in a Manhattan office building and tabulated logarithms and exponential functions. The project published twenty-eight volumes of the results of complex functions, with titles such as *Tables of Reciprocals of the Integers from 100,000 Through 200,009*, presenting 201 pages covered in tables of numbers.

Organized groups of human calculators showed the promise of computation, but also the limits of using brains to compute. Even when brains were enhanced by using mechanical calculators, humans worked slowly. A person looking to use the results of the Mathematical Tables Project had to flip through the pages of one of the twenty-eight volumes to find the result of a specific logarithm or exponent. The more calculations that were needed, the more pages had to be flipped through.

Meanwhile, the demand for calculations kept growing. Even before World War II, money was flowing into projects to produce more capable mechanical computers, but the war accelerated the hunt for computing power. Several countries' air forces developed mechanical bombsights to help aviators hit their targets. Bomber crews entered the wind speed and altitude by turning knobs, which moved metal levers that adjusted glass mirrors. These knobs and levers "computed" altitudes and angles more exactly than any pilot could, focusing the sight as the plane homed in on its target. However, the limitations were obvious. Such bombsights only considered a few inputs and provided a single output: when to drop the bomb. In perfect test conditions, America's bombsights were more accurate than pilots' guesswork. When deployed in the skies above Germany, though, only 20 percent of American bombs fell within one thousand feet of their target. The war was decided by the quantity of bombs dropped and artillery shells fired, not by the knobs on the mechanical computers that tried and usually failed to guide them.

More accuracy required more calculations. Engineers eventually began replacing mechanical gears in early computers with electrical charges. Early electric computers used the vacuum tube, a lightbulb-like metal filament enclosed in glass. The electric current running through the tube could be switched on and off, performing a function not unlike an abacus bead moving back and forth across a wooden rod. A tube turned on was coded as a 1 while a vacuum tube turned off was a 0. These two digits could produce any number using a system of binary counting—and therefore could theoretically execute many types of computation.

Moreover, vacuum tubes made it possible for these digital computers to be reprogrammed. Mechanical gears such as those in a bombsight could only perform a single type of calculation because each knob was physically attached to levers and gears. The beads on an abacus were constrained by the rods on which they moved back and forth. However, the connections between vacuum tubes could be reorganized, enabling the computer to run different calculations.

This was a leap forward in computing—or it would have been, if not for the moths. Because vacuum tubes glowed like lightbulbs, they attracted insects, requiring regular "debugging" by their engineers. Also like lightbulbs, vacuum tubes often burned out. A state-of-the-art computer called ENIAC, built for the U.S. Army at the University of Pennsylvania in 1945 to calculate artillery trajectories, had eighteen thousand vacuum tubes. On average, one tube malfunctioned every two days, bringing the entire machine to a halt and sending technicians scrambling to find and replace the broken part. ENIAC could multiply hundreds of numbers per second, faster than any mathematician. Yet it took up an entire room because each of its eighteen thousand tubes was the size of a fist. Clearly, vacuum tube technology was too cumbersome, too slow, and too unreliable. So long as computers were moth-ridden monstrosities, they'd only be useful for niche applications like code breaking, unless scientists could find a smaller, faster, cheaper switch.

CHAPTER 2

The Switch

William Shockley had long assumed that if a better "switch" was to be found, it would be with the help of a type of material called semiconductors. Shockley, who'd been born in London to a globe-trotting mining engineer, had grown up amid the fruit trees of the sleepy California town of Palo Alto. An only child, he was utterly convinced of his superiority over anyone around him—and he let everyone know it. He went to college at Caltech, in Southern California, before completing a PhD in physics at MIT and starting work at Bell Labs in New Jersey, which at the time was one of the world's leading centers of science and engineering. All his colleagues found Shockley obnoxious, but they also admitted he was a brilliant theoretical physicist. His intuition was so accurate that one of Shockley's coworkers said it was as if he could actually *see* electrons as they zipped across metals or bonded atoms together.

Semiconductors, Shockley's area of specialization, are a unique class of materials. Most materials either let electric current flow freely (like copper wires) or block current (like glass). Semiconductors are different. On their own, semiconductor materials like silicon and germanium are like glass, conducting hardly any electricity at all. But when certain materials are added and an electric field is applied, current can begin to flow. Adding phosphorous or antimony to semiconducting materials like silicon or germanium, for example, lets a negative current flow.

"Doping" semiconductor materials with other elements presented an opportunity for new types of devices that could create and control electric currents. However, mastering the flow of electrons across semiconductor materials like silicon or germanium was a distant dream so long as their electrical properties remained mysterious and unexplained. Until the late 1940s, despite all the physics brainpower accumulated at Bell Labs, no one could explain why slabs of semiconductor materials acted in such puzzling ways.

In 1945, Shockley first theorized what he called a "solid state valve," sketching in his notebook a piece of silicon attached to a ninety-volt battery. He hypothesized that placing a piece of semiconductor material like silicon in the presence of an electric field could attract "free electrons" stored inside to cluster near the edge of the semiconductor. If enough electrons were attracted by the electric field, the edge of the semiconductor would be transformed into a conductive material, like a metal, which always has large numbers of free electrons. If so, an electric current could begin flowing through a material that previously conducted no electricity at all. Shockley soon built such a device, expecting that applying and removing an electric field on top of the piece of silicon could make it function like a valve, opening and closing the flow of electrons across the silicon. When he ran this experiment, however, he was unable to detect a result. "Nothing measurable," he explained. "Quite mysterious." In fact, the simple instruments of the 1940s were too imprecise to measure the tiny current that was flowing.

Two years later, two of Shockley's colleagues at Bell Labs devised a similar experiment on a different type of device. Where Shockley was proud and obnoxious, his colleagues Walter Brattain, a brilliant experimental physicist from a cattle ranch in rural Washington, and John Bardeen, a Princeton-trained scientist who'd later become the only person to win two Nobel Prizes in physics, were modest and mild-mannered. Inspired by Shockley's theorizing, Brattain and Bardeen built a device that applied two gold filaments, each attached by wires to a power source and to a piece of metal, to a block of germanium, with each filament touching the germanium less than a millimeter apart from the other. On the afternoon of December 16, 1947, at Bell Labs' headquarters, Bardeen and Brattain switched on the power and were able to control the current surging across the germanium. Shockley's theories about semiconductor materials had been proven correct.

AT&T, which owned Bell Labs, was in the business of telephones, not computers, and saw this device—soon christened a "transistor"—as useful primarily for its ability to amplify signals that transmitted phone calls across its vast network. Because transistors could amplify currents, it was soon realized, they would be useful in devices such as hearing aids and radios, replacing less reliable vacuum tubes, which were also used for signal amplification. Bell Labs soon began arranging patent applications for this new device.

Shockley was furious that his colleagues had discovered an experiment to prove his theories, and he was committed to outdoing them. He locked himself in a Chicago hotel room for two weeks over Christmas and began imagining different transistor structures, based on his unparalleled understanding of semiconductor physics. By January 1948, he'd conceptualized a new type of transistor, made up of three chunks of semiconductor material. The outer two chunks would have a surplus of electrons; the piece sandwiched between them would have a deficit. If a tiny current was applied to the middle layer in the sandwich, it set a much larger current flowing across the entire device. This conversion of a small current into a large one was the same amplification process that Brattain and Bardeen's transistor had demonstrated. But Shockley began to perceive other uses, along the lines of the "solid state valve" he'd previously theorized. He could turn the larger current on and off by manipulating the small current applied to the middle of this transistor sandwich. On, off. On, off. Shockley had designed a switch.

When Bell Labs held a press conference in June 1948 to announce that its scientists had invented the transistor, it wasn't easy to understand why these wired blocks of germanium merited a special announcement. The *New York Times* buried the story on page 46. *Time* magazine did better, reporting the invention under the headline "Little Brain Cell." Yet even Shockley, who never underestimated his own importance, couldn't have imagined that soon thousands, millions, and billions of these transistors would be employed at microscopic scale to replace human brains in the task of computing.

CHAPTER 3

Noyce, Kilby, and the Integrated Circuit

The transistor could only replace vacuum tubes if it could be simplified and sold at scale. Theorizing and inventing transistors was simply the first step; now, the challenge was to manufacture them by the thousands. Brattain and Bardeen had little interest in business or mass production. They were researchers at heart, and after winning the Nobel, they continued their careers teaching and experimenting. Shockley's ambitions, by contrast, only grew. He wanted not only to be famous but also to be rich. He told friends he dreamed of seeing his name not only in academic publications like the *Physical Review* but in the *Wall Street Journal*, too. In 1955, he established Shockley Semiconductor in the San Francisco suburb of Mountain View, California, just down the street from Palo Alto, where his aging mother still lived.

Shockley planned to build the world's best transistors, which was possible because AT&T, the owner of Bell Labs and of the transistor patent, offered to license the device to other companies for $25,000, a bargain for the most cutting-edge electronics technology. Shockley assumed that there'd be a market for transistors, at least for replacing vacuum tubes in existing electronics. The potential size of the transistor market, though, was unclear. Everyone agreed transistors were a clever piece of technology based on the most advanced physics, but transistors would take off only if they did something better than vacuum tubes or could be produced more cheaply. Shockley would soon win the Nobel Prize for his theorizing about semiconductors, but the question of how to make transistors practical and useful was an engineering dilemma, not a matter of theoretical physics.

Transistors soon began to be used in place of vacuum tubes in computers, but the wiring between thousands of transistors created a jungle of complexity. Jack Kilby, an engineer at Texas Instruments, spent the summer of 1958 in his Texas lab fixated on finding a way to simplify the complexity created by all the wires that systems with transistors required. Kilby was soft-spoken, collegial, curious, and quietly brilliant. "He was never demanding," one colleague remembered. "You knew what he wanted to have happen and you tried your darndest to make it happen." Another colleague, who relished regular barbecue lunches with Kilby, said he was "as sweet a guy as you'd ever want to meet."

Kilby was one of the first people outside Bell Labs to use a transistor, after his first employer, Milwaukee-based Centralab, licensed the technology from AT&T. In 1958, Kilby left Centralab to work in the transistor unit of Texas Instruments. Based in Dallas, TI had been founded to produce equipment using seismic waves to help oilmen decide where to drill. During World War II, the company had been drafted by the U.S. Navy to build sonar devices to track enemy submarines. After the war, TI executives realized this electronics expertise could be useful in other military systems, too, so they hired engineers like Kilby to build them.

Kilby arrived in Dallas around the company's July holiday period, yet he'd accumulated no vacation time so he was left alone in the lab for a couple of weeks. With time to tinker, he wondered how to reduce the number of wires that were needed to string different transistors together. Rather than use a separate piece of silicon or germanium to build each transistor, he thought of assembling multiple components on the same piece of semiconductor material. When his colleagues returned from summer vacation, they realized that Kilby's idea was revolutionary. Multiple transistors could be built into a single slab of silicon or germanium. Kilby called his invention an "integrated circuit," but it became known colloquially as a "chip," because each integrated circuit was made from a piece of silicon "chipped" off a circular silicon wafer.

About a year earlier, in Palo Alto, California, a group of eight engineers employed by William Shockley's semiconductor lab had told their Nobel Prize–winning boss that they were quitting. Shockley had a knack for spotting talent, but he was an awful manager. He thrived on controversy and created a toxic atmosphere that alienated the bright young engineers he'd assembled. So these eight engineers left Shockley Semiconductor and decided to found their own company, Fairchild Semiconductor, with seed funding from an East Coast millionaire.

The eight defectors from Shockley's lab are widely credited with founding Silicon Valley. One of the eight, Eugene Kleiner, would go on to found Kleiner Perkins, one of the world's most powerful venture capital firms. Gordon Moore, who went on to run Fairchild's R&D process, would later coin the concept of Moore's Law to describe the exponential growth in computing power. Most important was Bob Noyce, the leader of the "traitorous eight," who had a charismatic, visionary enthusiasm for microelectronics and an intuitive sense of which technical advances were needed to make transistors tiny, cheap, and reliable. Matching new inventions with commercial opportunities was exactly what a startup like Fairchild needed to succeed—and what the chip industry needed to take off.

By the time Fairchild was founded, the science of transistors was broadly clear, but manufacturing them reliably was an extraordinary challenge. The first commercialized transistors were made of a block of germanium with different materials layered on top in the shape of a mesa from the Arizona desert. These layers were fabricated by covering a portion of the germanium with a drop of black wax, using a chemical to etch off the germanium that wasn't covered with wax, and then removing the wax, creating mesa shapes atop the germanium.

A downside of the mesa structure was that it allowed impurities like dust or other particles to become lodged on the transistor, reacting with the materials on the its surface. Noyce's colleague Jean Hoerni, a Swiss physicist and avid mountaineer, realized the mesas weren't necessary if the entire transistor could be built into, rather than on top of, the germanium. He devised a method of fabricating all the parts of a transistor by depositing a layer of protective silicon dioxide on top of a slab of silicon, then etching holes where needed and depositing additional materials. This method of depositing protective layers avoided exposing materials to air and impurities that could cause defects. It was a major advance in reliability.

Several months later, Noyce realized Hoerni's "planar method" could be used to produce multiple transistors on the same piece of silicon. Where Kilby, unbeknownst to Noyce, had produced a mesa transistor on a germanium base and then connected it with wires, Noyce used Hoerni's planar process to build multiple transistors on the same chip. Because the planar process covered the transistor with an insulating layer of silicon dioxide, Noyce could put "wires" directly on the chip by depositing lines of metal on top of it, conducting electricity between the chip's transistors. Like Kilby, Noyce had produced an integrated circuit: multiple electric components on a single piece of semiconductor material. However, Noyce's version had no freestanding wires at all. The transistors were built into a single block of material. Soon, the "integrated circuits" that Kilby and Noyce had developed would become known as "semiconductors" or, more simply, "chips."

Noyce, Moore, and their colleagues at Fairchild Semiconductor knew their integrated circuits would be vastly more reliable than the maze of wires that other electronic devices relied on. It seemed far easier to miniaturize Fairchild's "planar" design than standard mesa transistors. Smaller circuits, meanwhile, would require less electricity to work. Noyce and Moore began to realize that miniaturization and electric efficiency were a powerful combination: smaller transistors and reduced power consumption would create new use cases for their integrated circuits. At the outset, however, Noyce's integrated circuit cost fifty times as much to make as a simpler device with separate components wired together. Everyone agreed Noyce's invention was clever, even brilliant. All it needed was a market.

CHAPTER 4

Liftoff

Three days after Noyce and Moore founded Fairchild Semiconductor, at 8:55 p.m., the answer to the question of who would pay for integrated circuits hurtled over their heads through California's nighttime sky. Sputnik, the world's first satellite, launched by the Soviet Union, orbited the earth from west to east at a speed of eighteen thousand miles per hour. "Russ 'Moon' Circling Globe," declared the headline in the *San Francisco Chronicle*, reflecting Americans' fears that this satellite gave the Russians a strategic advantage. Four years later, the Soviet Union followed Sputnik with another shock when cosmonaut Yuri Gagarin became the first person in space.

Across America, the Soviet space program caused a crisis of confidence. Control of the cosmos would have serious military ramifications. The U.S. thought it was the world's science superpower, but now it seemed to have fallen behind. Washington launched a crash program to catch up with the Soviets' rocket and missile programs, and President John F. Kennedy declared the U.S. would send a man to the moon. Bob Noyce suddenly had a market for his integrated circuits: rockets.

The first big order for Noyce's chips came from NASA, which in the 1960s had a vast budget to send astronauts to the moon. As America set its sights on a lunar landing, engineers at the MIT Instrumentation Lab were tasked by NASA to design the guidance computer for the Apollo spacecraft, a device that was certain to be one of the most complicated computers ever made. Everyone agreed transistor-based computers were far better than the vacuum-tube equivalents that had cracked codes and calculated artillery trajectories during World War II. But could any of these devices really guide a spacecraft to the moon? One MIT engineer calculated that to meet the needs of the Apollo mission, a computer would need to be the size of a refrigerator and would consume more electricity than the entire Apollo spacecraft was expected to produce.

MIT's Instrumentation Lab had received its first integrated circuit, produced by Texas Instruments, in 1959, just a year after Jack Kilby had invented it, buying sixty-four of these chips for a price of $1,000 to test them as part of a U.S. Navy missile program. The MIT team ended up not using chips in that missile but found the idea of integrated circuits intriguing. Around the same time, Fairchild began marketing its own "Micrologic" chips. "Go out and buy large quantities of those things," one MIT engineer ordered a colleague in January 1962, "to see if they are real."

Fairchild was a brand-new company, run by a group of thirty-year-old engineers with no track record, but their chips were reliable and arrived on time. By November 1962, Charles Stark Draper, the famed engineer who ran the MIT lab, had decided to bet on Fairchild chips for the Apollo program, calculating that a computer using Noyce's integrated circuits would be one-third smaller and lighter than a computer based on discrete transistors. It would use less electricity, too. The computer that eventually took Apollo 11 to the moon weighed seventy pounds and took up about one cubic foot of space, a thousand times less than the University of Pennsylvania's ENIAC computer that had calculated artillery trajectories during World War II.

MIT considered the Apollo guidance computer one of its proudest accomplishments, but Bob Noyce knew that it was his chips that made the Apollo computer tick. By 1964, Noyce bragged, the integrated circuits in Apollo computers had run for 19 million hours with only two failures, one of which was caused by physical damage when a computer was being moved. Chip sales to the Apollo program transformed Fairchild from a small startup into a firm with one thousand employees. Sales ballooned from $500,000 in 1958 to $21 million two years later.

As Noyce ramped up production for NASA, he slashed prices for other customers. An integrated circuit that sold for $120 in December 1961 was discounted to $15 by next October. NASA's trust in integrated circuits to guide astronauts to the moon was an important stamp of approval. Fairchild's Micrologic chips were no longer an untested technology; they were used in the most unforgiving and rugged environment: outer space.

This was good news for Jack Kilby and Texas Instruments, even though their chips played only a small role in the Apollo program. At TI headquarters in Dallas, Kilby and TI president Pat Haggerty were looking for a big customer for their own integrated circuits. Haggerty was the son of a railroad telegrapher from small-town South Dakota who'd trained as an electrical engineer and worked on electronics for the U.S. Navy during World War II. Since the day he arrived at Texas Instruments in 1951, Haggerty had focused on selling electronic systems to the military.

Haggerty intuitively understood that Jack Kilby's integrated circuit could eventually be plugged into every piece of electronics the U.S. military used. A captivating public speaker, when he preached to Texas Instruments employees about the future of electronics, Haggerty was remembered by one TI veteran as "like a messiah speaking from the mountaintop. He seemed like he could predict everything." As the U.S. and the Soviet Union lurched between nuclear standoffs in the early 1960s—first over control of divided Berlin, then during the Cuban Missile Crisis—Haggerty had no better customer than the Pentagon. Just months after Kilby created the integrated circuit, Haggerty briefed Defense Department staff on Kilby's invention. The next year, the Air Force Avionics Lab agreed to sponsor TI's chip research. Several small contracts for military devices followed. But Haggerty was looking for a big fish.

In fall 1962, the Air Force began looking for a new computer to guide its Minuteman II missile, which was designed to hurl nuclear warheads through space before striking the Soviet Union. The first version of the Minuteman had just entered service, but it was so heavy it could barely hit Moscow from launch sites scattered across the American West. Its onboard guidance computer was a hulking monstrosity, based on discrete transistors, with the targeting program fed into the guidance computer via Mylar tape with holes punched in it.

Haggerty promised the Air Force that a computer using Kilby's integrated circuits could perform twice the computations with half the weight. He envisioned a computer that used twenty-two different types of integrated circuits. In his mind's eye, 95 percent of the computer's functions would be conducted by integrated circuits carved into silicon, which together weighed 2.2 ounces. The remaining 5 percent of the computer hardware, which TI's engineers couldn't yet figure out how to put on a chip, weighed 36 pounds. "It was just a matter of size and weight," explained one the engineers designing the computer, Bob Nease, regarding the decision to use integrated circuits. "There was really not much of a choice."

Winning the Minuteman II contract transformed TI's chip business. TI's integrated circuit sales had previously been measured in the dozens, but the firm was soon selling them by the thousands amid fear of an American "missile gap" with the Soviet Union. Within a year, TI's shipments to the Air Force accounted for 60 percent of all dollars spent buying chips to date. By the end of 1964, Texas Instruments had supplied one hundred thousand integrated circuits to the Minuteman program. By 1965, 20 percent of all integrated circuits sold that year went to the Minuteman program. Pat Haggerty's bet on selling chips to the military was paying off. The only question was whether TI could learn how to mass-produce them.

CHAPTER 5

Mortars and Mass Production

J ay Lathrop pulled into Texas Instruments' parking lot for his first day of work on September 1, 1958, just as Jack Kilby's fateful summer spent tinkering in TI's labs was coming to a close. After graduating from MIT, where he'd overlapped with Bob Noyce, Lathrop had worked at a U.S. government lab where he was tasked with devising a proximity fuse that would enable an 81mm mortar shell to detonate automatically above its target. Like engineers at Fairchild, he was struggling with mesa-shaped transistors, which were proving difficult to miniaturize. Existing manufacturing processes involved placing specially shaped globs of wax on certain portions of the semiconductor material, then washing away the uncovered portions using specialized chemicals. Making smaller transistors required smaller globs of wax, but keeping these globs in the correct shape proved challenging.

While looking through a microscope at one of their transistors, Lathrop and his assistant, chemist James Nall, had an idea: a microscope lens could take something small and make it look bigger. If they turned the microscope upside down, its lens would take something big and make it look smaller. Could they use a lens to take a big pattern and "print" it onto germanium, thereby making miniature mesas on their blocks of germanium? Kodak, the camera company, sold chemicals called photoresists, which reacted when exposed to light.

Lathrop covered a block of germanium with one of Kodak's photoresist chemicals that would disappear if exposed to light. Next, he turned his microscope upside down, covering the lens with a pattern so that light would only pass through a rectangle-shaped area. Light entered the pattern, shined in a rectangle shape through the lens, and was shrunk in size by the upside-down microscope as it focused onto the photoresist-coated germanium, with the rays of light creating a perfectly shaped, miniature version of the rectangular pattern. Where light struck the layer of photoresist, the chemical structure was altered, allowing it to be washed away, leaving a tiny rectangular hole, far smaller and more accurately shaped than any glob of wax could have been. Soon Lathrop discovered he could print "wires," too, by adding an ultra-thin layer of aluminum to connect the germanium with an external power source.

Lathrop called the process photolithography—printing with light. He produced transistors much smaller than had previously been possible, measuring only a tenth of an inch in diameter, with features as small as 0.0005 inches in height. Photolithography made it possible to imagine mass-producing tiny transistors. Lathrop applied for a patent on the technique in 1957. With the Army band playing, the military gave him a medal for his work and a $25,000 cash bonus, which he used to buy his family a Nash Rambler station wagon.

Pat Haggerty and Jack Kilby immediately realized Lathrop's photolithography process was worth a lot more than the $25,000 prize the Army had given him. The Minuteman II missile program needed thousands of integrated circuits. The Apollo spacecraft needed tens of thousands more. Haggerty and Kilby realized that light rays and photoresists could solve the mass-production problem, mechanizing and miniaturizing chipmaking in a way that soldering wires together by hand could not.

Implementing Lathrop's lithography process at Texas Instruments required new materials and new processes. Kodak's photoresist chemicals were insufficiently pure for mass production, so TI bought its own centrifuges and reprocessed the chemicals that Kodak supplied. Lathrop took trains across the country in search of "masks" that could be used to project precise patterns of light onto photoresist-covered slabs of semiconductor material to carve circuits. He eventually concluded that no existing mask company had sufficient precision, so TI decided to make masks itself, too. The slabs of silicon that Kilby's integrated circuits required had to be ultra-pure, beyond what any company sold. TI therefore also began producing its own silicon wafers.

Mass production works when everything is standardized. General Motors plugged many of the same car parts into all the Chevrolets that rolled off its assembly lines. When it came to semiconductors, companies like TI lacked the tools to know whether all the components of their integrated circuits were the same. Chemicals had impurities that at the time were impossible to test. Variation in temperature and pressure caused unexpected chemical reactions. The masks through which light was projected could be contaminated by particles of dust. A single impurity could ruin an entire production run. The only method of improvement was trial and error, with TI organizing thousands of experiments to assess the impact of different temperatures, chemical combinations, and production processes. Jack Kilby spent each Saturday pacing TI's hallways and checking on his engineers' experiments.

TI production engineer Mary Anne Potter spent months running round-the-clock tests. The first woman to earn a physics degree from Texas Tech, Potter was hired at TI to scale up chip production for the Minuteman missile. She often worked the night shift, from 11 p.m. until 8 a.m., to make sure experiments were progressing according to plan. Gathering data took days of experimentation. Then she ran regressions on the data, using her slide rule to calculate exponents and square roots, plot the results on a graph, and then interpret them— doing it all by hand. It was a slow, laborious, painful process, relying on human "computers" to crunch numbers. Yet trial and error was the only method Texas Instruments had.

Morris Chang arrived at TI in 1958, the same year as Jay Lathrop, and was put in charge of a production line of transistors. Nearly a decade had passed since Chang fled Shanghai to escape the advancing Communist armies, first to Hong Kong and then to Boston, having won admission to Harvard, where he was the only Chinese student in the freshman class. After a year spent studying Shakespeare, Chang began to worry about his career prospects. "There were Chinese-American laundry people, there were Chinese-American restaurant people," he recalled. "The only really serious . . . middle class profession that a Chinese American could pursue in the early fifties was technical." Mechanical engineering seemed safer than English literature, Chang decided, so he transferred to MIT.

After graduating, Chang was hired by Sylvania, a big electronics firm with facilities outside of Boston. He was tasked with improving Sylvania's manufacturing "yield"—the share of transistors that actually worked. Chang spent his days tinkering with Sylvania's production processes and his evenings studying Shockley's *Electrons and Holes in Semiconductors*, the bible of early semiconductor electronics. After three years at Sylvania, Chang received a job offer from TI, and moved to Dallas, Texas—"cowboy country," he remembered, and a land of "95-cent steaks." He was tasked with running a production line of transistors to be used in IBM computers, a type of transistor so unreliable that TI's yield was close to zero, he recalled. Almost all had manufacturing imperfections that caused circuits to short or to malfunction; they had to be tossed out.

A master bridge player, Chang approached manufacturing as methodically as he played his favorite card game. Upon arriving at TI, he began systematically tweaking the temperature and pressure at which different chemicals were combined, to determine which combinations worked best, applying his intuition to the data in a way that amazed and intimidated his colleagues. "You had to be careful when you worked with him," remembered one colleague. "He sat there and puffed on his pipe and looked at you through the smoke." The Texans who worked for him thought he was "like a Buddha." Behind the tobacco smoke was a brain second to none. "He knew enough about solid-state physics to lord it over anyone," one colleague recalled. He had a reputation for being a tough boss. "Morris was so bad for beating up on people," one subordinate recalled. "If you hadn't ever been chewed out by Morris, you hadn't been at TI." Chang's methods produced results, though. Within months, the yield on his production line of transistors jumped to 25 percent. Executives from IBM, America's biggest tech company, came to Dallas to study his methods. Soon he was placed in charge of TI's entire integrated circuit business.

Like Chang, Noyce and Moore saw no limits to the growth of the chip industry so long as they could figure out mass production. Noyce realized his MIT classmate Jay Lathrop, with whom he'd hiked New Hampshire's mountains while in graduate school, had discovered a technique that could transform transistor manufacturing. Noyce acted swiftly to hire Lathrop's lab partner, chemist James Nall, to develop photolithography at Fairchild. "Unless we could make it work," Noyce reasoned, "we did not have a company."

It was up to production engineers like Andy Grove to improve Fairchild's manufacturing process. After fleeing Hungary's Communist government in 1956 and arriving in New York as a refugee, Grove had worked his way into a PhD program at Berkeley. He'd written Fairchild in 1962 to ask for a job interview but was told to try again later: "We like our young men to interview with us when they have finished interviewing with everybody else," the rejection letter explained. Grove found Fairchild's rejection letter "condescendingly disgusting," he recalled, an early sign of the hubris that would come to define Silicon Valley. But as demand for Fairchild's semiconductors increased, the company suddenly had a desperate need for chemical engineers. One company executive rang Berkeley and asked for a list of the best students in the Chemistry Department. Grove was at the top of the list and was called to Palo Alto to meet Gordon Moore. "It was love at first sight," Grove remembered. He was hired in 1963 and would spend the rest of his life building the chip industry alongside Noyce and Moore.

The Nobel Prize for inventing the transistor went to Shockley, Bardeen, and Brattain. Jack Kilby later won a Nobel for creating the first integrated circuit; had Bob Noyce not died at the age of sixty-two, he'd have shared the prize with Kilby. These inventions were crucial, but science alone wasn't enough to build the chip industry. The spread of semiconductors was enabled as much by clever manufacturing techniques as academic physics. Universities like MIT and Stanford played a crucial role in developing knowledge about semiconductors, but the chip industry only took off because graduates of these institutions spent years tweaking production processes to make mass manufacturing possible. It was engineering and intuition, as much as scientific theorizing, that turned a Bell Labs patent into a world-changing industry.

Shockley, who was widely recognized as one of the greatest theoretical physicists of his generation, eventually abandoned his effort to make a fortune and get his name in the *Wall Street Journal*. His contribution in theorizing the transistor was important. But it was the traitorous eight young engineers who abandoned his company, as well as a similar group at Texas Instruments, who turned Shockley's transistors into a useful product—chips—and sold them to the U.S. military while learning how to mass-produce them. Armed with these capabilities, Fairchild and TI entered the mid-1960s with a new challenge: turning chips into a mass market product.

CHAPTER 6

"I...WANT...
TO...GET...RICH"

The computers that guided the Apollo spacecraft and the Minuteman II missile provided the initial liftoff for America's integrated circuit industry. By the mid-1960s, the U.S. military was deploying chips in weaponry of all types, from satellites to sonar, torpedoes to telemetry systems. Bob Noyce knew that military and space programs were crucial for Fairchild's early success, admitting in 1965 that military and space applications would use "over 95% of the circuits produced this year." But he always envisioned an even larger civilian market for his chips, though in the early 1960s no such market existed. He would have to create it, which meant keeping the military at arm's length so that he—not the Pentagon—set Fairchild's R&D priorities. Noyce declined most military research contracts, estimating that Fairchild never relied on the Defense Department for more than 4 percent of its R&D budget. "There are very few research directors anywhere in the world who are really adequate to the job" of assessing Fairchild's work, Noyce explained confidently, "and they are not often career officers in the Army."

Noyce had experienced government-directed R&D while fresh out of graduate school when he worked for Philco, an East Coast radio manufacturer with a big defense unit. "The direction of the research was being determined by people less competent," Noyce recalled, complaining about the time he wasted writing progress reports for the military. Now that he was running Fairchild, a company seeded by a trust-fund heir, he had flexibility to treat the military as a customer rather than a boss. He chose to target much of Fairchild's R&D not at the military, but at mass market products. Most of the chips used in rockets or satellites must have civilian uses, too, he reasoned. The first integrated circuit produced for commercial markets, used in a Zenith hearing aid, had initially been designed for a NASA satellite. The challenge would be making chips that civilians could afford. The military paid top dollar, but consumers were price sensitive. What remained tantalizing, though, was that the civilian market was far larger than even the bloated budgets of the Cold War Pentagon. "Selling R&D to the government was like taking your venture capital and putting it into a savings account," Noyce declared. "Venturing is venturing; you want to take the risk."

In Palo Alto, Fairchild Semiconductor was surrounded by firms that supplied the Pentagon, from aerospace to ammunition, radio to radar. Though the military bought chips from Fairchild, the Defense Department was more comfortable working with big bureaucracies than nimble startups. As a result, the Pentagon underestimated the speed at which Fairchild and other semiconductor startups would transform electronics. A Defense Department assessment from the late 1950s had praised radio giant RCA for having "the most ambitious microminiaturization program underway" while dismissively noting that Fairchild had only two scientists working on the company's leading circuit program. Defense contractor Lockheed Martin, which had a research facility just down the road in Palo Alto, had over fifty scientists in their microsystem electronics division, the Defense Department reported, implying that Lockheed was far ahead.

However, it was Fairchild's R&D team that, under Gordon Moore's direction, not only devised new technology but opened new civilian markets as well. In 1965, Moore was asked by *Electronics* magazine to write a short article on the future of integrated circuits. He predicted that every year for at least the next decade, Fairchild would double the number of components that could fit on a silicon chip. If so, by 1975, integrated circuits would have sixty-five thousand tiny transistors carved into them, creating not only more computing power but also lower prices per transistor. As costs fell, the number of users would grow. This forecast of exponential growth in computing power soon came to be known as Moore's Law. It was the greatest technological prediction of the century.

If the computing power on each chip continued to grow exponentially, Moore realized, the integrated circuit would revolutionize society far beyond rockets and radars. In 1965, defense dollars still bought 72 percent of all integrated circuits produced that year. However, the features the military demanded were useful in business applications, too. "Miniaturization and ruggedness," one electronics publication declared, "means good business." Defense contractors thought about chips mostly as a product that could replace older electronics in all the military's systems. At Fairchild, Noyce and Moore were already dreaming of personal computers and mobile phones.

When U.S. defense secretary Robert McNamara reformed military procurement to cut costs in the early 1960s, causing what some in the electronics industry called the "McNamara Depression," Fairchild's vision of chips for civilians seemed prescient. The company was the first to offer a full product line of off-the-shelf integrated circuits for civilian customers. Noyce slashed prices, too, gambling that this would drastically expand the civilian market for chips. In the mid-1960s, Fairchild chips that previously sold for $20 were cut to $2. At times Fairchild even sold products below manufacturing cost, hoping to convince more customers to try them.

Thanks to falling prices, Fairchild began winning major contracts in the private sector. Annual U.S. computer sales grew from 1,000 in 1957 to 18,700 a decade later. By the mid-1960s, almost all these computers relied on integrated circuits. In 1966, Burroughs, a computer firm, ordered 20 million chips from Fairchild—more than twenty times what the Apollo program consumed. By 1968, the computer industry was buying as many chips as the military. Fairchild chips served 80 percent of this computer market. Bob Noyce's price cuts had paid off, opening a new market for civilian computers that would drive chip sales for decades to come. Moore later argued that Noyce's price cuts were as big an innovation as the technology inside Fairchild's integrated circuits.

By the end of the 1960s, after a decade of development, Apollo 11 was finally ready to use its Fairchild-powered guidance computer to carry the first human to the moon. The semiconductor engineers in California's Santa Clara Valley had benefitted immensely from the space race, which provided a crucial early customer. Yet by the time of the first lunar landing, Silicon Valley's engineers had become far less dependent on defense and space contracts. Now they were focused on more earthly concerns. The chip market was booming. Fairchild's success had already inspired several top employees to defect to competing chipmakers. Venture capital funding was pouring into startups that focused not on rockets but on corporate computers.

Fairchild, however, was still owned by an East Coast multimillionaire who paid his employees well but refused to give them stock options, viewing the idea of giving away equity as a form of "creeping socialism." Eventually, even Noyce, one of Fairchild's cofounders, began wondering whether he had a future at the firm. Soon *everyone* began looking for the exit. The reason was obvious. Alongside new scientific discoveries and new manufacturing processes, this ability to make a financial killing was the fundamental force driving forward Moore's Law. As one of Fairchild's employees put it in the exit questionnaire he filled out when leaving the company: "I . . . WANT . . . TO . . . GET . . . RICH."

PART II

THE CIRCUITRY OF THE AMERICAN WORLD

CHAPTER 7

Soviet Silicon Valley

A couple months after Bob Noyce invented his integrated circuit at Fairchild Semiconductor, an unexpected visitor arrived in Palo Alto. In fall 1959, two years after Sputnik first orbited the earth, Anatoly Trutko, a semiconductor engineer from the Soviet Union, moved into a Stanford University dormitory called Crothers Memorial Hall. Though Cold War competition was near its peak, the two superpowers had agreed to begin student exchanges, and Trutko was one of a handful of students selected by the USSR and vetted by the U.S. State Department. He spent his year at Stanford studying America's most advanced technology with the country's leading scientists. He even attended lectures given by William Shockley, who'd abandoned his startup and was now a professor at the university. After one class, Trutko asked the Nobel Prize winner to sign a copy of his magnum opus *Electrons and Holes in Semiconductors*. "To Anatole," Shockley signed, before barking at the young scientist with complaints that the Soviet Union refused to pay royalties for the textbook's Russian translation.

America's decision to let Soviet scientists like Trutko study semiconductors at Stanford was surprising, given U.S. fears that the Soviet Union was catching up in science and technology. Yet every country's electronics industry was increasingly oriented toward Silicon Valley, which so totally set the standard and pace of innovation that the rest of the world had no choice but to follow—even America's adversaries. The Soviets didn't pay Shockley royalties, but they understood the value of semiconductors, translating Shockley's textbook into Russian just two years after it was published. As early as 1956, America's spies had been ordered to acquire Soviet semiconductor devices to test their quality and track their improvements. A CIA report in 1959 found that America was only two to four years ahead of the Soviets in quality and quantity of transistors produced. At least several of the early Soviet exchange students were KGB agents—suspected at the time, but not confirmed until decades later—forging an intimate connection between student exchanges and Soviet defense industrial goals.

Just like the Pentagon, the Kremlin realized that transistors and integrated circuits would transform manufacturing, computing, and military power. Beginning in the late 1950s, the USSR established new semiconductor facilities across the country and assigned its smartest scientists to build this new industry. For an ambitious young engineer like Yuri Osokin it was hard to imagine a more exciting assignment. Osokin had spent much of his childhood in China, where his father worked in a Soviet military hospital in the city of Dalian, on the shores of the Yellow Sea. From his youth, Osokin stood out for his encyclopedic memory for things like geography and the birthdays of famous people. After finishing school, he won entrance to a top academic institute in Moscow and specialized in semiconductors.

Osokin was soon assigned to a semiconductor plant in Riga, staffed with fresh graduates from the country's best universities, and ordered to build semiconductor devices for the Soviet space program and the military. Osokin was tasked by the factory's director to build a circuit with multiple components on the same piece of germanium, something no one in the Soviet Union had previously done. He produced his prototype integrated circuit in 1962. Osokin and his colleagues knew they were at the cutting edge of Soviet science. They spent their days tinkering in labs and their evenings debating the theory of solid-state physics, with Osokin occasionally breaking out his guitar to accompany his colleagues in song. They were young, their work was exciting, Soviet science was rising, and several of the USSR's Sputnik satellites were orbiting overhead, visible to the naked eye whenever Osokin put down his guitar and looked up into the night sky.

Soviet leader Nikita Khrushchev was committed to outcompeting the United States in every sphere, from corn production to satellite launches. Khrushchev himself was more comfortable on collective farms than in electronics labs. He understood nothing about technology but was obsessed with the notion of "catching up and overtaking" the United States, as he repeatedly promised to do. Alexander Shokin, first deputy chairman of the Soviet State Committee on Radioelectronics, realized Khrushchev's urge to compete with the United States could be used to win more investment in microelectronics. "Imagine, Nikita Sergeyevich," Shokin told the Soviet leader one day, "that a TV can be made the size of a cigarette box." Such was the promise of Soviet silicon. "Catching up and overtaking" the United States seemed like a real possibility. As with another sphere where the Soviets had caught up to the United States—nuclear weapons—the USSR had a secret weapon: a spy ring.

Joel Barr was the son of two Russian Jews who immigrated to the U.S. to flee tsarist oppression. Barr grew up in poverty in Brooklyn before winning admission to the City College of New York to study electrical engineering. As a student, he fell in with a group of Communists and found himself sympathizing with their critique of capitalism and their argument that the Soviet Union was best placed to stand up to the Nazis. Via Communist Party contacts, he was introduced to Alfred Sarant, a fellow electrical engineer and member of the Young Communist League. They'd spend the remainder of their lives working together to further the Communist cause.

In the 1930s, Barr and Sarant were integrated into an espionage ring led by Julius Rosenberg, the infamous Cold War spy. During the 1940s, Barr and Sarant worked on classified radars and other military systems at Western Electric and Sperry Gyroscope, two leading American technology firms. Unlike others in the Rosenberg ring, Barr and

Sarant didn't possess nuclear weapons secrets, but they had gained intimate knowledge about the electronics in new weapons systems. In the late 1940s, as the FBI began unraveling the KGB's spy networks in the U.S., Rosenberg was tried and sentenced to death by electrocution alongside his wife, Ethel. Before the FBI could catch them, Sarant and Barr fled the country, eventually reaching the Soviet Union.

When they arrived, they told KGB handlers they wanted to build the world's most advanced computers. Barr and Sarant weren't experts in computers, but nor was anyone else in the Soviet Union. Their status as spies was, in itself, a much admired credential, and their aura gave them access to resources. In the late 1950s, Barr and Sarant began building their first computer, called UM—the Russian word for "mind." Their work attracted the attention of Shokin, the bureaucrat who managed the Soviet electronics industry, and they partnered with him to convince Khrushchev that the USSR needed an entire city devoted to producing semiconductors, with its own researchers, engineers, labs, and production facilities. Even before the towns on the peninsula south of San Francisco had become known as Silicon Valley—a term that wasn't coined until 1971—Barr and Sarant had dreamt up their own version in a Moscow suburb.

To convince Khrushchev to fund this new city of science, Shokin arranged for the Soviet leader to visit Special Design Bureau of the Electronics Industry #2 in Leningrad. Behind the bulky, bureaucratic name—the Soviets never excelled at marketing—was an institute at the cutting edge of Soviet electronics. The Design Bureau spent weeks preparing for Khrushchev's visit, holding a dress rehearsal the day before to ensure that everything went according to plan. On May 4, 1962, Khrushchev arrived. To welcome the Soviet leader, Sarant dressed in a dark suit matching the color of his bushy eyebrows and carefully trimmed mustache. Barr stood nervously to Sarant's side, wiry glasses perched on his balding head. With Sarant in the lead, the two former spies showed Khrushchev the accomplishments of Soviet microelectronics. Khrushchev tested a tiny radio that fit in his ear and toyed with a simple computer that could print out his name. Semiconductor devices would soon be used in spacecraft, industry, government, aircraft—even "for the creation of a nuclear missile shield," Sarant confidently told Khrushchev. Then he and Barr led Khrushchev to an easel with pictures of a futuristic city devoted exclusively to producing semiconductor devices, with a vast fifty-two-story skyscraper at its center.

Khrushchev was enamored of grand projects, especially those that he could claim credit for, so he enthusiastically endorsed the idea of building a Soviet city for semiconductors. He embraced Barr and Sarant in a bear hug, promising his full support. Several months later, the Soviet government approved plans to build a semiconductor city in the outskirts of Moscow. "Microelectronics is a mechanical brain," Khrushchev explained to his fellow Soviet leaders. "It is our future."

The USSR soon broke ground on the city of Zelenograd, the Russian word for "green city"—and, indeed, it was designed to be a scientific paradise. Shokin wanted it to be a perfect scientific settlement, with research laboratories and production facilities, plus schools, day cares, movie theaters, libraries, and a hospital—everything a semiconductor engineer could need. Near the center was a university, the Moscow Institute of Electronic Technology, with a brick façade modeled on English and American college campuses. From the outside, it seemed just like Silicon Valley, only a little less sunny.

CHAPTER 8

"Copy It"

A round the same time that Nikita Khrushchev declared his support for building Zelenograd, a Soviet student named Boris Malin returned from a year studying in Pennsylvania with a small device in his luggage—a Texas Instruments SN-51, one of the first integrated circuits sold in the United States. A thin man with dark hair and deep-set eyes, Malin was one of the Soviet Union's leading experts on semiconductor devices. He saw himself as a scientist, not a spy. Yet Alexander Shokin, the bureaucrat in charge of Soviet microelectronics, believed the SN-51 was a device the Soviet Union must acquire by any means necessary. Shokin called Malin and a group of other engineers into his office, placed the chip under his microscope, and peered through the lens. "Copy it," he ordered them, "one-for-one, without any deviations. I'll give you three months."

Soviet scientists reacted angrily to the suggestion they were simply copying foreign advances. Their scientific understanding was as advanced as that of America's chemists and physicists. Soviet exchange students in the U.S. reported learning little from lectures by William Shockley that they couldn't have studied in Moscow. Indeed, the USSR had some of the world's leading theoretical physicists. When Jack Kilby was finally awarded the Nobel Prize in Physics in 2000 for inventing the integrated circuit (by then the co-inventor of the integrated circuit,

Bob Noyce, had died), he shared the prize with a Russian scientist named Zhores Alferov, who'd conducted fundamental research in the 1960s on ways semiconductor devices could produce light. The launch of Sputnik in 1957, the first space flight of Yuri Gagarin in 1961, and the fabrication of Osokin's integrated circuit in 1962 provided incontrovertible evidence that the Soviet Union was becoming a scientific superpower. Even the CIA thought the Soviet microelectronics industry was catching up rapidly.

Shokin's "copy it" strategy was fundamentally flawed, however. Copying worked in building nuclear weapons, because the U.S. and the USSR built only tens of thousands of nukes over the entire Cold War. In the U.S., however, TI and Fairchild were already learning how to mass-produce chips. The key to scaling production was reliability, a challenge that American chipmakers like Morris Chang and Andy Grove fixated on during the 1960s. Unlike their Soviet counterparts, they could draw on the expertise of other companies making advanced optics, chemicals, purified materials, and other production machinery. If no American companies could help, Fairchild and TI could turn to Germany, France, or Britain, each of which had advanced industries of their own.

The Soviet Union churned out coal and steel in vast quantities but lagged in nearly every type of advanced manufacturing. The USSR excelled in quantity but not in quality or purity, both of which were crucial to high-volume chipmaking. Moreover, the Western allies prohibited the transfer of many advanced technologies, including semiconductor components, to Communist countries via an organization called COCOM. The Soviets could often bypass COCOM restrictions using shell companies in neutral Austria or Switzerland, but this pathway was hard to use on a large-scale basis. So Soviet semiconductor facilities regularly had to work with machinery that was less sophisticated and with materials that were less pure, producing far fewer working chips as a result.

Spying could only get Shokin and his engineers so far. Simply stealing a chip didn't explain how it was made, just as stealing a cake can't explain how it was baked. The recipe for chips was already extraordinarily complicated. Foreign exchange students studying with Shockley at Stanford could become smart physicists, but it was engineers like Andy Grove or Mary Anne Potter who knew at what temperature certain chemicals needed to be heated, or how long photoresists should be exposed to light. Every step of the process of making chips involved specialized knowledge that was rarely shared outside of a specific company. This type of know-how was often not even written down. Soviet spies were among the best in the business, but the semiconductor production process required more details and knowledge than even the most capable agent could steal.

Moreover, the cutting edge was constantly changing, per the rate set out in Moore's Law. Even if the Soviets managed to copy a design, acquire the materials and machinery, and replicate the production process, this took time. TI and Fairchild were introducing new designs with more transistors every year. By the mid-1960s, the earliest integrated circuits were old news, too big and power-hungry to be very valuable. Compared to almost any other any type of technology, semiconductor technology was racing forward. The size of transistors and their energy consumption was shrinking, while the computing power that could be packed on a square inch of silicon roughly doubled every two years. No other technology moved so quickly—so there was no other sector in which stealing last year's design was such a hopeless strategy.

Soviet leaders never comprehended how the "copy it" strategy condemned them to backwardness. The entire Soviet semiconductor sector functioned like a defense contractor—secretive, top-down, oriented toward military systems, fulfilling orders with little scope for creativity. The copying process was "tightly controlled" by Minister Shokin, one of his subordinates remembered. Copying was literally hardwired into the Soviet semiconductor industry, with some chipmaking machinery using inches rather than centimeters to better replicate American designs, even though the rest of the USSR used the metric system. Thanks to the "copy it" strategy, the USSR started several years behind the U.S. in transistor technology and never caught up.

Zelenograd might have seemed like Silicon Valley without the sunshine. It had the country's best scientists and stolen secrets. Yet the two countries' semiconductor systems couldn't have been more different. Whereas Silicon Valley's startup founders job-hopped and gained practical "on the factory floor" experience, Shokin called the shots from his ministerial desk in Moscow. Yuri Osokin, meanwhile, lived in obscurity in Riga, highly respected by his colleagues but unable to speak about his invention with anyone who lacked a security clearance. Young Soviet students didn't pursue electrical engineering degrees, wanting to be like Osokin, because no one knew that he existed. Career advancement required becoming a better bureaucrat, not devising new products or identifying new markets. Civilian products were always an afterthought amid an overwhelming focus on military production.

Meanwhile, the "copy it" mentality meant, bizarrely, that the pathways of innovation in Soviet semiconductors were set by the United States. One of the most sensitive and secretive industries in the USSR therefore functioned like a poorly run outpost of Silicon Valley. Zelenograd was just another node in a globalizing network—with American chipmakers at the center.

CHAPTER 9

The Transistor Salesman

When Japanese prime minister Hayato Ikeda met French president Charles de Gaulle amid the splendor of the Elysée Palace in November 1962, he brought a small gift for his host: a Sony transistor radio. De Gaulle was formalistic and ceremonious, a tradition-minded military man who saw himself as the incarnation of French *grandeur*. Ikeda, by contrast, thought his country's voters were straightforwardly materialistic, and promised to double their incomes within a decade. Japan was nothing but an "economic power," de Gaulle declared, huffing to an aide after the meeting that Ikeda behaved like a "transistor salesman." But it wouldn't be long before all the world was looking enviously at Japan, because the country's success selling semiconductors would make it far wealthier and more powerful than de Gaulle ever imagined.

Integrated circuits didn't only connect electronic components in innovative ways, they also knit together nations in a network, with the United States at its center. The Soviets inadvertently made themselves part of this network by copying Silicon Valley's products. Japan, by contrast, was deliberately integrated into America's semiconductor industry, a process supported by Japanese business elites and the U.S. government.

When World War II ended, some Americans had envisioned stripping Japan of its high-tech industries as punishment for starting a brutal war. Yet within a couple years of Japan's surrender, defense officials in Washington adopted an official policy that "a strong Japan is a better risk than a weak Japan." Apart from a short-lived effort to shut down Japan's research into nuclear physics, the U.S. government supported Japan's rebirth as a technological and scientific power. The challenge was to help Japan rebuild its economy while binding it to an American-led system. Making Japan a transistor salesman was core to America's Cold War strategy.

News about the invention of the transistor first trickled into the country via the U.S. military authorities who governed occupied Japan. Makoto Kikuchi was a young physicist in the Japanese government's Electrotechnical Laboratory in Tokyo, which employed some of the country's most advanced scientists. One day his boss called him into his office with interesting news: American scientists, Kikuchi's boss explained, had attached two metal needles to a crystal and were able to amplify a current. Kikuchi knew an extraordinary device had been discovered.

In bombed-out Tokyo, it was easy to feel isolated from the world's leading physicists, but U.S. occupation headquarters in Tokyo provided Japan's scientists access to journals like *Bell System Technical Journal*, *Journal of Applied Physics*, and *Physical Review*, which published the papers of Bardeen, Brattain, and Shockley. These journals were otherwise impossible to obtain in postwar Japan. "I'd flick through the contents and whenever I saw the word 'semiconductor' or 'transistor,'" Kikuchi recounted, "my heart would start to pound." Several years later, in 1953, Kikuchi met John Bardeen when the American scientist traveled to Tokyo during a hot and humid September for a meeting of the International Union of Pure and Applied Physics. Bardeen was treated like a celebrity and was shocked by the number of people wanting to take his photo. "I've never seen so many flashbulbs in my life," he wrote his wife.

The same year Bardeen landed in Tokyo, Akio Morita took off from Haneda Airport for New York. The fifteenth-generation heir to one of Japan's most distinguished sake distilleries, Morita had been groomed since birth to take over the family business. Morita's father had wanted his son to become the sixteenth Morita to manage the sake business, but Akio Morita's childhood love of tinkering with electronics and a university degree in physics pointed in a different direction. During the war, this physics expertise may have saved his life, getting him sent to a research lab rather than the front lines.

Morita's physics degree proved useful in postwar Japan, too. In April 1946, with the country still in ruins, Morita partnered with a former colleague named Masaru Ibuka to build an electronics business, which they soon named Sony, from the Latin *sonus* (sound) and the American nickname "sonny." Their first device, an electric rice cooker, was a dud, but their tape recorder worked well and sold better. In 1948, Morita read about Bell Labs' new transistor and immediately grasped its potential. It seemed "miraculous," Morita recalled, dreaming of revolutionizing consumer devices.

Upon landing in the United States in 1953, Morita was shocked by the country's vast distances, open spaces, and extraordinary consumer wealth, especially compared to the deprivation of postwar Tokyo. *This country seems to have everything*, Morita thought. In New York, he met AT&T executives who agreed to issue him a license to produce the transistor. They told him to expect to manufacture nothing more useful than a hearing aid.

Morita understood what Charles de Gaulle did not: electronics were the future of the world economy, and transistors, soon embedded in silicon chips, would make possible unimaginable new devices. The smaller size and lower power consumption that transistors offered, Morita realized, were set to transform consumer electronics. He and Ibuka decided to bet the future of their company on selling these devices not only to Japanese customers, but to the world's richest consumer market, America.

Japan's government signaled its support for high tech, with Japan's crown prince visiting an American radio research lab the same year Morita traveled to Bell Labs. Japan's powerful Ministry of International

Trade and Industry also wanted to support electronics firms, but the ministry's impact was mixed, with bureaucrats at one point delaying Sony's application to license the transistor from Bell Labs by several months on the grounds that it was "inexcusably outrageous" for the company to have signed a contract with a foreign firm without the ministry's consent.

Sony had the benefit of cheaper wages in Japan, but its business model was ultimately about innovation, product design, and marketing. Morita's "license it" strategy couldn't have been more different from the "copy it" tactics of Soviet Minister Shokin. Many Japanese companies had reputations for ruthless manufacturing efficiency. Sony excelled by identifying new markets and targeting them with impressive products using Silicon Valley's newest circuitry technology. "Our plan is to lead the public with new products rather than ask them what kind of products they want," Morita declared. "The public does not know what is possible, but we do."

Sony's first major success was transistor radios, such as the radio Prime Minister Ikeda had given de Gaulle. Several years earlier, Texas Instruments had tried to market transistor radios, but though it had the necessary technology, TI bungled the pricing and marketing and quickly abandoned the business. Morita saw an opening and was soon churning out tens of thousands of the devices.

Nevertheless, U.S. chip firms like Fairchild continued to dominate the cutting edge of chip production, such as its business related to corporate mainframe computers. Throughout the 1960s, Japanese firms paid sizeable licensing fees on intellectual property, handing over 4.5 percent of all chip sales to Fairchild, 3.5 percent to Texas Instruments, and 2 percent to Western Electric. U.S. chipmakers were happy to transfer their technology because Japanese firms appeared to be years behind.

Sony's expertise wasn't in designing chips but devising consumer products and customizing the electronics they needed. Calculators were another consumer device transformed by Japanese firms. Pat

Haggerty, the TI Chairman, had asked Jack Kilby to build a handheld, semiconductor-powered calculator in 1967. However, TI's marketing department didn't think there'd be a market for a cheap, handheld calculator, so the project stagnated. Japan's Sharp Electronics disagreed, putting California-produced chips in a calculator that was far simpler and cheaper than anyone had thought possible. Sharp's success guaranteed most calculators produced in the 1970s were Japanese made. If only TI had found a way to market its own branded devices earlier, Haggerty later lamented, TI "would have been the Sony of consumer electronics." Replicating Sony's product innovation and marketing expertise, however, proved just as hard as replicating America's semiconductor expertise.

The semiconductor symbiosis that emerged between America and Japan involved a complex balancing act. Each country relied on the other for supplies and for customers. By 1964, Japan had overtaken the U.S. in production of discrete transistors, while American firms produced the most advanced chips. U.S. firms built the best computers, while electronics manufacturers like Sony and Sharp produced consumer goods that drove semiconductor consumption. Japan's exports of electronics—a mix of semiconductors and products that relied on them—boomed from $600 million in 1965 to $60 billion around two decades later.

Interdependence wasn't always easy. In 1959, the Electronics Industries Association appealed to the U.S. government for help lest Japanese imports undermine "national security"—and their own bottom line. But letting Japan build an electronics industry was part of U.S. Cold War strategy, so, during the 1960s, Washington never put much pressure on Tokyo over the issue. Trade publications like *Electronics* magazine—which might have been expected to take the side of U.S. companies—instead noted that "Japan is a keystone in America's Pacific policy. . . . If she cannot enter into healthy commercial intercourse with the Western hemisphere and Europe, she will seek economic sustenance elsewhere," like Communist China or the Soviet Union. U.S.

strategy required letting Japan acquire advanced technology and build cutting-edge businesses. "A people with their history won't be content to make transistor radios," President Richard Nixon later observed. They had to be allowed, even encouraged, to develop more advanced technology.

Japanese executives were no less committed to making this semiconductor symbiosis work. When Texas Instruments sought to become the first foreign chipmaker to open a plant in Japan, the company faced a thicket of regulatory barriers. Sony's Morita, who happened to be a friend of Haggerty, offered to help in exchange for a share of the profits. He told TI executives to visit Tokyo incognito, register at their hotel under false names, and never leave their hotel room. Morita visited the hotel clandestinely and proposed a joint venture: TI would produce chips in Japan, and Sony would manage the bureaucrats. "We will cover for you," he told the Texas Instruments executives. The Texans thought Sony was a "rogue operation," something they meant as a compliment.

With Morita's help, and after much red tape and green tea, Japan's bureaucrats finally approved TI's permits to open a semiconductor plant in Japan. For Morita, it was another coup, helping to make him one of the most famous Japanese businessmen on either side of the Pacific. For foreign policy strategists in Washington, more trade and investment links between the two countries tied Tokyo ever more tightly into a U.S.-led system. It was a victory for Japanese leaders like Prime Minister Ikeda, too. His goal of doubling Japanese incomes was achieved two years ahead of schedule. Japan won a new seat on the world stage thanks to intrepid electronics entrepreneurs like Morita. Transistor salesman was a position of far more influence than Charles de Gaulle could ever have imagined.

CHAPTER 10

"Transistor Girls"

"Their clothing was of the West, but their love rites were founded in the ancient pleasures of the East," read the cover of *The Transistor Girls*, a trashy Australian novel from 1964. The plot involved Chinese gangsters, international intrigue, and women assembly line workers who "added to their incomes by extracurricular night-time activity." The image on the front cover of *The Transistor Girls* showed a young Japanese woman, scantily clad, with a silhouette of a pagoda in the background. The back cover revealed a woman amid more orientalist imagery but with even less clothing.

It was mostly men who designed the earliest semiconductors, and mostly women who assembled them. Moore's Law predicted the cost of computing power was about to plummet. But making Moore's vision a reality wasn't only a question of shrinking the size of each transistor on a chip. It also required a larger and cheaper supply of workers to assemble them.

Many employees of Fairchild Semiconductor joined the firm in search of riches or because of a love of engineering. Charlie Sporck came to Fairchild after being chased out of his previous job. A cigar smoking, hard-driving New Yorker, Sporck was fixated on efficiency. In an industry full of brilliant scientists and technological visionaries, Sporck's expertise was in wringing productivity out of workers and machines alike. It was only thanks to tough managers like him that the cost of computing fell in line with the schedule Gordon Moore had predicted.

Sporck had studied engineering at Cornell before being hired by GE in the mid-1950s at the firm's factory in Hudson Falls, New York. He was tasked with improving GE's process for manufacturing capacitors and proposed changing the factory's assembly line process. He believed his new technique would improve productivity, but the labor union that controlled GE's assembly line workers saw him as threatening their control over the production process. The union revolted, staging a rally against Sporck and burning him in effigy. The factory's management timidly backed down, promising the union that Sporck's changes would never be implemented.

To hell with this, Sporck thought. That night, he arrived home and started looking for other jobs. In August 1959, he saw an ad in the *Wall Street Journal* for a production manager role at a small company called Fairchild Semiconductor and sent in an application. Soon he was called into New York City for an interview in a hotel on Lexington Avenue. The two Fairchild employees who interviewed him were drunk after a boozy lunch and offered him a job on the spot. It was one of the best hiring decisions Fairchild made. Sporck had never been west of Ohio, but he accepted immediately, reporting for duty in Mountain View shortly thereafter.

Upon arrival in California, Sporck recalled, he was surprised that the firm "had virtually no competence in the handling of labor and labor unions. I brought this competence to my new employer." Many companies wouldn't have described a strategy of labor relations that culminated in management getting burned in effigy as "competent." But in Silicon Valley, unions were weak, and Sporck was committed to keeping it that way. He and his colleagues at Fairchild were "dead set" against unions, he declared. A practical, down-to-earth engineer, Sporck wasn't a stereotypical union buster. He kept his offices so austere that they were compared to an army barracks. Sporck was proud of giving most employees stock options, a practice that was virtually unknown in the old East Coast electronics firms. But he'd ruthlessly insist, in exchange, that these same employees commit to maximizing their productivity.

Unlike East Coast electronics firms whose workforces tended to be male-dominated, most of the new chip startups south of San Francisco staffed their assembly lines with women. Women had worked in assembly line jobs in the Santa Clara Valley for decades, first in the fruit canneries that drove the valley's economy in the 1920s and 1930s, then in the aerospace industry during World War II. Congress's decision to ease immigration rules in 1965 added many foreign-born women to the valley's labor pool.

Chip firms hired women because they could be paid lower wages and were less likely than men to demand better working conditions. Production managers also believed women's smaller hands made them better at assembling and testing finished semiconductors. In the 1960s, the process of attaching a silicon chip to the piece of plastic on which it would sit first required looking through a microscope to position the silicon onto the plastic. The assembly worker then held the two pieces together as a machine applied heat, pressure, and ultrasonic vibration to bond the silicon to the plastic base. Thin gold wires were attached, again by hand, to conduct electricity to and from the chip. Finally, the chip had to be tested by plugging it into a meter—another step that at the time could only be done by hand. As demand for chips skyrocketed, so did the demand for pairs of hands that could assemble them.

Wherever they looked across California, semiconductor executives like Sporck couldn't find enough cheap workers. Fairchild scoured the U.S., eventually opening facilities in Maine—where workers had "a hatred for the labor unions," Sporck reported—and on a Navajo reservation in New Mexico that provided tax incentives. Even in the poorest parts of America, however, labor costs were substantial. Bob Noyce had made a personal investment in a radio assembly factory in Hong Kong, the British colony just across the border from Mao Zedong's Communist

China. Wages were a tenth of the American average—around 25 cents an hour. "Why don't you go take a look," Noyce told Sporck, who was soon on a plane to check it out.

Some colleagues at Fairchild were apprehensive. "The Red Chinese are down your nose," one warned, eying the thousands of People's Liberation Army soldiers stationed on Hong Kong's northern border. "You're going to get run over." But the radio factory Noyce had invested in illustrated the opportunity. "The Chinese labor, the girls working there, were exceeding everything that was ever known," one of Sporck's colleagues recalled. Assembly workers in Hong Kong seemed twice as fast as Americans, Fairchild executives thought, and more "willing to tolerate monotonous work," one executive reported.

Fairchild rented space in a sandal factory on Hang Yip Street, next to the old Hong Kong airport, right on the shore of Kowloon Bay. Soon a huge Fairchild logo several stories tall was mounted on the building, illuminating the junks sailing around Hong Kong's harbor. Fairchild continued to make its silicon wafers in California but began shipping semiconductors to Hong Kong for final assembly. In 1963, its first year of operation, the Hong Kong facility assembled 120 million devices. Production quality was excellent, because low labor costs meant Fairchild could hire trained engineers to run assembly lines, which would have been prohibitively expensive in California.

Fairchild was the first semiconductor firm to offshore assembly in Asia, but Texas Instruments, Motorola, and others quickly followed. Within a decade, almost all U.S. chipmakers had foreign assembly facilities. Sporck began looking beyond Hong Kong. The city's 25-cent hourly wages were only a tenth of American wages but were among the highest in Asia. In the mid-1960s, Taiwanese workers made 19 cents an hour, Malaysians 15 cents, Singaporeans 11 cents, and South Koreans only a dime.

Sporck's next stop was Singapore, a majority ethnic Chinese city-state whose leader, Lee Kuan Yew, had "pretty much outlawed" unions, as one Fairchild veteran remembered. Fairchild followed by opening a facility in the Malaysian city of Penang shortly thereafter. The semiconductor industry was globalizing decades before anyone had heard of the word, laying the grounds for the Asia-centric supply chains we know today.

Managers like Sporck had no game plan for globalization. He'd just as happily have kept building factories in Maine or California had they cost the same. But Asia had millions of peasant farmers looking for factory jobs, keeping wages low and guaranteeing they'd stay low for some time. Foreign policy strategists in Washington saw ethnic Chinese workers in cities like Hong Kong, Singapore, and Penang as ripe for Mao Zedong's Communist subversion. Sporck saw them as a capitalist's dream. "We had union problems in Silicon Valley," Sporck noted. "We never had any union problems in the Orient."

CHAPTER 11

Precision Strike

About halfway on the flight between the company's semi-conductor plants in Singapore and Hong Kong during the early 1970s, Texas Instruments employees would occasionally peer out their aircraft window and look down on puffs of smoke rising from the battlefields on Vietnam's coastal plains. TI's staff across Asia were focused on making chips, not on the war. Many of their colleagues in Texas, however, thought about nothing else. TI's first major contract for integrated circuits had been for massive nuclear missiles like the Minuteman II, but the war in Vietnam required different types of weapons. The early bombing campaigns in Vietnam, like Operation Rolling Thunder, which stretched from 1965 to 1968, dropped over eight hundred thousand tons of bombs, more than was dropped in the Pacific Theater during all of World War II. This firepower had only a marginal impact on North Vietnam's military, however, because most of the bombs missed their targets.

The Air Force realized it needed to fight smarter. The military had experimented with a variety of techniques for guiding its missiles and bombs, from using remote control to infrared seekers. Some of these weapons, like the Shrike missile, which was launched from planes and homed in on enemy radar facilities using a simple guidance system that pointed the missile toward the source of the radar's radio waves, proved reasonably effective. But many other guidance systems seemed hardly ever to work. As late as 1985, a Defense Department study found only four examples of air-to-air missiles downing an enemy aircraft outside of visual range. With limitations like these, it seemed impossible that guided munitions would ever decide the outcome of a war.

The problem with many guided munitions, the military concluded, was the vacuum tubes. The Sparrow III anti-aircraft missiles that U.S. fighters used in the skies over Vietnam relied on vacuum tubes that were hand-soldered. The humid climate of Southeast Asia, the force of takeoff and landings, and the rough-and-tumble of fighter combat caused regular failures. The Sparrow missile's radar system broke on average once every five to ten hours of use. A postwar study found that only 9.2 percent of Sparrows fired in Vietnam hit their target, while 66 percent malfunctioned, and the rest simply missed.

The military's biggest challenge in Vietnam, however, was striking ground targets. At the start of the Vietnam War, bombs fell on average within 420 feet of their target, according to Air Force data. Attacking a vehicle with a bomb was therefore basically impossible. Weldon Word, a thirty-four-year-old project engineer at TI, wanted to change this. Word had penetrating blue eyes, a loud, deep, hypnotic voice, and a unique vantage point for thinking about the future of war. He'd just concluded a yearlong stint aboard a Navy ship gathering data for a new TI-developed sonar, an assignment that was mind-numbingly monotonous, but that demonstrated how much data military systems could collect with the right sensors and instrumentation. As early as the mid-1960s, Word was already envisioning using microelectronics to transform the military's kill chain. Advanced sensors on satellites and in airplanes would acquire targets, track them, guide missiles toward them, and confirm they were destroyed. It sounded like science fiction. But TI already produced the necessary components in its research labs.

The intercontinental ballistic missiles that TI had built chips for presented a relatively straightforward guidance challenge. They were launched from a fixed position on the ground, not from a plane flying at several hundred miles per hour while maneuvering to avoid enemy fire. ICBM targets didn't move either. The missiles themselves were only slightly impacted by wind and weather conditions as they careened downward from outer space at multiple times the speed of sound. They carried warheads big enough to make even a slight miss immensely destructive. It was vastly easier to hit Moscow from Montana than it was to hit a truck with a bomb dropped by an F-4 flying at a couple thousand feet.

This was a complex task, but Word understood that the best weapons were "cheap and familiar," one of his colleagues explained, guaranteeing that they could be used often in training and on the battlefield. The microelectronics had to be designed with as little complexity as possible. Every connection that had to be soldered increased the risks to reliability. The simpler the electronics, the more reliable and more power-efficient a system would be.

Many defense contractors were trying to sell the Pentagon expensive missiles, but Word told his team to build weapons priced like an inexpensive family sedan. He was on the lookout for a device that was simple and easy to use, enabling it to be quickly deployed on every type of airplane, embraced by each military service, and quickly adopted by U.S. allies, too.

In June 1965, Word flew to Florida's Eglin Air Force Base, where he met Colonel Joe Davis, the officer in charge of a program to acquire new equipment for use in Vietnam. Davis had learned to fly at age fifteen before joining the military and piloting both fighter and bomber missions in World War II and Korea. Afterward he commanded Air Force units both in Europe and the Pacific. He understood better than anyone what type of weapons would work in Air Force missions. When Word sat down in his office, Davis opened his desk drawer and pulled out a photo of the Thanh Hoa Bridge, a 540-foot-long metallic structure stretching across North Vietnam's Song Ma river, ringed with air defenses. Word and Davis counted eight hundred pockmarks around the bridge, each caused by an American bomb or rocket that missed its target. Dozens, maybe hundreds more bombs had fallen in the river and left no mark. The bridge was still standing. Could Texas Instruments do anything to help? Davis asked.

Word thought TI's expertise in semiconductor electronics could make the Air Force's bombs more accurate. Texas Instruments knew nothing about designing bombs, so Word started with a standard-issue bomb—the 750-pound M-117, 638 of which already had been dropped unsuccessfully around the Thanh Hoa Bridge. He added a small set of wings that could direct the bomb's flight as it fell from the sky. Finally, he installed a simple laser-guidance system that would control the wings. A small silicon wafer was divided into four quadrants and placed behind a lens. The laser reflecting off the target would shine through the lens onto the silicon. If the bomb veered off course, one quadrant would receive more of the laser's energy than the others, and circuitry would move the wings to reorient the bomb's trajectory so that the laser was shining straight through the lens.

Colonel Davis gave Texas Instruments nine months and $99,000 to deliver this laser-guided bomb, which, thanks to its simple design, quickly passed the Air Force's tests. On May 13, 1972, U.S. aircraft dropped twenty-four of the bombs on the Thanh Hoa Bridge, which until that day had been still standing amid hundreds of craters, like a monument to the inaccuracy of mid-century bombing tactics. This time, American bombs scored direct hits. Dozens of other bridges, rail junctions, and other strategic points were hit with new precision bombs. A simple laser sensor and a couple of transistors had turned a weapon with a zero-for-638 hit ratio into a tool of precision destruction.

In the end, the guerilla war in Vietnam's countryside wasn't a fight that aerial bombing could win. The arrival of TI's Paveway laser-guided bombs coincided with America's defeat in the war. When military leaders like General William Westmoreland predicted "combat areas that are under real- or near real-time surveillance" and "automated fire control," many people heard echoes of the hubris that had dragged America into Vietnam in the first place. Outside a small number of military theorists and electrical engineers, therefore, hardly anyone realized Vietnam had been a successful testing ground for weapons that married microelectronics and explosives in ways that would revolutionize warfare and transform American military power.

CHAPTER 12

Supply Chain Statecraft

Though Texas Instruments executive Mark Shepherd had served in the Navy in Asia during World War II, Morris Chang quipped that his expertise in the region didn't extend beyond "bars and dancing girls." The son of a Dallas police officer, Shepherd had assembled his first vacuum tube at age six. He'd played a central role in building TI's semiconductor business, including supervising the division Jack Kilby worked in when the first integrated circuit was invented. With broad shoulders, a starched collar, slicked-back hair, and a taut smile, Shepherd looked like the Texas corporate titan that he was. Now he was poised to lead TI's strategy of offshoring some of its production to Asia.

Chang and Shepherd first visited Taiwan in 1968 as part of an Asian tour to select a location for a new chip assembly facility. The visit couldn't have gone worse. Shepherd reacted furiously when his steak was served with soy sauce, not the way it was usually prepared in Texas. His first meeting with Taiwan's powerful and savvy economy minister, K. T. Li, ended acrimoniously when the minister declared that intellectual property was something "imperialists used to bully less-advanced countries."

Li wasn't wrong to see Shepherd as an agent of America's empire. But unlike the North Vietnamese, who were trying to oust the United States from their country, Li eventually realized that Taiwan would benefit from integrating itself more deeply with the United States. Taiwan and the U.S. had been treaty allies since 1955, but amid the defeat in Vietnam, America's security promises were looking shaky. From South Korea to Taiwan, Malaysia to Singapore, anti-Communist governments were seeking assurance that America's retreat from Vietnam wouldn't leave them standing alone. They were also seeking jobs and investment that could address the economic dissatisfaction that drove some of their populations toward Communism. Minister Li realized that Texas Instruments could help Taiwan solve both problems at once.

In Washington, U.S. strategists feared the coming collapse of American-backed South Vietnam would send shock waves across Asia. Foreign policy strategists perceived ethnic Chinese communities all over the region as ripe for Communist penetration, ready to fall to Communist influence like a cascade of dominoes. Malaysia's ethnic Chinese minority formed the backbone of that country's Communist Party, for example. Singapore's restive working class was majority ethnic Chinese. Beijing was searching for allies—and probing for U.S. weakness.

No one was more worried about the impending Communist victory in Vietnam than the government in Taiwan, which still claimed to rule all of China. The 1960s had been a good decade for Taiwan's economy but disastrous for its foreign policy. The island's dictator, Chiang Kaishek, still dreamed of reconquering the mainland, but the military balance had shifted decisively against him. In 1964, Beijing tested its first atomic weapon. A thermonuclear weapon test shortly followed. Facing a nuclear China, Taiwan needed American security guarantees more than ever. Yet as the war in Vietnam dragged on, the U.S. cut economic aid for its friends in Asia, including in Taiwan, an ominous sign for a country so dependent on American support.

Taiwanese officials like K. T. Li, who'd studied nuclear physics at Cambridge and ran a steel mill before steering Taiwan's economic development through the postwar decades, began crystallizing a strategy to integrate economically with the United States. Semiconductors were at the center of this plan. Li knew there were plenty of Taiwanese-American semiconductor engineers willing to help. In Dallas, Morris Chang urged his colleagues at TI to set up a facility in Taiwan. Many people would later describe the mainland-born Chang as "returning" to Taiwan, but 1968 was the first time he stepped foot on the island, having lived in the U.S. since fleeing the Communist takeover of China. Two of Chang's PhD classmates at Stanford were from Taiwan, however, and they convinced him the island had a favorable business climate and that wages would stay low.

After initially accusing Mark Shepherd of being an imperialist, Minister Li quickly changed his tune. He realized a relationship with Texas Instruments could transform Taiwan's economy, building industry and transferring technological know-how. Electronics assembly, meanwhile, would catalyze other investments, helping Taiwan produce more higher-value goods. As Americans grew skeptical of military commitments in Asia, Taiwan desperately needed to diversify its connections with the United States. Americans who weren't interested in defending Taiwan might be willing to defend Texas Instruments. The more semiconductor plants on the island, and the more economic ties with the United States, the safer Taiwan would be. In July 1968, having smoothed over relations with the Taiwanese government, TI's board of directors approved construction of the new facility in Taiwan. By August 1969, this plant was assembling its first devices. By 1980, it had shipped its billionth unit.

Taiwan wasn't alone in thinking that semiconductor supply chains could provide economic growth and bolster political stability. In 1973, Singapore's leader Lee Kuan Yew told U.S. president Richard Nixon he was counting on exports to "sop up unemployment" in Singapore. With the Singapore government's support, TI and National Semiconductors built assembly facilities in the city-state. Many other chipmakers followed. By the end of the 1970s, American semiconductor firms employed tens of thousands of workers internationally, mostly in Korea, Taiwan, and Southeast Asia. A new international alliance emerged between Texan and Californian chipmakers, Asian autocrats, and the often ethnic-Chinese workers who staffed many of Asia's semiconductor assembly facilities.

Semiconductors recast the economies and politics of America's friends in the region. Cities that had been breeding grounds for political radicalism were transformed by diligent assembly line workers, happy to trade unemployment or subsistence farming for better paying jobs in factories. By the early 1980s, the electronics industry accounted for 7 percent of Singapore's GNP and a quarter of its manufacturing jobs. Of electronics production, 60 percent was semiconductor devices, and much of the rest was goods that couldn't work without semiconductors. In Hong Kong, electronics manufacturing created more jobs than any sector except textiles. In Malaysia, semiconductor production boomed in Penang, Kuala Lumpur, and Melaka, with new manufacturing jobs providing work for many of the 15 percent of Malaysian workers who had left farms and moved to cities between 1970 and 1980. Such vast migrations are often politically destabilizing, but Malaysia kept its unemployment rate low with many relatively well-paid electronics assembly jobs.

From South Korea to Taiwan, Singapore to the Philippines a map of semiconductor assembly facilities looked much like a map of American military bases across Asia. Yet even after the U.S. finally admitted defeat in Vietnam and drew down its military presence in the region, these trans-Pacific supply chains endured. By the end of the 1970s, rather than dominoes falling to Communism, America's allies in Asia were even more deeply integrated with the U.S.

In 1977, Mark Shepherd returned to Taiwan and met again with K. T. Li, nearly a decade after their first meeting. Taiwan still faced a risk of Chinese invasion, but Shepherd told Li, "We consider this risk to be more than offset by the strength and dynamism of Taiwan's economy. TI will stay and continue to grow in Taiwan," he promised. The company still has facilities on the island today. Taiwan, meanwhile, has made itself an irreplaceable partner to Silicon Valley.

CHAPTER 13

Intel's Revolutionaries

The year 1968 seemed like a revolutionary moment. From Beijing to Berlin to Berkeley, radicals and leftists were poised to tear down the established order. North Vietnam's Tet Offensive tested the limits of American military power. Yet it was the *Palo Alto Times* that scooped the world's biggest newspapers by reporting on page 6 what, in hindsight, was the most revolutionary event of the year: "Founders Leave Fairchild; Form Own Electronics Firm."

The rebellion of Bob Noyce and Gordon Moore didn't look like the protests in California's East Bay, where Berkeley students and Black Panthers plotted violent uprisings and dreamt of abolishing capitalism. At Fairchild, Noyce and Moore were unhappy about their lack of stock options and sick of meddling from the company's head office in New York. Their dream wasn't to tear down the established order, but to remake it.

Noyce and Moore abandoned Fairchild as quickly as they'd left Shockley's startup a decade earlier, and founded Intel, which stood for Integrated Electronics. In their vision, transistors would become the cheapest product ever produced, but the world would consume trillions and trillions of them. Humans would be empowered by semiconductors while becoming fundamentally dependent on them. Even as the world was being wired to the United States, America's internal

67

circuitry was changing. The industrial era was ending. Expertise in etching transistors into silicon would now shape the world's economy. Small California towns like Palo Alto and Mountain View were poised to become new centers of global power.

Two years after its founding, Intel launched its first product, a chip called a dynamic random access memory, or DRAM. Before the 1970s, computers generally "remembered" data using not silicon chips but a device called a magnetic core, a matrix of tiny metal rings strung together by a grid of wires. When a ring was magnetized, it stored a 1 for the computer; a non-magnetized ring was a 0. The jungle of wires that strung the rings together could turn each ring's magnetism off and on and could "read" whether a given ring was a 1 or a 0. The demand for remembering 1s and 0s was exploding, however, and wires and rings could only shrink so far. If the components got any smaller, the assemblers who weaved them together by hand would find them impossible to produce. As demand for computer memory exploded, magnetic cores couldn't keep up.

In the 1960s, engineers like IBM's Robert Dennard began envisioning integrated circuits that could "remember" more efficiently than little metal rings. Dennard had long, dark hair that flowed below his ears, then shot out at a right angle, parallel to the ground, giving him the look of an eccentric genius. He proposed coupling a tiny transistor with a capacitor, a miniature storage device that is either charged (1) or not (0). Capacitors leak over time, so Dennard envisioned repeatedly charging the capacitor via the transistor. The chip would be called a dynamic (due to the repeated charging) random access memory, or DRAM. These chips form the core of computer memory up to the present day.

A DRAM chip worked like the old magnetic core memories, storing 1s and 0s with the help of electric currents. But rather than relying on wires and rings, DRAM circuits were carved into silicon. They didn't need to be weaved by hand, so they malfunctioned less often and could be made far smaller. Noyce and Moore bet that their new company, Intel, could take Dennard's insight and put it on a chip far denser than a magnetic core could ever be. It only took one glance at a graph of Moore's Law to know that so long as Silicon Valley could keep shrinking transistors, DRAM chips would conquer the business of computer memory.

Intel planned to dominate the business of DRAM chips. Memory chips don't need to be specialized, so chips with the same design can be used in many different types of devices. This makes it possible to produce them in large volumes. By contrast, the other main type of chips—those tasked with "computing" rather than "remembering"—were specially designed for each device, because every computing problem was different. A calculator worked differently than a missile's guidance computer, for example, so until the 1970s, they used different types of logic chips. This specialization drove up cost, so Intel decided to focus on memory chips, where mass production would produce economies of scale.

Bob Noyce could never resist an engineering puzzle, however. Even though he'd just raised several million dollars on the promise that his new company would build memory chips, he was quickly convinced to add a product line. In 1969, a Japanese calculator firm called Busicom approached Noyce with a request to design a complicated set of circuits for its newest calculator. Handheld calculators were the iPhones of the 1970s, a product that used the most advanced computing technologies to drive down price and put a powerful piece of plastic in everyone's pocket. Many Japanese firms built calculators, but they often relied on Silicon Valley to design and manufacture their chips.

Noyce asked Ted Hoff, a soft-spoken engineer who'd arrived at Intel after an academic career studying neural networks, to handle Busicom's request. Unlike most Intel employees, who were physicists or chemists focused on the electrons zipping across chips, Hoff's background in computer architectures let him see semiconductors from the perspective of the systems they powered. Busicom told Hoff they'd need twelve different chips with twenty-four thousand transistors, all arranged in a bespoke design. He thought this sounded impossibly complicated for a small startup like Intel.

As he considered Busicom's calculator, Hoff realized computers face a tradeoff between customized logic circuits and customized software. Because chipmaking was a custom business, delivering specialized circuits for each device, customers didn't think hard about software. However, Intel's progress with memory chips—and the prospect they would become exponentially more powerful over time—meant computers would soon have the memory capacity needed to handle complex software. Hoff bet it would soon be cheaper to design a standardized logic chip that, coupled with a powerful memory chip programmed with different types of software, could compute many different things. After all, Hoff knew, no one was building memory chips more powerful than Intel's.

Intel wasn't the first company to think about producing a generalized logic chip. A defense contractor had produced a chip much like Intel's for the computer on the F-14 fighter jet. However, that chip's existence was kept secret until the 1990s. Intel, however, launched a chip called the 4004 and described it as the world's first microprocessor—"a micro-programmable computer on a chip," as the company's advertising campaign put it. It could be used in many different types of devices and set off a revolution in computing.

At his parents' fiftieth wedding anniversary party in 1972, Bob Noyce interrupted the festivities, held up a silicon wafer, and declared to his family: "This is going to change the world." Now general logic could be mass-produced. Computing was ready for its own industrial revolution and Intel had the world's most advanced assembly lines.

The person who best understood how mass-produced computing power would revolutionize society was a Caltech professor named Carver Mead. With piercing eyes and a goatee, Mead looked more like a Berkeley philosopher than an electrical engineer. He had struck up a friendship with Gordon Moore just after the founding of Fairchild, after Moore waltzed into Mead's Caltech office, pulled out a sock filled with Raytheon 2N706 transistors, and gave them to Mead for use in his electrical engineering classes. Moore soon hired Mead as a consultant, and for many years, the Caltech visionary spent each Wednesday at Intel's facilities in Silicon Valley. Though Gordon Moore had first graphed the exponential increase in transistor density in his famous 1965 article, Mead coined the term "Moore's Law" to describe it.

"In the next ten years," Mead predicted in 1972, "every facet of our society will be automated to some degree." He envisioned "a tiny computer deep down inside of our telephone, or our washing machine, or our car" as these silicon chips became pervasive and inexpensive. "In the past 200 years we have improved our ability to manufacture goods and move people by a factor of 100," Mead calculated. "But in the last 20 years there has been an increase of 1,000,000 to 10,000,000 in the rate at which we process and retrieve information." A revolutionary explosion of data processing was coming. "We have computer power coming out of our ears."

Mead was prophesying a revolution with profound social and political consequences. Influence in this new world would accrue to people who could produce computing power and manipulate it with software. The semiconductor engineers of Silicon Valley had the specialized knowledge, networks, and stock options that let them write the rules of the future—rules everyone else would have to follow. Industrial society was giving way to a digital world, with 1s and 0s stored and processed on many millions of slabs of silicon spread throughout society. The era of the tech tycoons was dawning. "Society's fate will hang in the balance," Carver Mead declared. "The catalyst is the microelectronics technology and its ability to put more and more components into less and less space." Industry outsiders only dimly perceived how the world was changing, but Intel's leaders knew that if they succeeded in drastically expanding the availability of computing power, radical changes would follow. "We are really the revolutionaries in the world today," Gordon Moore declared in 1973, "not the kids with the long hair and beards who were wrecking the schools a few years ago."

CHAPTER 14

The Pentagon's Offset Strategy

No one benefitted more from Noyce and Moore's revolution than a cornerstone of the old order—the Pentagon. Upon arriving in Washington in 1977, William Perry felt "like a kid in a candy store." For a Silicon Valley entrepreneur like Perry, serving as undersecretary of defense for research and engineering was, he said, the "best job in the world." No one had a larger budget to buy technology than the Pentagon. And hardly anyone in Washington had so clear a view of how microprocessors and powerful memory chips could transform all the weapons and systems the Defense Department relied on.

Unlike Bob Noyce or Gordon Moore, who were making a fortune by ignoring the government and selling chips for mass market calculators and mainframe computers, Perry knew the Pentagon intimately. The son of a Pennsylvania baker, he began his career as a Silicon Valley scientist working for Sylvania Electronic Defense Laboratories, a unit of the same electronics company that had hired Morris Chang after he graduated MIT. Working for Sylvania in California, Perry was tasked with designing highly classified electronics that monitored Soviet missile launches. In fall 1963, he'd been one of ten experts urgently called to Washington to examine new photographs taken by U-2 spy planes showing Soviet missiles in Cuba. At a young age, Perry was already seen as one of the country's top experts on military affairs.

Perry's job at Sylvania had catapulted him into America's defense establishment. But he still lived in Mountain View. For an engineer surrounded by startups, old-school Sylvania began to seem bureaucratic and stodgy. Its technology was quickly becoming outdated. Its consumer and military products alike relied on vacuum tubes long after Silicon Valley's chipmakers were churning out integrated circuits. Perry was intimately familiar with the advances in solid-state electronics all around him. He sang in the same Palo Alto madrigals choir as Bob Noyce. So, sensing the revolution that was underway, in 1963, Perry had set off on his own, founding his own firm to design surveillance devices for the military. To get the processing power he needed, Perry bought chips from his singing partner, Intel's CEO.

In sunny Silicon Valley it felt like "everything was new and anything was possible," Perry would later remember. Viewed from the Pentagon upon his arrival in 1977, the world looked far darker. The U.S. had just lost the Vietnam War. Worse, the Soviet Union had almost completely eroded America's military advantage, warned Pentagon analysts like Andrew Marshall. Born in Detroit, Marshall was a small man, with a bald head and a beaky nose, who stared inscrutably at the world from behind his glasses. He'd worked in a machine tools factory during World War II, before becoming one of the most influential government officials of the last half century. Marshall had been hired in 1973 to establish the Pentagon's Office of Net Assessment and was tasked with forecasting the future of war.

Marshall's grim conclusion was that after a decade of pointless fighting in Southeast Asia, the U.S. had lost its military advantage. He was fixated on regaining it. Though Washington had been shocked by Sputnik and the Cuban Missile Crisis, it wasn't until the early 1970s that the Soviets had built a big enough stockpile of intercontinental ballistic missiles to guarantee that enough of their atomic weapons could survive a U.S. nuclear strike to retaliate with a devastating atomic barrage of their own. More worrisome, the Soviet army had far more tanks and planes, which were already deployed on potential battle-grounds in Europe. The U.S.—facing pressure at home to cut military spending—simply couldn't keep up.

Strategists like Marshall knew the only answer to the Soviet quantitative advantage was to produce better quality weapons. But how? As early as 1972, Marshall wrote that the U.S. needed to take advantage of its "substantial and durable lead" in computers. "A good strategy would be to develop that lead and to shift concepts of warfare in ways that capitalize on it," he wrote. He envisioned "rapid information gathering," "sophisticated command and control," and "terminal guidance" for missiles, imagining munitions that could strike targets with almost perfect accuracy. If the future of war became a contest for accuracy, Marshall wagered, the Soviets would fall behind.

Perry realized that Marshall's vision of the future of war would soon be possible due to the miniaturization of computing power. He was intimately familiar with Silicon Valley's semiconductor innovation, having used Intel's chips in his company's own devices. Many of the weapons systems used in the Vietnam War still relied on vacuum tubes, but chips in the newest handheld calculators offered vastly more computing power than an old Sparrow III missile. Put those chips in missiles, Perry wagered, and America's military would jump ahead of the Soviets.

Guided missiles would not only "offset" the USSR's quantitative advantage, he reasoned. They'd force the Soviets to undertake a ruinously expensive anti-missile effort in response. Perry calculated Moscow would need five to ten years and $30 to $50 billion to defend against the three thousand American cruise missiles that the Pentagon planned to field—and even then, the Soviets could only destroy half the incoming missiles if they were all fired at the USSR.

This was exactly the type of technology that Andrew Marshall had been looking for. Working with Jimmy Carter's secretary of defense, Harold Brown, Perry and Marshall pushed the Pentagon to invest heavily in new technologies: a new generation of guided missiles that used integrated circuits, not vacuum tubes; a constellation of satellites that could beam location coordinates to any point on earth; and—most important—a new program to jump-start the next generation of chips, to ensure that the U.S. kept its technological edge.

Led by Perry, the Pentagon poured money into new weapons systems that capitalized on America's advantage in microelectronics. Precision weapons programs like the Paveway were promoted, as were guided munitions of all types, from cruise missiles to artillery shells. Sensors and communications also began to leap forward with the application of miniaturized computing power. Detecting enemy submarines, for example, was largely a problem of developing accurate sensors and running the information they gathered through ever-more-complicated algorithms. With enough processing power, the military's acoustic experts wagered, it should be possible to distinguish a whale from a submarine from many miles away.

Guided weaponry became more complex. New systems like the Tomahawk missile relied on far more sophisticated guidance systems than the Paveway, using a radar altimeter to scan the ground and match it with terrain maps preloaded into the missile's computer. This way, the missile could redirect itself if it veered off course. This type of guidance had been theorized decades earlier but was only possible to implement now that powerful chips were small enough to fit in a cruise missile.

Individual guided munitions were a powerful innovation, but they'd be even more impactful if they could share information. Perry commissioned a special program, run via the Pentagon's Defense Advanced Research Projects Agency (DARPA), to see what would happen if all these new sensors, guided weapons, and communications devices were integrated. Called "Assault Breaker," it envisioned an aerial radar that could identify enemy targets and provide location information to a ground-based processing center, which would fuse the radar details with information from other sensors. Ground-based missiles would communicate with the aerial radar guiding them toward the target.

On final descent, the missiles would release submunitions that would individually home in on their targets.

Guided weapons were giving way to a vision of automated war, with computing power distributed to individual systems in a way never before imaginable. This was only possible because the U.S. was on track "to increase the density of chips ten to a hundredfold," as Perry told an interviewer in 1981, promising comparable increases in computing power. "We will be able to put computers, which only ten years ago would have filled up this entire room, on a chip" and field "'smart' weapons at all levels."

Perry's vision was as radical as anything Silicon Valley had cooked up. Could the Pentagon really implement a high-tech program? By the time Perry left office in 1981, as the Carter presidency ended, journalists and members of Congress were attacking his gamble on precision strike. "Cruise Missiles: Wonder Weapon or Dud?" asked one columnist in 1983. Another equated Perry's advanced technologies with "bells and whistles," pointing out the frequent malfunctions and dismal kill ratio of ostensibly "smart" weapons like the vacuum tube–powered Sparrow missile.

The advances in computing power that Perry's vision required seemed like science fiction to many critics, who assumed guided missile technology would improve slowly because tanks and planes changed slowly, too. Exponential increases, which Moore's Law dictated, are rarely seen and hard to comprehend. However, Perry wasn't alone in predicting a "ten to a hundredfold" improvement. Intel was promising the very same thing to its customers. Perry grumbled that his congressional critics were "Luddites," who simply didn't understand how rapidly chips were changing.

Even after Perry left office, the Defense Department continued to pour money into advanced chips and the military systems they powered. Andrew Marshall continued his work at the Pentagon, already dreaming of the new systems these next-generation chips would make possible. Could semiconductor engineers deliver the progress Perry promised?

Moore's Law predicted that they could—but this was only a prediction, not a guarantee. Moreover, unlike when integrated circuits were first invented, the chip industry had become less focused on military production. Firms like Intel targeted corporate computers and consumer goods, not missiles. Only consumer markets had the volume to fund the vast R&D programs that Moore's Law required.

In the early 1960s, it had been possible to claim the Pentagon had created Silicon Valley. In the decade since, the tables had turned. The U.S. military lost the war in Vietnam, but the chip industry won the peace that followed, binding the rest of Asia, from Singapore to Taiwan to Japan, more closely to the U.S. via rapidly expanding investment links and supply chains. The entire world was more tightly connected to America's innovation infrastructure, and even adversaries like the USSR spent their time copying U.S. chips and chipmaking tools. Meanwhile, the chip industry had catalyzed an array of new weapons systems that were remaking how the U.S. military would fight future wars. American power was being recast. Now the entire nation depended on Silicon Valley's success.

PART III

LEADERSHIP LOST?

CHAPTER 15

"That Competition Is Tough"

"Ever since you've written that paper, my life has been hell!" one chip salesman grumbled to Richard Anderson, a Hewlett-Packard executive tasked with deciding which chips met HP's stringent standards. The 1980s were a hellish decade for the entire U.S. semiconductor sector. Silicon Valley thought it sat atop the world's tech industry, but after two decades of rapid growth it now faced an existential crisis: cutthroat competition from Japan. When Anderson took the stage at an industry conference at Washington, D.C.'s historic Mayflower Hotel on March 25, 1980, the audience listened carefully, because everyone was trying to sell him their chips. Hewlett-Packard, the company he worked for, had invented the concept of a Silicon Valley startup in the 1930s, when Stanford grads Dave Packard and Bill Hewlett began tinkering with electronic equipment in a Palo Alto garage. Now it was one of America's biggest tech companies—and one of the largest buyers of semiconductors.

Anderson's judgment about a chip could shape the fate of any semiconductor company, but Silicon Valley's salesmen were never allowed to wine and dine him. "Sometimes I let them take me out to lunch," he admitted sheepishly. But the entire valley knew that he was the gatekeeper to almost everyone's most important customer. His job gave him a panoramic view of the semiconductor industry, including how each company was performing.

In addition to American companies like Intel and TI, Japanese firms like Toshiba and NEC were now building DRAM memory chips—though most people in Silicon Valley didn't take these players seriously. U.S. chipmakers were run by the people who'd invented high-tech. They joked that Japan was the country of "click, click"—the sound made by cameras that Japanese engineers brought to chip conferences to better copy the ideas. The fact that major American chipmakers were embroiled in intellectual property lawsuits with Japanese rivals was interpreted as evidence that Silicon Valley was still well ahead.

At HP, however, Anderson didn't simply take Toshiba and NEC seriously—he tested their chips and found that they were of far better quality than American competitors. None of the three Japanese firms reported failure rates above 0.02 percent during their first one thousand hours of use, he reported. The lowest failure rate of the three American firms was 0.09 percent—which meant four-and-a-half times as many U.S.-made chips were malfunctioning. The worst U.S. firm produced chips with 0.26 percent failure rates—over *ten* times as bad as the Japanese results. American DRAM chips worked the same, cost the same, but malfunctioned far more often. So why should anyone buy them?

Chips weren't the only U.S. industry facing pressure from high-quality, ultra-efficient Japanese competitors. In the immediate postwar years, "Made in Japan" had been a synonym for "cheap." But entrepreneurs like Sony's Akio Morita had cast off this reputation for low price, replacing it with products that were as high quality as those of any American competitor. Morita's transistor radios were the first prominent challenger to American economic preeminence, and their success emboldened Morita and his Japanese peers to set their sights even higher. American industries from cars to steel were facing intense Japanese competition.

By the 1980s, consumer electronics had become a Japanese specialty, with Sony leading the way in launching new consumer goods, grabbing market share from American rivals. At first Japanese firms succeeded by replicating U.S. rivals' products, manufacturing them at higher quality and lower price. Some Japanese played up the idea that they excelled at implementation, whereas America was better at innovation. "We have no Dr. Noyces or Dr. Shockleys," one Japanese journalist wrote, though the country had begun to accumulate its share of Nobel Prize winners. Yet prominent Japanese continued to downplay their country's scientific successes, especially when speaking to American audiences. Sony's research director, the famed physicist Makoto Kikuchi, told an American journalist that Japan had fewer geniuses than America, a country with "outstanding elites." But America also had "a long tail" of people "with less than normal intelligence," Kikuchi argued, explaining why Japan was better at mass manufacturing.

American chipmakers clung to their belief that Kikuchi was right about America's innovation advantage, even though contradictory data was piling up. The best evidence against the thesis that Japan was an "implementer" rather than an "innovator" was Kikuchi's boss, Sony CEO Akio Morita. Morita knew that replication was a recipe for second-class status and second-rate profits. He drove his engineers not only to build the best radios and TVs, but to imagine new types of products entirely.

In 1979, just months before Anderson's presentation about quality problems in American chips, Sony introduced the Walkman, a portable music player that revolutionized the music industry, incorporating five of the company's cutting-edge integrated circuits in each device. Now teenagers the world over could carry their favorite music in their pockets, powered by integrated circuits that had been pioneered in Silicon Valley but developed in Japan. Sony sold 385 million units worldwide, making the Walkman one of the most popular consumer devices in history. This was innovation at its purest, and it had been made in Japan.

The U.S. had supported Japan's postwar transformation into a transistor salesman. U.S. occupation authorities transferred knowledge about the invention of the transistor to Japanese physicists, while policymakers in Washington ensured Japanese firms like Sony could easily sell into U.S. markets. The aim of turning Japan into a country of democratic capitalists had worked. Now some Americans were asking whether it had worked too well. The strategy of empowering Japanese businesses seemed to be undermining America's economic and technological edge.

Charlie Sporck, the executive who'd been burned in effigy while managing a GE production line, found Japan's productivity fascinating and frightening. After starting in the chip industry at Fairchild, Sporck left to run National Semiconductor, then a large producer of memory chips. Ultra-efficient Japanese competition seemed certain to put him out of business. Sporck had a hard-earned reputation for his ability to squeeze efficiency out of assembly line workers, but Japan's productivity levels were far ahead of anything his workers could accomplish.

Sporck sent one of his foremen and a group of assembly line workers to spend several months in Japan touring semiconductor facilities. When they returned to California, Sporck made a film about their experience. They reported that Japanese workers were "amazingly pro-company" and that "the foreman put a priority to the company over his family." Bosses in Japan didn't have to worry about getting burned in effigy. It was a "beautiful story," Sporck declared. "It was something for all of our employees to see how that competition is tough."

CHAPTER 16

"At War with Japan"

"I don't want to pretend I'm in a fair fight," complained Jerry Sanders, CEO of Advanced Micro Devices. "I'm not." Sanders knew something about fights. At age eighteen, he'd almost died after a brawl on Chicago's South Side, where he grew up. After his body was found in a garbage can, a priest administered last rites, though he miraculously emerged from a coma three days later. He eventually landed a job in sales and marketing at Fairchild Semiconductor, working alongside Noyce, Moore, and Andy Grove before they left Fairchild to found Intel. Though his colleagues were mostly modest engineers, Sanders flashed expensive watches and drove a Rolls-Royce. He commuted weekly to Silicon Valley from Southern California, where he lived, because, one colleague recalled, he and his wife only really felt at home in Bel Air. After founding his own chip firm, AMD, in 1969, he spent much of the next three decades in a legal brawl with Intel over intellectual property disputes. "I can't walk away from a fight," he admitted to a journalist.

"The chip industry was an incredibly competitive industry," remembered Charlie Sporck, the executive who'd led the offshoring of chip assembly throughout Asia. "Knock 'em down, fight 'em, kill 'em," Sporck explained, hitting his fists together to illustrate his point. With pride, patents, and millions of dollars at stake, the brawls between U.S.

chipmakers often got personal, but there was still plenty of growth to go around. Japanese competition seemed different, however. If Hitachi, Fujitsu, Toshiba, and NEC succeeded, Sporck thought, they'd move the whole industry across the Pacific. "I worked specifically on TVs at GE," Sporck warned. "You can drive by that facility now, it's still empty. . . . We knew the dangers and we damn right well weren't gonna let that happen to us." Everything was at stake—jobs, fortunes, legacies, pride. "We're at war with Japan," Sporck insisted. "Not with guns and ammunition, but an economic war with technology, productivity, and quality."

Sporck saw Silicon Valley's internal battles as fair fights, but thought Japan's DRAM firms benefitted from intellectual property theft, protected markets, government subsidies, and cheap capital. Sporck had a point about the spies. After a 5 a.m. rendezvous in the lobby of a Hartford, Connecticut, hotel on a cold November morning in 1981, Hitachi employee Jun Naruse handed over an envelope of cash and received in exchange a badge from a "consultant" at a company called Glenmar that promised to help Hitachi obtain industrial secrets. With the badge, Naruse gained entrance to a secret facility run by aircraft maker Pratt & Whitney and photographed the company's newest computer.

After the photo shoot, Naruse's colleague on the West Coast, Kenji Hayashi, sent a letter to Glenmar proposing a "consultation service contract." Hitachi's senior executives authorized half a million dollars in payments to Glenmar to continue the relationship. But Glenmar was a front company; its employees were FBI agents. "It seems that Hitachi stepped into the trap," the company's spokesman sheepishly admitted, after Hitachi's employees were arrested and the story made the front page of the business section of the *New York Times*.

Hitachi wasn't alone. Mitsubishi Electric faced similar charges. It wasn't only in semiconductors and computers that accusations of Japanese espionage and double-dealing swirled. Toshiba, the Japanese industrial conglomerate that by the mid-1980s was a world-leading DRAM producer, spent years fighting claims—true, it turned out—that the company sold the Soviets machinery that helped them build quieter submarines. There was no direct link between Toshiba's Soviet submarine deal and the company's semiconductor business, but many Americans saw the submarine case as further evidence of Japanese dirty dealing. The number of documented cases of illegal Japanese industrial espionage was low. But was this a sign that stealing secrets played only a small role in Japan's success, or evidence that Japanese firms were skilled at spycraft?

Sneaking into rivals' facilities was illegal but keeping tabs on competitors was normal practice in Silicon Valley. So, too, was accusing rivals of pilfering employees, ideas, and intellectual property. America's chipmakers were constantly suing each other, after all. It took a decade of litigation between Fairchild and Texas Instruments to resolve the question of whether Noyce or Kilby had invented the integrated circuit, for example. Chip firms regularly poached rivals' star engineers, too, hoping not only to acquire experienced workers but also knowledge about their competitors' production processes. Noyce and Moore had left Shockley Semiconductor to found Fairchild, then left Fairchild to found Intel, where they hired dozens of Fairchild employees, including Andy Grove. Fairchild considered suing before deciding that it was unlikely to win a lawsuit against the geniuses who had built the chip industry. Tracking and emulating rivals was key to Silicon Valley's business model. Was Japan's strategy any different?

Sporck and Sanders pointed out that Japanese firms benefitted from a protected domestic market, too. Japanese firms could sell to the U.S., but Silicon Valley struggled to win market share in Japan. Until 1974, Japan imposed quotas limiting the number of chips U.S. firms could sell there. Even after these quotas were lifted, Japanese companies still bought few chips from Silicon Valley, even though Japan consumed a quarter of the world's semiconductors, which companies like Sony plugged into TVs and VCRs that were sold worldwide. Some big Japanese chip consumers such as NTT, Japan's national telecom monopoly, bought almost exclusively from Japanese suppliers. This was ostensibly a business decision, but NTT was government-owned, so politics likely played a role. Silicon Valley's low market share in Japan cost American companies billions of dollars in sales.

Japan's government subsidized its chipmakers, too. Unlike in the U.S., where antitrust law discouraged chip firms from collaborating, the Japanese government pushed companies to work together, launching a research consortium called the VLSI Program in 1976 with the government funding around half the budget. America's chipmakers cited this as evidence of unfair Japanese competition, though the $72 million the VLSI Program spent annually on R&D was about the same as Texas Instruments' R&D budget, and less than Motorola's. Moreover, the U.S. government was itself deeply involved in supporting semiconductors, though Washington's funding took the form of grants from DARPA, the Pentagon unit that invests in speculative technologies and has played a crucial role in funding chipmaking innovation.

Jerry Sanders saw Silicon Valley's biggest disadvantage as its high cost of capital. The Japanese "pay 6 percent, maybe 7 percent, for capital. I pay 18 percent on a good day," he complained. Building advanced manufacturing facilities was brutally expensive, so the cost of credit was hugely important. A next-generation chip emerged roughly once every two years, requiring new facilities and new machinery. In the 1980s, U.S. interest rates reached 21.5 percent as the Federal Reserve sought to fight inflation.

By contrast, Japanese DRAM firms got access to far cheaper capital. Chipmakers like Hitachi and Mitsubishi were part of vast conglomerates with close links to banks that provided large, long-term loans. Even when Japanese companies were unprofitable, their banks kept them afloat by extending credit long after American lenders would have driven them to bankruptcy. Japanese society was structurally geared to produce massive savings, because its postwar baby boom and rapid shift to one-child households created a glut of middle-aged families focused on saving for retirement. Japan's skimpy social safety net provided a further incentive for saving. Meanwhile, tight restrictions on stock markets and other investments left people with little choice but to stuff savings in bank accounts. As a result, banks were flush with deposits, extending loans at low rates because they had so much cash on hand. Japanese companies had more debt than American peers but nevertheless paid lower rates to borrow.

With this cheap capital, Japanese firms launched a relentless struggle for market share. Toshiba, Fujitsu, and others were just as ruthless in competing with each other, despite the cooperative image painted by some American analysts. Yet with practically unlimited bank loans available, they could sustain losses as they waited for competitors to go bankrupt. In the early 1980s, Japanese firms invested 60 percent more than their U.S. rivals in production equipment, even though everyone in the industry faced the same cutthroat competition, with hardly anyone making much profit. Japanese chipmakers kept investing and producing, grabbing more and more market share. Because of this, five years after the 64K DRAM chip was introduced, Intel—the company that had pioneered DRAM chips a decade earlier—was left with only 1.7 percent of the global DRAM market, while Japanese competitors' market share soared.

Japan's firms doubled down on DRAM production as Silicon Valley was pushed out. In 1984, Hitachi spent 80 billion yen on capital expenditure for its semiconductor business, compared to 1.5 billion a decade earlier. At Toshiba, spending grew from 3 billion to 75 billion; at NEC, from 3.5 billion to 110 billion. In 1985, Japanese firms spent 46 percent of the world's capital expenditure on semiconductors, compared to America's 35 percent. By 1990, the figures were even more lopsided, with Japanese firms accounting for half the world's investment in chipmaking facilities and equipment. Japan's CEOs kept building new facilities so long as their banks were happy to foot the bill.

The Japanese chipmakers argued that none of this was unfair. America's semiconductor firms got plenty of help from the government, especially via defense contracts. Anyway, American consumers of chips, like

HP, had hard evidence that Japanese chips were simply better quality. So Japan's market share in DRAM chips grew every year during the 1980s, at the expense of American rivals. Japan's semiconductor surge seemed unstoppable, no matter the apocalyptic predictions of American chipmakers. Soon all of Silicon Valley would be left for dead, like teenage Jerry Sanders in a South Side garbage can.

CHAPTER 17

"Shipping Junk"

A s the Japanese juggernaut tore through America's high-tech industry, it wasn't only companies producing DRAM chips that struggled. Many of their suppliers did, too. In 1981, GCA Corporation was being celebrated as one of America's "hottest high-technology corporations," growing rapidly by selling equipment that made possible Moore's Law. In the two decades since physicist Jay Lathrop had first turned his microscope upside down to shine light on photoresist chemicals and "print" patterns on semiconductor wafers, the process of photolithography had become vastly more complicated. Long gone were the days of Bob Noyce driving up and down California's Highway 101 in his old jalopy in search of movie camera lenses for Fairchild's makeshift photolithography equipment. Now lithography was big business, and at the start of the 1980s, GCA was at the top.

Though photolithography had become far more precise than in the days of Jay Lathrop's upside-down microscope, the principles remained the same. A light shined through masks and lenses, projecting focused shapes onto a silicon wafer covered with photoresist chemicals. Where light struck, the chemicals reacted with the light, allowing them to be washed away, exposing microscopic indentations on top of the silicon wafer. New materials were added in these holes, building circuits on the silicon. Specialized chemicals etched away the photoresist, leaving behind perfectly formed shapes. It often took five, ten, or twenty iterations of lithography, deposition, etching, and polishing to fabricate an integrated circuit, with the result layered like a geometric wedding cake. As transistors were miniaturized, each part of the lithography process—from the chemicals to the lenses to the lasers that perfectly aligned the silicon wafers with the light source—became even more difficult.

The world's leading lens makers were Germany's Carl Zeiss and Japan's Nikon, though the U.S. had a few specialized lens makers, too. Perkin Elmer, a small manufacturer in Norwalk, Connecticut, had made bombsights for the U.S. military during World War II and lenses for Cold War satellites and spy planes. The company realized this technology could be used in semiconductor lithography and developed a chip scanner that could align a silicon wafer and a lithographic light source with almost perfect precision, which was crucial if the light was to hit the silicon exactly as intended. The machine moved the light across the wafer like a copy machine, exposing the photoresist-covered wafer as if it were being painted with lines of light. Perkin Elmer's scanner could create chips with features approaching one micron—a millionth of a meter—in width.

Perkin Elmer's scanner dominated the lithography market in the late 1970s, but by the 1980s, it had been displaced by GCA, a company led by an Air Force officer–turned-geophysicist named Milt Greenberg, an ambitious, stubborn, foul-mouthed genius. Greenberg and an Air Force buddy founded GCA after World War II with seed capital from the Rockefellers. Trained as a military meteorologist, Greenberg had parlayed his knowledge of the atmosphere and his Air Force connections into work as a defense contractor, producing devices like high-altitude balloons that made measurements and took photographs of the Soviet Union.

Greenberg's ambitions soon flew even higher. The growth in the semiconductor industry showed that the real money was in the mass market, not in specialized military contracts. Greenberg thought his company's high-tech optical systems—useful for military reconnaissance—could be deployed on civilian chips. At an industry conference in the late 1970s, where GCA was advertising its systems for chipmakers, Texas Instruments' Morris Chang walked up to the GCA booth, started looking at the company's equipment, and inquired whether, rather than scanning light across the length of a wafer, the firm's equipment could move step-by-step, exposing each chip on the silicon wafer. Such a "stepper" would be far more accurate than the existing scanners. Though a stepper had never been devised, GCA's engineers believed they could create one, providing higher-resolution imaging and thus smaller transistors.

Several years later, in 1978, GCA introduced its first stepper. Sales orders began rolling in. Before the stepper, GCA had never made more than $50 million a year in revenue on its military contracts, but now it had a monopoly on an extraordinarily valuable machine. Revenue soon hit $300 million and the company's stock price surged.

As Japan's chip industry rose, however, GCA began to lose its edge. Greenberg, the CEO, imagined himself as a business titan, but he spent less time running the business and more hobnobbing with politicians. He broke ground on a major new manufacturing facility, betting that the early 1980s semiconductor boom would continue indefinitely. Costs spun out of control. Inventory was wildly mismanaged. One employee stumbled onto a million dollars' worth of precision lenses sitting forgotten in a closet. Stories circulated of executives buying Corvettes on company credit cards. One of Greenberg's founding partners admitted that the company was spending money like a "drunken sailor."

The firm's excesses were poorly timed. The semiconductor industry had always been ferociously cyclical, with the industry skyrocketing upward when demand was strong, and slumping back when it was not. It didn't take a rocket scientist—and GCA had a handful on staff—to figure out that after the boom of the early 1980s, a downturn would eventually follow. Greenberg chose not to listen. "He didn't want to hear from the marketing department that 'there's going to be a downturn,'" one employee remembered. So the company entered the mid-1980s semiconductor slump heavily overextended. Global sales of lithography equipment fell by 40 percent between 1984 and 1986. GCA's revenue fell by over two-thirds. "If we had a competent economist on staff, we might have predicted it," one employee remembered. "But we didn't. We had Milt."

Just as the market slumped, GCA lost its position as the only company building steppers. Japan's Nikon had initially been a partner of GCA, providing the precision lenses for its stepper. But Greenberg had decided to cut Nikon out, buying his own lens maker, New York–based Tropel, which made lenses for the U2 spy planes but which struggled to produce the number of high-quality lenses GCA needed. Meanwhile, GCA's customer service atrophied. The company's attitude, one analyst recounted, was "buy what we build and don't bother us." The company's own employees admitted that "customers got fed up." This was the attitude of a monopolist—but GCA was no longer a monopoly. After Greenberg stopped buying Nikon lenses, the Japanese company decided to make its own stepper. It acquired a machine from GCA and reverse engineered it. Soon Nikon had more market share than GCA.

Many Americans blamed Japan's industrial subsidies for GCA's loss of lithography leadership. It was true that Japan's VLSI program, which boosted the country's producers of DRAM chips, also helped equipment suppliers like Nikon. As U.S. and Japanese firms traded accusations of unfair government help, commercial relations grew stormy. But GCA employees admitted that, though their technology was world class, the company struggled with mass production. Precision manufacturing was essential, since lithography was now so exact that a thunderstorm rolling through could change air pressure—and thus the angle at which light refracted—enough to distort the images carved on chips. Building hundreds of steppers a year required a laser focus on manufacturing and quality control. But GCA's leaders were focused elsewhere.

It was popular to interpret the decline of GCA as an allegory about Japan's rise and America's fall. Some analysts saw evidence of a broader manufacturing decay that started in steel, then afflicted cars, and was now spreading to high-tech industries. In 1987, Nobel Prize–winning MIT economist Robert Solow, who pioneered the study of productivity and economic growth, argued that the chip industry suffered from an "unstable structure," with employees job hopping between firms and companies declining to invest in their workers. Prominent economist Robert Reich lamented the "paper entrepreneurialism" in Silicon Valley, which he thought focused too much on the search for prestige and affluence rather than technical advances. At American universities, he declared, "science and engineering programs are foundering."

American chipmakers' DRAM disaster was somewhat related to GCA's collapsing market share. The Japanese DRAM firms that were outcompeting Silicon Valley preferred to buy from Japanese toolmakers, benefitting Nikon at the expense of GCA. However, most of GCA's problems were homegrown, driven by unreliable equipment and bad customer service. Academics devised elaborate theories to explain how Japan's huge conglomerates were better at manufacturing than America's small startups. But the mundane reality was that GCA didn't listen to its customers, while Nikon did. Chip firms that interacted with GCA found it "arrogant" and "not responsive." No one said that about its Japanese rivals.

By the mid-1980s, therefore, Nikon's systems were far better than GCA's—even when the skies were sunny. Nikon's machines produced meaningfully better yields and broke down far less often. Before IBM transitioned to Nikon steppers, it hoped each machine it used would work seventy-five hours before needing downtime for adjustments or repairs, for example. Nikon's customers averaged ten times that duration of continuous use.

Greenberg, GCA's CEO, could never figure out how to fix the company. Up to the day he was ousted, he didn't realize just how many of his company's problems were internal. As he flew around the world on sales visits, drinking a Bloody Mary in first class, customers thought the firm was "shipping junk." Employees complained that Greenberg was in hock to Wall Street, focused as much on the stock price as on the business model. To make end-of-year numbers, the company would collude with customers, shipping an empty crate with a user's manual in December before delivering the machines themselves the subsequent year. However, it was impossible to cover up the company's loss of market share. U.S. firms, with GCA as the leader, controlled 85 percent of the global market for semiconductor lithography equipment in 1978. A decade later this figure had dropped to 50 percent. GCA had no plan to turn things around.

Greenberg himself aimed criticism at the company's employees. "He would use unbelievable four-letter words," one subordinate remembered. Another recalled a decision to ban high-heeled shoes, which Greenberg thought ruined the company's carpets. As tension grew, the receptionist developed a code with fellow employees, turning on a ceiling light to denote that Greenberg was in the building, and turning it off when he left. Everyone could breathe a bit easier when he was out. But this couldn't stop America's lithography leader from hurtling toward crisis.

CHAPTER 18

The Crude Oil of the 1980s

On a chilly spring evening in Palo Alto, Bob Noyce, Jerry Sanders, and Charlie Sporck met under a sloping, pagoda-style roof. Ming's Chinese Restaurant was a staple of the Silicon Valley lunch circuit. But America's tech titans weren't at Ming's for its famous Chinese chicken salad. Noyce, Sanders, and Sporck had all started their careers at Fairchild: Noyce the technological visionary; Sanders the marketing showman; Sporck the manufacturing boss barking at his employees to build faster, cheaper, better. A decade later they'd become competitors as CEOs of three of America's biggest chipmakers. But as Japan's market share grew, they decided it was time to band together again. At stake was the future of America's semiconductor industry. Huddled over a table in a private dining room at Ming's, they devised a new strategy to save it. After a decade of ignoring the government, they were turning to Washington for help.

Semiconductors are the "crude oil of the 1980s," Jerry Sanders declared, "and the people who control the crude oil will control the electronics industry." As CEO of AMD, one of America's biggest chipmakers, Sanders had plenty of self-interested reasons to describe his main product as strategically crucial. But was he wrong? Throughout the 1980s, America's computer industry expanded rapidly, as PCs were made small enough and cheap enough for an individual home or office.

Every business was coming to rely on them. Computers couldn't work without integrated circuits. Nor, by the 1980s, could planes, automobiles, camcorders, microwaves, or the Sony Walkman. Every American now had semiconductors in their houses and cars; many used dozens of chips daily. Like oil, they were impossible to live without. Didn't this make them "strategic"? Shouldn't America be worried Japan was becoming "the Saudi Arabia of semiconductors"?

The oil embargoes of 1973 and 1979 had demonstrated to many Americans the risks of relying on foreign production. When Arab governments cut oil exports to punish America for supporting Israel, the U.S. economy plunged into a painful recession. A decade of stagflation and political crises followed. American foreign policy fixated on the Persian Gulf and securing its oil supplies. President Jimmy Carter declared the region one of "the vital interests of the United States of America." Ronald Reagan deployed the U.S. Navy to escort oil tankers in and out of the Gulf. George H. W. Bush went to war with Iraq in part to liberate Kuwait's oil fields. When America said that oil was a "strategic" commodity, it backed the claim with military force.

Sanders wasn't asking for the U.S. to send the Navy halfway across the world to secure supplies of silicon. But shouldn't the government find a way to help its struggling semiconductor firms? In the 1970s, Silicon Valley firms had forgotten about the government as they replaced defense contracts with civilian computer and calculator markets. In the 1980s, they crawled sheepishly back to Washington. After their dinner at Ming's, Sanders, Noyce, and Sporck joined other CEOs to create the Semiconductor Industry Association to lobby Washington to support the industry.

When Jerry Sanders described chips as "crude oil," the Pentagon knew exactly what he meant. In fact, chips were even more strategic than petroleum. Pentagon officials knew just how important semiconductors were to American military primacy. Using semiconductor technology to "offset" the Soviet conventional advantage in the Cold War had been American strategy since the mid-1970s, when Bob Noyce's singing partner Bill Perry ran the Pentagon's research and engineering division. American defense firms had been instructed to pack their newest planes, tanks, and rockets with as many chips as possible, enabling better guidance, communication, and command and control. In terms of producing military power, the strategy was working better than anyone except Bill Perry had thought possible.

There was only one problem. Perry had assumed that Noyce and his other Silicon Valley neighbors would remain on top of the industry. But in 1986, Japan had overtaken America in the number of chips produced. By the end of the 1980s, Japan was supplying 70 percent of the world's lithography equipment. America's share—in an industry invented by Jay Lathrop in a U.S. military lab—had fallen to 21 percent. Lithography is "simply something we can't lose, or we will find ourselves completely dependent on overseas manufacturers to make our most sensitive stuff," one Defense Department official told the *New York Times*. But if the trends of the mid-1980s continued, Japan would dominate the DRAM industry and drive major U.S. producers out of business. The U.S. might find itself even more reliant on foreign chips and semiconductor manufacturing equipment than it was on oil, even at the depths of the Arab embargo. Suddenly Japan's subsidies for its chip industry, widely blamed for undermining American firms like Intel and GCA, seemed like a national security issue.

The Defense Department recruited Jack Kilby, Bob Noyce, and other industry luminaries to prepare a report on how to revitalize America's semiconductor industry. Noyce and Kilby spent hours at brainstorming sessions in the Washington suburbs, working with defense industrial experts and Pentagon officials. Kilby had long worked closely with the Defense Department, given Texas Instruments' role as a major supplier of electronics for weapons systems. IBM and Bell Labs also had deep connections with Washington. But Intel's leaders had previously portrayed themselves as "Silicon Valley cowboys who didn't need anybody's help," as one defense official put it. The fact that Noyce was willing to spend time at the Defense Department was a sign of how serious a threat the semiconductor industry faced—and how dire the impact on the U.S. military could be.

The U.S. military was more dependent on electronics—and thus on chips—than ever before. By the 1980s, the report found, around 17 percent of military spending went toward electronics, compared to 6 percent at the end of World War II. Everything from satellites to early warning radars to self-guided missiles depended on advanced chips. The Pentagon's task force summarized the ramifications in four bullet points, underlining the key conclusions:

- U.S. military forces depend heavily on technological superiority to win.
- Electronics is the technology that can be leveraged most highly.
- Semiconductors are the key to leadership in electronics.
- U.S. defense will soon depend on foreign sources for state-of-the-art technology in semiconductors.

Of course, Japan was officially a Cold War ally—at least for now. When the U.S. had occupied Japan in the years immediately after World War II, it had written Japan's constitution to make militarism impossible. But after the two countries had signed a mutual defense pact in 1951, the U.S. began cautiously to encourage Japanese rearmament, seeking military support against the Soviet Union. Tokyo agreed, but it capped its military spending around 1 percent of Japan's GDP. This was intended to reassure Japan's neighbors, who viscerally remembered the country's wartime expansionism. However, because Japan didn't spend heavily on arms, it had more funds to invest elsewhere. The U.S. spent five to ten times more on defense relative to the size of its economy. Japan focused on growing its economy, while America shouldered the burden of defending it.

The results were more spectacular than anyone had expected. Once derided as a country of transistor salesmen, Japan was now the world's second-largest economy. It was challenging American industrial dominance in areas that were crucial to U.S. military power. Washington had long urged Tokyo to let the United States contain the Communists while Japan expanded its foreign trade, but this division of labor no longer seemed very favorable to the United States. Japan's economy had grown at unprecedented speed, while Tokyo's success in high-tech manufacturing was now threatening America's military edge. Japan's advance had caught everyone by surprise. "You don't want the same thing to happen to semiconductors as happened to the TV industry, to the camera industry," Sporck told the Pentagon. "Without semiconductors you're in nowheresville."

CHAPTER 19

Death Spiral

"We're in a death spiral," Bob Noyce told a reporter in 1986. "Can you name a field in which the U.S. is not falling behind?" In his more pessimistic moments, Noyce wondered whether Silicon Valley would end up like Detroit, its flagship industry withering under the impact of foreign competition. Silicon Valley had a schizophrenic relationship with the government, simultaneously demanding to be left alone and requesting that it help. Noyce exemplified the contradiction. He'd spent his earliest days at Fairchild avoiding Pentagon bureaucracy while benefitting from the Cold War–era space race. Now he thought the government needed to help the semiconductor industry, but he still feared that Washington would impede innovation. Unlike in the days of the Apollo program, by the 1980s over 90 percent of semiconductors were bought by companies and consumers, not the military. It was hard for the Pentagon to shape the industry because the Defense Department was no longer Silicon Valley's most important customer.

Moreover, in Washington there was little agreement on whether Silicon Valley merited government help. After all, many industries were suffering from Japanese competition, from car factories to steel mills. The chip industry and the Defense Department argued that semiconductors were "strategic." But many economists argued that there was no good definition of what "strategic" meant. Were semiconductors more "strategic" than jet engines? Or industrial robots? "Potato chips, computer chips, what's the difference?" one Reagan Administration economist was widely quoted as saying. "They're all chips. A hundred dollars of one or a hundred dollars of the other is still a hundred." The economist in question denies having ever compared potatoes to silicon. But the point was a reasonable one. If Japanese firms could produce DRAM chips at a lower price, perhaps the U.S. was better off buying them and pocketing the cost savings. If so, American computers would be cheaper as a result—and the computer industry might advance more quickly.

The question of support for semiconductors was decided by lobbying in Washington. One issue on which Silicon Valley and free market economists agreed was taxes. Bob Noyce testified to Congress in favor of cutting the capital gains tax from 49 percent to 28 percent and advocated loosening financial regulation to let pension funds invest in venture capital firms. After these changes, a flood of money rushed into the venture capital firms on Palo Alto's Sand Hill Road. Next, Congress tightened intellectual property protections via the Semiconductor Chip Protection Act, after Silicon Valley executives like Intel's Andy Grove testified to Congress that legal copying by Japanese firms was undermining America's market position.

As Japan's DRAM market share grew, however, tax cuts and copyright changes seemed insufficient. The Pentagon was unwilling to bet its defense industrial base on the future impact of copyright law. Silicon Valley CEOs lobbied for even more help. Noyce estimated that he spent half his time in the 1980s in Washington. Jerry Sanders attacked the "subsidies and nurturing, targeting and protection of markets" that Japan had pursued. "The Japanese subsidies have been in the billions," Sanders declared. Even after the U.S. and Japan reached an agreement to eliminate tariffs on semiconductor trade, Silicon Valley struggled to sell Japan more chips. Trade negotiators compared negotiating with the Japanese to peeling an onion. "The whole thing is a rather zen experience," one U.S. trade negotiator reported, with discussions ending with philosophical questions like "what is an onion, anyway." U.S. DRAM sales into Japan barely budged.

Prodded by the Pentagon and lobbied by industry, the Reagan administration eventually decided to act. Even former free traders like Reagan's secretary of state George Shultz concluded that Japan would only open its market if the U.S. threatened tariffs. America's chip industry lodged a series of formal complaints against Japanese firms for "dumping" cheap chips in the U.S. market. The claim that Japanese firms were selling below production cost was hard to prove. U.S. firms cited Japanese competitors' low cost of capital; Japan responded by saying that interest rates were lower across Japan's economy. Both sides had a point.

In 1986, with the threat of tariffs looming, Washington and Tokyo cut a deal. Japan's government agreed to put quotas on its exports of DRAM chips, limiting the number that were sold to the U.S. By decreasing supply, the agreement drove up the price of DRAM chips everywhere outside of Japan, to the detriment of American computer producers, which were among the biggest buyers of Japan's chips. Higher prices actually benefitted Japan's producers, which continued to dominate the DRAM market. Most American producers were already in the process of exiting the memory chip market. So despite the trade deal, only a few U.S. firms continued to produce DRAM chips. The trade restrictions redistributed profits within the tech industry, but they couldn't save most of America's memory chip firms.

Congress tried one final way to help. One of Silicon Valley's complaints was that Japan's government helped firms coordinate their R&D efforts and provided funds for this purpose. Many people in America's high-tech industry thought Washington should replicate these tactics. In 1987, a group of leading chipmakers and the Defense Department created a consortium called Sematech, funded half by the industry and half by the Pentagon.

Sematech was based on the idea that the industry needed more collaboration to stay competitive. Chipmakers needed better manufacturing equipment, while the firms that produced this equipment needed to know what chipmakers were looking for. CEOs of equipment firms complained that "companies like TI, Motorola, and IBM . . . just would not open up about their technology." Without an understanding of what technology these companies were working on, it was impossible to sell to them. Chipmakers, meanwhile, grumbled about the reliability of the machines they depended on. In the late 1980s, Intel's equipment was running only 30 percent of the time due to maintenance and repairs, one employee estimated.

Bob Noyce volunteered to lead Sematech. He was already de facto retired from Intel, having turned over the reins to Gordon Moore and Andy Grove a decade earlier. As the co-inventor of the integrated circuit and founder of two of America's most successful startups, he had the best technical and business credentials in the industry. No one could match his charisma or his connections in Silicon Valley. If anyone could resuscitate the chip industry, it was the person with the strongest claim to have created it.

Under Noyce's leadership, Sematech was a strange hybrid, neither a company nor a university nor a research lab. No one knew exactly what it was supposed to do. Noyce started by trying to help manufacturing equipment companies like GCA, many of which had strong technology but struggled to create durable businesses or effective manufacturing processes. Sematech organized seminars on reliability and good management skills, offering a sort of mini-MBA. It also began coordinating between equipment companies and chipmakers to align their production schedules. There was no point in a chipmaker preparing a new generation of chipmaking technology if the lithography or deposition equipment wasn't ready. Equipment firms didn't want to launch a new piece of machinery unless chipmakers were prepared to use it. Sematech helped them agree on production schedules. This wasn't exactly the free market, but Japan's biggest firms had excelled with this type of coordination. Anyway, what other choice did Silicon Valley have?

Noyce's focus, however, was saving America's lithography industry. Fifty-one percent of Sematech funding went to American lithography firms. Noyce explained the logic simply: lithography got half the money because it was "half the problem" facing the chip industry. It was impossible to make semiconductors without lithography tools, but the only remaining major U.S. producers were struggling to survive. America might soon be reliant on foreign equipment. Testifying to Congress in 1989, Noyce declared that "Sematech may likely be judged, in large part, as to how successful it is in saving America's optical stepper makers."

This was exactly what employees at GCA, the ailing Massachusetts manufacturer of lithography tools, were hoping to hear. After the company had invented the wafer stepper, a half decade of mismanagement and bad luck had left GCA a small player, far behind Japan's Nikon and Canon and the Netherlands' ASML. But when Peter Simone, GCA's president, called Noyce to discuss whether Sematech could help GCA, Noyce told him flatly: "You're done."

Few people in the chip industry could see how GCA could recover. Intel, which Noyce had founded, relied heavily on Nikon, GCA's primary Japanese competitor. "Why don't you come for one day," Simone proposed, hoping to convince Noyce that GCA could still produce cutting-edge machinery. Noyce agreed, and when he arrived in Massachusetts he decided that day to buy $13 million worth of GCA's newest equipment, as part of a program to share American-built semiconductor equipment with U.S. chipmakers and encourage them to buy more domestically produced tools.

Sematech bet hugely on GCA, giving the company contracts to produce deep-ultraviolet lithography equipment that was at the cutting edge of the industry's capabilities. GCA delivered far beyond expectations, living up to its earlier reputation for technological brilliance. Soon independent industry analysts were describing GCA's newest steppers as "the best in the world." The company even won a customer service award, casting off its reputation for being mediocre in that department. The software that GCA's machines used was far better than the company's Japanese rivals. "They were ahead of their time," recalled one lithography expert at Texas Instruments who tested GCA's newest machines.

But GCA still didn't have a viable business model. Being "ahead of your time" is good for scientists but not necessarily for manufacturing firms seeking sales. Customers had already gotten comfortable with equipment from competitors like Nikon, Canon, and ASML, and didn't want to take a risk on new and unfamiliar tools from a company whose future was uncertain. If GCA went bankrupt, customers might struggle to get spare parts. Unless a big customer could be convinced to sign a major contract with GCA, the company would spiral toward collapse. It lost $30 million between 1988 and 1992, despite $70 million in support from Sematech. Even Noyce could never convince Intel, the company he'd founded, to switch its allegiance from Nikon.

In 1990, Noyce, GCA's greatest supporter at Sematech, died of a heart attack after his morning swim. He'd built Fairchild and Intel, invented the integrated circuit, and commercialized the DRAM chips and microprocessors that undergird all modern computing. Lithography, however, proved immune to Noyce's magic. By 1993, GCA's owner, a company called General Signal, announced it would sell GCA or close it. As the clock ticked toward this self-imposed deadline, no buyer could be found. Sematech, which had already provided millions in funding for GCA, decided to pull the plug. GCA appealed one final time to the government for help, with top national security officials considering whether U.S. foreign policy required saving GCA. They concluded nothing could be done. The company shut its doors and sold off its equipment, joining a long list of firms vanquished by Japanese competition.

CHAPTER 20

The Japan That Can Say No

After decades of making millions by selling Americans electronics, Sony's Akio Morita began to detect "a certain arrogance" in his American friends. When he first licensed transistor technology in the 1950s, the U.S. was the world's tech leader. Since then, America had faced crisis after crisis. The disastrous war in Vietnam, racial tension, urban unrest, the humiliation of Watergate, a decade of stagflation, a gaping trade deficit, and now industrial malaise. After each new shock, America's allure dimmed.

On his first trip abroad in 1953, Morita had seen America as a country "that seemed to have everything." He was served ice cream with a tiny paper umbrella on the top. "This is from your country," the waiter told him, a humiliating reminder of how far behind Japan was. Three decades later, however, everything had changed. New York had seemed "glamorous" on Morita's first visit in the 1950s. Now it was dirty, crime-ridden, and bankrupt.

Sony, meanwhile, had become a global brand. Morita redefined Japan's image abroad. The country was no longer seen as a producer of paper umbrellas for ice cream sundaes. Now it built the world's most high-tech goods. Morita, whose family owned a major stake in Sony, had gotten rich. He had a powerful network of friends on Wall Street and in Washington. He cultivated the art of the New York dinner party as meticulously as other Japanese approached a traditional tea ceremony. Whenever Morita was in New York, he hosted the city's rich and famous at his apartment on 82nd and Fifth, just across from the Metropolitan Museum of Art. Morita's wife Yoshiko even wrote a book explaining American dinner party customs to unfamiliar Japanese readers, titled *My Thoughts on Home Entertaining*. (Kimonos were discouraged; "whenever everyone wears the same kind of outfit, harmony is enhanced.")

The Moritas enjoyed entertaining, but their dinner parties served a professional purpose, too. As commercial tension between the U.S. and Japan increased, Morita served as informal ambassador, explaining Japan to American powerbrokers. David Rockefeller was a personal friend. Morita dined with Henry Kissinger whenever the former secretary of state visited Japan. When private equity titan Pete Peterson took Morita to Augusta National, a golf club popular with CEOs, he was shocked to discover that "Akio had met them all." Not only that—Morita arranged a dinner with each of his acquaintances while at Augusta. "He must have had about ten meals a day while he was staying here," Peterson recounted.

Morita at first found the power and wealth represented by his American friends seductive. As America lurched from crisis to crisis, however, the aura around men like Henry Kissinger and Pete Peterson began to wane. Their country's system wasn't working—but Japan's was. By the 1980s, Morita perceived deep problems in America's economy and society. America had long seen itself as Japan's teacher, but Morita thought America had lessons to learn as it struggled with a growing trade deficit and the crisis in its high-tech industries. "The United States has been busy creating lawyers," Morita lectured, while Japan has "been busier creating engineers." Moreover, American executives were too focused on "this year's profit," in contrast to Japanese management, which was "long range." American labor relations were hierarchical and "old style," without enough training or motivation for shop-floor employees. Americans should stop complaining about Japan's success, Morita believed. It was time to tell his American friends: Japan's system simply worked better.

In 1989, Morita set out his views in a collection of essays titled *The Japan That Can Say No*: *Why Japan Will Be First Among Equals*. The book was coauthored with Shintaro Ishihara, a controversial far-right politician. While just a university student, Ishihara had risen to fame by publishing a sexually charged novel titled *Season of the Sun*, which was awarded Japan's most prestigious literary prize for new writers. He parlayed this fame, enhanced by derogatory diatribes against foreigners, into a parliamentary seat as a member of the ruling Liberal Democratic Party. In parliament, Ishihara agitated for Japan to assert itself internationally and to change the country's constitution, which had been dictated by U.S. occupation authorities after World War II, to let Tokyo build a powerful military.

It was hard to imagine a more provocative coauthor for Morita to have chosen as he lectured the United States about its internal crises. The book itself was a series of essays, some written by Morita and others by Ishihara. Morita's essays mostly rehashed his arguments about the failings of American business practices, though chapter titles such as "America, You Had Better Give Up Certain Arrogance" had a harsher tone than Morita usually expressed at New York dinner parties. Even the always gracious Morita found it difficult to mask his view that Japan's technological prowess had earned it a position among the world's great powers. "Militarily we could never defeat the United States," Morita told an American colleague at the time, "but economically we can overcome the United States and become number one in the world."

Ishihara never hesitated to say exactly what he was thinking. His first novel was a story of unconstrained sexual urges. His political career embraced the most unsavory instincts of Japanese nationalism. His essays in *The Japan That Can Say No* called for Japan to declare independence from an overbearing America that had bossed Japan around for too long. "Let's not give into America's bluster!" one of Ishihara's essays proclaimed. "Restrain America!" declared another. Japan's far right had always been unhappy with their country's secondary status in an America-led world. Morita's willingness to coauthor a book with someone like Ishihara shocked many Americans, showing that a threatening nationalism still lurked within the capitalist class that Washington had cultivated. The U.S. strategy since 1945 had been to bind Japan to the U.S. via exchanges of trade and technology. Akio Morita was arguably the greatest beneficiary of America's tech transfers and its market openness. If even *he* was questioning America's leading role, Washington needed to rethink its game plan.

What made *The Japan That Can Say No* truly frightening to Washington was not only that it articulated a zero-sum Japanese nationalism, but that Ishihara had identified a way to coerce America. Japan didn't need to submit to U.S. demands, Ishihara argued, because America relied on Japanese semiconductors. American military strength, he noted, required Japanese chips. "Whether it be mid-range nuclear weapons or inter-continental ballistic missiles, what ensures the accuracy of weapons is none other than compact, high-precision computers," he wrote. "If Japanese semiconductors are not used, this accuracy cannot be assured." Ishihara speculated that Japan could even provide advanced semiconductors to the USSR, tipping the military balance in the Cold War.

"The 1-megabit semiconductors which are used in the hearts of computers, which carry hundreds of millions of circuits in an area which is one-third the size of your little fingernail, are only made in Japan," Ishihara noted. "Japan has nearly a 100 percent share of these 1-megabit semiconductors. "Now Japan is at least five years ahead of the U.S. in this area and the gap is widening," he continued. Computers using Japan's chips were "central to military strength and therefore central to Japanese power . . . in that sense, Japan has become a very important country."

Other Japanese leaders appeared to take a similarly defiant nationalist view. One senior Foreign Ministry official was quoted as arguing that "Americans simply don't want to recognize that Japan has won the economic race against the West." Soon-to-be-prime-minister Kiichi Miyazawa publicly noted that cutting off Japanese electronics exports would cause "problems in the U.S. economy," and predicted that "the Asian economic zone will outdo the North American zone." Amid the collapse of its industries and its high-tech sector, America's future, a Japanese professor declared, was that of "a premier agrarian power, a giant version of Denmark."

In the U.S., *The Japan That Can Say No* sparked fury. It was translated and circulated in unofficial form by the CIA. One irate congressman entered the entire book—still published in English only unofficially—into the Congressional Record to publicize it. Bookstores reported that customers in Washington were "going absolutely bananas" trying to find bootleg copies. Morita sheepishly had the official English translation published only with Ishihara's essays, without his contributions. "I now regret my association with this project," Morita told reporters, "because it has caused so much confusion. I don't feel U.S. readers understand that my opinions are separate from Ishihara's. My 'essays' express my opinions and his 'essays' express his opinions."

Yet *The Japan That Can Say No* was controversial not because of its opinions, but because of the facts. The U.S. had fallen decisively behind in memory chips. If this trend persisted, geopolitical shifts would inevitably follow. It didn't take a far-right provocateur like Ishihara to recognize this; American leaders foresaw similar trends. The same year that Ishihara and Morita published *The Japan That Can Say No*, former defense secretary Harold Brown published an article that drew much the same conclusions. "High Tech Is Foreign Policy," Brown titled the article. If America's high-tech position was deteriorating, its foreign policy position was at risk, too.

This was an embarrassing admission for Brown, the Pentagon leader who'd hired Bill Perry in 1977 and empowered him to put semiconductors and computing power at the core of the military's most important new weapons systems. Brown and Perry succeeded in convincing the military to embrace microprocessors, but they hadn't anticipated Silicon Valley losing its lead. Their strategy paid off in terms of new weapons systems, but many of these now depended on Japan.

"Japan leads in memory chips, which are at the heart of consumer electronics," Brown admitted. "The Japanese are rapidly catching up in logic chips and application-specific integrated circuits." Japan also led in certain types of tools, like lithography equipment, needed to build chips. The best result Brown could foresee was a future in which the U.S. would protect Japan, but would do so with weapons powered by Japanese tech. America's strategy to turn Japan into a transistor salesman seemed to have gone horribly wrong.

Would Japan, a first-class technological power, be satisfied with second-class military status? If Japan's success in DRAM chips was any guide, it was set to overtake the United States in almost every industry that mattered. Why wouldn't it seek military dominance, too? If so, what would the U.S. do? In 1987, the CIA tasked a team of analysts with forecasting Asia's future. They saw Japanese dominance of semiconductors as evidence of an emerging "Pax Niponica"—an East Asian economic and political bloc led by Japan. American power in Asia had been built on technological dominance, military might, and trade and investment links that knit together Japan, Hong Kong, South Korea, and the countries of Southeast Asia. From the first Fairchild assembly plant on Hong Kong's Kowloon Bay, integrated circuits had been an integral feature of America's position in Asia. U.S. chipmakers built facilities from Taiwan to South Korea to Singapore. These territories were defended from Communist incursions not only by military force but also by economic integration, as the electronics industry sucked the region's peasants off farms—where rural poverty often inspired guerilla opposition—into good jobs assembling electronic devices for American consumption.

America's supply chain statecraft had worked brilliantly in fending off Communists, but by the 1980s, the primary beneficiary looked to have been Japan. Its trade and foreign investment had grown massively. Tokyo's role in Asia's economics and politics was expanding inexorably. If Japan could so swiftly establish dominance over the chip industry, what would stop it from dethroning America's geopolitical preeminence, too?

PART IV

AMERICA RESURGENT

CHAPTER 21

The Potato Chip King

Micron made "the best damn widgets in the whole world," Jack Simplot used to say. The Idaho billionaire didn't know much about the physics of how his company's main product, DRAM chips, actually worked. The chip industry was full of PhDs, but Simplot hadn't finished eighth grade. His expertise was potatoes, as everyone knew from the white Lincoln Town Car he drove around Boise. "Mr. Spud," the license plate declared. Yet Simplot understood business in a way Silicon Valley's smartest scientists didn't. As America's chip industry struggled to adjust to Japan's challenge, cowboy entrepreneurs like him played a fundamental role in reversing what Bob Noyce had called a "death spiral" and executing a surprise turnaround.

Silicon Valley's resurgence was driven by scrappy startups and by wrenching corporate transformations. The U.S. overtook Japan's DRAM behemoths not by replicating them but by innovating around them. Rather than cutting itself off from trade, Silicon Valley offshored even more production to Taiwan and South Korea to regain its competitive advantage. Meanwhile, as America's chip industry recovered, the Pentagon's bet on microelectronics began to pay off as it fielded new weapons systems that no other country could match. America's unrivaled power during the 1990s and 2000s stemmed from its resurgent dominance in computer chips, the core technology of the era.

117

Of all the people to help revive America's chip industry, Jack Simplot was the least likely candidate. He'd made his first fortune in potatoes, pioneering the use of machines to sort potatoes, dehydrate them, and freeze them for use in french fries. This wasn't Silicon Valley–style innovation, but it earned him a massive contract to sell spuds to McDonald's. At one point he supplied half the potatoes that McDonald's used to make fries.

Micron, the DRAM firm that Simplot backed, at first seemed guaranteed to fail. When twin brothers Joe and Ward Parkinson founded Micron in the basement of a Boise dentist office in 1978, it was the worst possible time to start a memory chip company. Japanese firms were ramping up production of high-quality, low-priced memory chips. Micron's first contract was to design a 64K DRAM chip for a Texas company called Mostek, but like every other American DRAM producer, it was beaten to the market by Fujitsu. Soon Mostek—the only customer for Micron's chip design services—went bust. Amid an onslaught of Japanese competition, AMD, National Semiconductor, Intel, and other industry leaders abandoned DRAM production, too. Facing billion-dollar losses and bankruptcies, it seemed like all Silicon Valley might go bankrupt. America's smartest engineers would be left flipping burgers. At least, the country still had plenty of french fries.

As Japanese firms grabbed market share, CEOs of America's biggest chip firms spent more and more time in Washington, lobbying Congress and the Pentagon. They set aside their free-market beliefs the moment Japanese competition mounted, claiming the competition was unfair. Silicon Valley angrily rejected the claim that there was no difference between potato chips and computer chips. Their chips merited government help, they insisted, because they were strategic in a way spuds weren't.

Jack Simplot didn't see anything wrong with potatoes. The argument that Silicon Valley deserved special help didn't go very far in Idaho, a state with few tech companies. Micron had had to raise funds the hard way. Micron cofounder Ward Parkinson had gotten to know a

Boise businessman named Allen Noble when he waded through Noble's muddy potato field in a business suit trying to find a malfunctioning electric component in an irrigation system. The Parkinson brothers parlayed this connection into $100,000 in seed funding from Noble and a couple of his wealthy Boise friends. When Micron lost its contract to design chips for Mostek and decided to make its own chips, the Parkinsons needed more capital. So they turned to Mr. Spud, the richest man in the state.

The Parkinson brothers first met Simplot at the Royal Café in downtown Boise, pouring sweat as they delivered their pitch to Idaho's potato plutocrat. Transistors and capacitors didn't mean much to Simplot, who was as close to the opposite of a Silicon Valley venture capitalist as you could get. He'd later preside over impromptu Micron board meetings each Monday at 5:45 a.m. at Elmer's, a local greasy spoon that served stacks of buttermilk pancakes for $6.99. However, as all of Silicon Valley's tech titans were fleeing DRAM chips amid the Japanese onslaught, Simplot instinctively understood that Ward and Joe Parkinson were entering the memory market at exactly the right time. A potato farmer like him saw clearly that Japanese competition had turned DRAM chips into a commodity market. He'd been through enough harvests to know that the best time to buy a commodity business was when prices were depressed and everyone else was in liquidation. Simplot decided to back Micron with $1 million. He'd later pour in millions more.

America's technology titans thought the Idaho country bumpkins didn't have a clue. "I'd hate to say it's over in memory chips," said L. J. Sevin, a former Texas Instruments engineer who'd become an influential venture capitalist. "But it's over." At Intel, Andy Grove and Gordon Moore had reached the same conclusion. Texas Instruments and National Semiconductor announced losses and layoffs in their DRAM divisions. The future of the U.S. chip industry, the *New York Times* declared, was "grim." So Simplot dove right in.

The Parkinson brothers played up their backcountry image, telling long, winding stories with a slight country drawl. In fact, they were as sophisticated as the founder of any Silicon Valley startup. Both had studied at Columbia University in New York, after which Joe worked as a corporate lawyer, while Ward designed chips at Mostek. But they embraced their Idaho outsider image. Their business model was to sweep into a market that America's biggest chip firms were abandoning, so they weren't going to make many friends anyway in Silicon Valley, which was still licking its wounds from the DRAM battles with Japan.

At first, Micron mocked Silicon Valley's efforts to secure government help against the Japanese. The company sanctimoniously declined to join the Semiconductor Industry Association, the lobby group started by Bob Noyce, Jerry Sanders, and Charlie Sporck. "It was very clear to me that they had a different agenda," Joe Parkinson declared. "Their strategy was, whatever the Japanese get into, let's get out. The people who are dominant in the SIA are not taking the Japanese on. In my opinion, it's a self-defeating strategy."

Micron decided to challenge the Japanese DRAM makers at their own game, but to do so by aggressively cutting costs. Soon the company realized that tariffs might help, and reversed course, leading the charge for tariffs on imported Japanese DRAM chips. They accused Japanese producers of "dumping" chips in the U.S. below cost, harming American producers. Simplot was furious about Japan's trade policies hurting his potato sales and his memory chips. "They've got a big tariff on potatoes," he grumbled. "We're paying through the nose on potatoes. We can out-tech 'em and we can out produce 'em. We'll beat the hell out of 'em. But they're giving those chips away." That's why he was demanding the government impose tariffs. "You ask why we go to the government? Cuz the law says they can't do that."

The allegation that Japanese firms were cutting prices by too much was a bit rich coming from Simplot. Whether spud or semiconductor, he'd always said business success required being "the lowest-cost producer of the highest-quality product." Anyway, Micron had a knack for cost cuts that none of its Silicon Valley or Japanese competitors could match. Ward Parkinson—"the engineering brains behind the organization," one early employee remembered—had a talent for designing DRAM chips as efficiently as possible. While most of his competitors were fixated on shrinking the size of transistors and capacitors on each chip, Ward realized that if he shrunk the size of the chip itself, Micron could put more chips on each of the circular silicon wafers that it processed. This made manufacturing far more efficient. "It was by far the worst product on the market," Ward joked, "but by far the least expensive to produce."

Next, Parkinson and his lieutenants simplified the manufacturing processes. The more steps in manufacturing, the more time each chip took to make and the more room for errors. By the mid-1980s, Micron used far fewer production steps than its competitors, letting the company use less equipment, cutting costs further. They tweaked the lithography machines they bought from Perkin Elmer and ASML to make them more accurate than the manufacturers themselves thought possible. Furnaces were modified to bake 250 silicon wafers per load rather than the 150 wafers that was industry standard. Every step of the fabrication process that could handle more wafers or reduce production times meant lower prices. "We were figuring it out on the fly," one early employee explained, so unlike other chipmakers, "we were prepared to do things that hadn't been written in a paper before." More than any of its Japanese or American competitors, the engineering expertise of Micron's employees was directed toward cost cuts.

Micron focused ruthlessly on costs because it had no choice. There was simply no other way for a small Idaho startup to win customers. It helped that land and electricity were cheaper in Boise than in California or in Japan, thanks in part to low-cost hydroelectric power. Survival was still a struggle. At one point, in 1981, the company's cash balances fell so low it could cover only two weeks of payroll. Micron scraped through that crisis, but amid another downturn a few years later it had to lay off half of its employees and cut salaries for the remainder. Since the earliest days of the business, Joe Parkinson had made sure employees realized that their survival depended on efficiency, going so far as to dim hallway lights at night to save on power bills when DRAM prices fell. Employees thought he was "maniacally" focused on costs—and it showed.

Micron's employees had no choice but to keep the company alive. In Silicon Valley, if your employer went bust you could drive down Route 101 to the next chip firm or computer maker. Micron, by contrast, was in Boise. "We didn't have something else to do," one employee explained. "We either made DRAMs, or game over." It was a "hardworking, blue collar work ethic," another remembered, a "sweatshop mentality." "Memory chips is a brutal, brutal business," recalled an early employee who survived a series of painful DRAM market downturns.

Jack Simplot never lost faith. He'd survived downswings in every business he'd ever owned. He wasn't going to abandon Micron because of short-term price swings. Despite entering the DRAM market just as Japanese competition was peaking, Micron survived and eventually thrived. Most other American DRAM producers were forced out of the market in the late 1980s. TI kept manufacturing DRAM chips but struggled to make any money, and eventually sold its operations to Micron. Simplot's first $1 million investment eventually ballooned into a billion-dollar stake.

Micron learned to compete with Japanese rivals like Toshiba and Fujitsu when it came to the storage capacity of each generation of DRAM chip and to outcompete them on cost. Like the rest of the DRAM industry, Micron's engineers bent the laws of physics as they made ever denser DRAM chips, providing the memory chips needed in personal computers. But advanced technology on its own wasn't enough to save America's DRAM industry. Intel and TI had plenty of technology but couldn't make the business work. Micron's scrappy Idaho engineers outmaneuvered rivals on both sides of the Pacific with their creativity and cost-cutting skill. After a decade of pain, the U.S. chip industry finally scored a win—and it was only possible thanks to the market wisdom of America's greatest potato farmer.

CHAPTER 22

Disrupting Intel

"Look, Clayton, I'm a busy man and I don't have time to read drivel from academics," Andy Grove told Harvard Business School's most famous professor, Clayton Christensen. When the two of them made the cover of *Forbes* several years later, Christensen—six feet, eight inches tall—towered over Grove, whose balding head barely reached Christensen's shoulder. But Grove's intensity outshone that of everyone around him. He was a "butt-kicking Hungarian," his longtime deputy explained, "chewing on people's ankles, and yelling at them, and challenging them, and pushing as hard as he could." More than anything else did, Grove's tenacity saved Intel from bankruptcy and made it one of the world's most profitable and powerful companies.

Professor Christiansen was famous for his theory of "disruptive innovation," in which a new technology displaces incumbent firms. As the DRAM business slumped, Grove realized that Intel—once synonymous with innovation—was now being disrupted. By the early 1980s, Grove was Intel's president, in charge of day-to-day operations, though Moore still played a major role. Grove described his management philosophy in his bestselling book *Only the Paranoid Survive*: "Fear of competition, fear of bankruptcy, fear of being wrong and fear of losing can all be powerful motivators." After a long day of work, it was fear that kept Grove flipping through his correspondence or on the phone with subordinates, worried he'd missed news of product delays or unhappy customers. On the outside, Andy Grove was living the American dream: a once-destitute refugee transformed into a tech titan. Inside this Silicon Valley success story was a Hungarian exile scarred by a childhood spent hiding from the Soviet and Nazi armies marching down Budapest streets.

Grove realized Intel's business model of selling DRAM chips was finished. DRAM prices might recover from the price slump, but Intel would never win back market share. It had been "disrupted" by Japanese producers. Now it would either disrupt itself or fail. Exiting the DRAM market felt impossible. Intel had pioneered memory chips, and admitting defeat would be humiliating. It was like Ford deciding to get out of cars, one employee said. "How could we give up our identity?" Grove wondered. He spent much of 1985 sitting in Gordon Moore's office at Intel's Santa Clara headquarters, the two of them staring out the window at the Ferris wheel in the Great America amusement park in the distance, hoping that like one of the cabins on the Ferris wheel, the memory market would eventually hit bottom and begin circling up again.

However, the disastrous DRAM numbers were impossible to deny. Intel would never make enough money in memory to justify new investments. It was a leader, though, in the small microprocessor market, where Japanese firms still lagged. And one development in that arena provided a glimmer of hope. In 1980, Intel had won a small contract with IBM, America's computer giant, to build chips for a new product called a personal computer. IBM contracted with a young programmer named Bill Gates to write software for the computer's operating system. On August 12, 1981, with the ornate wallpaper and thick drapes of the Waldorf Astoria's grand ballroom in the background, IBM announced the launch of its personal computer, priced at $1,565 for a bulky computer, a big-box monitor, a keyboard, a printer, and two diskette drives. It had a small Intel chip inside.

The microprocessor market seemed almost certain to grow. But the prospect that microprocessor sales could overtake DRAMs, which constituted the bulk of chip sales, seemed mind-boggling, one of Grove's deputies recalled. Grove saw no other choice. "If we got kicked out and the board brought in a new CEO, what do you think he would do?" Grove asked Moore, who wanted to keep producing DRAM chips. "He would get us out of memories," Moore admitted sheepishly. Finally, Intel decided to leave memories, surrendering the DRAM market to the Japanese and focusing on microprocessors for PCs. It was a gutsy gamble for a company that had been built on DRAMs. "Disruptive innovation" sounded attractive in Clayton Christensen's theory, but it was gut-wrenching in practice, a time of "gnashing of teeth," Grove remembered, and "bickering and arguments." The disruption was obvious. The innovation would take years to pay off, if it ever did.

While waiting to see if his bet on PCs would work, Grove applied his paranoia with a ruthlessness Silicon Valley had rarely seen. Workdays started at 8 a.m. sharp and anyone who signed in late was criticized publicly. Disagreements between employees were resolved via a tactic Grove called "constructive confrontation." His go-to management technique, quipped his deputy Craig Barrett, was "grabbing someone and slamming them over the head with a sledgehammer."

This wasn't the freewheeling culture Silicon Valley was known for, but Intel needed a drill sergeant. Its DRAM chips faced the same quality problems as those of other American chipmakers. When it had made money in DRAMs, it did so by being first to the market with a new design, not by being the leader in mass production. Bob Noyce and Gordon Moore had always fixated on maintaining cutting-edge tech. But Noyce admitted that he always found "the venture part" more fun than "the control part." Grove loved control as much as anything, which is why Gordon Moore had first brought him to Fairchild in 1963: to solve the company's production problems. When he followed Noyce and Moore to Intel, he was given the same role. Grove spent the rest of his life immersed in every detail of the company's manufacturing processes and its business, driven by a nagging sense of fear.

In Grove's restructuring plan, step one was to lay off over 25 percent of Intel's workforce, shutting facilities in Silicon Valley, Oregon, Puerto

Rico, and Barbados. Grove's deputy described his boss's approach as: "Oh my god. Fire these two people, burn the ships, kill the business." He was ruthless and decisive in a way that Noyce and Moore never could have been. Step two was to make manufacturing work. He and Barrett relentlessly copied Japanese manufacturing methods. "Barrett basically took a baseball [bat] to manufacturing and said: 'Damn it! We are not going to get beaten by the Japanese,'" one subordinate recalled. He forced factory managers to visit Japan and told them: "This is how you are supposed to do it."

Intel's new manufacturing method was called "copy exactly." Once Intel determined that a specific set of production processes worked best, they were replicated in all other Intel facilities. Before then, engineers had prided themselves on fine-tuning Intel's processes. Now they were asked not to think, but to replicate. "It was a huge cultural issue," one remembered, as a freewheeling Silicon Valley style was replaced with assembly line rigor. "I was perceived as a dictator," Barrett admitted. But "copy exactly" worked: Intel's yields rose substantially, while its manufacturing equipment was used more efficiently, driving down costs. Each of the company's plants began to function less like a research lab and more like a finely tuned machine.

Grove and Intel got lucky, too. Some of the structural factors that had favored Japanese producers in the early 1980s began to shift. Between 1985 and 1988, the value of the Japanese yen doubled against the dollar, making American exports cheaper. Interest rates in the U.S. fell sharply over the 1980s, reducing Intel's capital costs. Meanwhile, Texas-based Compaq Computer muscled in on IBM's PC market, driven by the realization that though it was hard to write operating systems or build microprocessors, assembling PC components into a plastic box was relatively straightforward. Compaq launched its own PCs using Intel chips and Microsoft software, priced far below IBM's PCs. By the mid-1980s, Compaq and other firms building "clones" of IBM's PC sold more units than IBM itself. Prices fell precipitously as computers were installed in every office and many homes. Except for Apple's computers, almost every PC used Intel's chips and Windows software, both of which had been designed to work smoothly together. Intel entered the personal computer era with a virtual monopoly on chip sales for PCs.

Grove's restructuring of Intel was a textbook case of Silicon Valley capitalism. He recognized that the company's business model was broken and decided to "disrupt" Intel himself by abandoning the DRAM chips it had been founded to build. The firm established a stranglehold on the market for PC chips, issuing a new generation of chip every year or two, offering smaller transistors and more processing power. Only the paranoid survive, Andy Grove believed. More than innovation or expertise, it was his paranoia that saved Intel.

CHAPTER 23

"My Enemy's Enemy": The Rise of Korea

Lee Byung-Chul could make a profit selling almost anything. Born in 1910, just a year after Jack Simplot, Lee launched his business career in March 1938, a time when his native Korea was part of Japan's empire, at war with China and soon with the United States. Lee's first products were dried fish and vegetables, which he gathered from Korea and shipped to northern China to feed Japan's war machine. Korea was an impoverished backwater, with no industry or technology, but Lee was already dreaming of building a business that would be "big, strong, and eternal," he declared. He would turn Samsung into a semiconductor superpower thanks to two influential allies: America's chip industry and the South Korean state. A key part of Silicon Valley's strategy to outmaneuver the Japanese was to find cheaper sources of supply in Asia. Lee decided this was a role Samsung could easily play.

South Korea was used to navigating between bigger rivals. Seven years after Lee founded Samsung, it could have been crushed in 1945, following Japan's defeat by the United States. Yet Lee deftly pivoted, trading political patrons as smoothly as he hawked dried fish. He forged ties with the Americans who occupied the southern half of Korea after the war and fended off South Korean politicians who wanted to break up big business groups like his. He even kept hold of his assets when the Communist government in North Korea invaded the South—though, when the enemy briefly captured Seoul, a Communist Party chief seized Lee's Chevrolet and drove it around the occupied capital.

Lee expanded his business empire despite the war, navigating South Korea's complicated politics with finesse. When a military regime took power in 1961, the generals stripped Lee of his banks, but he survived with his other companies intact. He insisted Samsung was working for the good of the nation—and that the good of the nation depended on Samsung becoming a world-class company. "Serving the nation through business," the first part of the Lee family motto read. From fish and vegetables, he diversified into sugar, textiles, fertilizer, construction, banking, and insurance. He saw Korea's economic boom during the 1960s and 1970s as proof he was serving the nation. Critics, who noted that by 1960 he had become the richest person in South Korea, thought his wealth was evidence the nation—and its venal politicians—were serving him.

Lee had long wanted to break into the semiconductor industry, watching companies like Toshiba and Fujitsu take DRAM market share in the late 1970s and early 1980s. South Korea was already an important location for outsourced assembly and packaging of chips made in the U.S. or Japan. Moreover, the U.S. government had helped fund the creation in 1966 of the Korea Institute of Science and Technology, and a growing number of Koreans were graduating from top U.S. universities or being trained in Korea by U.S.-educated professors. Even with a skilled workforce, though, it wasn't easy for firms to jump from basic assembly to cutting-edge chipmaking. Samsung had previously dabbled in simple semiconductor work but struggled to make money or produce advanced technology.

In the early 1980s, however, Lee sensed the environment changing. The brutal DRAM competition between Silicon Valley and Japan during the 1980s provided an opening. The South Korean government, meanwhile, had identified semiconductors as a priority. As Lee pondered Samsung's future, he traveled to California in spring 1982, visiting Hewlett-Packard's facilities and marveling at the company's technology. If HP could grow from a Palo Alto garage to a tech behemoth, surely a fish-and-vegetables shop like Samsung could, too. "It's all thanks to semiconductors," one HP employee told him. He also toured an IBM computer factory and was shocked he was allowed to take photographs. "There must be many secrets in your factory," he told the IBM employee giving him the tour. "They can't be replicated by mere observation," the employee confidently responded. Replicating Silicon Valley's success, though, was exactly what Lee planned to do.

Doing so would require many millions of dollars in capital expenditure, yet there was no guarantee it would work. Even for Lee, this was a big bet. He hesitated for months. Failure could bring down his entire business empire. South Korea's government, however, signaled it was willing to provide financial support. It had promised to invest $400 million to develop its semiconductor industry. Korea's banks would follow the government's direction and lend millions more. As in Japan, therefore, Korea's tech companies emerged not from garages, but from massive conglomerates with access to cheap bank loans and government support. In February 1983, after a nervous, sleepless night, Lee picked up the phone, called the head of Samsung's electronics division, and proclaimed: "Samsung will make semiconductors." He bet the company's future on semiconductors, and was ready to spend at least $100 million, he declared.

Lee was a canny entrepreneur, and South Korea's government stood firmly behind him. Yet Samsung's all-in bet on chips wouldn't have worked without support from Silicon Valley. The best way to deal with international competition in memory chips from Japan, Silicon Valley wagered, was to find an even cheaper source in Korea, while focusing America's R&D efforts on higher-value products rather than commoditized DRAMs. U.S. chipmakers therefore saw Korean upstarts as potential partners. "With the Koreans around," Bob Noyce told Andy Grove, Japan's strategy of "dump no matter what the costs" wouldn't succeed in monopolizing the world's DRAM production, because the Koreans would undercut Japanese producers. The result would be "deadly" to Japanese chipmakers, Noyce predicted.

Intel therefore cheered the rise of Korean DRAM producers. It was one of several Silicon Valley firms to sign a joint venture with Samsung in the 1980s, selling chips Samsung manufactured under Intel's own brand and wagering that helping Korea's chip industry would reduce Japan's threat to Silicon Valley. Moreover, Korea's costs and wages were substantially lower than Japan's, so Korean firms like Samsung had a shot at winning market share even if their manufacturing processes weren't as perfectly tuned as the ultra-efficient Japanese.

U.S.-Japan trade tension helped Korean companies, too. After Washington threatened tariffs unless Japan stopped "dumping"—selling DRAM chips cheaply on the U.S. market—in 1986, Tokyo agreed to limit its sales of chips to the U.S. and promised not to sell at low prices. This provided an opening for Korean companies to sell more DRAM chips at higher prices. The Americans didn't intend for the deal to benefit Korean firms, but they were happy to see anyone but Japan producing the chips they needed.

The U.S. didn't simply provide a market for South Korean DRAM chips; it provided technology, too. With Silicon Valley's DRAM producers mostly near collapse, there was little hesitation about transferring top-notch technology to Korea. Lee proposed to license a design for a 64K DRAM from Micron, the cash-strapped memory chip startup, befriending its founder Ward Parkinson in the process. The Idahoans, looking for any money they could get, eagerly agreed even if it meant Samsung would learn many of their processes. "Whatever we did, Samsung did," Parkinson remembered, seeing the cash infusion that Samsung provided as "not crucial, but close" in helping Micron survive. Some industry leaders, like Gordon Moore, worried that some chip firms were so desperate they'd "part with increasingly valuable bits of technology." However, it was hard to make the case that DRAM technology was particularly valuable when most U.S. firms making memory chips were nearly bankrupt. Most of Silicon Valley was happy to work with Korean companies, undercutting Japanese competitors and helping make South Korea one of the world's leading centers of memory chipmaking. The logic was simple, as Jerry Sanders explained: "my enemy's enemy is my friend."

CHAPTER 24

"This Is the Future"

The rebirth of America's chip industry after Japan's DRAM onslaught was only possible thanks to Andy Grove's paranoia, Jerry Sanders's bare-knuckle brawling, and Jack Simplot's cowboy competitiveness. Silicon Valley's testosterone and stock option–fueled competition often felt less like the sterile economics described in textbooks and more like a Darwinian struggle for the survival of the fittest. Many firms failed, fortunes were lost, and tens of thousands of employees were laid off. The companies like Intel and Micron that survived did so less thanks to their engineering skills—though these were important—than their ability to capitalize on technical aptitude to make money in a hypercompetitive, unforgiving industry.

Yet Silicon Valley's rebirth isn't solely a story of heroic entrepreneurs and creative destruction. Alongside the rise of these new industrial titans, a new set of scientists and engineers were preparing a leap forward in chipmaking and devising revolutionary new ways to use processing power. Many of these developments occurred in coordination with government efforts, usually not the heavy hand of Congress or the White House, but the work of small, nimble organizations like DARPA that were empowered to take big bets on futuristic technologies—and to build the educational and R&D infrastructure that such gambles required.

Competition from Japan's high-quality, low-cost DRAM chips wasn't the only problem Silicon Valley faced in the 1980s. Gordon Moore's famous law predicted exponential growth in the number of transistors on each chip, but this dream was getting ever more difficult to realize. Through the late 1970s, many integrated circuits had been designed by the same process Intel's Federico Faggin used to produce the first microprocessor. In 1971, Faggin had spent half a year crouched over his drafting table, sketching the design with Intel's most advanced tools: a straightedge and color pencils. Then, this design was cut into Rubylith, a red film, using a penknife. A special camera projected the patterns carved in Rubylith onto a mask, a glass plate with a chrome covering that perfectly replicated the Rubylith's pattern. Finally, light was shined through the mask and a set of lenses to project a tiny version of the pattern on a silicon wafer. After months of sketching and carving, Faggin had created a chip.

The problem was, while pencils and tweezers were adequate tools for an integrated circuit with a thousand components, something more sophisticated was needed for a chip with a million transistors. Carver Mead, the goateed physicist who was a friend of Gordon Moore, was puzzling over this dilemma when he was introduced to Lynn Conway, a computer architect at Xerox's Palo Alto Research Center, where the concept of the personal computer with a mouse and a keyboard was just then being invented.

Conway was a brilliant computer scientist, but anyone who spoke with her discovered a mind that glistened with insights from diverse fields, astronomy to anthropology to historical philosophy. She had arrived at Xerox in 1973 in "stealth mode," she explained, following being fired from IBM in 1968 after undergoing a gender transition. She was shocked to find that the Valley's chipmakers were more like artists than engineers. High-tech tools were paired with simple tweezers. Chipmakers produced marvelously complex patterns on each block of silicon, but their design methods were those of medieval artisans. Each company's fab (fabrication plant) had a long, complicated, proprietary set of instructions for how chips must be designed if they were to be produced in that specific facility. Conway, whose training as a computer architect had taught her to think in terms of the standardized instructions on which any computer program is built, found this method bizarrely backward.

Conway realized that the digital revolution Mead prophesied needed algorithmic rigor. After she and Mead were introduced by a mutual colleague, they began discussing how to standardize chip design. Why couldn't you program a machine to design circuits, they wondered. "Once you can write a program to do something," Mead declared, "you don't need anybody's tool kit, you write your own."

Conway and Mead eventually drew up a set of mathematical "design rules," paving the way for computer programs to automate chip design. With Conway and Mead's method, designers didn't have to sketch out the location of each transistor but could draw from a library of "interchangeable parts" that their technique made possible. Mead liked to think of himself as Johannes Gutenberg, whose mechanization of book production had let writers focus on writing and printers on printing. Conway was soon invited by MIT to teach a course on this chip design methodology. Each of her students designed their own chips, then shipped the design to a fabrication facility for manufacturing. Six weeks later, having never stepped foot in a fab, Conway's students received fully functioning chips in the mail. The Gutenberg moment had arrived.

No one was more interested in what soon became known as the "Mead-Conway Revolution" than the Pentagon. DARPA financed a program to let university researchers send chip designs to be produced at cutting-edge fabs. Despite its reputation for funding futuristic weapons systems, when it came to semiconductors DARPA focused as much on building educational infrastructure so that America had an ample supply of chip designers. DARPA also helped universities acquire advanced computers and convened workshops with industry officials and academics to discuss research problems over fine wine. Helping companies and professors keep Moore's Law alive, DARPA reasoned, was crucial to America's military edge.

The chip industry also funded university research on chip design techniques, establishing the Semiconductor Research Corporation to distribute research grants to universities like Carnegie Mellon and the University of California, Berkeley. Over the 1980s, a cadre of students and faculty from these two universities founded a series of startups that created a new industry—software tools for semiconductor design—that had never previously existed. Today, every chip company uses tools from each of three chip design software companies that were founded and built by alumni of these DARPA- and SRC-funded programs.

DARPA also backed researchers studying a second set of challenges: finding new uses for chips' growing processing power. Irwin Jacobs, an expert in wireless communication, was one such researcher. Born in Massachusetts to a family of restaurant owners, Jacobs had planned to follow his parents into the hospitality industry before falling in love with electrical engineering. He spent the 1950s playing around with vacuum tubes and IBM calculators. While pursuing his master's degree at MIT, Jacobs studied antennas and electromagnetic theory and decided to focus his research on information theory—the study of how information can be stored and communicated.

Radios had been transmitting wirelessly for decades, but the demands for wireless communication were growing and spectrum space was limited. If you wanted a radio station at 99.5 FM, you had to ensure there wasn't one at 99.7 already, or the interference would make yours incomprehensible. The same principle applied to other forms of radio communication. The more information that was packed into a given slice of spectrum, the less room there was for error created by muddled signals bouncing off buildings and interfering with each other as they careened through airspace toward a radio receiver.

Jacobs's longtime University of California, San Diego, colleague Andrew Viterbi had devised a complex algorithm in 1967 to decode a messy set of digital signals reverberating through noisy airwaves. It was praised by scientists as an excellent piece of theory, but Viterbi's algorithm seemed difficult to use in practice. The idea that normal radios would ever have the computing power to run complicated algorithms seemed implausible.

In 1971, Jacobs flew to St. Petersburg, Florida, to attend a conference of academics working on communications theory. Many of the professors had glumly concluded that their scholarly subfield—encoding data into radio waves—had reached its practical limits. The radio spectrum could only hold a limited number of signals before they became impossible to sort and interpret. Viterbi's algorithms provided a theoretical way to pack more data into the same radio spectrum, but no one had the computing power to apply these algorithms at scale. The process of sending data through the air seemed to have hit a wall. "Coding is dead," one professor declared.

Jacobs completely disagreed. Standing up from the back row, he held aloft a small chip and declared: "This is the future." Chips, Jacobs realized, were improving so rapidly that they'd soon be able to encode orders of magnitude more data in the same spectrum space. Because the number of transistors on a square inch of silicon was increasing exponentially, the amount of data that could be sent through a given slice of the radio spectrum was about to take off, too.

Jacobs, Viterbi, and several colleagues set up a wireless communications business called Qualcomm—quality communications—betting that ever-more-powerful microprocessors would let them stuff more signals into existing spectrum bandwidth. Jacobs initially won contracts from DARPA and NASA to build space communications systems. In the late 1980s, Qualcomm diversified into the civilian market, launching a satellite communications system for the trucking industry. But even by the early 1990s, using chips to send large quantities of data through the air seemed like a niche business.

For a professor-turned-entrepreneur like Irwin Jacobs, DARPA funding and Defense Department contracts were crucial in keeping his startups afloat. But only some government programs worked.

Sematech's effort to save America's lithography leader was an abject failure, for example. Government efforts were effective not when they tried to resuscitate failing firms, but when they capitalized on preexisting American strengths, providing funding to let researchers turn smart ideas into prototype products. Members of Congress would no doubt have been furious had they learned that DARPA—ostensibly a defense agency—was wining and dining professors of computer science as they theorized about chip design. But it was efforts like these that shrank transistors, discovered new uses for semiconductors, drove new customers to buy them, and funded the subsequent generation of smaller transistors. When it came to semiconductor design, no country in the world had a better innovation ecosystem. By the end of the 1980s, a chip with a million transistors—unthinkable in the early 1970s, when Lynn Conway had arrived in Silicon Valley—had become a reality, when Intel announced its 486 microprocessor, a small piece of silicon packed with 1.2 million microscopic switches.

CHAPTER 25

The KGB's Directorate T

Vladimir Vetrov was a KGB spy, but his life felt more like a Chekhov story than a James Bond film. His KGB work was bureaucratic, his mistress far from a supermodel, and his wife more affectionate toward her shih tzu puppies than toward him. By the end of the 1970s, Vetrov's career, and his life, had hit a dead end. He despised his desk job and was ignored by his bosses. He detested his wife, who was having an affair with one of his friends. For recreation, he escaped to his log cabin in a village north of Moscow, which was so rustic that there was no electricity. Or he'd simply stay in Moscow and get drunk.

Vetrov's life hadn't always been so dull. In the early 1960s, he'd earned a plum foreign posting in Paris, where as a "foreign trade official" he was tasked with gathering secrets from France's high-tech industries, per Minister Shokin's "copy it" strategy. In 1963, the same year the USSR established Zelenograd, the city of scientists working on microelectronics, the KGB established a new division, Directorate T, which stood for *teknologia*. The mission: "acquire Western equipment and technology," a CIA report warned, "and improve its ability to produce integrated circuits."

In the early 1980s, the KGB reportedly employed around one thousand people to steal foreign technology. Around three hundred worked at foreign posts, with most of the rest on the eighth floor of the KGB's imposing headquarters on Moscow's Lubyanka Square, sitting atop the Stalin-era prison and torture chambers. Other Soviet intelligence services, like the military's GRU, also had spies who focused on technology theft. The Soviet consulate in San Francisco reportedly had a team of sixty agents targeting the tech firms of Silicon Valley. They stole chips directly and bought them from the black market, supplied by thieves like the man called "One Eyed Jack," who was caught in California in 1982 and accused of stealing chips from an Intel facility by hiding them in his leather jacket. Soviet spies also blackmailed Westerners with access to advanced technology. At least one British employee of a UK computer company living in Moscow died after "falling" from the window of his high-rise apartment building.

Spying continued to play a fundamental role in Soviet semiconductors, as a group of Rhode Island fishermen discovered after pulling a strange metallic buoy out of the waters of the North Atlantic in fall 1982. They hadn't expected to pick up advanced chips in their haul. When the mysterious buoy was sent to a military lab, however, it was identified as a Soviet listening device that used perfect replicas of Texas Instruments Series 5400 semiconductors. After Intel commercialized the microprocessor, meanwhile, Minister Shokin shut down a Soviet research unit trying to produce a similar device, in favor of copying American microprocessors.

However, the "copy it" strategy was far less successful than Soviet surveillance buoys suggested. It was easy enough to steal a couple examples of Intel's latest chips, or even to have an entire shipment of integrated circuits diverted to the USSR, usually via shell companies in neutral Austria or Switzerland. However, American counterintelligence occasionally unmasked the USSR's agents operating in third countries, so this was never a reliable source of supply.

Stealing chip designs was only useful if they could be produced at scale in the USSR. This was difficult to do during the early Cold War but almost impossible by the 1980s. As Silicon Valley crammed more transistors onto silicon chips, building them became steadily harder. The KGB thought its campaign of theft provided Soviet semi-conductor producers with extraordinary secrets, but getting a copy of a new chip didn't guarantee Soviet engineers could produce it. The KGB began stealing semiconductor manufacturing equipment, too. The CIA claimed that the USSR had acquired nearly every facet of the semiconductor manufacturing process, including nine hundred Western machines for preparing materials needed for semiconductor fabrication; eight hundred machines for lithography and etching; and three hundred machines each for doping, packaging, and testing chips.

However, a factory needed a full suite of equipment, and when machines broke down, they needed spare parts. Sometimes spare parts for foreign machines could be produced in the USSR, but this intro-duced new inefficiencies and defects. The system of theft and replication never worked well enough to convince Soviet military leaders they had a steady supply of quality chips, so they minimized the use of electronics and computers in military systems.

It took time for the West to realize the scale of the theft. When the KGB first sent Vetrov to Paris in 1965, Directorate T was all but unknown. Vetrov and his colleagues worked undercover, often as employees of the Soviet Ministry of Foreign Trade. When Soviet agents visited foreign research labs, befriended executives, and tried to siphon the secrets of foreign industry, it looked as if they were simply conduct-ing their "day job" as foreign trade officials.

The operations of Directorate T might have remained a state secret had Vetrov not decided to add intrigue to his otherwise dull existence upon moving back to Moscow. By the early 1980s, his career had stalled, his marriage was ruined, and his life was falling apart. He was a spy like James Bond, but with more desk work and fewer martinis. He decided to make life more interesting by sending a postcard to a Parisian acquaintance who, he knew, was connected with the French intelligence services.

Soon Vetrov was passing dozens of documents about Directorate T to his French handler in Moscow. French intelligence code-named him

"Farewell." In total, he appears to have provided thousands of pages of documents from the heart of the KGB, unveiling a vast bureaucracy focused on stealing Western industrial secrets. A key priority: "advanced microprocessors," for which the Soviet Union lacked not only skilled engineers but also the software needed to design cutting-edge processors and the equipment needed to produce them. Western spies were shocked at just how much the Soviets stole.

In his routine of rendezvousing with French agents Vetrov had found a new activity, but he hadn't found fulfillment. The French provided him with gifts from abroad, to keep Vetrov's mistress happy, yet what Vetrov really wanted was for his wife to love him. He grew ever more delusional. On February 22, 1982, having told his son he planned to break off the relationship with his mistress, Vetrov stabbed her repeatedly in his car while parked along Moscow's ring road. Only after he was apprehended by police did the KGB realize Vetrov had betrayed his country and handed the secrets of Directorate T to Western intelligence.

The French quickly shared information about Vetrov with U.S. and other allied intelligence services. The Reagan administration responded by launching Operation Exodus, which tightened customs checks on advanced technology. By 1985, the program had seized around $600 million worth of goods and resulted in around one thousand arrests. However, when it came to semiconductors, the Reagan administration's claim to have stopped the "massive hemorrhage of American technology to the Soviet Union" probably overstated the impact of tighter controls. The USSR's "copy it" strategy had actually benefitted the United States, guaranteeing the Soviets faced a continued technological lag. In 1985, the CIA conducted a study of Soviet microprocessors and found that the USSR produced replicas of Intel and Motorola chips like clockwork. They were always half a decade behind.

CHAPTER 26

"Weapons of Mass Destruction": The Impact of the Offset

"Long-range, highly accurate, terminally guided combat systems, unmanned flying machines, and qualitatively new electronic control systems," Soviet Marshal Nikolai Ogarkov predicted, would transform conventional explosives into "weapons of mass destruction." Ogarkov served as chief of the general staff of the Soviet military from 1977 to 1984. In the West, he was most famous for leading the media offensive after the Soviets accidentally shot down a civilian airliner from South Korea in 1983. Rather than admit a mistake, he accused the plane's pilots of being on a "deliberate, thoroughly planned intelligence mission" and declared that the airliner was "asking for it." This wasn't a message likely to win Ogarkov any friends in the West, but that was likely of little consequence to him since his life purpose was preparing for war with the United States.

The Soviet Union had kept up with the Americans in the race to develop the crucial technologies of the early Cold War, building powerful rockets and a formidable nuclear stockpile. Now brawn was being replaced by computerized brains. When it came to the silicon chips undergirding this new driver of military power, the Soviet Union had fallen hopelessly behind. One popular Soviet joke from the 1980s recounted a Kremlin official who declared proudly, "Comrade, we have built the world's biggest microprocessor!"

By traditional metrics like numbers of tanks or troops, the Soviet Union had a clear advantage in the early 1980s. Ogarkov saw things differently: quality was overtaking quantity. He was fixated on the threat posed by America's precision weapons. Combined with better surveillance and communication tools, the ability to strike targets accurately hundreds or even thousands of miles away was producing a "military-technical revolution," Ogarkov argued to anyone who'd listen. The days of vacuum tube–guided Sparrow missiles missing 90 percent of their targets in the skies over Vietnam were long gone. The Soviet Union had many more tanks than the United States, but Ogarkov realized his tanks would soon be many times more vulnerable in a fight with the U.S.

Bill Perry's "offset strategy" was working, and the Soviet Union didn't have a response. It lacked the miniaturized electronics and computing power that American and Japanese chipmakers produced. Zelenograd and other Soviet chipmaking facilities couldn't keep up. Whereas Perry pushed the Pentagon to embrace Moore's Law, the inadequacies of Soviet chipmaking taught the country's weapons designers to limit use of complex electronics whenever possible. This was a viable approach in the 1960s, but by the 1980s this unwillingness to keep pace with advances in microelectronics guaranteed Soviet systems would remain "dumb" even as American weapons were learning to think. The U.S. had put a guidance computer powered by Texas Instruments' chips onboard the Minuteman II missile in the early 1960s, but the Soviets' first missile guidance computer using integrated circuits wasn't tested until 1971.

Accustomed to low-quality microelectronics, Soviet missile designers devised elaborate workarounds. Even the mathematics they plugged into their guidance computers was simpler, to minimize the strain on the onboard computer. Soviet ballistic missiles were generally told to follow a specific flight path toward their target, with the guidance computer adjusting the missile to put it back on the preprogrammed route if it deviated. By contrast, by the 1980s, American missiles calculated their own path to the target.

By the mid-1980s, America's new MX missile was publicly estimated to land within 364 feet of its target 50 percent of the time. A roughly comparable Soviet missile, the SS-25, on average fell within twelve hundred feet of its target, according to estimates from a former Soviet defense official. In the grim logic of Cold War military planners, a difference of several hundred feet mattered hugely. It was easy enough to destroy a city, but both superpowers wanted the ability to knock out each other's nuclear arsenals. Even nuclear warheads needed a reasonably direct hit to disable a hardened missile silo. Enough direct hits, and one side could potentially compromise the adversary's nuclear forces in a surprise first strike. The most pessimistic Soviet estimates suggested that if the U.S. launched a nuclear first strike in the 1980s, it could have disabled or destroyed 98 percent of Soviet ICBMs.

The USSR didn't have any margin for error. The Soviet military had two other systems that could launch a nuclear attack on America: long-range bombers and missile submarines. Bomber fleets were widely agreed to be the weakest delivery system because they could be identified by radar shortly after taking off and shot down before launching their nuclear weapons. America's nuclear missile submarines, by contrast, were practically undetectable and therefore invincible. Soviet submarines were less secure, because the U.S. was learning to apply computing power to make its submarine detection systems far more accurate.

The challenge in finding a submarine is to make sense of a cacophony of sound waves. Sound bounces off the seafloor at different angles and refracts differently through water depending on the temperature or the presence of schools of fish. By the early 1980s it was publicly admitted that the U.S. had plugged its submarine sensors into the Illiac IV, one of the most powerful supercomputers and the first using semiconductor memory chips, which were built by Fairchild. Illiac IV and other processing centers were connected via satellite to an array of sensors on ships, planes, and helicopters to track Soviet subs, which were highly vulnerable to American detection.

When Ogarkov ran the numbers, he concluded that America's semiconductor-powered advantage in missile accuracy, antisubmarine warfare, surveillance, and command and control could enable a surprise strike to threaten the survivability of the Soviet nuclear arsenal. Nukes were supposed to be the ultimate insurance policy, but the Soviet military now felt "substantially inferior in strategic weapons," as one general put it.

Soviet military leaders feared a conventional war, too. Military analysts previously thought the Soviets' superiority in numbers of tanks and troops provided a decisive advantage in a conventional war. However, the Paveway bomb first used over Vietnam had been supplemented by a suite of new guided systems. Tomahawk cruise missiles could strike deep into Soviet territory. Soviet defense planners feared American conventionally armed cruise missiles and stealth bombers could disable Soviet command and control over their nuclear forces. The challenge threatened the very survival of the Soviet state.

The Kremlin wanted to revitalize its microelectronics industry but didn't know how to do so. In 1987, Soviet leader Mikhail Gorbachev visited Zelenograd and called for "more discipline" in the city's work. Discipline was part of Silicon Valley's success, evident in Charlie Sporck's fixation on productivity and Andy Grove's paranoia. However, discipline alone couldn't solve the Soviets' basic problems.

One issue was political meddling. In the late 1980s, Yuri Osokin was removed from his job at the Riga semiconductor plant. The KGB had demanded that he fire several of his employees, one of whom had mailed letters to a woman in Czechoslovakia, a second who refused to work as an informant for the KGB, and a third who was a Jew. When Osokin refused to punish these workers for their "crimes," the KGB ousted him and tried to have his wife fired, too. It was hard enough to design chips in normal times. Doing so while battling the KGB was impossible.

A second issue was overreliance on military customers. The U.S., Europe, and Japan had booming consumer markets that drove chip demand. Civilian semiconductor markets helped fund the specialization of the semiconductor supply chain, creating companies with expertise in everything from ultra-pure silicon wafers to the advanced optics in lithography equipment. The Soviet Union barely had a consumer market, so it produced only a fraction of the chips built in the West. One Soviet source estimated that Japan alone spent eight times as much on capital investment in microelectronics as the USSR.

A final challenge was that the Soviets lacked an international supply chain. Working with America's Cold War allies, Silicon Valley had forged an ultra-efficient globalized division of labor. Japan led the production of memory chips, the U.S. produced more microprocessors, while Japan's Nikon and Canon and the Netherland's ASML split the market for lithography equipment. Workers in Southeast Asia conducted much of the final assembly. American, Japanese, and European companies jostled over their position in this division of labor, but they all benefitted from the ability to spread R&D costs over a far larger semiconductor market than the USSR ever had.

The USSR had only a handful of allies, most of whom weren't much help. Soviet-dominated East Germany, which had a chip industry as advanced as Zelenograd, made a last-ditch effort in the mid-1980s to revitalize its semiconductor sector, drawing on a long tradition of precision manufacturing as well as world-leading optics produced by the Carl Zeiss company in the city of Jena. East German chip output grew rapidly in the late 1980s, but the industry was only able to produce memory chips less advanced than Japan's, at ten times the price. Advanced Western manufacturing equipment remained hard to access, while East Germany had none of the cheap labor that Silicon Valley firms hired across Asia.

The Soviet Union's effort to reinvigorate its chipmakers failed completely. Neither the Soviets nor their socialist allies could ever catch up, despite vast espionage campaigns and huge sums poured into research facilities like those in Zelenograd. And just as the Kremlin's response to Bill Perry's "offset" was beginning to sputter out, the world was given a terrifying glimpse of the future of war on the battlefields of the Persian Gulf.

CHAPTER 27

War Hero

E arly in the morning on January 17, 1991, the first wave of American F-117 stealth bombers took off from their airbases in Saudi Arabia, their black airframes quickly disappearing in the dark desert sky. Their target: Baghdad. The United States hadn't fought a major war since Vietnam, but now it had several hundred thousand troops along Saudi Arabia's northern border, tens of thousands of tanks awaiting orders to storm forward, dozens of naval ships positioned offshore, their guns and missile batteries aimed at Iraq. The American general leading the assault, Norman Schwarzkopf, was an infantryman by training, having served two tours in Vietnam. This time, he was trusting in stand-off weapons to deliver the first strike.

The twelve-story tall telephone exchange building on Baghdad's Rashid Street was the only target deemed important enough to be attacked by two F-117s. General Schwarzkopf's war plan depended on it being destroyed, knocking out part of Iraq's communications infrastructure. The two planes homed in on their target, releasing two-thousand-pound Paveway laser-guided bombs that tore through the facility and set it aflame. Suddenly the TV feed of CNN's reporters in Baghdad went dark. Schwarzkopf's pilots had scored a hit. Almost simultaneously, 116 Tomahawk cruise missiles fired from naval ships offshore slammed into their targets in and around Baghdad. The Persian Gulf War had begun.

A communications tower, a military command post, air force head-quarters, power stations, and Saddam Hussein's country retreat—the first U.S. airstrikes sought to decapitate the Iraqi leadership and cut their communications, limiting their ability to track the war or communicate with their forces. Soon their military was in a disorganized retreat. CNN broadcast videos of hundreds of bombs and missiles striking Iraqi tanks. Warfare looked like a video game. But watching from Texas, Weldon Word knew this futuristic technology actually dated to the Vietnam War.

The Paveway laser-guided bombs that slammed into Baghdad's telephone exchange used the same basic system design as the first generation of Paveways that destroyed the Thanh Hoa Bridge in 1972. Those were built with a handful of transistors, a laser sensor, and a couple of wings strapped to an old "dumb" bomb. By 1991, Texas Instruments had updated the Paveway multiple times, with each new version replacing existing circuitry with more advanced electronics, reducing the number of components, increasing reliability, and adding new features. By the start of the Persian Gulf War, the Paveway had become the military's weapon of choice for the same reason Intel's microprocessors were used across the computer industry: they were widely understood, easy to use, and cost-effective. Paveways were always cheap, but they got cheaper over the course of the 1970s and 1980s. Thanks to their low cost, every pilot had dropped Paveways in training exercises. And they were highly versatile, too. Targets didn't need to be selected in advance but could be chosen on the battlefield. The hit rates, meanwhile, were almost as good as they looked on TV. Air Force studies conducted after the war found that non-precision munitions were far less accurate than pilots often claimed, while precision munitions like the Paveway bombs actually did better than claimed. Planes using laser guidance for their bomb strikes hit thirteen times as many targets as comparable planes without guided munitions.

U.S. airpower proved decisive in the Persian Gulf War, decimating Iraqi forces while minimizing U.S. casualties. Weldon Word received an award for inventing the Paveway, improving its electronics, and driving down its cost so that each one was never more expensive than a jalopy, just as he had originally promised. It took several decades for people outside the U.S. military to realize how the Paveway and other weapons like it were changing war. But pilots who used these bombs knew just how transformative they were. "There are about ten thousand Americans who didn't get killed because of you guys," an Air Force officer told Word at the Pentagon award ceremony. Advanced microelectronics and a set of wings strapped to a bomb had transformed the nature of military power.

As Bill Perry watched the Persian Gulf War unfold, he knew laser-guided bombs were just one of dozens of military systems that had been revolutionized by integrated circuits, enabling better surveillance, communication, and computing power. The Persian Gulf War was the first major test of Perry's "offset strategy," which had been devised after the Vietnam War but never deployed in a sizeable battle.

In the years after Vietnam, the U.S. military had talked about its new capabilities, but many people didn't take them seriously. Military leaders like General William Westmoreland, who commanded American forces in Vietnam, promised that future battlefields would be automated. But the Vietnam War had gone disastrously despite America's wide technological advantage over the North Vietnamese. So why would more computing power change things? America's military mostly sat in its barracks during the 1980s, except for a few small operations against third-rate opponents like Libya and Grenada. No one was sure how the Pentagon's advanced gadgets would perform on real battlefields.

Videos of Iraqi buildings, tanks, and airfields being destroyed by precision weapons made it impossible to deny: the character of war was changing. Even the vacuum tube–powered Sidewinder air-to-air missiles that had missed most of their targets above Vietnam were now upgraded with more powerful, semiconductor-based guidance systems. They were six times as accurate in the Persian Gulf War as in Vietnam.

The new technologies Perry had pushed the Pentagon to develop during the late 1970s performed even beyond his expectations. The Iraqi military—armed with some of the best equipment the Soviet Union's defense industry produced—was helpless in the face of the American assault. "High-tech works," Perry proclaimed. "What's making all this work is weapons based on information instead of the volume of fire power," one military analyst explained to the media. "It's the triumph of silicon over steel," declared a *New York Times* headline. "War Hero Status Possible for the Computer Chip," read another.

The reverberations from the explosions of Paveway bombs and Tomahawk missiles were felt as powerfully in Moscow as in Baghdad. The war was a "technological operation," one Soviet military analyst declared. It was "a struggle over the airwaves," another said. The result—Iraq's easy defeat—was exactly what Ogarkov had predicted. Soviet Defense Minister Dmitri Yazov admitted the Gulf War made the Soviet Union nervous about its air defense capabilities. Marshal Sergey Akhromeyev was embarrassed after his predictions of a protracted conflict were promptly disproven by Iraq's speedy surrender. CNN videos of American bombs guiding themselves through the sky and slamming through the walls of Iraqi buildings proved Ogarkov's forecasts about the future of war.

CHAPTER 28

"The Cold War Is Over and You Have Won"

Sony's Akio Morita had spent the 1980s jetting around the world, dining with Henry Kissinger, golfing at Augusta National, hobnobbing with other global elites in groups like the Trilateral Commission. He was treated as a business oracle and a representative of Japan—the world's rising economic power—on the global stage. Morita found "Japan as Number One" easy to believe in because he was personally living it. Thanks to Sony's Walkman and other consumer electronics, Japan had become prosperous and Morita had gotten rich.

Then in 1990 crisis hit. Japan's financial markets crashed. The economy slumped into a deep recession. Soon the Tokyo stock market was trading at half its 1990 level. Real estate prices in Tokyo fell even further. Japan's economic miracle seemed to screech to a halt. Meanwhile, America was resurgent, in business and in war. In just a few short years, "Japan as Number One" no longer seemed very accurate. The case study in Japan's malaise was the industry that had been held up as exemplary of Japan's industrial prowess: semiconductors.

Morita, now sixty-nine years old, watched Japan's fortunes decline alongside Sony's slumping stock price. He knew his country's problems cut deeper than its financial markets. Morita had spent the previous decade lecturing Americans about their need to improve production quality, not focus on "money games" in financial markets. But as Japan's stock market crashed, the country's vaunted long-term thinking no longer looked so visionary. Japan's seeming dominance had been built on an unsustainable foundation of government-backed overinvestment. Cheap capital had underwritten the construction of new semiconductor fabs, but also encouraged chipmakers to think less about profit and more about output. Japan's biggest semiconductor firms doubled down on DRAM production even as lower cost producers like Micron and South Korea's Samsung undercut Japanese rivals.

Japan's own media perceived overinvestment in the semiconductor sector, with newspaper headlines warning of "reckless investment competition" and "investment they cannot stop." CEOs of Japan's memory chip producers couldn't bring themselves to stop building new chip fabs, even if they weren't profitable. "If you start worrying" about overinvestment, one Hitachi executive admitted, "you can't sleep at night." So long as banks kept lending, it was easier for CEOs to keep spending than to admit they had no path to profitability. America's arm's-length capital markets hadn't felt like an advantage in the 1980s, but the risk of losing financing helped keep American firms on their toes. Japanese DRAM makers would have benefitted from Andy Grove's paranoia or Jack Simplot's wisdom about commodity market volatility. Instead, they all poured investment into the same market, guaranteeing that few made much money.

Sony, which was unique among Japanese semiconductor firms in never betting heavily on DRAMs, succeeded in developing innovative new products, like specialized chips for image sensors. When photons strike their silicon, these chips create electric charges that are correlated to the strength of the light, letting the chips convert images into digital data. Sony was therefore well placed to lead the digital camera revolution, and the company's chips that sense images today remain world-class. Even still, the company failed to cut investment in loss-making segments, and its profitability slumped beginning in the early 1990s.

Most of Japan's big DRAM producers, however, failed to take advantage of their influence in the 1980s to drive innovation. At Toshiba, a DRAM giant, a mid-ranking factory manager named Fujio Masuoka developed a new type of memory chip in 1981 that, unlike DRAM, could continue "remembering" data even after it was powered off. Toshiba ignored this discovery, so it was Intel that brought this new type of memory chip, commonly called "flash" or NAND, to market.

The biggest error that Japan's chip firms made, however, was to miss the rise of PCs. None of the Japanese chip giants could replicate Intel's pivot to microprocessors or its mastery of the PC ecosystem. Only one Japanese firm, NEC, really tried, but it never won more than a tiny share of the microprocessor market. For Andy Grove and Intel, making money on microprocessors was a matter of life or death. Japan's DRAM firms, with massive market share and few financial constraints, ignored the microprocessor market until it was too late. As a result, the PC revolution mostly benefitted American chip firms. By the time Japan's stock market crashed, Japan's semiconductor dominance was already eroding. In 1993, the U.S. retook first place in semiconductor shipments. In 1998, South Korean firms had overtaken Japan as the world's largest producers of DRAM, while Japan's market share fell from 90 percent in the late 1980s to 20 percent by 1998.

Japan's semiconductor ambitions had underwritten the country's expanding sense of its global position, but this foundation now looked brittle. In *The Japan That Can Say No*, Ishihara and Morita had argued Japan could use chip dominance to exert power over both the United States and the USSR. But when war finally came, in the unexpected arena of the Persian Gulf, American military might astounded most observers. In the first war of the digital era, Japan declined to join the twenty-eight countries that sent troops to the Gulf to eject Iraqi forces from Kuwait. Instead, Tokyo participated by sending checks to pay for coalition armies and to support Iraq's neighbors. As American Paveway laser-guided bombs pummeled Iraqi tank columns, this financial diplomacy looked impotent.

Morita suffered a stroke in 1993 that caused debilitating health problems. He retreated from public view and spent most of the remainder of his life in Hawaii, before dying in 1999. Morita's coauthor, Ishihara, kept insisting that Japan needed to assert itself on the world stage. Like a broken record, he published *The Asia That Can Say No* in 1994 followed by *The Japan That Can Say No Again* several years later. But to most Japanese, Ishihara's argument no longer made sense. In the 1980s, he'd been right to predict chips would shape the military balance and define the future of technology. But he was wrong to think those chips would be made in Japan. The country's semiconductor firms spent the 1990s shrinking in the face of America's resurgence. The technological basis for Japan's challenge to American hegemony began to crumble.

The only other serious challenger to the United States, meanwhile, was careening toward collapse. In 1990, having recognized that efforts to overcome technological backwardness via command methods and the "copy it" strategy were hopeless, Soviet leader Mikhail Gorbachev arrived in Silicon Valley for an official visit. The city's tech tycoons treated him with a feast fit for a tsar. David Packard and Apple's Steve Wozniak sat alongside Gorbachev as he was wined and dined. Gorbachev made no secret of why he chose to visit California's Bay Area. "The ideas and technologies of tomorrow are born here in California," he declared in a speech at Stanford. This was exactly what Marshal Ogarkov had been warning his fellow Soviet leaders of for over a decade.

Gorbachev promised to end the Cold War by withdrawing Soviet troops from Eastern Europe, and he wanted access to American technologies in exchange. Meeting with America's tech executives, he encouraged them to invest in the USSR. When Gorbachev visited Stanford University, he high-fived spectators as he walked around campus. "The Cold War is now behind us," the Soviet leader told an audience at Stanford. "Let's not wrangle over who won it."

But it was obvious who won, and why. Ogarkov had identified the dynamic a decade earlier, though at the time he hoped the USSR might overcome it. Like the rest of the Soviet military leadership, he'd grown more pessimistic over time. As early as 1983, Ogarkov had gone so far as to tell American journalist Les Gelb—off the record—that "the Cold War is over and you have won." The Soviet Union's rockets were as powerful as ever. It had the world's largest nuclear arsenal. But its semiconductor production couldn't keep up, its computer industry fell behind, its communications and surveillance technologies lagged, and the military consequences were disastrous. "All modern military capability is based on economic innovation, technology, and economic strength," Ogarkov explained to Gelb. "Military technology is based on computers. You are far, far ahead of us with computers. . . . In your country, every little child has a computer from age 5."

After the easy defeat of Saddam Hussein's Iraq, America's vast new fighting power was visible to everyone. This caused a crisis in the Soviet military and the KGB, who were embarrassed yet afraid to admit how decisively they were outgunned. The security chiefs led a demoralized coup attempt against Gorbachev that sputtered out after three days. It was a pathetic end for a once-powerful country, which couldn't come to terms with the painful decline in its military power. The Russian chip industry faced humiliation of its own, with one fab reduced in the 1990s to producing tiny chips for McDonald's Happy Meal toys. The Cold War was over; Silicon Valley had won.

PART V

INTEGRATED CIRCUITS, INTEGRATED WORLD?

CHAPTER 29

"We Want a Semiconductor Industry in Taiwan"

n 1985, Taiwan's powerful minister K. T. Li called Morris Chang into his office in Taipei. Nearly two decades had passed since Li had helped convince Texas Instruments to build its first semiconductor facility on the island. In the twenty years since then, Li had forged close ties with Texas Instrument's leaders, visiting Pat Haggerty and Morris Chang whenever he was in the U.S. and convincing other electronics firms to follow TI and open factories in Taiwan. In 1985, he hired Chang to lead Taiwan's chip industry. "We want to promote a semiconductor industry in Taiwan," he told Chang. "Tell me," he continued, "how much money you need."

The 1990s were the years when the word "globalization" first became commonly used, though the chip industry had relied on international production and assembly since the earliest days of Fairchild Semiconductor. Taiwan had deliberately inserted itself into semiconductor supply chains since the 1960s, as a strategy to provide jobs, acquire advanced technology, and to strengthen its security relationship with the United States. In the 1990s, Taiwan's importance began to grow, driven by the spectacular rise of the Taiwan Semiconductor Manufacturing

Company, which Chang founded with strong backing from the Taiwanese government.

When Chang was hired by Taiwan's government in 1985 to lead the country's preeminent electronics research institute, Taiwan was one of Asia's leaders in assembling semiconductor devices—taking chips made abroad, testing them, and attaching them to plastic or ceramic packages. Taiwan's government had tried breaking into the chipmaking business by licensing semiconductor manufacturing technology from America's RCA and founding a chipmaker called UMC in 1980, but the company's capabilities lagged far behind the cutting edge. Taiwan boasted plenty of semiconductor industry jobs, but captured only a small share of the profit, since most money in the chip industry was made by firms designing and producing the most advanced chips. Officials like Minister Li knew the country's economy would keep growing only if it advanced beyond simply assembling components designed and fabricated elsewhere.

When Morris Chang had first visited Taiwan in 1968, the island was competing with Hong Kong, South Korea, Singapore, and Malaysia. Now Samsung and South Korea's other big conglomerates were pouring funds into the most advanced memory chips. Singapore and Malaysia were trying to replicate South Korea's shift from assembling semiconductors to fabricating them, though with less success than Samsung. Taiwan had to improve its capabilities constantly simply to maintain its position in the bottom rungs of the semiconductor supply chain.

The biggest threat was the People's Republic of China. Across the Taiwan Strait, Mao Zedong had died in 1976, reducing the threat of imminent invasion. But China now posed an economic challenge. Under its new, post-Mao leadership, China began integrating into the global economy by attracting some of the basic manufacturing and assembly jobs that Taiwan had used to lift itself out of poverty. With lower wages and several hundred million peasants eager to trade subsistence farming for factory jobs, China's entry into electronics assembly threatened to put Taiwan out of business. It amounted to economic "warfare,"

Taiwanese officials complained to visiting Texas Instruments executives. It was impossible to compete with China on price. Taiwan had to produce advanced technology itself.

K. T. Li turned to the person who'd first helped bring semiconductor assembly to Taiwan: Morris Chang. After over two decades with Texas Instruments, Chang had left the company in the early 1980s after being passed over for the CEO job and "put out to pasture," he'd later say. He spent a year running an electronics company in New York called General Instrument, but resigned soon after, dissatisfied with the work. He'd personally helped build the world's semiconductor industry. TI's ultra-efficient manufacturing processes were the result of his experimentation and expertise in improving yields. The job he'd wanted at TI—CEO—would have placed him at the top of the chip industry, on par with Bob Noyce or Gordon Moore. So when the government of Taiwan called, offering to put him in charge of the island's chip industry and providing a blank check to fund his plans, Chang found the offer intriguing. At age fifty-four, he was looking for a new challenge.

Though most people speak of Chang "returning" to Taiwan, his strongest connection to the island was the Texas Instruments facilities that he helped establish, and by Taiwan's claim to be the legitimate government of China, the country that Chang grew up in, but that he hadn't visited since fleeing nearly four decades earlier. By the mid-1980s, the place Chang had lived the longest was Texas. He held a U.S. security clearance for defense-related work at TI. He was arguably more Texan than Taiwanese. "Taiwan was a strange place to me," he'd later recall.

However, building Taiwan's semiconductor industry sounded like an exciting challenge. Directing the Taiwanese government's Industrial Technology Research Institute, the position that Chang was formally offered, would place him at the center of Taiwan's chip development efforts. The promise of government financing sweetened the deal. Being placed de facto in charge of the island's semiconductor sector guaranteed Chang wouldn't have to answer to anyone except ministers like K. T. Li, who promised to give him wide leeway. Texas Instruments never handed out blank checks like this. Chang knew he'd need a lot of money, because his business plan was based on a radical idea. If it worked, it would upend the electronics industry, placing him—and Taiwan—in control of the world's most advanced technology.

As early as the mid-1970s, while still at TI, Chang had toyed with the idea of creating a semiconductor company that would manufacture chips designed by customers. At the time, chip firms like TI, Intel, and Motorola mostly manufactured chips they had designed in-house. Chang pitched this new business model to fellow TI executives in March 1976. "The low cost of computing power," he explained to his TI colleagues, "will open up a wealth of applications that are not now served by semiconductors," creating new sources of demand for chips, which would soon be used in everything from phones to cars to dishwashers. The firms that made these goods lacked the expertise to produce semiconductors, so they'd prefer to outsource fabrication to a specialist, he reasoned. Moreover, as technology advanced and transistors shrank, the cost of manufacturing equipment and R&D would rise. Only companies that produced large volumes of chips would be cost-competitive.

TI's other executives weren't convinced. At the time, in 1976, there weren't any "fabless" companies that designed chips but lacked their own fabs, though Chang predicted such companies would soon emerge. Texas Instruments was already making plenty of money, so gambling on markets that didn't yet exist seemed risky. The idea was quietly binned.

Chang never forgot the foundry concept. He thought it was ripening as time passed, particularly after Lynn Conway and Carver Mead's revolution in chip design made it far easier to separate chip design from manufacturing, which they thought would create a Gutenberg moment for semiconductors.

In Taiwan, some of the island's electrical engineers were thinking along similar lines. Chintay Shih, who helped run Taiwan's Industrial Technology Research Institute, had invited Mead to visit Taiwan in the mid-1980s to share his vision of Gutenberg for semiconductors. The idea of separating chip design and manufacturing had therefore already been percolating in Taiwan for several years before Minister K. T. Li offered Morris Chang a blank check to build Taiwan's chip industry.

Minister Li followed through on his promise to find the money for the business plan Chang drew up. The Taiwanese government provided 48 percent of the startup capital for TSMC, stipulating only that Chang find a foreign chip firm to provide advanced production technology. He was turned down by his former colleagues at TI and by Intel. "Morris, you've had a lot of good ideas in your time," Gordon Moore told him. "This isn't one of them." However, Chang convinced Philips, the Dutch semiconductor company, to put up $58 million, transfer its production technology, and license intellectual property in exchange for a 27.5 percent stake in TSMC.

The rest of the capital was raised from wealthy Taiwanese who were "asked" by the government to invest. "What generally happened was that one of the ministers in the government would call a businessman in Taiwan," Chang explained, "to get him to invest." The government asked several of the island's wealthiest families, who owned firms that specialized in plastics, textiles, and chemicals, to put up the money. When one businessman declined to invest after three meetings with Chang, Taiwan's prime minister called the stingy executive and reminded him, "The government has been very good to you for the last twenty years. You better do something for the government now." A check for Chang's chip foundry arrived soon after. The government also provided generous tax benefits for TSMC, ensuring the company had plenty of money to invest. From day one, TSMC wasn't really a private business: it was a project of the Taiwanese state.

A crucial ingredient in TSMC's early success was deep ties with the U.S. chip industry. Most of its customers were U.S. chip designers, and many top employees had worked in Silicon Valley. Morris Chang hired Don Brooks, another former Texas Instruments executive, to work as

TSMC's president from 1991 to 1997. "Most of the guys who reported to me, down two levels," Brooks recalled, "all had some experience in the U.S . . . they all worked for Motorola, Intel, or TI." Throughout much of the 1990s, half of TSMC's sales were to American companies. Most of the company's executives, meanwhile, trained in top doctoral programs at U.S. universities.

This symbiosis benefitted Taiwan and Silicon Valley. Before TSMC, a couple of small companies, mostly based in Silicon Valley, had tried building businesses around chip design, avoiding the cost of building their own fabs by outsourcing the manufacturing. These "fabless" firms were sometimes able to convince a bigger chipmaker with spare capacity to manufacture their chips. However, they always had second-class status behind the bigger chipmakers' own production plans. Worse, they faced the constant risk that their manufacturing partners would steal their ideas. In addition, they had to navigate manufacturing processes that were slightly different at each big chipmaker. Not having to build fabs dramatically reduced startup costs, but counting on competitors to manufacture chips was always a risky business model.

The founding of TSMC gave all chip designers a reliable partner. Chang promised never to design chips, only to build them. TSMC didn't compete with its customers; it succeeded if they did. A decade earlier, Carver Mead had prophesied a Gutenberg moment in chipmaking, but there was one key difference. The old German printer had tried and failed to establish a monopoly over printing. He couldn't stop his technology from quickly spreading across Europe, benefitting authors and print shops alike.

In the chip industry, by lowering startup costs, Chang's foundry model gave birth to dozens of new "authors"—fabless chip design firms— that transformed the tech sector by putting computing power in all sorts of devices. However, the democratization of authorship coincided with a monopolization of the digital printing press. The economics of chip manufacturing required relentless consolidation. Whichever company produced the most chips had a built-in advantage, improving its yield and spreading capital investment costs over more customers. TSMC's business boomed during the 1990s and its manufacturing processes improved relentlessly. Morris Chang wanted to become the Gutenberg of the digital era. He ended up vastly more powerful. Hardly anyone realized it at the time, but Chang, TSMC, and Taiwan were on a path toward dominating the production of the world's most advanced chips.

CHAPTER 30

"All People Must Make Semiconductors"

n 1987, the same year that Morris Chang founded TSMC, a couple hundred miles to the southeast a then-unknown engineer named Ren Zhengfei established an electronics trading company called Huawei. Taiwan was a small island with big ambitions. It had deep connections not just with the world's most advanced chip companies but also thousands of engineers who'd been educated at universities like Stanford and Berkeley. China, by contrast, had a vast population but was impoverished and technologically backward. A new policy of economic openness had caused trade to boom, however, particularly via Hong Kong, through which goods could be imported or smuggled. Shenzhen, where Huawei was founded, sat just across the border.

In Taiwan, Morris Chang set his sights on building some of the world's most advanced chips and winning Silicon Valley giants as his customers. In Shenzhen, Ren Zhengfei bought cheap telecommunications equipment in Hong Kong and sold it for a higher price across China. The equipment he traded used integrated circuits, but the idea of producing his own chips would have seemed absurd. In the 1980s, the Chinese government, led by minister of the electronics industry and later president of China Jiang Zemin, identified electronics as a priority. At the time, the most advanced, widely used chip that China produced domestically was a DRAM with roughly the same storage capacity as the first DRAM Intel had brought to market in the early 1970s, putting China over a decade behind the cutting edge.

Were it not for Communist rule, China might have played a much larger role in the semiconductor industry. When the integrated circuit was invented, China had many of the ingredients that helped Japan, Taiwan, and South Korea attract American semiconductor investment, like a vast, low-cost workforce and a well-educated scientific elite. However, after seizing power in 1949, the Communists looked at foreign connections with suspicion. For someone like Morris Chang, returning to China after finishing his studies at Stanford would have meant certain poverty and possible imprisonment or death. Many of the best graduates from China's universities before the revolution ended up working in Taiwan or in California, building the electronics capabilities of the PRC's primary rivals.

China's Communist government, meanwhile, made the same mistakes the Soviet Union did, though in more extreme forms. As early as the mid-1950s, Beijing had identified semiconductor devices as a scientific priority. Soon, they were calling on the skills of researchers at Peking University and other scientific centers—including some scientists who'd been trained before the revolution at Berkeley, MIT, Harvard, or Purdue. By 1960, China had established its first semiconductor research institute, in Beijing. Around the same time, the country began manufacturing simple transistor radios. In 1965, Chinese engineers forged their first integrated circuit, a half decade after Bob Noyce and Jack Kilby.

However, Mao's radicalism made it impossible to attract foreign investment or conduct serious science. The year after China produced its first integrated circuit, Mao plunged the country into the Cultural Revolution, arguing that expertise was a source of privilege that undermined socialist equality. Mao's partisans waged war on the country's educational system. Thousands of scientists and experts were sent to work as farmers in destitute villages. Many others were simply killed. Chairman Mao's "Brilliant Directive issued on July 21, 1968" insisted that "it is essential to shorten the length of schooling, revolutionize education, put proletarian politics in command. . . . Students should be selected from among workers and peasants with practical experience, and they should return to production after a few years study."

The idea of building advanced industries with poorly educated employees was absurd. Even more so was Mao's effort to keep out foreign technology and ideas. U.S. restrictions prevented China from buying advanced semiconductor equipment, but Mao added his own self-imposed embargo. He wanted complete self-reliance and accused his political rivals of trying to infect China's chip industry with foreign parts, even though China couldn't produce many advanced components itself. His propaganda machine urged support for "the earth-shaking mass movement for the . . . independent and self-reliant development of the electronic industry."

Mao wasn't simply skeptical of foreign chips; at times he worried that all electronic goods were intrinsically anti-socialist. His political rival Liu Shaoqi had endorsed the idea that "modern electronic technology" would "bring about a big leap forward for our industry" and would "make China the first newly industrialized socialist power with first-rate electronic technology." Mao, who always associated socialism with smokestacks, attacked the idea. It was "reactionary," one of Mao's supporters argued, to see electronics as the future, when it was obvious that "only the iron and steel industry should play a leading role" in building a socialist utopia in China.

In the 1960s, Mao won the political struggle over the Chinese semiconductor industry, downplaying its importance and cutting its ties with foreign technology. Most of China's scientists resented the chairman for ruining their research—and their lives—by sending them to live on peasant farms to study proletarian politics rather than semiconductor engineering. One leading Chinese expert in optics who was sent to the countryside survived rural reeducation on a diet of rough grains, boiled cabbage, and an occasional grilled snake, as he waited for Mao's radicalism to subside. While China's small cadre of semiconductor engineers were hoeing China's fields, Maoists exhorted the country's workers that "all people must make semiconductors," as if every member of the Chinese proletariat could forge chips at home.

One tiny speck of Chinese territory escaped the horrors of the Cultural Revolution. Thanks to a quirk of colonialism, Hong Kong was still governed temporarily by the British. As most Chinese were meticulously memorizing the quotations of their crazed chairman, Hong Kong workers were diligently assembling silicon components at Fairchild's plant overlooking Kowloon Bay. A couple hundred miles away in Taiwan, multiple U.S. chip firms had facilities employing thousands of workers in jobs that were low-paying by California's standards but far better than peasant farming. Just as Mao was sending China's small set of skilled workers to the countryside for socialist reeducation, the chip industry in Taiwan, South Korea, and across Southeast Asia was pulling peasants from the countryside and giving them good jobs at manufacturing plants.

The Cultural Revolution began to wane as Mao's health declined in the early 1970s. Communist Party leaders eventually called scientists back from the countryside. They tried picking up the pieces in their labs. But China's chip industry, which had lagged far behind Silicon Valley before the Cultural Revolution, was now far behind China's neighbors, too. During the decade in which China had descended into revolutionary chaos, Intel had invented microprocessors, while Japan had grabbed a large share of the global DRAM market. China accomplished nothing beyond harassing its smartest citizens. By the mid-1970s, therefore, its chip industry was in a disastrous state. "Out of every 1,000 semiconductors we produce, only one is up to standard," one party leader complained in 1975. "So much is being wasted."

On September 2, 1975, John Bardeen landed in Beijing, two decades after he'd won his first Nobel Prize with Shockley and Brattain for inventing the transistor. In 1972, he had become the only person to win a second Nobel in physics, this time for work on superconductivity. In the world of physics, no one was more renowned, though Bardeen was the same modest man who'd been unfairly outshone by Shockley in the late 1940s. As he approached retirement, he devoted more time to building connections between American and foreign universities. When a delegation of prominent American physicists was being assembled to visit China in 1975, Bardeen was asked to join.

With the Cultural Revolution winding down, China's leaders were trying to set aside their revolutionary fervor and befriend the Americans. At the time of Bardeen's visit, Mao was ill; he would die the next year. Bardeen's delegation reminded the Chinese of the technology that friendship with America could provide. This visit was a sign of how much had changed since the depths of the Cultural Revolution. A decade earlier, the Nobel Prize winner would have been denounced as a counterrevolutionary agent and not welcomed by China's leading research institutes in Beijing, Shanghai, Nanjing, and Xian. But still, much of the Maoist legacy remained. The Americans were told that Chinese scientists didn't publish their research because they opposed "self-glorification."

Bardeen knew something about scientists obsessed with self-glorification from his work with Shockley, who unfairly claimed all the credit for inventing the transistor. The example of Shockley—a brilliant scientist but a failed businessman—demonstrated that the link between capitalism and self-glorification wasn't as straightforward as Maoist doctrine suggested. Bardeen told his wife that despite claims of equality he found Chinese society regimented and hierarchical. The political minders who watched over China's semiconductor scientists certainly had no parallel in Silicon Valley.

Bardeen and his colleagues left China impressed with the country's scientists, but China's semiconductor manufacturing ambitions seemed hopeless. Asia's electronics revolution had completely passed by mainland China. Silicon Valley chip firms employed thousands of workers, often ethnic Chinese, in plants from Hong Kong to Taiwan, Penang to Singapore. But the People's Republic had spent the 1960s denouncing capitalists while its neighbors were trying desperately to attract them. A study in 1979 found that China had hardly any commercially viable semiconductor production and only fifteen hundred computers in the entire country.

Mao Zedong died the year after Bardeen's visit to China. The old dictator was replaced, after a few years, by Deng Xiaoping, who promised a policy of "Four Modernizations" to transform China. Soon China's government declared that "science and technology" were "the crux of the Four Modernizations." The rest of the world was being transformed by a technological revolution, and China's scientists realized that chips were at the core of this change. The National Science Conference held in March 1978, just as Deng Xiaoping was consolidating power, placed semiconductors at the center of its agenda, hoping that China could use advances in semiconductors to help develop new weapons systems, consumer electronics, and computers.

The political goal was clear: China needed its own semiconductors, and it couldn't rely on foreigners. Newspaper *Guangming Ribao* set the tone, calling on readers in 1985 to abandon "the formula of 'the first machine imported, the second machine imported, and the third machine imported'" and replace it with "'the first machine imported, the second made in China, and the third machine exported.'" This "Made in China" obsession was hardwired into the Communist Party's worldview, but the country was hopelessly behind in semiconductor technology—something that neither Mao's mass mobilization nor Deng's diktat could easily change.

Beijing called for more semiconductor research, but government decrees alone couldn't produce scientific inventions or viable industries. The government's insistence that chips were strategically important caused China's officials to try to control chipmaking, embroiling the sector in bureaucracy. When rising entrepreneurs like Huawei's Ren Zhengfei began building electronics businesses in the late 1980s, they had no choice but to rely on foreign chips. China's electronics assembly industry was built on a foundation of foreign silicon, imported from the United States, Japan, and increasingly Taiwan—which the Communist Party still considered part of "China," but which remained outside its control.

CHAPTER 31

"Sharing God's Love
with the Chinese"

R ichard Chang just wanted to "share God's love with the Chinese." The Bible didn't say much about semiconductors, but Chang had a missionary's zeal to bring advanced chipmaking to China. A devout Christian, the Nanjing-born, Taiwan-raised, Texas-trained semiconductor engineer convinced Beijing's rulers in 2000 to give him vast subsidies to build a semiconductor foundry in Shanghai. The facility was designed exactly to his specifications, even including a church, thanks to special permission from China's normally atheist government. The country's leaders were willing to compromise on their opposition to religion if Chang could finally bring them modern semiconductor fabrication. Yet even with the full-fledged support of the government, Chang still felt like David as he struggled with the semiconductor industry's goliaths, especially Taiwan's TSMC.

The geography of chip fabrication shifted drastically over the 1990s and 2000s. U.S. fabs made 37 percent of the world's chips in 1990, but this number fell to 19 percent by 2000 and 13 percent by 2010. Japan's market share in chip fabrication collapsed, too. South Korea, Singapore, and Taiwan each poured funds into their chip industries and rapidly increased output. For example, Singapore's government funded fabrication facilities and chip design centers in partnership with companies like Texas Instruments, Hewlett-Packard, and Hitachi, building a vibrant semiconductor sector in the city-state. The Singaporean government also tried replicating TSMC, establishing a foundry called Chartered Semiconductor, though the company never performed as well as its Taiwanese rival.

South Korea's semiconductor industry did even better. After dethroning Japan's DRAM producers and becoming the world's leading memory chipmaker in 1992, Samsung grew rapidly through the rest of that decade. It fended off competition in the DRAM market from Taiwan and Singapore, benefitting from formal government support and from unofficial government pressure on South Korea's banks to provide credit. This financing mattered because Samsung's main product, DRAM memory chips, required brute financial force to reach each successive technology node—spending that had to be sustained even during industry downturns. The DRAM market was like a game of chicken, one Samsung executive explained. In good times, the world's DRAM companies would pour money into new factories, pushing the market toward overcapacity, driving down prices. Carrying on spending was ruinously expensive, but stopping investments, even for a single year, risked ceding market share to rivals. No one wanted to blink first. Samsung had the capital to keep investing after its rivals were forced to cut back. Its memory chip market share grew inexorably.

China had the most potential to upend the semiconductor industry, given its growing role assembling the electronic devices into which most of the world's chips were slotted. By the 1990s, decades had passed since the country's first ill-fated efforts at semiconductor production were interrupted by Maoist radicalism. China had become the world's workshop, and cities like Shanghai and Shenzhen were centers of electronics assembly—the type of work that had propelled Taiwan's economy several decades earlier. However, China's leaders knew the real money was in the components that powered electronics, above all in semiconductors.

China's chip manufacturing capabilities in the 1990s lagged far behind Taiwan and South Korea, to say nothing of the United States. Even though China's economic reforms were in full swing, smugglers still found it profitable to bring chips illegally into the country by stuffing suitcases full of them and crossing the border from Hong Kong. But as China's electronics industry matured, smuggling chips began to seem less appealing than making them.

Richard Chang saw bringing chips to China as his life's calling. Born in 1948 to a military family in Nanjing, the former capital, his family fled China after the Communists took power, arriving in Taiwan when he was only one year old. In Taiwan, he grew up in a community of mainlanders who treated residence on the island as a temporary sojourn. The expected collapse of the People's Republic never came, leaving people like Chang in a permanent state of identity crisis, seeing themselves as Chinese but living on an island that, in political terms, was drifting ever further away from the land of their birth. After finishing university, Chang moved to the U.S., completing a graduate degree in Buffalo, New York, before taking a job at Texas Instruments, where he worked with Jack Kilby. He became an expert in operating fabs, running TI's facilities around the world, from the U.S. to Japan, Singapore to Italy.

Most of the early results of China's government efforts to subsidize the construction of a domestic semiconductor industry weren't impressive. Some fabs were built in China, such as a joint venture in Shanghai between China's Huahong and Japan's NEC. NEC received a sweet financial deal from the Chinese government in exchange for promising to bring its technology to China. However, NEC made sure that Japanese experts were in charge; Chinese workers were only allowed to undertake basic activities. "We cannot say this industry is a Chinese industry," one analyst was quoted as saying. It was just a "wafer fab located in China." China gained little expertise from the joint venture.

Grace Semiconductor, another chip firm founded in Shanghai, in 2000, involved a similar mix of foreign investment, state subsidies, and failed technology transfer. Grace was a venture between Jiang

Mianheng, son of Chinese president Jiang Zemin, and Winston Wang, scion of a Taiwanese plastics dynasty. The idea of attracting Taiwanese participation in China's chip industry made sense given the island's success in semiconductors, while the involvement of a child of a Chinese president helped secure government support. The company even hired Neil Bush, a younger brother of President George W. Bush, to advise on "business strategies," paying him $400,000 annually for his insight. This star-studded leadership team may have kept Grace out of political trouble, but the company's technology lagged and it struggled to acquire customers, never winning more than a small share of China's foundry business, a sliver of the world's total.

If anyone could build a chip industry in China, it was Richard Chang. He wouldn't rely on nepotism or on foreign help. All the knowledge needed for a world-class fab was already in his head. While working at Texas Instruments, he'd opened new facilities for the company around the world. Why couldn't he do the same in Shanghai? He founded the Semiconductor Manufacturing International Corporation (SMIC) in 2000, raising over $1.5 billion from international investors like Goldman Sachs, Motorola, and Toshiba. One analyst estimated that half of SMIC's startup capital was provided by U.S. investors. Chang used these funds to hire hundreds of foreigners to operate SMIC's fab, including at least four hundred from Taiwan.

Chang's strategy was simple: do as TSMC had done. In Taiwan, TSMC had hired the best engineers it could find, ideally with experience at American or other advanced chip firms. TSMC bought the best tools it could afford. It focused relentlessly on training its employees in the industry's best practices. And it took advantage of all the tax and subsidy benefits that Taiwan's government was willing to provide.

SMIC followed this road map religiously. It hired aggressively from overseas chipmakers, especially from Taiwan. For much of its first decade of operation, a third of SMIC's engineering personnel were hired from overseas. In 2001, according to analyst Doug Fuller, SMIC employed 650 local engineers compared with 393 who were recruited from overseas, mostly from Taiwan and the U.S. Through the end of the decade, roughly a third of engineering employees were hired from abroad. The company even had a slogan, "one old staffer brings along two new ones," emphasizing the need for experienced foreign-trained employees to help local engineers learn. SMIC's local engineers learned quickly, and were soon perceived to be so capable they began receiving job offers from foreign chipmakers. The company's success in domesticating technology was only possible thanks to this foreign-trained workforce.

Like China's other chip startups, SMIC benefitted from vast government support, like a five-year corporate tax holiday and reduced sales tax on chips sold in China. SMIC milked these benefits, but at first it didn't depend on them. Unlike rivals who focused more on hiring politicians' children than on manufacturing quality, Chang ramped up production capacity and adopted technology that was near the cutting edge. By the end of the 2000s SMIC was only a couple years behind the world's technology leaders. The company seemed on track to become a top-notch foundry, perhaps eventually capable of threatening TSMC. Richard Chang soon won contracts to build chips for industry leaders like his former employer, Texas Instruments. SMIC listed its shares on the New York Stock Exchange in 2004.

Now TSMC had competition from multiple foundries in different countries in East Asia. Singapore's Chartered Semiconductor, Taiwan's UMC and Vanguard Semiconductor, and South Korea's Samsung—which entered the foundry business in 2005—were also competing with TSMC to produce chips designed elsewhere. Most of these companies were subsidized by their governments, but this made chip production cheaper, benefitting the mostly American fabless semiconductor designers they served. Fabless firms, meanwhile, were in the early stages of launching a revolutionary new product chock-full of complex chips: the smartphone. Offshoring had reduced manufacturing costs and spurred more competition. Consumers benefitted from low prices and from previously unthinkable devices. Wasn't this exactly how globalization was designed to work?

CHAPTER 32

Lithography Wars

When John Carruthers sat down in a meeting room at Intel's headquarters in Santa Clara, California, in 1992, he didn't expect that asking Intel CEO Andy Grove for $200 million was going to be easy. As a leader of Intel's R&D efforts, Carruthers was used to making big bets. Some worked, and others didn't, but Intel's engineers had as good a batting average as anyone in the industry. By 1992, Intel was again the world's biggest chipmaker, on the strength of Grove's decision to focus Intel's efforts on microprocessors for PCs. It was flush with cash and as committed as ever to Moore's Law.

Carruthers's request stretched far beyond the usual for R&D projects, however. Along with everyone else in the industry, Carruthers knew existing lithography methods would soon be unable to produce the ever-smaller circuits that next-generation semiconductors required. Lithography companies were rolling out tools using deep ultraviolet light, with wavelengths of 248 or 193 nanometers, invisible to the human eye. But it wouldn't be long before chipmakers would be asking for even more lithographic precision. He wanted to target "extreme ultraviolet" (EUV) light, with a wavelength of 13.5 nanometers. The smaller the wavelength, the smaller the features that could be carved onto chips. There was only one problem: most people thought extreme ultraviolet light was impossible to mass-produce.

"You mean to tell me you're going to spend money on something that we don't even know if it's gonna work?" Grove asked skeptically. "Yeah, Andy, that's called research," Carruthers retorted. Grove turned to Gordon Moore, Intel's former CEO, who remained an advisor to the company. "What would you do, Gordon?" "Well, Andy, what other choices do you have?" Moore asked. The answer was obvious: none. The chip industry would either learn to use ever smaller wavelengths for lithography, or the shrinking of transistors—and the law named after Moore—would come to a halt. Such an outcome would be devastating for Intel's business and humiliating for Grove. He gave Carruthers $200 million to spend developing EUV lithography. Intel would eventually spend billions of dollars on R&D and billions more learning how to use EUV to carve chips. It never planned to make its own EUV equipment, but needed to guarantee that at least one of the world's advanced lithography firms would bring EUV machines to market so that Intel would have the tools needed to carve ever-smaller circuits.

More than at any point since Jay Lathrop had turned his microscope upside down in his U.S. military lab, in the 1990s the future of lithography was in doubt. Three existential questions hung over the lithography industry: engineering, business, and geopolitics. In the early days of chipmaking, transistors were so big that the size of the light waves used by lithography tools barely mattered. But Moore's Law had progressed to the point where the scale of light waves—a couple hundred nanometers, depending on the color—impacted the precision with which circuits could be etched. By the 1990s, the most advanced transistors were measured in the hundreds of nanometers (billionths of a meter), but it was already possible to envision far smaller transistors with features just a dozen nanometers in length.

Producing chips at this scale, most researchers believed, required more precise lithography tools to shoot light at photoresist chemicals and carve shapes on silicon. Some researchers sought to use beams of electrons to carve chips, but electron beam lithography was never fast enough for mass production. Others placed their bet on X-rays or extreme ultraviolet light, each of which reacted with different sets of photoresist chemicals. At the annual international conference of lithography experts, scientists debated which technique would win out. It was a time of "lithography wars," one participant put it, between competing groups of engineers.

The "war" to find the next, best type of beam to shoot at silicon wafers was only one of three contests underway over the future of lithography. The second battle was commercial, over which company would build the next generation of lithography tools. The enormous cost of developing new lithography equipment pushed the industry toward concentration. One or at most two companies would dominate the market. In the United States, GCA had been liquidated, while Silicon Valley Group, a lithography firm descended from Perkin Elmer, lagged far behind the market leaders, Canon and Nikon. U.S. chipmakers had fended off the Japanese challenge of the 1980s, but American lithography toolmakers hadn't.

The only real competitor to Canon and Nikon was ASML, the small but growing Dutch lithography company. In 1984, Philips, the Dutch electronics firm, had spun out its internal lithography division, creating ASML. Coinciding with the collapse in chip prices that sank GCA's business, the spinoff was horribly timed. What's more, Veldhoven, a town not far from the Dutch border with Belgium, seemed an unlikely place for a world-class company in the semiconductor industry. Europe was a sizeable producer of chips, but it was very clearly behind Silicon Valley and Japan.

When Dutch engineer Frits van Hout joined ASML in 1984 just after completing his master's degree in physics, the company's employees asked whether he'd joined voluntarily or was forced to take the job. Beyond its tie with Philips, "we had no facilities and no money," van Hout remembered. Building vast in-house manufacturing processes for lithography tools would have been impossible. Instead, the company decided to assemble systems from components meticulously sourced from suppliers around the world. Relying on other companies for key components brought obvious risks, but ASML learned to manage them. Whereas Japanese competitors tried to build everything in-house, ASML could buy the best components on the market. As it began to focus on developing EUV tools, its ability to integrate components from different sources became its greatest strength.

ASML's second strength, unexpectedly, was its location in the Netherlands. In the 1980s and 1990s, the company was seen as neutral in the trade disputes between Japan and the United States. U.S. firms treated it like a trustworthy alternative to Nikon and Canon. For example, when Micron, the American DRAM startup, wanted to buy lithography tools, it turned to ASML rather than relying on one of the two main Japanese suppliers, each of which had deep ties with Micron's DRAM competitors in Japan.

ASML's history of being spun out of Philips helped in a surprising way, too, facilitating a deep relationship with Taiwan's TSMC. Philips had been the cornerstone investor in TSMC, transferring its manufacturing process technology and intellectual property to the young foundry. This gave ASML a built-in market, because TSMC's fabs were designed around Philips's manufacturing processes. An accidental fire in TSMC's fab in 1989 helped, too, causing TSMC to buy an additional nineteen new lithography machines, paid for by the fire insurance. Both ASML and TSMC started as small firms on the periphery of the chip industry, but they grew together, forming a partnership without which advances in computing today would have ground to a halt.

The partnership between ASML and TSMC pointed to the third "lithography war" of the 1990s. This was a political contest, though few people in industry or government preferred to think in those terms. At the time, the U.S. was celebrating the end of the Cold War and cashing in its peace dividend. Measured by technological, military, or economic power, the U.S. towered above the rest of the world, allies and adversaries alike. One influential commentator declared the 1990s a "unipolar moment," in which America's dominance was unquestioned.

The Persian Gulf War had demonstrated America's terrifying techno-logical and military might.

When Andy Grove was preparing to approve Intel's first major investment in EUV lithography research in 1992, it was easy to see why even the chip industry, which had emerged out of the Cold War military-industrial complex, had concluded politics no longer mattered. Management gurus promised a future "borderless world" in which profits not power would shape the global business landscape. Econo-mists spoke of accelerating globalization. CEOs and politicians alike embraced these new intellectual fashions. Intel, meanwhile, was again on top of the semiconductor business. It had fended off its Japanese rivals and now all but monopolized the global market for the chips that powered personal computers. It has made a profit every year since 1986. Why should it worry about politics?

In 1996, Intel forged a partnership with several of the laboratories operated by the U.S. Department of Energy, which had expertise in optics and other fields needed to make EUV work. Intel assembled a half dozen other chipmakers to join the consortium, but Intel paid for most of it and was the "95 percent gorilla" in the room, one participant remembered. Intel knew that the researchers at Lawrence Livermore and Sandia National Labs had the expertise to build a prototype EUV system, but their focus was on the science, not on mass production.

Intel's goal was "to make stuff, not just to measure it," Carruthers explained, so the company began searching for a company to commer-cialize and mass-produce EUV tools. It concluded no American firm could do it. GCA was no more. America's biggest remaining lithography firm was Silicon Valley Group (SVG), which lagged technologically. The U.S. government, still sensitive from the trade wars of the 1980s, didn't want Japan's Nikon and Canon to work with the national labs, though Nikon itself didn't think EUV technology would work. ASML was the only lithography firm left.

The idea of giving a foreign company access to the most advanced research coming out of America's national labs raised some questions in Washington. There was no immediate military application for EUV technology, and it still wasn't clear that EUV would work. Nevertheless, if it did, the U.S. would be reliant on ASML for a tool fundamental to all computing. Except for a few officials in the Defense Department, hardly anyone in Washington was concerned. Most people saw ASML and the Dutch government as reliable partners. More important to political leaders was the impact on jobs, not geopolitics. The U.S. government required ASML to build a facility in the U.S. to manufacture components for its lithography tools and supply American customers and employ American staff. However, much of ASML's core R&D would take place in the Netherlands. Key decision makers from the Commerce Department, the National Labs, and the companies involved say they don't recall political considerations playing much if any role in the government's decision to let this arrangement proceed.

Despite long delays and huge cost overruns, the EUV partnership slowly made progress. Locked out of the research at the U.S. national labs, Nikon and Canon decided not to build their own EUV tools, leaving ASML as the world's only producer. In 2001, meanwhile, ASML bought SVG, America's last major lithography firm. SVG already lagged far behind industry leaders, but again questions were raised about whether the deal suited America's security interests. Inside DARPA and the Defense Department, which had funded the lithography industry for decades, some officials opposed the sale. Congress raised concerns, too, with three senators writing President George W. Bush that "ASML will wind up with all of the U.S. government's EUV technology."

This was undeniably true. But America's power was at its peak. Most people in Washington thought globalization was a good thing. The dominant belief in the U.S. government was that expanding trade and supply chain connections would promote peace by encouraging powers like Russia or China to focus on acquiring wealth rather than geopolitical power. Claims that the decline of America's lithography industry would imperil security were seen as out of touch with this new era of globalization and interconnection. The chip industry, meanwhile, simply wanted to build semiconductors as efficiently as possible. With no large-scale U.S. lithography firms remaining, what choice did they have but to bet on ASML?

Intel and other big chipmakers argued that the sale of SVG to ASML was crucial to developing EUV—and thus fundamental to the future of computing. "Without the merger," Intel's new CEO Craig Barrett argued in 2001, "the development path to the new tools in the U.S. will be delayed." With the Cold War over, the Bush administration, which had just taken power, wanted to loosen technology export controls on all goods except those with direct military applications. The administration described the strategy as "building high walls around technologies of the highest sensitivity." EUV didn't make the list.

The next-generation EUV lithography tools would therefore be mostly assembled abroad, though some components continued to be built in a facility in Connecticut. Anyone who raised the question of how the U.S. could guarantee access to EUV tools was accused of retaining a Cold War mindset in a globalizing world. Yet the business gurus who spoke about technology spreading globally misrepresented the dynamic at play. The scientific networks that produced EUV spanned the world, bringing together scientists from countries as diverse as America, Japan, Slovenia, and Greece. However, the manufacturing of EUV wasn't globalized, it was monopolized. A single supply chain managed by a single company would control the future of lithography.

CHAPTER 33

The Innovator's Dilemma

teve Jobs stood alone on a dark stage at the 2006 Macworld conference, wearing his trademark blue jeans and a black turtleneck. An audience of hundreds of tech buffs waited anxiously for Silicon Valley's prophet to speak. Jobs turned toward his left, and blue smoke erupted on the far side of the stage. A man in a white bunny suit—the type used by semiconductor workers to keep their fabs ultra-clean—walked through the smoke, across the stage, right up to Jobs. He took off his head covering and grinned: it was Intel CEO Paul Otellini. He handed Jobs a large silicon wafer. "Steve, I want to report that Intel is ready."

This was classic Steve Jobs theater, but it was a typical Intel business coup. By 2006, Intel already supplied the processors for most PCs, having spent the previous decade successfully fending off AMD, the only other major company producing chips on the x86 instruction set architecture—a foundational set of rules that govern how chips compute—that was the industry standard for PCs. Apple was the only major computer-maker that didn't use x86-based chips. Now, Jobs and Otellini announced, this would change. Mac computers would have Intel chips inside. Intel's empire would grow, and its stranglehold on the PC industry would tighten.

Jobs was already a Silicon Valley icon, having invented the Macintosh and pioneered the idea that computers could be intuitive and easy to use. In 2001, Apple released the iPod, a visionary product showing how digital technology could transform any consumer device. Intel's Otellini couldn't have been more different from Jobs. He was hired to be a manager, not a visionary. Unlike Intel's prior CEOs—Bob Noyce, Gordon Moore, Andy Grove, and Craig Barrett—Otellini's background was not in engineering or physics, but in economics. He'd graduated with an MBA, not a PhD. His time as CEO saw influence shift from chemists and physicists toward managers and accountants. This was barely perceptible at first, though employees noted that executives' shirts became steadily whiter and they wore ties more often. Otellini inherited a company that was enormously profitable. He saw his primary task as keeping profit margins as high as possible by milking Intel's de facto monopoly on x86 chips, and he applied textbook management practices to defend it.

The x86 architecture dominated PCs not because it was the best, but because IBM's first personal computer happened to use it. Like Microsoft, which provided the operating system for PCs, Intel controlled this crucial building block for the PC ecosystem. This was partially by luck—IBM could have chosen Motorola's processors for its first PCs— but also partly due to Andy Grove's strategic foresight. At staff meetings in the early 1990s, Grove would sketch an image illustrating his vision of the future of computing: a castle surrounded by a moat. The castle was Intel's profitability; the moat, defending the castle, was x86.

In the years since Intel first adopted the x86 architecture, computer scientists at Berkeley had devised a newer, simpler chip architecture called RISC that offered more efficient calculations and thus lower power consumption. The x86 architecture was complex and bulky by comparison. In the 1990s, Andy Grove had seriously considered switching Intel's main chips to a RISC architecture, but ultimately decided against it. RISC was more efficient, but the cost of change was high, and the threat to Intel's de facto monopoly was too serious. The computer industry was designed around x86 and Intel dominated the ecosystem. So x86 defines most PC architectures to this day.

Intel's x86 instruction set architecture also dominates the server business, which boomed as companies built ever larger data centers in the 2000s and then as businesses like Amazon Web Services, Microsoft Azure, and Google Cloud constructed the vast warehouses of servers that create "the cloud," on which individuals and companies store data and run programs. In the 1990s and early 2000s, Intel had only a small share of the business of providing chips for servers, behind companies like IBM and HP. But Intel used its ability to design and manufacture cutting-edge processor chips to win data center market share and establish x86 as the industry standard there, too. By the mid-2000s, just as cloud computing was emerging, Intel had won a near monopoly over data center chips, competing only with AMD. Today, nearly every major data center uses x86 chips from either Intel or AMD. The cloud can't function without their processors.

Some companies tried challenging x86's position as the industry standard in PCs. In 1990, Apple and two partners established a joint venture called Arm, based in Cambridge, England. The aim was to design processor chips using a new instruction set architecture based on the simpler RISC principles that Intel had considered but rejected. As a startup, Arm faced no costs of shifting away from x86, because it had no business and no customers. Instead, it wanted to replace x86 at the center of the computing ecosystem. Arm's first CEO, Robin Saxby, had vast ambitions for the twelve-person startup. "We have got to be the global standard," he told his colleagues. "That's the only chance we've got."

Saxby had climbed the ranks at Motorola's European semiconductor divisions before working at a European chip startup that failed because its manufacturing processes underperformed. He understood the limits of relying on in-house manufacturing. "Silicon is like steel," he insisted in the early debates over Arm's strategy. "It's a commodity. . . . We should build chips over my dead body." Instead, Arm adopted a business model of selling licenses for use of its architecture and letting any other chip designer buy them. This presented a new vision of a disaggregated chip industry. Intel had its own architecture (x86) on which it designed and produced many different chips. Saxby wanted to sell his Arm architecture to fabless design firms that would customize Arm's architecture for their own purposes, then outsource the manufacturing to a foundry like TSMC.

Saxby didn't simply dream of rivaling Intel, but of disrupting its business model. However, Arm failed to win market share in PCs in the 1990s and 2000s, because Intel's partnership with Microsoft's Windows operating system was simply too strong to challenge. However, Arm's simplified, energy-efficient architecture quickly became popular in small, portable devices that had to economize on battery use. Nintendo chose Arm-based chips for its handheld video games, for example, a small market that Intel never paid much attention to. Intel's computer processor oligopoly was too profitable to justify thinking about niche markets. Intel didn't realize until too late that it ought to compete in another seemingly niche market for a portable computing device: the mobile phone.

The idea that mobile devices would transform computing wasn't new. Carver Mead, the visionary Caltech professor, had predicted as much in the early 1970s. Intel, too, knew that PCs wouldn't be the final stage in the evolution of computing. The company invested in a series of new products over the course of the 1990s and 2000s, like a Zoom-esque video conferencing system that was two decades ahead of its time. But few of these new products caught on, less for technical reasons than because they were all far less profitable than Intel's core business of building chips for PCs. They never attracted support from inside Intel.

Mobile devices had been a regular source of discussion at the company since the early 1990s, when Andy Grove was still CEO. At one meeting at Intel's Santa Clara headquarters in the early 1990s, an executive waved his Palm Pilot in the air and declared: "These devices will grow up and replace the PC." But the idea of pouring money into mobile devices seemed like a wild gamble at a time when there was far more money to be made selling processors for PCs. So Intel decided not to enter the mobile business until it was too late.

Intel's dilemma could have been easily diagnosed by the Harvard professor who'd advised Andy Grove. Everyone at Intel knew Clayton Christensen and his concept of "the innovator's dilemma." However, the company's PC processor business looked likely to print money for a very long time. Unlike in the 1980s, when Grove reoriented Intel away from DRAM at a time when the company was bleeding money, in the 1990s and 2000s, Intel was one of America's most profitable firms. The problem wasn't that no one realized Intel ought to consider new products, but that the status quo was simply too profitable. If Intel did nothing at all, it would still own two of the world's most valuable castles—PC and server chips—surrounded by a deep x86 moat.

Shortly after the deal to put Intel's chips in Mac computers, Jobs came back to Otellini with a new pitch. Would Intel build a chip for Apple's newest product, a computerized phone? All cell phones used chips to run their operating systems and manage communication with cell phone networks, but Apple wanted its phone to function like a computer. It would need a powerful computer-style processor as a result. "They wanted to pay a certain price," Otellini told journalist Alexis Madrigal after the fact, "and not a nickel more. . . . I couldn't see it. It wasn't one of these things you can make up on volume. And in hindsight, the forecasted cost was wrong and the volume was 100× what anyone thought." Intel turned down the iPhone contract.

Apple looked elsewhere for its phone chips. Jobs turned to Arm's architecture, which unlike x86 was optimized for mobile devices that had to economize on power consumption. The early iPhone processors were produced by Samsung, which had followed TSMC into the foundry business. Otellini's prediction that the iPhone would be a niche product proved horribly wrong. By the time he realized his mistake, however, it was too late. Intel would later scramble to win a share of the smartphone business. Despite eventually pouring billions of dollars into products for smartphones, Intel never had much to show for it.

Apple dug a deep moat around its immensely profitable castle before Otellini and Intel realized what was happening.

Just a handful of years after Intel turned down the iPhone contract, Apple was making more money in smartphones than Intel was selling PC processors. Intel tried several times to scale the walls of Apple's castle but had already lost first-mover advantage. Spending billions for second place was hardly appealing, especially since Intel's PC business was still highly profitable and its data center business was growing quickly. So Intel never found a way to win a foothold in mobile devices, which today consume nearly a third of chips sold. It still hasn't.

Intel's missed opportunities in the years since Grove left the scene all had a common cause. Since the late 1980s, Intel has made a quarter trillion dollars in profit, even before adjusting for inflation, a track record that few other companies have matched. It has done this by charging a ton for PC and server chips. Intel could sustain high prices because of the optimized design processes and advanced manufacturing that Grove had honed and bequeathed to his successors. The company's leadership consistently prioritized the production of chips with the highest profit margin.

This was a rational strategy—no one wants products with low profit margins—but it made it impossible to try anything new. A fixation on hitting short-term margin targets began to replace long-term technology leadership. The shift in power from engineers to managers accelerated this process. Otellini, Intel's CEO from 2005 to 2013, admitted he turned down the contract to build iPhone chips because he worried about the financial implications. A fixation on profit margins seeped deep into the firm—its hiring decisions, its product road maps, and its R&D processes. The company's leaders were simply more focused on engineering the company's balance sheet than its transistors. "It had the technology, it had the people," one former finance executive at Intel reminisced. "It just didn't want to take the margin hit."

Today's computers and smartphones run on chips containing billions of microscopic transistors, the tiny electric switches that flip on and off to represent information. As such, they are unfathomably more capable than the U.S. Army's ENIAC computer, which was state of the art for 1945. That device contained a mere 18,000 "switches." (Getty Images)

Bob Noyce (*center*) cofounded Fairchild Semiconductor in 1957 with the goal of building silicon transistors. Also pictured is Noyce's longtime partner Gordon Moore (*far left*) as well as Eugene Kleiner (*third from left*), who later founded Kleiner Perkins, America's most powerful venture capital firm. (Wayne Miller/Magnum Photos)

In 1958, Jack Kilby at Texas Instruments built multiple electronic components on a single block of semiconductor material—the first "integrated circuit," or "chip." (*Dallas Morning News*)

Bob Noyce realized it was the civilian computer market, not the military, that would drive chip demand. He aggressively cut prices so that chips could be plugged into civilian computers, fueling the industry's growth. (Ted Streshinsky/Getty Images)

The first major order for Texas Instruments' chips was for the guidance computer on the Minuteman II missile, pictured here. (Dave Fields)

KGB spies Alfred Sarant and Joel Barr, both of whom grew up in New York, defected to the USSR to help build the Soviet computer industry. Despite the Soviets' pilfering, they failed to find the cutting edge. (Barr Papers/Steven Usdin)

At Texas Instruments, Weldon Word used microelectronics to build the first laser-guided bomb, which was first used to strike a bridge in Vietnam that had previously been missed by hundreds of "dumb" bombs. (Mark Perlstein/Getty Images)

In the 1980s Japan challenged the U.S. for semiconductor dominance. Akio Morita and Masaru Ibuka, cofounders of Sony, pioneered transformative products like the Sony Walkman, which proved that Asian firms could not only manufacture effectively but also win lucrative consumer markets. (Sony)

American semiconductor assembly plants across Asia provided thousands of jobs for America's allies. Pictured here are women at an Intel facility in Penang, Malaysia, that opened in 1972. "The workers were predominantly women," Intel explained, "because they performed better on dexterity tests." (Intel)

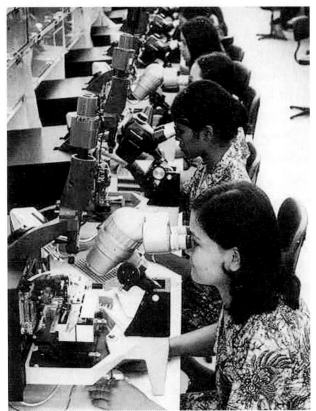

When Morris Chang was passed over for the CEO job at Texas Instruments, he moved to Taiwan where he founded Taiwan Semiconductor Manufacturing Company and built the country's chip industry. TSMC is one of Asia's most valuable companies. (Bloomberg/Getty Images)

Facing competition from Asia, American chipmakers competed on innovation. Intel's Andy Grove, who took over as CEO after Gordon Moore, forged an alliance with Bill Gates. Forty years later, Microsoft's Windows software and Intel's x86 chips continue to dominate the PC business. (AP Photo/Paul Sakuma)

In what proved to be a colossally bad decision, Intel turned down Steve Jobs's proposal to build chips for Apple's mobile phones. "I couldn't see it," Intel CEO Paul Otellini would later say. (Karl Mondon/Abaca Press)

The most advanced lithography machines, which are used to pattern millions of microscopic transistors, each far smaller than a human cell, are made by ASML in the Netherlands. Each machine costs well over $100 million dollars and is built from hundreds of thousands of components. (ASML)

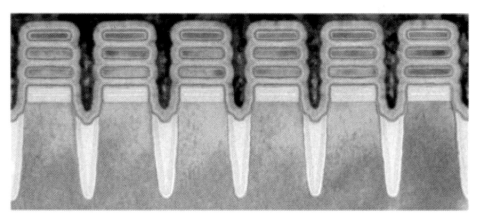

Today, advanced chips possess tiny, three-dimensional transistors, each smaller than a coronavirus, measuring a handful of nanometers (billionths of a meter) wide. (IBM)

EAST ASIA PRODUCES:

90 percent of all memory chips, 75 percent of all processor (logic) chips, and 80 percent of all silicon wafers

CHINA produces 15 percent of all chips, mostly low-tech, though, with government help, China's chip industry is growing rapidly

KOREA produces 44 percent of all memory chips and 8 percent of all processor chips

Dalian

Seoul

KOREA

JAPAN

Xian

Nanjing

Kumamoto

Wuhan

Shanghai

CHINA

JAPAN produces 17 percent of all chips

Hsinchu

TAIWAN

Shenzhen

Tainan

TAIWAN produces 41 percent of all processor chips and more than 90 percent of the most advanced chips

Penang

MALAYSIA

SINGAPORE

SINGAPORE produces around 5 percent of all chips

Source: Data from the Center for Security and Emerging Technology and the Semiconductor Industry Association

CHAPTER 34

Running Faster?

A ndy Grove was dining at a Palo Alto restaurant in 2010 when he was introduced to three Chinese venture capitalists who were touring Silicon Valley. He'd stepped down as Intel's chairman in 2005 and was now a simple retiree. The company he'd built and then rescued was still immensely profitable. It made money even in 2008 and 2009, though Silicon Valley's unemployment rate spiked above 9 percent. However, Grove didn't view Intel's past success as an argument for complacency. He was as paranoid as ever. Seeing Chinese venture capitalists investing in Palo Alto made him wonder: Was Silicon Valley smart to be offshoring production at a time of mass unemployment?

As a Jewish refugee from Nazi and Soviet armies, Grove was no nativist. Intel hired engineers from the world over. It operated facilities on multiple continents. However, Grove was worried about the offshoring of advanced manufacturing jobs. The iPhone, which had been introduced just three years earlier, exemplified the trend. Few of the iPhone's components were built in the U.S. Though offshoring started with low-skilled jobs, Grove didn't think it would stop there, whether in semiconductors or any other industry. He worried about lithium batteries needed for electric vehicles, where the U.S. made up a tiny share of the market despite having invented much of the core technology. His solution: "Levy an extra tax on the product of offshored labor. If the result is a trade war, treat it like other wars—fight to win."

Many people chose to write off Grove as a representative of a bygone era. He'd built Intel a generation earlier, before the internet existed. His company missed the mobile phone and was living off the fruits of its x86 monopoly. In the early 2010s, Intel retained the world's most advanced semiconductor process technology, introducing smaller transistors before rivals, with the same regular cadence it had been known for since the days of Gordon Moore. However, the gap between Intel and rivals like TSMC and Samsung had begun to shrink.

Moreover, Intel's business was now overshadowed by other tech firms with different business models. Intel had been one of the world's most valuable companies in the early 2000s, but had been overtaken by Apple, whose new mobile ecosystem didn't rely on Intel's chips. Intel missed the rise of the internet economy. Facebook, founded in 2006, was by 2010 worth nearly half as much as Intel. It would soon become several times more valuable. The Valley's biggest chipmaker could retort that the internet's data was processed on its server chips and accessed on PCs reliant on its processors. Yet producing chips was less profitable than selling ads on apps. Grove idolized "disruptive innovation," but by the 2010s, Intel's business was being disrupted. His lament of Apple's offshored assembly lines fell on deaf ears.

Even in the semiconductor space, Grove's doom-filled prophesies were widely rejected. True, new semiconductor foundries like TSMC were largely offshore. Yet foreign foundries produced chips largely designed by American fabless firms. Moreover, their fabs were full of U.S.-made manufacturing equipment. Offshoring to Southeast Asia had been central to the chip industry's business model since Fairchild Semiconductor—Andy Grove's first employer—opened its initial assembly plant in Hong Kong.

Grove wasn't convinced. "Abandoning today's 'commodity' manufacturing can lock you out of tomorrow's emerging industry," he declared, pointing to the electric battery industry. The U.S. "lost its lead in batteries thirty years ago when it stopped making consumer electronics devices," Grove wrote. Then it missed PC batteries, and now was far behind on batteries for electric vehicles. "I doubt they will ever catch up," he predicted in 2010.

Even within the semiconductor industry, it was easy to find counterpoints to Grove's pessimism about offshoring expertise. Compared to the situation in the late 1980s, when Japanese competitors were beating Silicon Valley in terms of DRAM design and manufacturing, America's chip ecosystem looked healthier. It wasn't only Intel that was printing immense profits. Many fabless chip designers were, too. Except for the loss of cutting-edge lithography, America's semiconductor manufacturing equipment firms generally thrived during the 2000s. Applied Materials remained the world's largest semiconductor toolmaking company, building equipment like the machines that deposited thin films of chemicals on top of silicon wafers as they were processed. Lam Research had world-beating expertise in etching circuits into silicon wafers. And KLA, also based in Silicon Valley, had the world's best tools for finding nanometer-sized errors on wafers and lithography masks. These three toolmakers were rolling out new generations of equipment that could deposit, etch, and measure features at the atomic scale, which would be crucial for making the next generation of chips. A couple Japanese firms—notably, Tokyo Electron—had some comparable capabilities to America's equipment makers. Nevertheless, it was basically impossible to make a leading-edge chip without using some American tools.

The same was true for designing chips. By the early 2010s, the most advanced microprocessors had a billion transistors on each chip. The software capable of laying out these transistors was provided by three American firms, Cadence, Synopsys, and Mentor, which controlled around three-quarters of the market. It was impossible to design a chip without using at least one of these firms' software. Moreover, most of the smaller firms providing chip design software were U.S.-based, too. No other country came close.

When analysts on Wall Street and in Washington looked at Silicon Valley, they saw a chip industry that was profitable and advancing technologically. There were, of course, some risks of relying so heavily on a couple of facilities in Taiwan to manufacture a large share of the world's chips. In 1999, an earthquake measuring 7.3 on the Richter scale struck Taiwan, knocking out power across much of the country, including from two nuclear power plants. TSMC's fabs lost power, too, threatening the company's production and many of the world's chips.

Morris Chang was quickly on the phone with Taiwanese officials to ensure the company got preferential access to electricity. It took a week to get four of the company's five fabs back online; the fifth took even longer. However, disruptions were limited and the market for consumer electronics reverted to normal within a month. However, the 1999 earthquake was only the third strongest the island had suffered in the twentieth century; it was easy to imagine stronger seismic shocks. TSMC's customers were told that the company's facilities could tolerate earthquakes measuring 9 on the Richter scale, of which the world has experienced five since 1900. This was not a claim that anyone wanted to test. However, TSMC could always point out that Silicon Valley sat atop the San Andreas Fault, so bringing manufacturing back to California wasn't much safer.

A more difficult question was how the U.S. government should adjust its controls on foreign sales of semiconductor technology to account for an increasingly international supply chain. Except for a couple of small chipmakers that produced specialized semiconductors for the U.S. military, Silicon Valley giants downgraded their relations with the Pentagon during the 1990s and 2000s. When they'd faced Japanese competition in the 1980s, Silicon Valley CEOs spent plenty of time in the halls of Congress. Now they didn't think they needed government help. Their main concern was for government to get out of the way, by signing trade deals with other countries and removing controls on exports. Many officials in Washington backed the industry's calls for looser controls. China had ambitious companies like SMIC, but the consensus in Washington was that trade and investment would encourage China to become a "responsible stakeholder" of the international system, as influential diplomat Robert Zoellick put it.

Moreover, popular theories about globalization made it sound almost impossible to impose strict controls. Controls had been hard enough to enforce during the Cold War, sparking regular disputes between the U.S. and allies about what equipment could be sold to the Soviets. Unlike the USSR, China in the 2000s was far more integrated into the world economy. Washington concluded that export controls would do more harm than good, hurting U.S. industry without preventing China from buying goods from firms in other countries. Japan and Europe were eager to sell almost anything to the PRC. No one in Washington had the stomach for a fight with allies about export controls, especially as U.S. leaders were focused on befriending their Chinese counterparts.

A new consensus in Washington formed around the idea that the best policy was to "run faster" than America's rivals. "The likelihood that the United States will grow dependent on any one country, much less China, for any one product, especially semiconductors, is exceedingly small," predicted one American expert. The U.S. went so far as to give China's SMIC special status as a "validated end-user," certifying that the company didn't sell to the Chinese military and was thus exempt from certain export controls. Other than a handful of legislators—mostly Southern Republicans who still looked at China as though the Cold War had never ended—almost everyone in Washington backed the strategy of "running faster" than rivals.

"Run faster" was an elegant strategy with only a single problem: by some key metrics, the U.S. *wasn't* running faster, it was losing ground. Hardly anyone in government bothered to do the analysis, but Andy Grove's gloomy predictions about the offshoring of expertise were partially coming true. In 2007, the Defense Department commissioned a study from former Pentagon official Richard Van Atta and several colleagues to assess the impact of semiconductor industry "globalization" on the military's supply chains. Van Atta had worked on defense microelectronics for several decades and had lived through the rise and fall of Japan's chip industry. He wasn't prone to overreaction and understood how a multinational supply chain made the industry more efficient. In peacetime, this system worked smoothly. However, the Pentagon had to think about worst-case scenarios. Van Atta reported that the Defense Department's access to cutting-edge chips would soon depend on foreign countries because so much advanced fabrication was moving abroad.

Amid the hubris of America's unipolar moment, hardly anyone was willing to listen. Most people in Washington simply concluded the U.S. was "running faster" without even glancing at the evidence. However, the history of the semiconductor industry didn't suggest that U.S. leadership was guaranteed. America hadn't outrun the Japanese in the 1980s, though it did in the 1990s. GCA hadn't outrun Nikon or ASML in lithography. Micron was the only DRAM producer able to keep pace with East Asian rivals, while many other U.S. DRAM producers went bust. Through the end of the 2000s, Intel retained a lead over Samsung and TSMC in producing miniaturized transistors, but the gap had narrowed. Intel was running more slowly, though it still benefitted from its more advanced starting point. The U.S. was a leader in most types of chip design, though Taiwan's MediaTek was proving that other countries could design chips, too. Van Atta saw few reasons for confidence and none for complacency. "The U.S. leadership position," he warned in 2007, "will likely erode seriously over the next decade." No one was listening.

PART VI

OFFSHORING INNOVATION?

CHAPTER 35

"Real Men Have Fabs"

Jerry Sanders, the Rolex-clad, Rolls Royce–driving brawler who founded AMD, liked to compare owning a semiconductor fab with putting a pet shark in your swimming pool. Sharks cost a lot to feed, took time and energy to maintain, and could end up killing you. Even still, Sanders was sure of one thing: he'd never give up his fabs. Though he had studied electrical engineering as an undergraduate at the University of Illinois, he was never a manufacturing guy. He moved up the ranks in sales and marketing at Fairchild Semiconductor, making his name as the company's most flamboyant and successful salesman.

His specialty was sales, but Sanders never dreamed of giving up AMD's manufacturing facilities, even as the rise of foundries like TSMC made it possible for big chip firms to consider divesting their manufacturing operations and outsourcing to a foundry in Asia. Having brawled with the Japanese for DRAM market share in the 1980s and with Intel for the PC market in the 1990s, Sanders was committed to his fabs. He thought they were crucial to AMD's success.

Even he admitted, though, that it was becoming harder to make money while owning and operating a fab. The problem was simple: each generation of technological improvement made fabs more expensive. Morris Chang had drawn a similar conclusion several decades earlier, which is why he thought TSMC's business model was superior.

A foundry like TSMC could fabricate chips for many chip designers, wringing out efficiencies from its massive production volumes that other companies would find difficult to replicate.

Not all sectors of the chip industry faced similar dynamics, but many did. By the 2000s, it was common to split the semiconductor industry into three categories. "Logic" refers to the processors that run smartphones, computers, and servers. "Memory" refers to DRAM, which provides the short-term memory computers need to operate, and flash, also called NAND, which remembers data over time. The third category of chips is more diffuse, including analog chips like sensors that convert visual or audio signals into digital data, radio frequency chips that communicate with cell phone networks, and semiconductors that manage how devices use electricity.

This third category has not been primarily dependent on Moore's Law to drive performance improvements. Clever design matters more than shrinking transistors. Today around three-quarters of this category of chips are produced on processors at or larger than 180 nanometers, a manufacturing technology that was pioneered in the late 1990s. As a result, the economics of this segment are different from logic and memory chips that must relentlessly shrink transistors to remain on the cutting edge. Fabs for these types of chips generally don't need to race toward the smallest transistors every couple of years, so they're substantially cheaper, on average requiring a quarter the capital investment of an advanced fab for logic or memory chips. Today, the biggest analog chipmakers are American, European, or Japanese. Most of their production occurs in these three regions, too, with only a sliver offshored to Taiwan and South Korea. The largest analog chipmaker today is Texas Instruments, which failed to establish an Intel-style monopoly in the PC, data center, or smartphone ecosystems but remains a medium-sized, highly profitable chipmaker with a vast catalog of analog chips and sensors. There are many other U.S.-based analog chipmakers now, like Onsemi, Skyworks, and Analog Devices, alongside comparable companies in Europe and Japan.

The memory market, by contrast, has been dominated by a relentless push toward offshoring production to a handful of facilities, mostly in East Asia. Rather than a diffuse set of suppliers centered in advanced economies, the two main types of memory chip—DRAM and NAND—are produced by only a couple of firms. For DRAM memory chips, the type of semiconductor that defined Silicon Valley's clash with Japan in the 1980s, an advanced fab can cost $20 billion. There used to be dozens of DRAM producers, but today there are only three major producers. In the late 1990s, several of Japan's struggling DRAM producers were consolidated into a single company, called Elpida, which sought to compete with Idaho's Micron and with Korea's Samsung and SK Hynix. By the end of the 2000s, these four companies controlled around 85 percent of the market. Yet Elpida struggled to survive and in 2013 was bought by Micron. Unlike Samsung and Hynix, which produce most of their DRAM in South Korea, Micron's long string of acquisitions left it with DRAM fabs in Japan, Taiwan, and Singapore as well as in the United States. Government subsidies in countries like Singapore encouraged Micron to maintain and expand fab capacity there. So even though an American company is one of the world's three biggest DRAM producers, most DRAM manufacturing is in East Asia.

The market for NAND, the other main type of memory chip, is also Asia-centric. Samsung, the biggest player, supplies 35 percent of the market, with the rest produced by Korea's Hynix, Japan's Kioxia, and two American firms—Micron and Western Digital. The Korean firms produce chips almost exclusively in Korea or China, but only a portion of Micron and Western Digital's NAND production is in the U.S., with other production in Singapore and Japan. As with DRAM, while U.S. firms play a major role in NAND production, the share of U.S.-based fabrication is substantially lower.

America's second-rate status in memory chip output, however, is nothing new. It dates to the late 1980s, when Japan first overtook the U.S. in DRAM output. The big shift in recent years is the collapse in the share of logic chips produced in the United States. Today, building an advanced logic fab costs $20 billion, an enormous capital investment that few firms can afford. As with memory chips, there's a correlation between the number of chips a firm produces and its yield—the number of chips that actually work. Given the benefits of scale, the number of firms fabricating advanced logic chips has shrunk relentlessly.

With the prominent exception of Intel, many key American logic chipmakers have given up their fabs and outsourced manufacturing. Other formerly major players, like Motorola or National Semiconductor, went bankrupt, were purchased, or saw their market share shrink. They were replaced by fabless firms, which often hired chip designers from legacy semiconductor firms but outsourced fabrication to TSMC or other foundries in Asia. This let fabless companies focus on their strength—chip design—without requiring simultaneous expertise in fabricating semiconductors.

So long as Sanders was CEO, AMD, the company he founded, stayed in the business of manufacturing logic chips, like processors for PCs. Old-school Silicon Valley CEOs kept insisting that separating the fabrication of semiconductors from their design caused inefficiencies. But it was culture, not business reasoning, that kept chip design and chip fabrication integrated for so long. Sanders could still remember the days of Bob Noyce tinkering away in Fairchild's lab. His argument in favor of keeping AMD's manufacturing in-house relied on macho-man posturing that was quickly going out of date. When he heard a quip from a journalist in the 1990s that "real men have fabs," he adopted the phrase as his own. "Now hear me and hear me well," Sanders declared at one industry conference. "Real men have fabs."

CHAPTER 36

The Fabless Revolution

"Real men" might have fabs, but Silicon Valley's new wave of semiconductor entrepreneurs didn't. Since the late 1980s, there's been explosive growth in the number of fabless chip firms, which design semiconductors in-house but outsource their manufacturing, commonly relying on TSMC for this service. When Gordon Campbell and Dado Banatao founded Chips and Technologies, which is generally considered the first fabless firm, in 1984, one friend alleged it "wasn't a real semiconductor company," since it didn't build its own chips. However, the graphics chips they designed for PCs proved popular, competing with products built by some of the industry's biggest players. Eventually Chips and Technologies faded and was purchased by Intel. However, it had proved that a fabless business model could work, requiring only a good idea and a couple of million dollars in startup capital, a tiny fraction of the money needed to build a fab.

Computer graphics remained an appealing niche for semiconductor startups, because unlike PC microprocessors, in graphics Intel didn't have a de facto monopoly. Every PC maker, from IBM to Compaq, had to use an Intel or an AMD chip for their main processor, because these two firms had a de facto monopoly on the x86 instruction set that PCs required. There was a lot more competition in the market for chips that rendered images on screens. The emergence of semiconductor foundries, and the driving down of startup costs, meant that it wasn't only Silicon Valley aristocracy that could compete to build the best graphics processors. The company that eventually came to dominate the market for graphics chips, Nvidia, had its humble beginnings not in a trendy Palo Alto coffeehouse but in a Denny's in a rough part of San Jose.

Nvidia was founded in 1993 by Chris Malachowsky, Curtis Priem, and Jensen Huang, the latter of whom remains CEO today. Priem had done fundamental work on how to compute graphics while at IBM, then worked at Sun Microsystems alongside Malachowsky. Huang, who was originally from Taiwan but had moved to Kentucky as a child, worked for LSI, a Silicon Valley chipmaker. He became the CEO and the public face of Nvidia, always wearing dark jeans, a black shirt, and a black leather jacket, and possessing a Steve Jobs–like aura suggesting that he'd seen far into the future of computing.

Nvidia's first set of customers—video and computer game companies—might not have seemed like the cutting edge, yet the firm wagered that the future of graphics would be in producing complex, 3D images. Early PCs were a dull, drab, 2D world, because the computation required to display 3D images was immense. In the 1990s, when Microsoft Office introduced an animated, paperclip called Clippy that sat at the side of the screen and dispensed advice, it represented a leap forward in graphics—and often caused computers to freeze.

Nvidia not only designed chips called graphics processor units (GPUs) capable of handling 3D graphics, it also devised a software ecosystem around them. Making realistic graphics requires use of programs called shaders, which tell all the pixels in an image how they should be portrayed in, say, a given shade of light. The shader is applied to each of the pixels in an image, a relatively straightforward calculation conducted over many thousands of pixels. Nvidia's GPUs can render images quickly because, unlike Intel's microprocessors or other general-purpose CPUs, they're structured to conduct lots of simple calculations—like shading pixels—simultaneously.

In 2006, realizing that high-speed parallel computations could be used for purposes besides computer graphics, Nvidia released CUDA, software that lets GPUs be programmed in a standard programming language, without any reference to graphics at all. Even as Nvidia was churning out top-notch graphics chips, Huang spent lavishly on this software effort, at least $10 billion, according to a company estimate in 2017, to let any programmer—not just graphics experts—work with Nvidia's chips. Huang gave away CUDA for free, but the software only works with Nvidia's chips. By making the chips useful beyond the graphics industry, Nvidia discovered a vast new market for parallel processing, from computational chemistry to weather forecasting. At the time, Huang could only dimly perceive the potential growth in what would become the biggest use case for parallel processing: artificial intelligence.

Today Nvidia's chips, largely manufactured by TSMC, are found in most advanced data centers. It's a good thing the company didn't need to build its own fab. At the startup stage, it would probably have been impossible to raise the necessary sums. Giving a couple million dollars to chip designers working in a Denny's was already a gamble. Betting over a hundred million dollars—the cost of a new fab at the time—would have been a stretch even for Silicon Valley's most adventurous investors. Moreover, as Jerry Sanders noted, running a fab well is expensive and time-consuming. It's hard enough simply to design top-notch chips, as Nvidia did. If it had also had to manage its own manufacturing processes, it probably wouldn't have had the resources or the bandwidth to plow money into building a software ecosystem.

Nvidia wasn't the only fabless company pioneering new use cases for specialized logic chips. Irwin Jacobs, the communications theory professor who'd held aloft a microprocessor and declared "This is the future!" at an academic conference in the early 1970s, now believed the future had arrived. Mobile phones—big, black bricks of plastic that were attached to the dashboard or floor of a car—were about to enter their second generation (2G) of technology. Phone companies were trying to agree on a technology standard that would let their phones communicate with one other. Most companies wanted a system called "time-division multiple access," whereby data from multiple phone calls would be transmitted on the same radio-wave frequency, with data from one call slotted into the radio-wave spectrum when there was a moment of silence in a different call.

Jacobs, whose faith in Moore's Law was as strong as ever, thought a more complicated system of frequency-hopping would work better. Rather than keeping a given phone call on a certain frequency, he proposed moving call data between different frequencies, letting him cram more calls into available spectrum space. Most people thought he was right in theory, but that such a system would never work in practice. Voice quality would be low, they argued, and calls would be dropped. The amount of processing needed to move call data between frequencies and have it interpreted by a phone on the other end seemed enormous.

Jacobs disagreed, founding a company called Qualcomm—Quality Communications—in 1985 to prove the point. He built a small network with a couple cell towers to prove it would work. Soon the entire industry realized Qualcomm's system would make it possible to fit far more cell phone calls into existing spectrum space by relying on Moore's Law to run the algorithms that make sense of all the radio waves bouncing around.

For each generation of cell phone technology after 2G, Qualcomm contributed key ideas about how to transmit more data via the radio spectrum and sold specialized chips with the computing power capable of deciphering this cacophony of signals. The company's patents are so fundamental it's impossible to make a cell phone without them. Qualcomm soon diversified into a new business line, designing not only the modem chips in a phone that communicate with a cell network, but also the application processors that run a smartphone's core systems. These chip designs are monumental engineering accomplishments, each built on tens of millions of lines of code. Qualcomm has made hundreds of billions of dollars selling chips and licensing intellectual property. But it hasn't fabricated any chips: they're all designed in-house but fabricated by companies like Samsung or TSMC.

It's easy to lament the offshoring of semiconductor manufacturing. But companies like Qualcomm might not have survived if they'd had to invest billions of dollars each year building fabs. Jacobs and his engineers were wizards at cramming data into the radio-wave spectrum and devising ever-more-clever chips to decode the meaning of these signals. As was the case with Nvidia, it was a good thing they didn't have to try to be semiconductor manufacturing experts, too. Qualcomm repeatedly considered opening its own fabrication facilities, but always decided against it, given the cost and complexity involved. Thanks to TSMC, Samsung, and other companies willing to produce their chips, Qualcomm's engineers could focus on their core strengths in managing spectrum and in semiconductor design.

There were many other U.S. chip firms that benefitted from a fabless model, letting them produce new chip designs without having to spend billions building an in-house fab. Entire new categories of chips emerged that were fabricated only at TSMC and other foundries rather than in-house. Field-programmable gate arrays, chips that can be programmed for different uses, were pioneered by companies like Xilinx and Altera, both of which relied on outsourced manufacturing from their earliest days. The biggest change, however, wasn't simply new types of chips. By making possible mobile phones, advanced graphics, and parallel processing, fabless firms enabled entirely new types of computing.

CHAPTER 37

Morris Chang's Grand Alliance

J erry Sanders may have promised never to give up his fabs, but the generation of engineers who came of age designing chips with penknives and tweezers was leaving the scene. Their replacements had been trained in the new discipline of computer science, and many knew semiconductors primarily through the new chip design software programs that emerged out of the 1980s and 1990s. To many people in Silicon Valley, Sanders's romantic attachment to fabs seemed as out of touch as his macho swagger. The new class of CEOs who took over America's semiconductor firms in the 2000s and 2010s tended to speak the language of MBAs as well as PhDs, chatting casually about capex and margins with Wall Street analysts on quarterly earnings calls. By most measures this new generation of executive talent was far more professional than the chemists and physicists who'd built Silicon Valley. But they often seemed stale in comparison to the giants who preceded them.

An era of wild wagers on impossible technologies was being superseded by something more organized, professionalized, and rationalized. Bet-the-house gambles were replaced by calculated risk management. It was hard to escape the sense that something was lost in the process. Of the chip industry's founders, only Morris Chang remained, smoking his pipe in his office in Taiwan, a habit he defended as good for his health, or at least for his mood. In the 2000s, even Chang began to think about succession planning. In 2005, aged seventy-four, he stepped down from the role of CEO, though he remained chairman of TSMC. Soon there'd be no one left who remembered working in the lab alongside Jack Kilby or drinking beers with Bob Noyce.

The changing of the guard atop the chip industry accelerated the splitting of chip design and manufacturing, with much of the latter offshored. Five years after Sanders retired from AMD, the company announced it was dividing its chip design and fabrication businesses. Wall Street cheered, reckoning the new AMD would be more profitable without the capital-intensive fabs. AMD spun out these facilities into a new company that would operate as a foundry like TSMC, producing chips not only for AMD but other customers, too. The investment arm of the Abu Dhabi government, Mubadala, became the primary investor in the new foundry, an unexpected position for a country known more for hydrocarbons than for high-tech. CFIUS, the U.S. government body that reviews foreign purchases of strategic assets, waved the sale through, judging that it had no national security implications. But the fate of AMD's production capabilities would end up shaping the chip industry—and guaranteeing that the most advanced chipmaking would take place offshore.

GlobalFoundries, as this new company that inherited AMD's fabs was known, entered an industry that was as competitive and unforgiving as ever. Moore's Law marched forward through the 2000s and early 2010s, forcing cutting-edge chipmakers to spend ever larger sums rolling out a new, more advanced manufacturing process roughly once every two years. Smartphone, PC, and server chips quickly migrated to each new "node," taking advantage of increased processing power and lower power consumption as transistors were more densely packed. Each node transition required ever more expensive machinery to produce.

For many years, each generation of manufacturing technology was named after the length of the transistor's gate, the part of the silicon chip whose conductivity would be turned on and off, creating and interrupting the circuit. The 180nm node was pioneered in 1999, followed by 130nm, 90nm, 65nm, and 45nm, with each generation shrinking transistors enough to make it possible to cram roughly twice as many in the same area. This reduced power consumption per transistor, because smaller transistors needed fewer electrons to flow through them.

Around the early 2010s, it became unfeasible to pack transistors more densely by shrinking them two dimensionally. One challenge was that, as transistors were shrunk according to Moore's Law, the narrow length of the conductor channel occasionally caused power to "leak" through the circuit even when the switch was off. On top of this, the layer of silicon dioxide atop each transistor became so thin that quantum effects like "tunneling"— jumping through barriers that classical physics said should be insurmountable—began seriously impacting transistor performance. By the mid-2000s, the layer of silicon dioxide on top of each transistor was only a couple of atoms thick, too small to keep a lid on all the electrons sitting in the silicon.

To better control the movement of electrons, new materials and transistor designs were needed. Unlike the 2D design used since the 1960s, the 22nm node introduced a new 3D transistor, called a FinFET (pronounced finfet), that sets the two ends of the circuit and the channel of semiconductor material that connects them on top of a block, looking like a fin protruding from a whale's back. The channel that connects the two ends of the circuit can therefore have an electric field applied not only from the top but also from the sides of the fin, enhancing control over the electrons and overcoming the electricity leakage that was threatening the performance of new generations of tiny transistors. These nanometer-scale 3D structures were crucial for the survival of Moore's Law, but they were staggeringly difficult to make, requiring even more precision in deposition, etching, and lithography. This added uncertainty about whether the major chipmakers would all flawlessly execute the switch to FinFET architectures or whether one might fall behind.

When GlobalFoundries was established as an independent company in 2009, industry analysts thought it was well placed to win market share amid this race toward 3D transistors. Even TSMC was worried, the company's former executives admit. GlobalFoundries had inherited a massive fab in Germany and was building a new, cutting-edge facility in New York. Unlike its rivals, it would be basing its most advanced production capacity in advanced economies, not in Asia. The company had a partnership with IBM and Samsung to jointly develop technology, making it straightforward for customers to contract with either GlobalFoundries or with Samsung to produce their chips. Moreover, fabless chip design firms were hungry for a credible competitor to TSMC, because the Taiwanese behemoth already had around half of the world's foundry market.

The only other major competitor was Samsung, whose foundry business had technology that was roughly comparable to TSMC's, though the company possessed far less production capacity. Complications arose, though, because part of Samsung's operation involved building chips that it designed in-house. Whereas a company like TSMC builds chips for dozens of customers and focuses relentlessly on keeping them happy, Samsung had its own line of smartphones and other consumer electronics, so it was *competing* with many of its customers. Those firms worried that ideas shared with Samsung's chip foundry might end up in other Samsung products. TSMC and GlobalFoundries had no such conflicts of interest.

The move to FinFET transistors wasn't the only shock to the chip industry that coincided with the establishment of GlobalFoundries. TSMC faced substantial manufacturing problems with its 40nm process, giving GlobalFoundries a chance to distinguish itself from its large rival. Moreover, the 2008–2009 financial crisis was threatening to reorder the chip industry. Consumers stopped buying electronics, so tech firms stopped ordering chips. Semiconductor purchases slumped. It felt like an elevator careening down an empty shaft, one TSMC executive recalled. If anything could disrupt the chip industry, a global financial crisis was it.

Morris Chang wasn't about to give up dominance of the foundry business, though. He'd lived through every industry cycle since his old colleague Jack Kilby invented the integrated circuit. He was sure this downturn would eventually end, too. Companies that were over-extended would be pushed out of business, leaving those that invested during the downturn positioned to grab market share. Moreover, Chang realized as early as anyone how smartphones would transform computing—and therefore how they would change the chip industry, too. The media focused on young tech tycoons like Facebook's Mark Zuckerberg, but seventy-seven-year-old Chang had a perspective that few could match. Mobile devices would be a "game-changer" for the chip industry, he told *Forbes*, perceiving them as heralding shifts as significant as the PC had brought. He was committed to winning the lion's share of this business, whatever the cost.

Chang realized that TSMC could pull ahead of rivals technologi-cally because it was a neutral player around which other companies would design their products. He called this TSMC's "Grand Alliance," a partnership of dozens of companies that design chips, sell intellectual property, produce materials, or manufacture machinery. Many of these companies compete with each other, but since none fabricate wafers, none compete with TSMC. TSMC could therefore coordinate between them, setting standards that most other companies in the chip industry would agree to use. They had no choice, because compatibility with TSMC's processes was crucial for almost every company. For fabless firms, TSMC was their most competitive source of manufacturing ser-vices. For equipment companies and materials firms, TSMC was often their biggest customer. As smartphones began to take off, driving up demand for silicon, Morris Chang sat at the center. "TSMC knows it is important to use everyone's innovation," Chang declared, "ours, that of the equipment makers, of our customers, and of the IP providers. That's the power of the Grand Alliance." The financial implications of this were profound. "The combined R&D spending of TSMC and its ten biggest customers," he bragged "exceeds that of Samsung and

Intel together." The old model of integrating design and manufacture would struggle to compete when the rest of the industry was coalescing around TSMC.

TSMC's position at the center of the semiconductor universe required it to have capacity to produce chips for all its biggest customers. Doing so wouldn't be cheap. Amid the financial crisis, Chang's handpicked successor, Rick Tsai, had done what nearly every CEO did—lay off employees and cut costs. Chang wanted to do the opposite. Getting the company's 40nm chipmaking back on track required investing in personnel and technology. Trying to win more smartphone business—especially that of Apple's iPhone, which launched in 2007 and which initially bought its key chips from TSMC's archrival, Samsung—required massive investment in chipmaking capacity. Chang saw Tsai's cost cutting as defeatist. "There was very, very little investment," Chang told journalists afterward. "I had always thought that the company was capable of more. . . . It didn't happen. There was stagnation."

So Chang fired his successor and retook direct control of TSMC. The company's stock price fell that day, as investors worried he'd launch a risky spending program with uncertain returns. Chang thought the real risk was accepting the status quo. He wasn't about to let a financial crisis threaten TSMC in the race for industry leadership. He had a half-century-long track record at chipmaking, a reputation he'd honed since the mid-1950s. So at the depths of the crisis Chang rehired the workers the former CEO had laid off and doubled down on investment in new capacity and R&D. He announced several multibillion-dollar increases to capital spending in 2009 and 2010 despite the crisis. It was better "to have too much capacity than the other way around," Chang declared. Anyone who wanted to break into the foundry business would face the full force of competition from TSMC as it raced to capture the booming market for smartphone chips. "We're just at the start," Chang declared in 2012, as he launched into his sixth decade atop the semiconductor industry.

CHAPTER 38

Apple Silicon

The greatest beneficiary of the rise of foundries like TSMC was a company that most people don't even realize designs chips: Apple. The company Steve Jobs built has always specialized in hardware, however, so it's no surprise that Apple's desire to perfect its devices includes controlling the silicon inside. Since his earliest days at Apple, Steve Jobs had thought deeply about the relationship between software and hardware. In 1980, when his hair nearly reached his shoulders and his mustache covered his upper lip, Jobs gave a lecture that asked, "What is software?" "The only thing I can think of," he answered, "is software is something that is changing too rapidly, or you don't exactly know what you want yet, or you didn't have time to get it into hardware."

Jobs didn't have time to get all his ideas into the hardware of the first-generation iPhone, which used Apple's own iOS operating system but outsourced design and production of its chips to Samsung. The revolutionary new phone had many other chips, too: an Intel memory chip, an audio processor designed by Wolfson, a modem to connect with the cell network produced by Germany's Infineon, a Bluetooth chip designed by CSR, and a signal amplifier from Skyworks, among others. All were designed by other companies.

As Jobs introduced new versions of the iPhone, he began etching his vision for the smartphone into Apple's own silicon chips. A year after launching the iPhone, Apple bought a small Silicon Valley chip design firm called PA Semi that had expertise in energy-efficient processing. Soon Apple began hiring some of the industry's best chip designers. Two years later, the company announced it had designed its own application processor, the A4, which it used in the new iPad and the iPhone 4. Designing chips as complex as the processors that run smartphones is expensive, which is why most low- and midrange smartphone companies buy off-the-shelf chips from companies like Qualcomm. However, Apple has invested heavily in R&D and chip design facilities in Bavaria and Israel as well as Silicon Valley, where engineers design its newest chips. Now Apple not only designs the main processors for most of its devices but also ancillary chips that run accessories like AirPods. This investment in specialized silicon explains why Apple's products work so smoothly. Within four years of the iPhone's launch, Apple was making over 60 percent of all the world's profits from smartphone sales, crushing rivals like Nokia and BlackBerry and leaving East Asian smartphone makers to compete in the low-margin market for cheap phones.

Like Qualcomm and the other chip firms that powered the mobile revolution, even though Apple designs ever more silicon, it doesn't build any of these chips. Apple is well known for outsourcing assembly of its phones, tablets, and other devices to several hundred thousand assembly line workers in China, who are responsible for screwing and gluing tiny pieces together. China's ecosystem of assembly facilities is the world's best place to build electronic devices. Taiwanese companies, like Foxconn and Wistron, that run these facilities for Apple in China are uniquely capable of churning out phones, PCs, and other electronics. Though the electronics assembly facilities in Chinese cities like Dongguan and Zhengzhou are the world's most efficient, however, they aren't irreplaceable. The world still has several hundred million subsistence farmers who'd happily fasten components into an iPhone for a dollar an hour. Foxconn assembles most of its Apple products in China, but it builds some in Vietnam and India, too.

Unlike assembly line workers, the chips inside smartphones are very difficult to replace. As transistors have shrunk, they've become ever harder to fabricate. The number of semiconductor companies that can build leading-edge chips has dwindled. By 2010, at the time Apple launched its first chip, there were just a handful of cutting-edge foundries: Taiwan's TSMC, South Korea's Samsung, and—perhaps—GlobalFoundries, depending on whether it could succeed in winning market share. Intel, still the world's leader at shrinking transistors, remained focused on building its own chips for PCs and servers rather than processors for other companies' phones. Chinese foundries like SMIC were trying to catch up but remained years behind.

Because of this, the smartphone supply chain looks very different from the one associated with PCs. Smartphones and PCs are both assembled largely in China with high-value components mostly designed in the U.S., Europe, Japan, or Korea. For PCs, most processors come from Intel and are produced at one of the company's fabs in the U.S., Ireland, or Israel. Smartphones are different. They're stuffed full of chips, not only the main processor (which Apple designs itself), but modem and radio frequency chips for connecting with cellular networks, chips for WiFi and Bluetooth connections, an image sensor for the camera, at least two memory chips, chips that sense motion (so your phone knows when you turn it horizontal), as well as semiconductors that manage the battery, the audio, and wireless charging. These chips make up most of the bill of materials needed to build a smartphone.

As semiconductor fabrication capacity migrated to Taiwan and South Korea, so too did the ability to produce many of these chips. Application processors, the electronic brain inside each smartphone, are mostly produced in Taiwan and South Korea before being sent to China for final assembly inside a phone's plastic case and glass screen. Apple's iPhone processors are fabricated exclusively in Taiwan. Today, no company besides TSMC has the skill or the production capacity to build the chips Apple needs. So the text etched onto the back of each iPhone—"Designed by Apple in California. Assembled in China"—is highly misleading. The iPhone's most irreplaceable components are indeed designed in California and assembled in China. But they can only be made in Taiwan.

CHAPTER 39

EUV

Apple isn't the only company in the semiconductor business with a bewilderingly complex supply chain. By the late-2010s, ASML, the Dutch lithography company, had spent nearly two decades trying to make extreme-ultraviolet lithography work. Doing so required scouring the world for the most advanced components, the purest metals, the most powerful lasers, and the most precise sensors. EUV was one of the biggest technological gambles of our time. In 2012, years before ASML had produced a functional EUV tool, Intel, Samsung, and TSMC had each invested directly in ASML to ensure the company had the funding needed to continue developing EUV tools that their future chipmaking capabilities would require. Intel alone invested $4 billion in ASML in 2012, one of the highest-stakes bets the company ever made, an investment that followed billions of dollars of previous grants and investments Intel had spent on EUV, dating back to the era of Andy Grove.

The idea behind EUV lithography tools was little changed from when Intel and a consortium of other chip firms had given several of America's national labs "what felt like infinite money for solving an impossible problem," as one of the scientists who worked on the project put it. The concept remained much the same as Jay Lathrop's upside-down microscope: create a pattern of light waves by using a "mask" to block some of the light, then project the light onto photoresist chemicals applied to a silicon wafer. The light reacts with photoresists, making it possible to deposit material or etch it away in perfectly formed shapes, producing a working chip.

Lathrop had used simple visible light and off-the-shelf photoresists produced by Kodak. Using more complex lenses and chemicals, it eventually became possible to print shapes as small as a couple hundred nanometers on silicon wafers. The wavelength of visible light is itself several hundred nanometers, depending on the color, so it eventually faced limits as transistors were made ever smaller. The industry later moved to different types of ultraviolet light with wavelengths of 248 and 193 nanometers. These wavelengths could carve shapes more precise than visible light, but they, too, had limits, so the industry placed its hope on extreme ultraviolet light with a wavelength of 13.5 nanometers.

Using EUV light introduced new difficulties that proved almost impossible to resolve. Where Lathrop used a microscope, visible light, and photoresists produced by Kodak, all the key EUV components had to be specially created. You can't simply buy an EUV lightbulb. Producing enough EUV light requires pulverizing a small ball of tin with a laser. Cymer, a company founded by two laser experts from the University of California, San Diego, had been a major player in lithographic light sources since the 1980s. The company's engineers realized the best approach was to shoot a tiny ball of tin measuring thirty-millionths of a meter wide moving through a vacuum at a speed of around two hundred miles per hour. The tin is then struck twice with a laser, the first pulse to warm it up, the second to blast it into a plasma with a temperature around half a million degrees, many times hotter than the surface of the sun. This process of blasting tin is then repeated fifty thousand times per second to produce EUV light in the quantities necessary to fabricate chips. Jay Lathrop's lithography process had relied on a simple bulb for a light source. The increase in complexity since then was mind-boggling.

Cymer's light source only worked, though, thanks to a new laser that could pulverize the tin droplets with sufficient power. This required a carbon dioxide–based laser more powerful than any that previously existed. In summer 2005, two engineers at Cymer approached a German precision tooling company called Trumpf to see if it could build such a laser. Trumpf already made the world's best carbon dioxide–based lasers for industrial uses like precision cutting. These lasers were monuments of machining in the best German industrial tradition. Because around 80 percent of the energy a carbon dioxide laser produces is heat and only 20 percent light, extracting heat from the machine is a key challenge. Trumpf had previously devised a system of blowers with fans that turned a thousand times a second, too fast to rely on physical bearings. Instead, the company learned to use magnets, so the fans floated in air, sucking heat out of the laser system without grinding against other components and imperiling reliability.

Trumpf had a reputation and a track record for delivering the precision and reliability Cymer needed. Could it deliver the power? Lasers for EUV needed to be substantially more powerful than the lasers Trumpf already produced. Moreover, the precision Cymer demanded was more exacting than anything Trumpf had previously dealt with. The company proposed a laser with four components: two "seed" lasers that are low power but accurately time each pulse so that the laser can hit 50 million tin drops a second; four resonators that increase the beam's power; an ultra-accurate "beam transport system" that directs the beam over thirty meters toward the tin droplet chamber; and a final focusing device to ensure the laser scores a direct hit, millions of times a second.

Every step required new innovations. Specialized gases in the laser chamber had to be kept at constant densities. The tin droplets themselves reflected light, which threatened to shine back into the laser and interfere with the system; to prevent this, special optics were required. The company needed industrial diamonds to provide the "windows" through which the laser exited the chamber, and had to work with partners to develop new, ultra-pure diamonds. It took Trumpf a decade to master these challenges and produce lasers with sufficient power and reliability. Each one required exactly 457,329 component parts.

After Cymer and Trumpf found a way to blast tin so it emits sufficient EUV light, the next step was to create mirrors that collected the light and directed it toward a silicon chip. Zeiss, the German company that builds the world's most advanced optical systems, had built mirrors and lenses for lithography systems since the days of Perkin Elmer and GCA. The difference between the optics used in the past and those required by EUV, however, was about as vast as the contrast between Lathrop's lightbulb and Cymer's system of blasting tin droplets.

Zeiss's primary challenge was that EUV is difficult to reflect. The 13.5nm wavelength of EUV is closer to X-rays than to visible light, and as is the case with X-rays, many materials absorb EUV rather than reflect it. Zeiss began developing mirrors made of one hundred alternating layers of molybdenum and silicon, each layer a couple nanometers thick. Researchers in Lawrence Livermore National Lab had identified this as an optimal EUV mirror in a paper published in 1998, but building such a mirror with nanoscale precision proved almost impossible. Ultimately, Zeiss created mirrors that were the smoothest objects ever made, with impurities that were almost imperceptibly small. If the mirrors in an EUV system were scaled to the size of Germany, the company said, their biggest irregularities would be a tenth of a millimeter. To direct EUV light with precision, they must be held perfectly still, requiring mechanics and sensors so exact that Zeiss boasted they could be used to aim a laser to hit a golf ball as far away as the moon.

For Frits van Houts, who took over leadership of ASML's EUV business in 2013, the most crucial input into an EUV lithography system wasn't any individual component, but the company's own skill in supply chain management. ASML engineered this network of business relationships "like a machine," van Houts explained, producing a finely tuned system of several thousand companies capable of meeting ASML's exacting requirements. ASML itself only produced 15 percent of an EUV tool's components, he estimated, buying the rest from other firms. This let it access the world's most finely engineered goods, but it also required constant surveillance.

The company had no choice but to rely on a single source for the key components of an EUV system. To manage this, ASML drilled down into its suppliers' suppliers to understand the risks. ASML rewarded certain suppliers with investment, like the $1 billion it paid Zeiss in 2016 to fund that company's R&D process. It held all of them, however, to exacting standards. "If you don't behave, we're going to buy you," ASML's CEO Peter Wennink told one supplier. It wasn't a joke: ASML ended up buying several suppliers, including Cymer, after concluding it could better manage them itself.

The result was a machine with hundreds of thousands of components that took tens of billions of dollars and several decades to develop. The miracle isn't simply that EUV lithography works, but that it does so reliably enough to produce chips cost-effectively. Extreme reliability was crucial for any component that would be put in the EUV system. ASML had set a target for each component to last on average for at least thirty thousand hours—around four years—before needing repair. In practice, repairs would be needed more often, because not every part breaks at the same time. EUV machines cost over $100 million each, so every hour one is offline costs chipmakers thousands of dollars in lost production.

EUV tools work in part because their software works. ASML uses predictive maintenance algorithms to guess when components need to be replaced before they break, for example. It also uses software for a process called computational lithography to print patterns more exactly. The atomic-level unpredictability in light waves' reaction with photoresist chemicals created new problems with EUV that barely existed with larger-wavelength lithography. To adjust for anomalies in the way light refracts, ASML's tools project light in a pattern that differs from what chipmakers want imprinted on a chip. Printing an "X" requires using a pattern with a very different shape but which ends up creating an "X" when the light waves hit the silicon wafer.

The final product—chips—work so reliably because they only have a single component: a block of silicon topped with other metals. There are no moving parts in a chip, unless you count the electrons zipping around inside. Producing advanced semiconductors, however, has relied on some of the most complex machinery ever made. ASML's EUV lithography tool is the most expensive mass-produced machine tool in history, so complex it's impossible to use without extensive training from ASML personnel, who remain on-site for the tool's entire life span. Each EUV scanner has an ASML logo on its side. But ASML's expertise, the company readily admits, was its ability to orchestrate a far-flung network of optics experts, software designers, laser companies, and many others whose capabilities were needed to make the dream of EUV a reality.

It's easy to lament the offshoring of manufacturing, as Andy Grove did during the final years of his life. That a Dutch company, ASML, had commercialized a technology pioneered in America's National Labs and largely funded by Intel would undoubtedly have rankled America's economic nationalists, had any been aware of the history of lithography or of EUV technology. Yet ASML's EUV tools weren't really Dutch, though they were largely assembled in the Netherlands. Crucial components came from Cymer in California and Zeiss and Trumpf in Germany. And even these German firms relied on critical pieces of U.S.-produced equipment. The point is that, rather than a single country being able to claim pride of ownership regarding these miraculous tools, they are the product of many countries. A tool with hundreds of thousands of parts has many fathers.

"Will it work?" Andy Grove had asked John Carruthers, before investing his first $200 million in EUV. After three decades of investment, billions of dollars, a series of technological innovations, and the establishment of one of the world's most complex supply chains, by the mid-2010s, ASML's EUV tools were finally ready to be deployed in the world's most advanced chip fabs.

CHAPTER 40

"There Is No Plan B"

I n 2015, Tony Yen was asked what would happen if the new extreme-ultraviolet lithography tool that ASML was developing didn't work. Yen had spent the prior twenty-five years working at the cutting edge of lithography. In 1991 he'd been hired fresh out of MIT by Texas Instruments, where he tinkered with one of the final lithography tools GCA produced before going bankrupt. He then joined TSMC in the late 1990s just as deep-ultraviolet lithography tools, which produced light with a wavelength of 193 nanometers, were coming online. For nearly two decades, the industry relied on these tools to fabricate ever-smaller transistors, using a series of optical tricks like shooting light through water or through multiple masks to enable light waves measuring 193nm to pattern shapes a fraction of the size. These tricks kept Moore's Law alive, as the chip industry shrank transistors from the 180nm node in the late 1990s through the early stages of 3D FinFET chips, which were ready for high-volume manufacturing by the mid-2010s.

However, there were only so many optical tricks that could help 193nm light carve smaller features. Each new workaround added time and cost money. By the mid-2010s, it might have been possible to eke out a couple additional improvements, but Moore's Law needed better lithography tools to carve smaller shapes. The only hope was that the hugely delayed EUV lithography tools, which had been in development since the early 1990s, could finally be made to work at a commercial scale. What was the alternative? "There is no Plan B," Yen knew.

Morris Chang bet more heavily on EUV than anyone else in the semiconductor industry. The company's lithography team was divided over whether EUV tools were ready for high-volume manufacturing, but Shang-yi Chiang, the soft-spoken engineer who headed TSMC's R&D and was widely credited for the company's top-notch manufacturing technology, was convinced EUV was the only path forward. Chiang was born in Chongqing where, like Morris Chang, his family had fled from Japanese armies during World War II. He grew up in Taiwan before studying electrical engineering at Stanford and landing jobs at TI in Texas and then at HP in Silicon Valley. When TSMC called out of the blue with a job offer—and a massive signing bonus—he moved back to Taiwan in 1997 to help build the company. In 2006, he tried retiring in California, but when TSMC faced a delay with its 40nm manufacturing process in 2009, a frustrated Morris Chang ordered Chiang back to Taiwan and over a meal of beef noodle soup asked him to again take up the responsibility of managing R&D.

Having worked in Texas and California as well as in Taiwan, Chiang was always struck by the ambition and the work ethic that drove TSMC. The ambition stemmed from Morris Chang's vision of world-beating technology, evident in his willingness to spend huge sums expanding TSMC's R&D team from 120 people in 1997 to 7,000 in 2013. This hunger permeated the entire company. "People worked so much harder in Taiwan," Chiang explained. Because manufacturing tools account for much of the cost of an advanced fab, keeping the equipment operating is crucial for profitability. In the U.S., Chiang said, if something broke at 1 a.m., the engineer would fix it the next morning. At TSMC, they'd fix it by 2 a.m. "They do not complain," he explained, and "their spouse does not complain" either. With Chiang back in charge of R&D, TSMC charged forward toward EUV. He had no difficulty finding employees to work all night long. He requested that three EUV scanners for testing purposes be built in the middle of one of the company's biggest facilities, Fab 12, and in the company's partnership with ASML he spared no expense in testing and improving EUV tools.

Like TSMC, Samsung, and Intel, GlobalFoundries was considering adopting EUV as it prepared for its own 7nm node. From its creation, GlobalFoundries knew it needed to grow if it was to thrive. The company had inherited AMD's fabs, but it was far smaller than its rivals. To grow, GlobalFoundries had bought Chartered Semiconductor, a Singapore-based foundry, in 2010. Several years later, in 2014, it bought IBM's microelectronics business, promising to produce chips for Big Blue, which had decided to go fabless for the same reason as AMD. IBM executives used to share an image of the computing ecosystem: an upside-down pyramid with semiconductors at the bottom, on which all other computing depended. Yet though IBM had played a fundamental role in the growth of the semiconductor business, its leaders concluded that fabricating chips made no financial sense. Facing a decision to invest billions to build a new advanced fab, or billions on high-margin software, they chose the latter, selling their chip division to GlobalFoundries.

By 2015, thanks to these acquisitions, GlobalFoundries was by far the biggest foundry in the United States and one of the largest in the world, but it was still a minnow compared to TSMC. GlobalFoundries competed with Taiwan's UMC for status as the world's second-largest foundry, with each company having about 10 percent of the foundry marketplace. However, TSMC had over 50 percent of the world's foundry market. Samsung only had 5 percent of the foundry market in 2015, but it produced more wafers than anyone when its vast production of chips designed in-house (for example, memory chips and chips for smartphone processors) were included. Measured by thousands of wafers per month, the industry standard, TSMC had a capacity of 1.8 million while Samsung had 2.5 million. GlobalFoundries had only 700,000.

TSMC, Intel, and Samsung were certain to adopt EUV, though they had different strategies about when and how to embrace it. Global-Foundries was less confident. The company had struggled with its 28nm process. To reduce the risk of delays, it decided to license its 14nm process from Samsung rather than develop it in-house, a decision that didn't suggest confidence in its R&D efforts.

By 2018, GlobalFoundries had purchased several EUV lithography tools and was installing them in its most advanced facility, Fab 8, when the company's executives ordered them to halt work. The EUV program was being canceled. GlobalFoundries was giving up production of new, cutting-edge nodes. It wouldn't pursue a 7nm process based on EUV lithography, which had already cost $1.5 billion in development and would have required a comparable amount of additional spending to bring online. TSMC, Intel, and Samsung had financial positions that were strong enough to roll the dice and hope they could make EUV work. GlobalFoundries decided that as a medium-sized foundry, it could never make a 7nm process financially viable. It announced it would stop building ever-smaller transistors, slashed R&D spending by a third, and quickly turned a profit after several years of losses. Building cutting-edge processors was too expensive for everyone except the world's biggest chipmakers. Even the deep pockets of the Persian Gulf royals who owned GlobalFoundries weren't deep enough. The number of companies capable of fabricating leading-edge logic chips fell from four to three.

CHAPTER 41

How Intel Forgot Innovation

A t least the United States could count on Intel. The company had an unparalleled position in the semiconductor industry. The old leadership was long gone—Andy Grove died in 2016, while Gordon Moore, now in his nineties, retired to Hawaii—but the reputation of having commercialized the DRAM and invented the microprocessor remained. No company had a better track record combining innovative chip design with manufacturing prowess. Intel's x86 architecture remained the industry standard for PCs and data centers. The PC market was stagnant, because it seemed nearly everyone already had a PC, but it remained remarkably profitable for Intel, providing billions of dollars a year that could be reinvested into R&D. The company spent over $10 billion a year on R&D throughout the 2010s, four times as much as TSMC and three times more than the entire budget of DARPA. Only a couple of companies in the world spent more.

As the chip industry entered the EUV era, Intel looked poised to dominate. The company had been crucial to EUV's emergence, thanks to Andy Grove's initial $200 million bet on the technology in the early 1990s. Now, after billions of dollars of investment—a substantial portion of which had come from Intel—ASML had finally made the technology a reality. Yet rather than capitalizing on this new era of shrinking transistors, Intel squandered its lead, missing major shifts in semiconductor architecture needed for artificial intelligence, then bungling its manufacturing processes and failing to keep up with Moore's Law.

Intel remains enormously profitable today. It's still America's biggest and most advanced chipmaker. However, its future is more in doubt than at any point since Grove's decision in the 1980s to abandon memory and bet everything on microprocessors. It still has a shot at regaining its leadership position over the next half decade, but it could just as easily end up defunct. What's at stake isn't simply one company, but the future of America's chip fabrication industry. Without Intel, there won't be a single U.S. company—or a single facility outside of Taiwan or South Korea—capable of manufacturing cutting-edge processors.

Intel entered the 2010s as an outlier in Silicon Valley. Most of America's biggest firms in the market for logic chips, including Intel's archrival AMD, had sold their fabs and focused only on design. Intel stuck stubbornly to its integrated model—combining semiconductor design and manufacturing in one company—which executives there thought was still the best way to churn out chips. The company's design and manufacturing processes were optimized for each other, Intel's leaders argued. TSMC, by contrast, had no choice but to adopt generic manufacturing processes that could work just as well for a Qualcomm smartphone processor as an AMD server chip.

Intel was right to perceive some benefits of an integrated model, but there were substantial downsides. Because TSMC manufactures chips for many different companies, it now fabricates nearly three times as many silicon wafers per year as Intel, so it has more chance to hone its process. Moreover, where Intel saw chip design startups as a threat, TSMC saw potential customers for manufacturing services. Because TSMC had only a single value proposition—effective manufacturing— its leadership focused relentlessly on fabricating ever-more-advanced semiconductors at lower cost. Intel's leaders had to split their attention between chip design and chip manufacturing. They ended up bungling both.

Intel's first problem was artificial intelligence. By the early 2010s, the company's core market, supplying PC processors, had stalled. Today, other than gamers, hardly anyone excitedly upgrades their PC when a new model is released, and most people don't think much about which type of processor is inside. Intel's other main market—selling processors for servers in data centers—boomed over the 2010s. Amazon Web Services, Microsoft Azure, Google Cloud, and other companies built networks of vast data centers, which provided the computing power that made possible "the cloud." Most of the data we use online is processed in one of these companies' data centers, each of which is full of Intel chips. But in the early 2010s, just as Intel completed its conquest of the data center, processing demands began to shift. The new trend was artificial intelligence—a task that Intel's main chips were poorly designed to address.

Since the 1980s, Intel has specialized in a type of chip called a CPU, a central processing unit, of which a microprocessor in a PC is one example. These are the chips that serve as the "brain" in a computer or data center. They are general-purpose workhorses, equally capable of opening a web browser or running Microsoft Excel. They can conduct many different types of calculations, which makes them versatile, but they do these calculations serially, one after another.

It's possible to run any AI algorithm on a general-purpose CPU, but the scale of computation required for AI makes using CPUs prohibitively expensive. The cost of *training* a single AI model—the chips it uses and the electricity they consume—can stretch into the millions of dollars. (To *train* a computer to recognize a cat, you have to show it a lot of cats and dogs so it learns to distinguish between the two. The more animals your algorithm requires, the more transistors you need.)

Because AI workloads often require running the same calculation repeatedly, using different data each time, finding a way to customize chips for AI algorithms is crucial to making them economically viable. Big cloud computing companies like Amazon and Microsoft, which operate the data centers on which most companies' algorithms run, spend tens of billions of dollars annually buying chips and servers. They also spend vast sums providing electricity for these data centers. Wringing efficiencies out of their chips is a necessity as they compete to sell companies space in their "cloud." Chips optimized for AI can work faster, take up less data center space, and use less power than general-purpose Intel CPUs.

In the early 2010s, Nvidia—the designer of graphic chips—began hearing rumors of PhD students at Stanford using Nvidia's graphics processing units (GPUs) for something other than graphics. GPUs were designed to work differently from standard Intel or AMD CPUs, which are infinitely flexible but run all their calculations one after the other. GPUs, by contrast, are designed to run multiple iterations of the same calculation at once. This type of "parallel processing," it soon became clear, had uses beyond controlling pixels of images in computer games. It could also train AI systems efficiently. Where a CPU would feed an algorithm many pieces of data, one after the other, a GPU could process multiple pieces of data simultaneously. To learn to recognize images of cats, a CPU would process pixel after pixel, while a GPU could "look" at many pixels at once. So the time needed to train a computer to recognize cats decreased dramatically.

Nvidia has since bet its future on artificial intelligence. From its founding, Nvidia outsourced its manufacturing, largely to TSMC, and focused relentlessly on designing new generations of GPUs and rolling out regular improvements to its special programming language called CUDA that makes it straightforward to devise programs that use Nvidia's chips. As investors bet that data centers will require ever more GPUs, Nvidia has become America's most valuable semiconductor company.

Its ascent isn't assured, however, because in addition to buying Nvidia chips the big cloud companies—Google, Amazon, Microsoft, Facebook, Tencent, Alibaba, and others—have also begun designing their own chips, specialized to their processing needs, with a focus on artificial intelligence and machine learning. For example, Google has designed its own chips called Tensor processing units (TPUs), which are optimized for use with Google's TensorFlow software library. You can rent the use of Google's simplest TPU in its Iowa data center for $3,000 per month, but prices for more powerful TPUs can reach over $100,000 monthly. The cloud may sound ethereal, but the silicon on which all our data lives is very real—and very expensive.

Whether it will be Nvidia or the big cloud companies doing the vanquishing, Intel's near-monopoly in sales of processors for data centers is ending. Losing this dominant position would have been less problematic if Intel had found new markets. However, the company's foray into the foundry business in the mid-2010s, where it tried to compete head-on with TSMC, was a flop. Intel tried opening its manufacturing lines to any customers looking for chipmaking services, quietly admitting that the model of integrated design and manufacturing wasn't nearly as successful as Intel's executives claimed. The company had all the ingredients to become a major foundry player, including advanced technology and massive production capacity, but succeeding would have required a major cultural change. TSMC was open with intellectual property, but Intel was closed off and secretive. TSMC was service-oriented, while Intel thought customers should follow its own rules. TSMC didn't compete with its customers, since it didn't design any chips. Intel was the industry giant whose chips competed with almost everyone.

Brian Krzanich, who was Intel's CEO from 2013 to 2018, insisted publicly that "I've been basically running our foundry business for the last few years" and described the effort as "strategically important." But it didn't look that way to customers, who thought the company failed to put foundry customers first. Inside Intel, the foundry business wasn't treated as a priority. Compared to making PC and data center chips—which remained highly profitable businesses—the new foundry venture had little internal support. So Intel's foundry business won only a single major customer while in operation in the 2010s. It was shuttered after just several years.

As Intel approached its fiftieth anniversary in 2018, decay had set in. The company's market share was shrinking. The bureaucracy was stultifying. Innovation happened elsewhere. The final straw was Intel's bungling of Moore's Law, as the company faced a series of delays to planned improvements in its manufacturing process, which it is still struggling to rectify. Since 2015, Intel has repeatedly announced delays to its 10nm and 7nm manufacturing processes, even as TSMC and Samsung have charged ahead.

The company has done little to explain what went wrong. Intel has now spent half a decade announcing "temporary" manufacturing delays, the technical details of which are obscured in the secrecy of employee nondisclosure agreements. Most people in the industry think many of the company's problems stem from Intel's delayed adoption of EUV tools. By 2020, half of all EUV lithography tools, funded and nurtured by Intel, were installed at TSMC. By contrast, Intel had only barely begun to use EUV in its manufacturing process.

As the decade ended, only two companies could manufacture the most cutting-edge processors, TSMC and Samsung. And so far as the United States was concerned, both were problematic for the same reason: their location. Now the entire world's production of advanced processors was taking place in Taiwan and Korea—just off the coast from America's emerging strategic competitor: the People's Republic of China.

PART VII

CHINA'S CHALLENGE

CHAPTER 42

Made in China

"Without cybersecurity there is no national security," declared Xi Jinping, general secretary of the Chinese Communist Party, in 2014, "and without informatization, there is no modernization." The son of one of China's earliest Communist Party leaders, Xi had studied engineering in college before ascending the ranks of Chinese politics thanks to his chameleonlike knack for appearing to be whatever a given audience thought it wanted. To Chinese nationalists, his program of a "Chinese Dream" promised national rejuvenation and great power status. To businesses, he pledged economic reform. Some foreigners even saw him as a closet democrat, with the *New Yorker* declaring right after he took power that Xi was "a leader who realizes that China must undertake real political reform." The only certainty was Xi's talent as a politician. His own views were hidden behind pursed lips and a feigned smile.

Behind this smile is a gnawing sense of insecurity that has driven Xi's policies during the decade he's ruled China. The primary risk, he believed, was the digital world. Most observers thought Xi had little to fear when it came to guaranteeing his own digital security. China's leaders have the world's most effective system of internet control, employing many thousands of censors to police online chatter. China's firewall made a huge swath of the internet inaccessible to its citizens, decisively disproving Western predictions that the internet would be a liberalizing political force. Xi felt strong enough online to mock the Western belief that the internet would spread democratic values. "The internet has turned the world into a global village," Xi declared, sidestepping the fact that many of the world's most popular websites, like Google and Facebook, were banned in China. He had a different type of global network in mind than the utopians of the early internet age—a network that China's government could use to project power. "We must march out, deepen international internet exchange and collaboration, and vigorously participate in the construction of 'One Belt, One Road,'" he declared on a different occasion, referring to his plan to enmesh the world in Chinese-built infrastructure that included not only roads and bridges but network equipment and censorship tools.

No country has been more successful than China at harnessing the digital world for authoritarian purposes. It has tamed America's tech giants. Google and Facebook were banned and replaced by homegrown firms like Baidu and Tencent, which, technologically, are close matches with their American rivals. The U.S. tech firms that have won access to the Chinese market, like Apple and Microsoft, were allowed in only after agreeing to collaborate with Beijing's censorship efforts. Far more than any other country, China has made the internet subservient to its leaders' wishes. Foreign internet and software companies either signed on to whatever censorship rules the Communist Party desired or lost access to a vast market.

Why, then, was Xi Jinping worried about digital security? The more China's leaders studied their technological capabilities, the less important their internet companies seemed. China's digital world runs on digits—1s and 0s—that are processed and stored mostly by imported semiconductors. China's tech giants depend on data centers full of foreign, largely U.S.-produced, chips. The documents that Edward Snowden leaked in 2013 before fleeing to Russia demonstrated American network-tapping capabilities that surprised even the cyber sleuths in Beijing. Chinese firms had replicated Silicon Valley's expertise in building software for e-commerce, online search, and digital payments. But all this software relies on foreign hardware. When it comes to the core technologies that undergird computing, China is staggeringly reliant on foreign products, many of which are designed in Silicon Valley and almost all of which are produced by firms based in the U.S. or one of its allies.

Xi thought this presented an untenable risk. "However great its size, however high its market capitalization, if an internet enterprise critically relies on the outside world for core components, the 'vital gate' of the supply chain is grasped in the hands of others," Xi declared in 2016. Which core technologies most worry Xi? One is a software product, Microsoft Windows, which is used by most PCs in China, despite repeated efforts to develop competitive Chinese operating systems. Yet even more important in Xi's thinking are the chips that power China's computers, smartphones, and data centers. As he noted, "Microsoft's Windows operating system can only be paired with Intel chips." So most computers in China needed American chips to function. During most years of the 2000s and 2010s, China spent more money importing semiconductors than oil. High-powered chips were as important as hydrocarbons in fueling China's economic growth. Unlike oil, though, the supply of chips is monopolized by China's geopolitical rivals.

Most foreigners struggled to comprehend why China felt nervous. Hadn't the country built vast tech firms worth hundreds of billions of dollars? Newspaper headlines repeatedly declared China one of the world's leading tech powers. When it came to artificial intelligence, the country was one of the world's two *AI Superpowers*, according to a widely discussed book by Kai-Fu Lee, former head of Google China. Beijing built a twenty-first-century fusion of AI and authoritarianism, maximizing use of surveillance technology. But even the surveillance systems that track China's dissidents and its ethnic minorities rely on chips from American companies like Intel and Nvidia. All of China's most important technology rests on a fragile foundation of imported silicon.

Chinese leaders didn't need to be paranoid to think their country should build more chips at home. It wasn't just about avoiding supply chain vulnerability. Like its neighbors, China can only win more valuable business if it produces what Beijing's leaders call "core technologies"—products the rest of the world can't live without. Otherwise, China risks continuing the low-profit pattern of what has occurred with the iPhone. Millions of Chinese are involved in assembling the phones, but when the devices are sold to end users Apple makes most of the money, with much of the rest accruing to the makers of the chips inside each phone.

The question for China's leaders was how to pivot to producing the kind of chips the world coveted. When Japan, Taiwan, and South Korea wanted to break into the complex and high-value portions of the chip industry, they poured capital into their semiconductor companies, organizing government investment but also pressing private banks to lend. Second, they tried to lure home their scientists and engineers who'd been trained at U.S. universities and worked in Silicon Valley. Third, they forged partnerships with foreign firms but required them to transfer technology or train local workers. Fourth, they played foreigners off each other, taking advantage of competition between Silicon Valley firms—and, later, between Americans and Japanese—to get the best deal for themselves. "We want to promote a semiconductor industry in Taiwan," the island's powerful minister, K. T. Li, had told Morris Chang while founding TSMC. Was it any surprise that Xi Jinping wanted one, too?

CHAPTER 43

"Call Forth the Assault"

I n January 2017, Xi took the stage at the World Economic Forum in the Swiss ski resort of Davos, three days before Donald Trump's inauguration as U.S. president, to outline China's economic vision. As Xi promised "win-win outcomes" via a "dynamic, innovation-driven growth model," the audience of CEOs and billionaires applauded politely. "No one will emerge as a winner in a trade war," the Chinese president declared, in a none-too-subtle dig at his incoming American counterpart. Three days later in Washington, Trump delivered a shockingly combative inaugural address, condemning "other countries making our products, stealing our companies and destroying our jobs." Rather than embracing trade, Trump declared that "protection will lead to great prosperity and strength."

Xi's speech was the sort of claptrap that global leaders were supposed to say when addressing business tycoons. The media fawned over his supposed defense of economic openness and globalization against populist shocks like Trump and Brexit. "Xi sounding rather more presidential than US president-elect," tweeted talking-head Ian Bremmer. "Xi Jinping Delivers a Robust Defence of Globalisation," reported the lead headline in the *Financial Times*. "World Leaders Find Hope for Globalization in Davos Amid Populist Revolt," the *Washington Post* declared. "The international community is looking to China," explained Klaus Schwab, the chair of the World Economic Forum.

Months before his Davos debut, Xi had struck a different tone in a speech to Chinese tech titans and Communist Party leaders in Beijing for a conference on "cyber security and informatization." To an audience that included Huawei founder Ren Zhengfei, Alibaba CEO Jack Ma, high-profile People's Liberation Army (PLA) researchers, and most of China's political elite, Xi exhorted China to focus on "gaining breakthroughs in core technology as quickly as possible." Above all, "core technology" meant semiconductors. Xi didn't call for a trade war, but his vision didn't sound like trade peace, either. "We must promote strong alliances and attack strategic passes in a coordinated manner. We must assault the fortifications of core technology research and development. . . . We must not only call forth the assault, we must also sound the call for assembly, which means that we must concentrate the most powerful forces to act together, compose shock brigades and special forces to storm the passes." Donald Trump, it turned out, wasn't the only world leader who mixed martial metaphors with economic policy. The chip industry faced an organized assault by the world's second-largest economy and the one-party state that ruled it.

China's leaders were counting on a mix of market and military methods to develop advanced chips at home. Though Xi had jailed his rivals and become China's most powerful leader since Mao Zedong, his control over China was far from absolute. He could lock up dissidents and censor even the most veiled criticism online. But many facets of Xi's economic agenda, from industrial restructuring to financial market reform, remained stillborn, obstructed by Communist Party bureaucrats and local government officials who preferred the status quo. Officials often dragged their feet when faced with instructions from Beijing that they disliked.

Xi's military rhetoric wasn't solely a tactic for mobilizing lazy bureaucrats, however. With every year that passed, the precariousness of China's technological position became clearer. China's imports of

semiconductors increased year after year. The chip industry was changing in ways that weren't favorable to China. "The scale of investment
has risen rapidly and market share has accelerated to the concentration
of dominant firms," China's State Council noted in one technology policy report. These dominant firms—TSMC and Samsung chief among
them—would be extremely difficult to displace. Yet demand for chips
was "exploding," China's leaders realized, driven by "cloud computing,
the Internet of Things, and big data." These trends were dangerous:
chips were becoming even more important, yet the design and production of the most advanced chips was monopolized by a handful of
companies, all located outside of China.

China's problem isn't only in chip fabrication. In nearly every step of
the process of producing semiconductors, China is staggeringly dependent on foreign technology, almost all of which is controlled by China's
geopolitical rivals—Taiwan, Japan, South Korea, or the United States.
The software tools used to design chips are dominated by U.S. firms,
while China has less than 1 percent of the global software tool market,
according to data aggregated by scholars at Georgetown University's
Center for Security and Emerging Technology. When it comes to core
intellectual property, the building blocks of transistor patterns from
which many chips are designed, China's market share is 2 percent;
most of the rest is American or British. China supplies 4 percent of
the world's silicon wafers and other chipmaking materials; 1 percent
of the tools used to fabricate chips; 5 percent of the market for chip
designs. It has only a 7 percent market share in the business of fabricating chips. None of this fabrication capacity involves high-value,
leading-edge technology.

Across the entire semiconductor supply chain, aggregating the
impact of chip design, intellectual property, tools, fabrication, and
other steps, Chinese firms have a 6 percent market share, compared to
America's 39 percent, South Korea's 16 percent, or Taiwan's 12 percent,
according to the Georgetown researchers. Almost every chip produced
in China can also be fabricated elsewhere. For advanced logic, memory,

and analog chips, however, China is crucially dependent on American software and designs; American, Dutch, and Japanese machinery; and South Korean and Taiwanese manufacturing. It's no wonder that Xi Jinping was worried.

As China's tech firms pushed further into spheres like cloud computing, autonomous vehicles, and artificial intelligence, their demand for semiconductors was guaranteed to grow. The x86 server chips that remain the workhorse of modern data centers are still dominated by AMD and Intel. There's no Chinese firm that produces a commercially competitive GPU, leaving China reliant on Nvidia and AMD for these chips, too. The more China becomes an AI superpower, as Beijing's boosters promise and as China's government hopes, the more the country's reliance on foreign chips will increase, unless China finds a way to design and manufacture its own. Xi's call to "compose shock brigades and special forces to storm the passes" seemed urgent. China's government set out a plan called Made in China 2025, which envisioned reducing China's imported share of its chip production from 85 percent in 2015 to 30 percent by 2025.

Every Chinese leader since the founding of the People's Republic wanted a semiconductor industry, of course. Mao's Cultural Revolution dream that every worker could produce their own transistors had been an abject failure. Decades later, Chinese leaders recruited Richard Chang to found SMIC and "share God's love with the Chinese." He built a capable foundry, but it struggled to make money and suffered a series of bruising intellectual property lawsuits with TSMC. Eventually Chang was ousted and private-sector investors were displaced by the Chinese state. By 2015, a former official from China's Ministry of Industry and Information was named chairman, solidifying the relationship between SMIC and the Chinese government. The firm continued to lag meaningfully behind TSMC in manufacturing prowess.

SMIC, meanwhile, was the comparative success story in China's fabrication industry. Huahong and Grace, two other Chinese foundries, won little market share, in large part because the state-owned firms and municipal governments that controlled them meddled incessantly in business decisions. One former CEO of a Chinese foundry explained that every governor wanted a chip fab in his province and offered a mix of subsidies and veiled threats to ensure a facility was built. So China's foundries ended up with an inefficient collection of small facilities spread across the country. Foreigners saw immense potential in the Chinese chip industry, but only if disastrous corporate governance and business processes could somehow be fixed. "When a Chinese firm said, 'Let's open a joint venture,'" one European semiconductor executive explained. "I heard, 'Let's lose money.'" The joint ventures that did emerge were generally addicted to government subsidies and rarely produced meaningful new technology.

China's subsidy strategy of the 2000s hadn't created a leading-edge domestic chip industry. Yet doing nothing—and tolerating continued dependence on foreign semiconductors—wasn't politically tolerable. So as early as 2014, Beijing had decided to double down on semiconductor subsidies, launching what became known as the "Big Fund" to back a new leap forward in chips. Key "investors" in the fund include China's Ministry of Finance, the state-owned China Development Bank, and a variety of other government-owned firms, including China Tobacco and investment vehicles of the Beijing, Shanghai, and Wuhan municipal governments. Some analysts hailed this as a new "venture capital" model of state support, but the decision to force China's state-owned cigarette company to fund integrated circuits was about as far from the operating model of Silicon Valley venture capital as could be.

Beijing was right to conclude the country's chip industry needed more money. In 2014, when the fund was launched, advanced fabs cost well over $10 billion. SMIC reported revenue of just a couple billion dollars per year throughout the 2010s, less than a tenth of TSMC. It would be impossible to replicate TSMC's investment plans with private-sector funding alone. Only a government could take such a gamble. The amount of money China's put into chip subsidies and "investments" is hard to calculate, since much of the spending is done by local governments and opaque state-owned banks, but it's widely thought to measure in the tens of billions of dollars.

China was disadvantaged, however, by the government's desire not to build connections with Silicon Valley, but to break free of it. Japan, South Korea, the Netherlands, and Taiwan had come to dominate important steps of the semiconductor production process by integrating deeply with the U.S. chip industry. Taiwan's foundry industry only grew rich thanks to America's fabless firms, while ASML's most advanced lithography tools only work thanks to specialized light sources produced at the company's San Diego subsidiary. Despite occasional tension over trade, these countries have similar interests and worldviews, so mutual reliance on each other for chip designs, tools, and fabrication services was seen as a reasonable price to pay for the efficiency of globalized production.

If China only wanted a bigger part in this ecosystem, its ambitions could've been accommodated. However, Beijing wasn't looking for a better position in a system dominated by America and its friends. Xi's call to "assault the fortifications" wasn't a request for slightly higher market share. It was about remaking the world's semiconductor industry, not integrating with it. Some economic policymakers and semiconductor industry executives in China would have preferred a strategy of deeper integration, yet leaders in Beijing, who thought more about security than efficiency, saw interdependence as a threat. The Made in China 2025 plan didn't advocate economic integration but the opposite. It called for slashing China's dependence on imported chips. The primary target of the Made in China 2025 plan is to reduce the share of foreign chips used in China.

This economic vision threatened to transform trade flows and the global economy. Since Fairchild Semiconductor's first facility in Hong Kong, trade in chips had helped build globalization. The dollar values at stake in China's vision of reworking semiconductor supply chains were staggering. China's import of chips—$260 billion in 2017, the year of Xi's Davos debut—was far larger than Saudi Arabia's export of oil or Germany's export of cars. China spends more money buying chips each year than the entire global trade in aircraft. No product is more central to international trade than semiconductors.

It wasn't only Silicon Valley's profits that were at risk. If China's drive for self-sufficiency in semiconductors succeeded, its neighbors, most of whom had export-dependent economies, would suffer even more. Integrated circuits made up 15 percent of South Korea's exports in 2017; 17 percent of Singapore's; 19 percent of Malaysia's; 21 percent of the Philippines'; and 36 percent of Taiwan's. Made in China 2025 called all this into question. At stake was the world's most dense network of supply chains and trade flows, the electronics industries that had undergirded Asia's economic growth and political stability over the past half century.

Made in China 2025 was just a plan, of course. Governments often have plans that fail abjectly. China's track record in spurring production of cutting-edge chips was far from impressive. Yet the tools China could bring to bear—vast government subsidies, state-backed theft of trade secrets, and the ability to use access to the world's second-largest consumer market to force foreign firms to follow its writ—gave Beijing unparalleled power to shape the future of the chip industry. If any country could pull off such an ambitious transformation of trade flows, it was China. Many countries in the region thought Beijing might succeed. Taiwan's tech industry began worrying about what Taiwanese called the "red supply chain"—the mainland firms muscling into high-value electronics components Taiwan had previously dominated. It was easy to imagine semiconductors would be next.

Xi Jinping's call for China's government and its companies to "assault the fortifications of core technology research" reverberated around East Asia long before it made much impact in the West. Donald Trump's proclamations about protectionism garnered millions of retweets, but Beijing had a plan, powerful tools, and a forty-year track record of surprising the world with China's economic and technological capabilities. This vision of semiconductor independence promised to upend globalization, transforming the production of one of the world's most widely traded and most valuable goods. No one in the audience of Xi's speech at Davos in 2017 noticed what was at stake behind the platitudes, but even a populist like Trump couldn't have imagined a more radical reworking of the global economy.

CHAPTER 44

Technology Transfer

" If you're a country, as China is, of 1.3 billion people, you would want an IT industry," IBM CEO Ginni Rometty told the audience at the 2015 China Development Forum, an annual event hosted by China's government in Beijing. "I think some firms find that perhaps frightening. We, though, at IBM . . . find that to be a great opportunity." Of all America's tech firms, none had a closer relationship to the U.S. government than IBM. For nearly a century, the company had built advanced computer systems for America's most sensitive national security applications. IBM staff had deep personal relationships with officials in the Pentagon and in U.S. intelligence agencies. When Edward Snowden stole and leaked documents about America's foreign intelligence operations before fleeing to Moscow, it wasn't a surprise to find IBM under suspicion for collaborating with American cyber sleuths.

After the Snowden leaks, IBM's sales in China slumped by 20 percent as Chinese firms turned elsewhere for servers and networking equipment. IBM's CFO, Martin Schroeter, told investors that "China is going through a very significant economic set of reforms," an eloquent way of explaining that the Chinese government was punishing IBM by restricting its sales. Rometty decided to offer Beijing an olive branch in the form of semiconductor technology. She made a series of visits to China in the years after 2014, meeting with top Chinese officials like

Premier Li Keqiang, Beijing mayor Wang Anshun, and Vice Premier Ma Kai, who was personally in charge of China's efforts to upgrade its chip industry. IBM told the media that Rometty's visits to Beijing were intended "to emphasize the tech giant's commitment to local partnerships, future cooperation, and information security," as a report by the Reuters news agency put it. China's state-run Xinhua news service was even more blunt about the quid pro quo, reporting that Rometty and Ma discussed "enhancing cooperation in integrated circuit" development.

In its drive for semiconductor self-sufficiency, one of Beijing's focus areas was chips for servers. The mid-2010s were very much like today where the world's data centers rely mostly on chips using the x86 instruction set architecture, though Nvidia's GPUs were beginning to win market share. Only three companies had the necessary intellectual property to produce x86 chips: America's Intel and AMD as well as a small Taiwanese company called Via. In practice, Intel dominated the market. IBM's "Power" chip architecture had once played a major role in corporate servers but had lost out in the 2010s. Some researchers thought that Arm's architecture—popular in mobile devices—might also play a role in future data centers, though at the time Arm-based chips had little server market share. Whatever the architecture, China had virtually no domestic capability to produce competitive data center chips. China's government set out to acquire this technology, strong-arming U.S. companies and pressuring them to transfer technology to Chinese partners.

Intel, which dominated sales of semiconductors for servers, had few incentives to cut deals with Beijing over data center processors (though it was separately doing deals with Chinese state-backed firms and local governments in the market for mobile chips and NAND memory chips, where Intel's position was weaker). The American chipmakers that had lost data center market share to Intel, however, were looking for a competitive advantage. At IBM, Rometty announced a change of strategy that would appeal to Beijing. Rather than trying to sell chips and servers to Chinese customers, she announced, IBM would open its chip technology to Chinese partners, enabling them, she explained, to "create a new and vibrant ecosystem of Chinese companies producing homegrown computer systems for the local and international markets." IBM's decision to trade technology for market access made business sense. The firm's technology was seen as second-rate, and without Beijing's imprimatur it was unlikely to reverse its post-Snowden market shrinkage. IBM was simultaneously trying to shift its global business from selling hardware to selling services, so sharing access to its chip designs seemed logical.

For China's government, however, this partnership wasn't solely about business. One of the individuals working with IBM's newly available chip technology was the former cyber security chief of China's nuclear missile arsenal, Shen Changxiang, the *New York Times* reported. Just a year earlier, Shen had been warning of the "huge security risks" in working with U.S. firms. Now he appeared to have concluded that IBM's offer to turn over chip technology supported Beijing's semiconductor strategy and China's national interests.

IBM wasn't the only company willing to help Chinese firms develop data center chips. Around the same time, Qualcomm, the company specializing in chips for smartphones, was trying to break into the data center chip business using an Arm architecture. Simultaneously, Qualcomm was battling Chinese regulators who wanted it to slash the fees it charged Chinese firms that licensed its smartphone chip technology, a key source of Qualcomm's revenue. As the biggest market for Qualcomm's chips, China had enormous leverage over the company. So some industry analysts saw a connection when, shortly after settling the pricing dispute with Beijing, Qualcomm agreed to a joint venture with a Chinese company called Huaxintong to develop server chips. Huaxintong didn't have a track record in advanced chip design, but it was based in Guizhou Province, then governed by an up-and-coming Chinese party official named Chen Min'er, industry analysts noted.

The Qualcomm-Huaxintong joint venture didn't last long. It was closed in 2019 after producing little of value. But some of the expertise developed appears to have transferred to other Chinese companies building Arm-based data center chips. For example, Huaxintong participated in a consortium to develop energy-efficient chips that included Phytium, another Chinese firm building Arm-based chips. At least one chip design engineer appears to have left Huaxintong in 2019 to work for Phytium, which the U.S. later alleged had helped the Chinese military design advanced weapons systems like hypersonic missiles.

The most controversial example of technology transfer, however, was by Intel's archrival, AMD. In the mid-2010s, the company was struggling financially, having lost PC and data center market share to Intel. AMD was never on the brink of bankruptcy, but it wasn't far from it, either. The company was looking for cash to buy time as it brought new products to market. In 2013, it sold its corporate headquarters in Austin, Texas, to raise cash, for example. In 2016, it sold to a Chinese firm an 85 percent stake in its semiconductor assembly, testing, and packaging facilities in Penang, Malaysia, and Suzhou, China, for $371 million. AMD described these facilities as "world-class."

That same year, AMD cut a deal with a consortium of Chinese firms and government bodies to license the production of modified x86 chips for the Chinese market. The deal, which was deeply controversial within the industry and in Washington, was structured in a way that didn't require the approval of CFIUS, the U.S. government committee that reviews foreign purchases of American assets. AMD took the transaction to the relevant authorities in the Commerce Department, who don't "know anything about microprocessors, or semiconductors, or China," as one industry insider put it. Intel reportedly warned the government about the deal, implying that it harmed U.S. interests and that it would threaten Intel's business. Yet the government lacked a straightforward way to stop it, so the deal was ultimately waved through, sparking anger in Congress and in the Pentagon.

Just as AMD finalized the deal, its new processor series, called "Zen," began hitting the market, turning around the company's fortunes, so AMD ended up not depending on the money from its licensing deal.

However, the joint venture had already been signed and the technology was transferred. The *Wall Street Journal* ran multiple stories arguing that AMD had sold "crown jewels" and "the keys to the kingdom." Other industry analysts suggested the transaction was designed to let Chinese firms claim to the Chinese government they were designing cutting-edge microprocessors in China, when in reality they were simply tweaking AMD designs. The transaction was portrayed in English-language media as a minor licensing deal, but leading Chinese experts told state-owned media the deal supported China's effort to domesticate "core technologies" so that "we no longer can be pulled around by our noses." Pentagon officials who opposed the deal agree that AMD scrupulously followed the letter of the law, but say they remain unconvinced the transaction was as innocuous as defenders claim. "I continue to be very skeptical we were getting the full story from AMD," one former Pentagon official says. The *Wall Street Journal* reported that the joint venture involved Sugon, a Chinese supercomputer firm that has described "making contributions to China's national defense and security" as its "fundamental mission." AMD described Sugon as a "strategic partner" in press releases as recently as 2017, which was guaranteed to raise eyebrows in Washington.

What's clear is that Sugon wanted help to build some of the world's leading supercomputers, which are commonly used for developing "nuclear weapons and hypersonic weapons," as Commerce Secretary Gina Raimondo explained in 2021. Sugon itself has advertised its links to the Chinese military, according to Elsa Kania, a leading American expert on the Chinese military. Even after the Trump administration decided to blacklist Sugon, severing the relationship with AMD, chip industry analyst Anton Shilov found Sugon circuit boards with AMD chips that it shouldn't have been able to buy. AMD told journalists it had not provided technical support for the device in question and wasn't sure how Sugon acquired the chips.

The Chinese market was so enticing that companies found it nearly impossible to avoid transferring technology. Some companies were even induced to transfer control of their entire China subsidiaries. In 2018, Arm, the British company that designs the chip architecture, spun out its China division, selling 51 percent of Arm China to a group of investors, while retaining the other 49 percent itself. Two years earlier, Arm had been purchased by Softbank, a Japanese company that has invested billions in Chinese tech startups. Softbank was therefore dependent on favorable Chinese regulatory treatment for the success of its investments. It faced scrutiny from U.S. regulators, who worried that its exposure to China made it vulnerable to political pressure from Beijing. Softbank had purchased Arm in 2016 for $40 billion, but it sold a 51 percent stake in the China division—which according to Softbank accounted for a fifth of Arm's global sales—for only $775 million.

What was the logic of spinning off Arm China? There's no hard evidence that Softbank faced pressure from Chinese officials to sell the company's Chinese subsidiary. Arm executives were open, however, in describing the logic. "If somebody was building [a system on a chip] for China military or China surveillance," one Arm executive told *Nikkei Asia*, "China wants to have it only inside China. With this kind of new joint venture, this company can develop that. In the past this is something we couldn't do." "China wants to be secure and controllable," this executive continued. "Ultimately they want to have control of their technology. . . . If it's based on the technology that we bring, we could benefit from that," he explained. Neither the Japanese officials who regulate Softbank, the UK officials who regulate Arm, nor the American officials with jurisdiction over a substantial portion of Arm's intellectual property chose to investigate the implications.

Chip firms simply can't ignore the world's largest market for semiconductors. Chipmakers jealously guard their critical technologies, of course. But almost every chip firm has non-core technology, in subsectors that they don't lead, that they'd be happy to share for a price. When companies are losing market share or in need of financing, moreover, they don't have the luxury of focusing on the long term. This gives China powerful levers to induce foreign chip firms to transfer technology, open production facilities, or license intellectual property, even when foreign companies realize they're helping develop competitors. For chip firms, its often easier to raise funds in China than on Wall Street. Accepting Chinese capital can be an implicit requirement for doing business in the country.

Viewed on their own terms, the deals that IBM, AMD, and Arm struck in China were driven by reasonable business logic. Collectively, they risk technology leakage. U.S. and UK chip architectures and designs as well as Taiwanese foundries have played a central role in the development of China's supercomputer programs. Compared to a decade ago, though its capabilities still meaningfully lag the cutting edge, China is substantially less reliant on foreigners to design and produce chips needed in data centers. IBM CEO Ginni Rometty was right to sense "great opportunity" in technology transfer agreements with China. She was only wrong in thinking her firm would be the beneficiary.

CHAPTER 45

"Mergers Are Bound
to Happen"

For Zhao Weiguo, it was a long, winding road from a childhood raising pigs and sheep along China's western frontier to being celebrated as a chip billionaire by Chinese media. Zhao ended up in rural China after his father was banished for writing subversive poems during the Cultural Revolution, but he never planned to accept a life rearing livestock in the countryside. He won entrance to Tsinghua University, one of the best in China, and pursued a degree in electrical engineering. Tsinghua had led China's semiconductor efforts since the industry's earliest days in China, but it isn't clear how much expertise in transistors and capacitors Zhao developed as a student. He worked at a tech firm after finishing his bachelor's degree, then pivoted toward investing as a vice president of Tsinghua Unigroup. This company was established by his alma mater to turn the university's scientific research into profitable businesses, but it appears to have invested heavily in real estate. Zhao built a reputation as a corporate dealmaker and set himself on a path toward a billion-dollar fortune.

In 2004, Zhao launched his own investment fund, Beijing Jiankun Group, investing in real estate, mining, and other sectors where high-level political connections are usually crucial to success. Rich financial returns followed, with Zhao reportedly turning 1 million yuan of initial invested capital into 4.5 billion. In 2009, Zhao used this wealth to buy a 49 percent stake in his former employer, Tsinghua Unigroup. The university continued to own the other 51 percent of shares. It was a bizarre transaction: a private real-estate investment firm now owned nearly half of a company that was supposed to be monetizing technologies produced by China's premier research university. But Tsinghua Unigroup was never simply a "normal" company. The son of former Chinese president Hu Jintao—said to be a "personal friend" of Zhao's—served as Communist Party secretary for the holding company that owned Unigroup. The president of Tsinghua University throughout the 2000s, meanwhile, was a college roommate of Xi Jinping.

In 2013, four years after buying his stake in Tsinghua Unigroup, and just before China's Communist Party announced new plans to provide vast subsidies to the country's semiconductor firms, Zhao decided it was time to invest in the chip industry. He denies that Tsinghua Unigroup's semiconductor strategy was a response to the government's wishes. "Everyone thinks that the government is pushing the development of the chip sector, but it's not like that," he told *Forbes* in 2015. Instead, he takes credit for attracting Beijing's attention to the sector. "Companies did some stuff first and then the government started to notice. . . . All our deals are market oriented."

"Market oriented" is not how most analysts would describe Zhao's strategy. Rather than investing in the best chip firms, he tried buying anything on the market. His explanation of Tsinghua's investment strategy didn't suggest nuance or sophistication. "If you carry your gun up the mountain, you just don't know if there's game there," he was quoted as saying. "Maybe you'll catch a deer, maybe a goat, you just don't know." Nevertheless, he was a confident hunter. The world's chip firms were his prey.

Even given his fortune, which was estimated at $2 billion, the sums Zhao spent building his chip empire were shocking. In 2013, Tsinghua Unigroup started its shopping spree at home, spending several billion

dollars buying two of China's most successful fabless chip design companies, Spreadtrum Communications and RDA Microelectronics, which
made low-end chips for smartphones. Zhao declared the merger would
produce "enormous synergies in China and abroad," though nearly a
decade on there's little evidence any synergies have materialized.

A year later, in 2014, Zhao cut a deal with Intel to couple Intel's
wireless modem chips with Tsinghua Unigroup's smartphone processors. Intel hoped the tie-up would boost its sales in China's smartphone
market, while Zhao wanted his companies to learn from Intel's chip
design expertise. He was open about Tsinghua Unigroup's goals: semiconductors were China's "national priority," he said. Working with Intel
would "accelerate the technology development and further strengthen
the competitiveness and market position of Chinese semiconductor
companies."

Zhao's partnership with Intel had some business logic behind it, but
many other decisions didn't appear driven by a desire to make a profit.
For example, Tsinghua Unigroup offered to fund XMC (later acquired
by YMTC), a Chinese firm trying to break into the NAND memory
chip market. The company's CEO admitted at one public event that
he initially asked for $15 billion to build a new fab but was told to take
$24 billion instead, "on the basis that if they were going to be serious
about being a world leader then they needed to match the world leaders'
investment." Even the goatherders Zhao grew up alongside in western
China would have recognized he was handing out multibillion-dollar
checks with reckless abandon. When it later emerged that in addition
to semiconductors, Tsinghua Unigroup was also investing in real estate
and online gambling, it was barely a surprise.

China's state-backed "Big Fund," meanwhile, announced plans to
invest an initial tranche of over $1 billion in Tsinghua Unigroup. This
provided a stamp of government approval for the company's strategy.
Zhao turned his efforts overseas. It wasn't enough to own China's fabless companies or attract foreign firms to invest in China. He wanted
to control the commanding heights of the world's chip industry. He

hired several leading Taiwanese semiconductor executives, including the former CEO of UMC, Taiwan's second biggest foundry. In 2015, Zhao visited Taiwan himself and pressed the island to lift its restrictions on Chinese investment in sectors like chip design and fabrication. He bought a 25 percent stake in Taiwan's Powertech Technology, which assembles and tests semiconductors, a transaction that was allowed under Taiwan's rules. He pursued stakes and joint ventures with several of Taiwan's other large chip assemblers.

However, Zhao's real interest was in buying the island's crown jewels—MediaTek, the leading chip designer outside the U.S., and TSMC, the foundry on which almost all the world's fabless chip firms rely. He floated the idea of buying a 25 percent stake in TSMC and advocated merging MediaTek with Tsinghua Unigroup's chip design businesses. Neither transaction was legal under Taiwan's existing foreign investment rules, but when Zhao returned from Taiwan he took the stage at a public conference in Beijing and suggested China should ban imports of Taiwanese chips if Taipei didn't change these restrictions.

This pressure campaign put TSMC and MediaTek in a bind. Both companies were crucially reliant on the Chinese market. Most of the chips TSMC produced were assembled into electronics goods in workshops across China. The idea of selling Taiwan's technological crown jewels to a state-backed investor on the mainland made little sense. The island would end up dependent on Beijing. Besides abolishing its military or welcoming occupation by the People's Liberation Army, it was hard to think of a step that would do more to undermine Taiwan's autonomy.

Both TSMC and MediaTek issued statements vaguely expressing openness to Chinese investment. Morris Chang said his only stipulations were "if the price is right and if it is beneficial to shareholders"—hardly the response one would expect about a deal that threatened to undermine Taiwan's economic independence. But Chang also warned that if Chinese investors could appoint members to Taiwanese companies' boards of directors, "it will not be that easy to protect intellectual property." MediaTek said it was supportive of efforts "to join hands and raise the status and competitiveness of the Chinese and Taiwanese enterprises in the global chip industry"—but only if the Taiwanese government allowed. In Taipei, the government seemed to be wobbling, however. John Deng, the island's economy minister, suggested relaxing Taiwan's restrictions on Chinese investment in the chip sector. Amid Chinese pressure, he signaled that greater Chinese control of Taiwan's chip sector was inevitable. "You cannot escape from this issue," Deng told journalists. But amid a contentious presidential election in Taiwan, the government delayed any policy changes.

Soon Zhao set his sights on America's semiconductor industry. In July 2015, Tsinghua Unigroup floated the idea of buying Micron, the American memory chip producer, for $23 billion, which would have been the largest ever Chinese purchase of a U.S. company in any industry. Unlike in the case of Taiwan's tech titans and its economic technocrats, Tsinghua's efforts to purchase Micron were firmly rebuffed. Micron said it didn't think the transaction was realistic given the U.S. government's security concerns. Soon after, in September 2015, Tsinghua Unigroup tried again, extending a $3.7 billion offer for a 15 percent stake in another U.S. company that made NAND memory chips. CFIUS, the U.S. government body that assesses foreign investment, rejected this on security grounds.

Then, in spring 2016, Tsinghua quietly bought 6 percent of the shares in Lattice Semiconductor, another U.S. chip firm. "This is purely a financial investment," Zhao told the *Wall Street Journal*. "We don't have any intention at all to try to acquire Lattice." Scarcely weeks after the investment was publicized, Tsinghua Unigroup began to sell its shares in Lattice. Shortly thereafter, Lattice received a buyout offer from a California-based investment firm called Canyon Bridge, which journalists from Reuters revealed had been discreetly funded by the Chinese government. The U.S. government firmly rejected the deal.

The same investment fund simultaneously bought Imagination, a UK-based chip designer in financial distress. The transaction was carefully structured to exclude Imagination's U.S. assets so that Washington didn't block it, too. British regulators waved the deal through, only to find themselves regretting the decision when, three years later, the new owners tried to restructure the board of directors with officials appointed by a Chinese government investment fund.

The problem wasn't simply that Chinese government-linked funds were buying up foreign chip firms. They were doing so in ways that violated laws about market manipulation and insider trading. While Canyon Bridge was maneuvering to purchase Lattice Semiconductor, for example, one of Canyon Bridge's cofounders tipped off a colleague in Beijing, passing along details about the transaction via WeChat and at meetings in a Starbucks in Beijing. His colleague bought stock based on this knowledge; the Canyon Bridge executive was convicted of insider trading.

For his part, Zhao saw himself as simply a committed entrepreneur. "Mergers between big U.S. and Chinese companies are bound to happen," he declared. "They should be viewed from a business perspective instead of being treated under nationalist or political contexts." But Tsinghua Unigroup's activities were impossible to comprehend from the perspective of business logic. There were too many Chinese state-owned and state-financed "private equity" firms circling the world's semiconductor companies to describe this as anything other than a government-led effort to seize foreign chip firms. "Call forth the assault," Xi Jinping had demanded. Zhao, Tsinghua Unigroup, and other government-backed "investment" vehicles were simply following these publicly announced instructions. Amid this frenzied deal-making, Tsinghua Unigroup announced in 2017 that it had received new "investment": around $15 billion from the China Development Bank and $7 billion from the Integrated Circuit Industry Investment Fund—both owned and controlled by the Chinese state.

CHAPTER 46

The Rise of Huawei

When Ren Zhengfei gives media interviews in the headquarters of Huawei, the Chinese technology company he founded, his crisply tailored jacket and slacks, unbuttoned collar, and vivacious smile make him seem just like any Silicon Valley executive. In some ways he is. His company's telecom equipment—the radios on cell towers that transmit calls, pictures, and emails to and from smartphones—forms the backbone of the world's mobile internet. Huawei's smartphone unit, meanwhile, was until recently one of the world's largest, rivaling Apple and Samsung in numbers of phones sold. The company provides other types of tech infrastructure, too, from undersea fiber-optic cables to cloud computing. In many countries it's impossible to use a phone without using some of Huawei's equipment—as difficult as it is to use a PC without Microsoft products or to surf the internet (outside of China) without Google. However, Huawei is different from the world's other big tech companies in one major way: its two-decade-long struggle with America's national security state.

Reading American newspaper headlines about Huawei's role in Chinese government spying, it would be easy to conclude that the company emerged as an appendage of China's security agencies. The ties between Huawei and the Chinese state are well documented but explain little about how the company built a globe-spanning business.

To understand the company's expansion, it's more helpful to compare Huawei's trajectory to a different tech-focused conglomerate, South Korea's Samsung. Ren was born a generation after Samsung's Lee Byung-Chul, but the two moguls have a similar operating model. Lee built Samsung from a trader of dried fish into a tech company churning out some of the world's most advanced processor and memory chips by relying on three strategies. First, assiduously cultivate political relationships to garner favorable regulation and cheap capital. Second, identify products pioneered in the West and Japan and learn to build them at equivalent quality and lower cost. Third, globalize relentlessly, not only to seek new customers but also to learn by competing with the world's best companies. Executing these strategies made Samsung one of the world's biggest companies, achieving revenues equivalent to 10 percent of South Korea's entire GDP.

Could a Chinese firm execute a similar set of strategies? Most of China's tech firms tried a different approach with a less global focus. For all the country's export prowess, China's internet firms make almost all their money inside of China's domestic market, where they're protected by regulation and censorship. Tencent, Alibaba, Pinduoduo, and Meituan would be minnows were it not for their home market dominance. When Chinese tech firms have gone abroad, they've often struggled to compete.

By contrast, Huawei has embraced foreign competition from its earliest days. Ren Zhengfei's business model has been fundamentally different from Alibaba's or Tencent's. He's taken concepts pioneered abroad, produced quality versions at lower cost, and sold them to the world, grabbing international market share from international rivals. This business model made Samsung's founders rich and put the company at the center of the world's tech ecosystem. Until very recently, Huawei seemed to be on the same path.

The company's international orientation was visible from its founding in 1987. Ren had grown up in a family of high school teachers in rural Guizhou Province in southern China. He'd trained as an engineer in Sichuan's capital of Chongqing before serving in the Chinese army, where he says he worked in a factory producing synthetic fiber for garments. After reportedly leaving the army (some skeptics wonder about the circumstances, and if he actually did cut ties with the military completely), he moved to Shenzhen, then a small town just across the border from Hong Kong. At the time, Hong Kong was still ruled by the British, a small outpost of prosperity along the otherwise impoverished South China coast. China's leaders had begun implementing economic reforms about a decade earlier, experimenting with letting individuals form private companies as a means of spurring economic growth. Shenzhen was one of several cities selected as a "special economic zone," where restrictive laws were canceled and foreign investment was encouraged. The city boomed as Hong Kong money flowed in and as China's would-be entrepreneurs flocked to the city in search of freedom from regulation.

Ren saw an opportunity to import telecom switches, the equipment that connects one caller to another. With $5,000 in startup capital, he began importing this gear from Hong Kong. When his partners across the border realized he was making good money by reselling their equipment, they cut him off, so Ren decided to build his own equipment. By the early 1990s, Huawei had several hundred people working in R&D, largely focused on building switching equipment. Since those days, the telecom infrastructure has merged with digital infrastructure. The same cell towers that transmit calls also send other types of data. So Huawei's equipment now plays an important—and in many countries, crucial—role in transmitting the world's data. Today it is one of the world's three biggest providers of equipment on cell towers, alongside Finland's Nokia and Sweden's Ericsson.

Huawei's critics often allege that its success rests on a foundation of stolen intellectual property, though this is only partly true. The company has admitted to some prior intellectual property violations and has been accused of far more. In 2003, for example, Huawei acknowledged that 2 percent of the code in one of its routers was copied directly from Cisco, an

American competitor. Canadian newspapers, meanwhile, have reported that the country's spy agencies believe there was a Chinese-government-backed campaign of hacking and espionage against Canadian telecom giant Nortel in the 2000s, which allegedly benefitted Huawei.

Theft of intellectual property may well have benefitted the company, but it can't explain its success. No quantity of intellectual property or trade secrets is enough to build a business as big as Huawei. The company has developed efficient manufacturing processes that have driven down costs and built products that customers see as high-quality. Huawei's spending on R&D, meanwhile, is world leading. The company spends several times more on R&D than other Chinese tech firms. Its roughly $15 billion annual R&D budget is paralleled by only a handful of firms, including tech companies like Google and Amazon, pharmaceutical companies like Merck, and carmakers like Daimler or Volkswagen. Even when weighing Huawei's track record of intellectual property theft, the company's multibillion-dollar R&D spending suggests a fundamentally different ethos than the "copy it" mentality of Soviet Zelenograd, or the many other Chinese firms that have tried to break into the chip industry on the cheap.

Huawei executives say they invest in R&D because they've learned from Silicon Valley. Ren reportedly brought a group of Huawei executives to tour the U.S. in 1997, visiting companies like HP, IBM, and Bell Labs. They left convinced of the importance not only of R&D, but also of effective management processes. Starting in 1999, Huawei hired IBM's consulting arm to teach it to operate like a world-class company. One former IBM consultant said Huawei spent $50 million in 1999 on consulting fees, at a time when its entire revenue was less than a billion dollars. At one point it employed one hundred IBM staff to redo business processes. "They weren't too daunted by the engineering tasks," this former consultant reported, but "they felt they were a hundred years behind when it came to economic knowledge and business knowledge." Thanks to IBM and other Western consultants, Huawei learned to manage its supply chain, anticipate customer demand, develop top-class marketing, and sell products worldwide.

Huawei coupled this with a militaristic ethos that the company celebrates as "wolf-culture." Calligraphy on the wall of one of the company's research lab reads "Sacrifice is a soldier's highest cause. Victory is a soldier's greatest contribution," according to a *New York Times* report. In the context of the chip industry, though, Ren Zhengfei's militarism wasn't that unique. Andy Grove wrote a bestseller about the benefits of paranoia. Morris Chang, meanwhile, said that he'd studied Stalingrad, the bloodiest battle of World War II, for lessons about business.

In addition to Western consulting firms, Huawei had help from another powerful institution: China's government. At different points in its development, Huawei has benefitted from support from the local government in Shenzhen, from state-owned banks, and from the central government in Beijing. A *Wall Street Journal* review of total subsidies provided by the Chinese government reached a figure of $75 billion, in the form of subsidized land, state-backed credit, and tax deductions at a scale far above what most Western companies get from their governments, though the benefits provided to Huawei might not be too different from what other East Asian governments provide to priority companies.

The scale of state support for an ostensibly private firm has raised red flags, especially in the United States. China's leaders have certainly been supportive of the company's global expansion. Even in the mid-1990s, when Huawei was still a small company, top Chinese officials like Vice Premier Wu Bangguo visited the company and promised to support it. Vice Premier Wu also traveled abroad with Ren Zhengfei to help Huawei sell telecom equipment in Africa. Yet it's hard to distinguish whether this amounted to special support for Huawei or was simply standard operating procedure given China's mercantilist approach to international trade and the fuzzy boundaries between public and private property.

The lack of clarity about Ren's transition from the People's Liberation Army to Huawei remains puzzling. The company's complex and opaque ownership structure has also provoked reasonable questions.

Huawei executive Ken Hu's argument to a U.S. congressional inquiry that Ren Zhengfei's membership in the Chinese Communist Party was just like how "some American businessmen are Democrat or Republican," sounded to U.S. analysts like willful obfuscation of the Communist Party's role in the company's governance. Nevertheless, the thesis that Huawei was purpose built by the Chinese state has never had strong evidence behind it.

Huawei's rise has, however, worked in the interests of the Chinese state, as the company grabbed market share and embedded its equipment in the world's telecom networks. For many years, despite the warning of America's spy agencies, Huawei spread rapidly across the world. As it grew, incumbent Western firms selling telecom equipment were forced to merge or pushed out of the market. Canada's Nortel went bankrupt. Alcatel-Lucent, the company that inherited Bell Labs after AT&T was broken up, sold its operations to Finland's Nokia.

Huawei's ambitions only grew. Having provided the infrastructure that makes phone calls possible, it started selling phones, too. Soon its smartphones were among the world's best sellers. By 2019 the company lagged only Samsung measured by number of units sold. Huawei still made substantially less money per phone than either Samsung or Apple, the latter of which had the marketing and the ecosystem to charge vastly higher prices. However, Huawei's ability to enter the smartphone market and quickly seize a leading position put Apple and Samsung on notice.

Moreover, Huawei was making progress designing some of the critical chips in its own phones. Company insiders say the firm's chip design ambitions accelerated in March 2011, when an earthquake off Japan's east coast caused a tsunami that slammed into the country. The world's attention focused on the Fukushima Daiichi nuclear reactor that was damaged by the flooding, but inside Huawei, executives worried about the threat to the company's supply chain. Like every major producer of electronics, Huawei relied on Japanese providers for crucial components in their telecom gear and smartphones and feared the disaster might cause immense delays. In the end, Huawei got lucky. Few of its component suppliers saw production knocked out for long. However, the company asked its consultants to determine its supply chain risk. They reported that the company had two key vulnerabilities: access to Google's Android operating system, the core software on which all non-Apple smartphones run, and the supply of the semiconductors that every smartphone requires.

The company identified the 250 most important semiconductors that its products required and began designing as many as possible in-house. These chips were largely related to the business of building telecom base stations but also included the application processors for the company's smartphones, semiconductors that were monstrously complex and required the most advanced chipmaking technology. Like Apple and most other leading chip firms, Huawei chose to outsource fabrication of these chips, because it needed to use manufacturing processes that, at most, a couple companies could provide. Taiwan's TSMC was the natural place to turn.

By the end of the 2010s, Huawei's HiSilicon unit was designing some of the world's most complex chips for smartphones and had become TSMC's second-largest customer. Huawei's phones still required chips from other companies, too, like memory chips or various types of signal processors. But mastering the production of cell phone processors was an impressive feat. America's near monopoly on the world's most profitable chip design businesses was under threat. This was more evidence that Huawei was successfully replicating what South Korea's Samsung or Japan's Sony had done decades earlier: learning to produce advanced technology, winning global markets, investing in R&D, and challenging America's tech leaders. Moreover, Huawei seemed uniquely well placed for a new era of ubiquitous computing that would accompany the rollout of the next generation of telecom infrastructure: 5G.

The 5G Future

When Ren Zhengfei started importing telephone switches from Hong Kong, network gear couldn't do much beyond connecting one phone to another. In the early days of telephones, switching had been done by hand, with rows of women seated in front of a wall of plugs, connecting them in different combinations depending on who was calling. By the 1980s, humans had been replaced by electronic switches, which often relied on semiconductor devices. Even still, it took switching gear the size of a closet to manage a single building's worth of telephone lines. Today, telecom providers are more reliant than ever on silicon, but a closet's worth of gear can process calls, texts, and video, now often sent via radio networks rather than landlines.

Huawei has mastered the latest generation of equipment to send calls and data via cell networks, called 5G. Yet 5G isn't really about phones—it's about the future of computing, and therefore, it's about semiconductors. The "G" in 5G stands for generation. We've already cycled through four generations of mobile networking standards, each of which required new hardware on phones and in cell towers. Just as Moore's Law has let us pack more transistors onto chips, there's been a steady increase in the number of 1s and 0s flying to and from cell phones via radio waves. 2G phones could send picture texts; 3G phones opened websites; and 4G made it possible to stream video from almost anywhere. 5G will provide a similar leap forward.

Most people today take their smartphone for granted, but it's only thanks to ever more powerful semiconductors that we no longer marvel at picture texts and are instead frustrated with split-second delays in video streaming. The modem chips that manage a phone's connection with cell networks make it possible to send many more 1s and 0s in the radio waves via a phone's antenna.

There's been a comparable change in the chips hidden inside a cell network and atop cell towers. Sending 1s and 0s through the air while minimizing dropped calls or delays to video streaming is staggeringly complicated. The amount of space available in the relevant part of the radio-wave spectrum is limited. There are only so many radio-wave frequencies, many of which aren't optimal for sending lots of data or transmitting over long distances. Telecom firms have therefore relied on semiconductors to pack ever more data into existing spectrum space. "Spectrum is far more expensive than silicon," explains Dave Robertson, a chip expert at Analog Devices, which specializes in semiconductors that manage radio transmission. Semiconductors have therefore been fundamental to the ability to send more data wirelessly. Chip designers like Qualcomm found new ways to optimize transmission of data via the radio spectrum, and chipmakers like Analog Devices have made semiconductors called radio frequency transceivers that can send and receive radio waves with more precision while using less power.

The next generation of network technology, 5G, will make possible the wireless transmission of even more data. Partly, this will be via even more intricate methods of sharing spectrum space, which require more complex algorithms and more computing power on phones and in cell towers so that 1s and 0s can be slotted in even the tiniest free space in the wireless spectrum. Partly, 5G networks will send more data by using a new, empty radio frequency spectrum that was previously considered impractical to fill. Advanced semiconductors make it possible not only to pack more 1s and 0s into a given frequency of radio waves, but also to send radio waves farther and target them with unprecedented accuracy. Cell networks will identify a phone's location and send radio waves directly toward a phone, using a technique called beamforming. A typical radio wave, like one that sends music to your car radio, sends signals out in every direction because it doesn't know where your car is. This wastes power and creates more waves and more interference. With beamforming, a cell tower identifies a device's location and sends the signal it needs only in that direction. Result: less interference and stronger signals for everyone.

Faster networks capable of carrying more data won't simply let existing phones run faster—they'll change the way we think about mobile computing. In the age of 1G networks, cell phones were too expensive for most people to own. With 2G networks, we came to assume that phones could send text messages as well as voice. Today, we expect phones and tablets to have almost all the features of PCs. As it becomes possible to send even more data over cell networks, we'll connect ever more devices to the cell network. The more devices we have, the more data they'll produce, which will require more processing power to make sense of.

The promise of connecting many more devices to cell networks and harvesting data from them may not sound revolutionary. You may not think a 5G network can brew better coffee, but it won't be long until your coffeemaker is collecting and processing data on the temperature and quality of each cup it produces. There are innumerable ways in business and industry that more data and more connectivity will produce better service and lower cost, from optimizing how tractors drive across fields to coordinating robots on assembly lines. Medical devices and sensors will track and diagnose more conditions. The world has far more sensory information than our current ability to digitize, communicate, and process.

There's no better case study showing how connectivity and computing power will turn old products into digitized machines than Tesla, Elon Musk's auto company. Tesla's cult following and soaring stock price have attracted plenty of attention, but what's less noticed is that Tesla is also a leading chip designer. The company hired star semiconductor designers like Jim Keller to build a chip specialized for its automated driving needs, which is fabricated using leading-edge technology. As early as 2014, some analysts were noting that Tesla cars "resemble a smartphone." The company has been often compared to Apple, which also designs its own semiconductors. Like Apple's products, Tesla's finely tuned user experience and its seemingly effortless integration of advanced computing into a twentieth-century product—a car—are only possible because of custom-designed chips. Cars have incorporated simple chips since the 1970s. However, the spread of electric vehicles, which require specialized semiconductors to manage the power supply, coupled with increased demand for autonomous driving features foretells that the number and cost of chips in a typical car will increase substantially.

Cars are only the most prominent example of how the ability to send and receive more data will create more demand for computing power—in devices on the "edge" of the network, in the cell network itself, and in vast data centers. Around 2017, as telecom companies around the world began signing contracts with equipment providers to build 5G networks, it emerged that China's Huawei was in a leading position, offering gear that was perceived by the industry to be high-quality and competitively priced. Huawei looked likely to play a bigger role in the construction of 5G networks than any other company, overtaking Sweden's Ericcson and Finland's Nokia, the only other main producers of the equipment on cell towers.

Inside Huawei's equipment on cell towers, like that of its rivals, is a large quantity of silicon. One study of Huawei's radio units, by the Japanese newspaper *Nikkei Asia*, found a heavy reliance on U.S.-made chips, like field-programmable gate arrays from Lattice Semiconductor, the Oregon company that Tsinghua Unigroup had bought and then sold a minority stake in several years earlier. Texas Instruments, Analog Devices, Broadcom, and Cypress Semiconductor also designed and built chips that Huawei's radio gear relied on. According to this analysis,

American chips and other components constitute nearly 30 percent of the cost of each Huawei system. However, the main processor chip was designed domestically by Huawei's HiSilicon chip design arm and fabricated at TSMC. Huawei hadn't reached technological self-sufficiency. It relied on multiple foreign chip firms to produce specialized semiconductors and on TSMC to fabricate the chips it designed in-house. Yet Huawei produced some of the most complex electronics in each radio system and understood the details of how to integrate all the components.

With Huawei's design arm proving itself world-class, it wasn't hard to imagine a future in which Chinese chip design firms were as important customers of TSMC as Silicon Valley giants. If the trends of the late 2010s were projected forward, by 2030 China's chip industry might rival Silicon Valley for influence. This wouldn't simply disrupt tech firms and trade flows. It would also reset the balance of military power.

CHAPTER 48

The Next Offset

From swarms of autonomous drones to invisible battles in cyber-space and across the electromagnetic spectrum, the future of war will be defined by computing power. The U.S. military is no longer the unchallenged leader. Long gone are the days when the U.S. had unrivaled access to the world's seas and airspace, guaranteed by preci-sion missiles and all-seeing sensors. The shock waves that reverberated around the world's defense ministries after the 1991 Persian Gulf War—and the fear that the surgical strikes that had defanged Saddam's army could be used against any military in the world—was felt in Beijing like a "psychological nuclear attack," according to one account. In the thirty years since that conflict, China has poured funds into high-tech weap-onry, abandoning Mao-era doctrines of waging a low-tech People's War and embracing the idea that the fights of the future will rely on advanced sensors, communications, and computing. Now China is developing the computing infrastructure an advanced fighting force requires.

Beijing's aim isn't simply to match the U.S. system-by-system, but to develop capabilities that could "offset" American advantages, taking the Pentagon's concept from the 1970s and turning it against the United States. China has fielded an array of weapons that sys-tematically undermine U.S. advantages. China's precision anti-ship missiles make it extremely dangerous for U.S. surface ships to transit the Taiwan Strait in a time of war, holding American naval power at bay. New air defense systems contest America's ability to dominate the airspace in a conflict. Long-range land attack missiles threaten the network of American military bases from Japan to Guam. China's anti-satellite weapons threaten to disable communications and GPS networks. China's cyberwar capabilities haven't been tested in wartime, but the Chinese would try to bring down entire U.S. military systems. Meanwhile, in the electromagnetic spectrum, China might try to jam American communications and blind surveillance systems, leaving the U.S. military unable to see enemies or communicate with allies.

Undergirding all these capabilities is a belief in Chinese military circles that warfare is not simply becoming "informationized" but "intelligentized"—inelegant military jargon that means applying artificial intelligence to weapons systems. Of course, computing power has been central to warfare for the past half century, though the quantity of 1s and 0s that can be harnessed to support military systems is millions of times larger than decades earlier. What's new today is that America now has a credible challenger. The Soviet Union could match the U.S. missile-for-missile but not byte-for-byte. China thinks it can do both. The fate of China's semiconductor industry isn't simply a question of commerce. Whichever country can produce more 1s and 0s will have a serious military advantage, too.

What factors will define this computing race? In 2021, a group of American tech and foreign policy grandees chaired by former Google CEO Eric Schmidt released a report predicting that "China could surpass the United States as the world's AI superpower." Chinese leaders appear to agree. As China military expert Elsa Kania notes, the PLA has been talking about "AI weapons" for at least a decade, referring to systems that use "AI to pursue, distinguish, and destroy enemy targets automatically." Xi Jinping himself has urged the PLA to "accelerate the development of military intelligentization" as a defense priority.

The idea of military AI evokes images of killer robots, but there are many spheres where applying machine learning can make military systems better. Predictive maintenance—learning when machines need to be fixed—is already helping keep planes in the sky and ships at sea. AI-enabled submarine sonars or satellite imagery can identify threats more accurately. New weapons systems can be designed more quickly. Bombs and missiles can be aimed more accurately, especially when it comes to moving targets. Autonomous vehicles in the air, underwater, and on land are already learning to maneuver, identify adversaries, and destroy them. Not all of this is as revolutionary as phrases like "AI weapons" might imply. We've had self-guided, fire-and-forget missiles for decades, for example. But as weapons get smarter and more autonomous, their demands for computing power only grow.

It isn't guaranteed that China will win the race to develop and deploy systems empowered by artificial intelligence, in part because this "race" isn't about a single technology but about complex systems. The Cold War arms race, it's worth remembering, wasn't won by the first country to shoot a satellite into space. Yet China's capabilities when it comes to AI systems are undeniably impressive. Georgetown University's Ben Buchanan has noted that a "triad" of data, algorithms, and computing power are needed to harness AI. With the exception of computing power, China's capabilities may already equal the United States'.

When it comes to accessing the type of data that can be fed into AI algorithms, neither China nor the U.S. has a clear advantage. Beijing's boosters argue the country's surveillance state and its massive population let it collect more data, though the ability to amass data about China's populace probably doesn't help much in the military sphere. No amount of data about online shopping habits or the facial structure of all of China's 1.3 billion citizens will train a computer to recognize the sounds of a submarine lurking in the Taiwan Strait, for example. China doesn't have any built-in advantages in gathering data relevant to military systems.

It's harder to say whether one side has an advantage when it comes to devising clever algorithms. Measured by the number of AI experts, China appears to have capabilities that are comparable to America's.

Researchers at MacroPolo, a China-focused think tank, found that 29 percent of the world's leading researchers in artificial intelligence are from China, as opposed to 20 percent from the U.S. and 18 percent from Europe. However, a staggering share of these experts end up working in the U.S., which employs 59 percent of the world's top AI researchers. The combination of new visa and travel restrictions plus China's effort to retain more researchers at home may neutralize America's historical skill at stripping geopolitical rivals of their smartest minds.

In the third part of Buchanan's "triad," computing power, the United States still has a substantial lead, though it has eroded significantly in recent years. China is still staggeringly dependent on foreign semiconductor technology—in particular, U.S.-designed, Taiwan-fabricated processors—to undertake complex computation. It isn't only Chinese smartphones and PCs that rely on foreign chips. So, too, do most Chinese data centers—which explains why the country has tried so hard to acquire technology from companies like IBM and AMD. One Chinese study has estimated that as many as 95 percent of GPUs in Chinese servers running artificial intelligence workloads are designed by Nvidia, for example. Chips from Intel, Xilinx, AMD, and others are crucially important in Chinese data centers. Even under the most optimistic projections, it will be half a decade before China can design competitive chips and the software ecosystem around them, and far longer before it can manufacture these chips domestically.

For many Chinese military systems, however, acquiring U.S.-designed, Taiwan-fabricated chips hasn't been difficult. A recent review of 343 publicly available AI-related People's Liberation Army procurement contracts, by researchers at Georgetown University, found that less than 20 percent of the contracts involved companies that are subject to U.S. export controls. In other words, the Chinese military has had little difficulty simply buying cutting-edge U.S. chips off-the-shelf and plugging them into military systems. The Georgetown researchers found that Chinese military suppliers even advertise on their websites their use of American chips. The Chinese government's controversial policy of

"Civil Military Fusion," an effort to apply advanced civilian technology to military systems, looks like it's working. Absent a major change in U.S. export restrictions, the People's Liberation Army will acquire much of the computing power it needs by simply buying it from Silicon Valley.

Of course, the People's Liberation Army isn't the only military trying to apply advanced computing to weapons systems. As the fighting power of China's military has grown, the Pentagon has realized it needs a new strategy. In the mid-2010s, officials like Secretary of Defense Chuck Hagel began speaking about a need for a new "offset," evoking the effort of Bill Perry, Harold Brown, and Andrew Marshall during the 1970s to overcome the USSR's quantitative advantage. The U.S. faces the same basic dilemma today: China can deploy more ships and planes than the U.S., especially in theaters that matter, like the Taiwan Strait. "We will never try to match our opponents or our competitors tank for tank, plane for plane, person for person," declared Bob Work, the former deputy defense secretary who is the intellectual godfather of this new offset, in a clear echo of the logic of the late 1970s. The U.S. military will only succeed, in other words, if it has a decisive technological advantage.

What will this technological advantage look like? The 1970s offset was driven by "digital microprocessors, information technologies, new sensors, stealth," Work has argued. This time, it will be "advances in Artificial Intelligence (AI) and autonomy." The U.S. military is already fielding the first generation of new autonomous vehicles, like Saildrone, an unmanned windsurfer that can spend months roving the oceans while tracking submarines or intercepting adversaries' communications. These devices cost a tiny fraction of a typical Navy ship, letting the military field many of them and providing platforms for sensors and communications across the world's oceans. Autonomous surface ships, planes, and submarines are also being developed and deployed. These autonomous platforms will require artificial intelligence to guide them and make decisions. The more computing power that can be put on board, the smarter decisions they'll make.

DARPA developed the technology that made the 1970s offset possible; now it's devising systems that promise new computing-enabled transformations in warfare. DARPA leaders envision "computers distributed across the battlespace that can all communicate and coordinate with one another," from the largest naval ship to the tiniest drone. The challenge isn't simply to embed computing power in a single device, like a guided missile, but to network thousands of devices across a battlefield, letting them share data and putting machines in a position to make more decisions. DARPA has funded research programs on "human-machine teaming," envisioning, for example, a piloted fighter jet flying alongside several autonomous drones that are an additional set of eyes and ears for the human pilot.

Just as the Cold War was decided by electrons zipping around the guidance computers of American missiles, the fights of the future may be decided in the electromagnetic spectrum. The more the world's militaries rely on electronic sensors and communication, the more they'll have to battle for access to the spectrum space needed to send messages or to detect and track adversaries. We've only had a glimpse of what wartime electromagnetic spectrum operations will look like. For example, Russia has used a variety of radar and signals jammers in its war against Ukraine. The Russian government also reportedly obstructs GPS signals around President Vladimir Putin's official travel, perhaps as a security measure. Not coincidentally, DARPA is researching alternative navigation systems that aren't reliant on GPS signals or satellites, to enable American missiles to hit their targets even if GPS systems are down.

The battle for the electromagnetic spectrum will be an invisible struggle conducted by semiconductors. Radar, jamming, and communications are all managed by complex radio frequency chips and digital-analog converters, which modulate signals to take advantage of open spectrum space, send signals in a specific direction, and try to confuse adversaries' sensors. Simultaneously, powerful digital chips will run complex algorithms inside a radar or jammer that assess the signals received and decide what signals to send out in a matter of milliseconds. At stake is a military's ability to see and to communicate. Autonomous drones won't be worth much if the devices can't determine where they are or where they're heading.

The warfare of the future will be more reliant than ever on chips—powerful processors to run AI algorithms, big memory chips to crunch data, perfectly tuned analog chips to sense and produce radio waves. In 2017, DARPA launched a new project called the Electronics Resurgence Initiative to help build the next wave of militarily relevant chip technology. In some ways, DARPA's renewed interest in chips stems naturally from its history. It funded pioneering scholars like Caltech's Carver Mead and catalyzed research into chip design software, new lithography techniques, and transistor structures.

Yet DARPA and the U.S. government have found it harder than ever to shape the future of the chip industry. DARPA's budget is a couple billion dollars per year, less than the R&D budgets of most of the industry's biggest firms. Of course, DARPA spends a lot more on far-out research ideas, whereas companies like Intel and Qualcomm spend most of their money on projects that are only a couple years from fruition. However, the U.S. government in general buys a smaller share of the world's chips than ever before. The U.S. government bought almost all the early integrated circuits that Fairchild and Texas Instruments produced in the early 1960s. By the 1970s, that number had fallen to 10–15 percent. Now it's around 2 percent of the U.S. chip market. As a buyer of chips, Apple CEO Tim Cook has more influence on the industry than any Pentagon official today.

Making semiconductors is so expensive that even the Pentagon can't afford to do it in-house. The National Security Agency used to have a chip fab at its headquarters in Maryland's Fort Meade. In the 2000s, however, the government decided it was too expensive to keep upgrading per the cadence dictated by Moore's Law. Today even *designing* a leading-edge chip—which can cost several hundred million dollars—is too expensive for all but the most important projects.

Both the U.S. military and the government's spy agencies outsource the production of their chips to "trusted foundries." This is relatively straightforward for many types of analog or radio frequency chips, where the U.S. has world-class capabilities. When it comes to logic chips, though, this poses a dilemma. Intel's production capabilities are just behind the leading edge, though the company mostly produces chips for its own PC and server businesses. TSMC and Samsung, meanwhile, keep their most cutting-edge fabrication capabilities in Taiwan and South Korea. And a large share of chip assembly and packaging also takes place in Asia. As the Defense Department tries to use more off-the-shelf components to reduce cost, it will buy even more devices from abroad.

The military worries that chips fabricated or assembled abroad are more susceptible to tampering, with back doors added or errors written in. However, even chips designed and produced domestically can have unintended vulnerabilities. In 2018, researchers discovered two fundamental errors in Intel's widely used microprocessor architecture called Spectre and Meltdown, which enabled the copying of data such as passwords—a huge security flaw. According to the *Wall Street Journal*, Intel first disclosed the flaw to customers, including Chinese tech companies, before notifying the U.S. government, a fact that only intensified Pentagon officials' concern about their declining influence over the chip industry.

DARPA is investing in technology that can guarantee chips are tamper-free or to verify they're manufactured exactly as intended. Long gone are the days when the military could count on firms like TI to design, manufacture, and assemble cutting-edge analog and digital electronics all onshore. Today there's simply no way to avoid buying some things from abroad—and buying many from Taiwan. So DARPA's betting on technology to enable a "zero trust" approach to microelectronics: trust nothing and verify everything, via technologies like tiny sensors implanted on a chip that can detect efforts to modify it.

All these efforts to use microelectronics to spur a new "offset" and reestablish a decisive military advantage over China and Russia, however, assume the U.S. will keep its lead in chips. That's now looking like a risky bet. The era of the "run faster" strategy saw the U.S. fall behind in certain segments of the chipmaking process, most notably in the growing dependence on Taiwan for building advanced logic chips. Intel, which for three decades had been America's chip champion, has now very clearly stumbled. Many people in the industry think it has fallen decisively behind. Meanwhile, China is pouring billions of dollars into its chip industry while pressuring foreign companies to turn over sensitive technology. For every major chip firm, the Chinese consumer market is far more important a customer than the U.S. government.

Beijing's efforts to acquire advanced technology, the deep inter-connections between the U.S. and Chinese electronics industries, and the two countries' mutual reliance on fabrication in Taiwan all raise questions. America was already running slower. It's now betting the future of its military on a technology over which its dominance is slipping. "This idea of pulling ahead with an offset," argues Matt Turpin, an official who worked on the issue at the Pentagon, "is nearly impossible if the Chinese are in the car with us."

"Call forth the assault," Xi Jinping declared. China's leaders have identified their reliance on foreign chipmakers as a critical vulnerability. They've set out a plan to rework the world's chip industry by buying foreign chipmakers, stealing their technology, and providing billions of dollars of subsidies to Chinese chip firms. The People's Liberation Army is now counting on these efforts to help it evade U.S. restrictions, though it can still buy legally many U.S. chips in its pursuit of "military intelligentization." For its part, the Pentagon has launched its own offset, after admitting that China's military modernization has closed the gap between the two superpowers' militaries, especially in the contested waters off China's coast. Taiwan isn't simply the source of the advanced chips that both countries' militaries are betting on. It's also the most likely future battleground.

PART VIII

THE CHIP CHOKE

CHAPTER 49

"Everything We're Competing On"

ntel's CEO Brian Krzanich couldn't hide his anxiety about China's push to seize a bigger share of the world's chip industry. As chairman in 2015 of the Semiconductor Industry Association, the U.S. chip industry's trade group, Krzanich was tasked with hobnobbing with U.S. government officials. Usually this meant asking for tax cuts or reduced regulation. This time, the topic was different: convincing the U.S. government to do something about China's massive semiconductor subsidies. America's chip firms were all caught in the same bind. China was a crucial market for almost every U.S. semiconductor firm, either because these firms sold directly to Chinese customers or because their chips were assembled into smartphones or computers in China. Beijing's strong-arm methods forced U.S. chip firms to stay silent about China's subsidies, even though the Chinese government had adopted a formal policy of trying to cut them out of China's supply chain.

Obama administration officials were used to complaints about China from industries like steel or solar panels. High tech was supposed to be America's specialty, a sphere where it had a competitive advantage. So when senior administration officials perceived a "palpable sense of fear in his eyes" when meeting with Krzanich, they were worried. Intel's

CEOs had a long history of paranoia, of course. But now there was more reason than ever for the company, and the entire U.S. chip industry, to be worried. China had driven U.S. solar panel manufacturing out of business. Couldn't it do the same in semiconductors? "This massive $250 billion fund is going to bury us," one Obama official worried, referencing the subsidies China's central and local governments have promised to support homegrown chipmakers.

By around 2015, from deep in the U.S. government, gears slowly began to shift. The government's trade negotiators saw China's chip subsidies as a flagrant violation of international agreements. The Pentagon nervously watched China's efforts to apply computing power to new weapons systems. The intelligence agencies and Justice Department unearthed more evidence of collusion between China's government and its industries to push out American chip firms. Yet the twin pillars of American tech policy—embracing globalization and "running faster"—were deeply ingrained, not only by the industry's lobbying, but also by Washington's intellectual consensus. Moreover, most people in Washington barely knew what a semiconductor was. The Obama administration moved slowly on semiconductors, one person involved in the effort recalled, because many senior officials simply didn't see chips as an important issue.

It wasn't until the final days of the Obama administration, therefore, that the government began to act. In late 2016, six days before that year's presidential election, Commerce Secretary Penny Pritzker gave a high-profile address in Washington on semiconductors, declaring it "imperative that semiconductor technology remains a central feature of American ingenuity and a driver of our economic growth. We cannot afford to cede our leadership." She identified China as the central challenge, condemning "unfair trade practices and massive, non-market-based state intervention" and cited "new attempts by China to acquire companies and technology based on their government's interest—not commercial objectives," an accusation driven by Tsinghua Unigroup's acquisition spree.

With little time left in the Obama administration, however, there wasn't much Pritzker could do. Rather, the administration's modest goal was to start a discussion that—it hoped—the incoming Hillary Clinton administration would carry forward. Pritzker also ordered the Commerce Department to conduct a study of the semiconductor supply chain and promised to "make clear to China's leaders at every opportunity that we will not accept a $150 billion industrial policy designed to appropriate this industry." But it was easy to condemn China's subsidies. It was far harder to make them stop.

Around the same time, the White House commissioned a group of semiconductor executives and academics to study the future of the industry. They issued a report days before Obama left office, which urged the U.S. to double down on its existing strategy. Its primary recommendation was: "win the race by running faster"—advice that could have been copied and pasted from the 1990s. The need to keep innovating was obviously important. The continuation of Moore's Law was a competitive necessity. But during the decades Washington thought it was "running faster," its adversaries had grown their market share while the entire world had become frighteningly reliant on a handful of vulnerable choke points, in particular Taiwan.

In Washington and in the chip industry, almost everyone had drunk their own Kool-Aid about globalization. Newspapers and academics alike reported that globalization was in fact "global," that technological diffusion was unstoppable, that other countries' advancing technological capabilities were in the U.S. interest, and that even if they weren't, nothing could halt technological progress. "Unilateral action is increasingly ineffective in a world where the semiconductor industry is globalized," the Obama administration's semiconductor report declared. "Policy can, in principle, slow the diffusion of technology, but it cannot stop the spread." Neither of these claims was backed by evidence; they were simply assumed to be true. However, "globalization" of chip fabrication hadn't occurred; "Taiwanization" had. Technology hadn't diffused. It was monopolized by a handful of irreplaceable companies.

American tech policy was held hostage to banalities about globalization that were easily seen to be false.

America's technological lead in fabrication, lithography, and other fields had dissipated because Washington convinced itself that companies should compete but that governments should simply provide a level playing field. A laissez-faire system works if every country agrees to it. Many governments, especially in Asia, were deeply involved in supporting their chip industries. However, U.S. officials found it easier to ignore other countries' efforts to grab valuable chunks of the chip industry, instead choosing to parrot platitudes about free trade and open competition. Meanwhile, America's position was eroding.

In polite company in Washington and Silicon Valley, it was easier simply to repeat words like multilateralism, globalization, and innovation, concepts that were too vacuous to offend anyone in a position of power. The chip industry itself—deeply fearful of angering China or TSMC—put its considerable lobbying resources behind repeating false platitudes about how "global" the industry had become. These concepts fit naturally with the liberal internationalist ethos that guided officials of both political parties amid America's unipolar moment. Meetings with foreign companies and governments were more pleasant when everyone pretended that cooperation was win-win. So Washington kept telling itself that the U.S. was running faster, blindly ignoring the deterioration in the U.S. position, the rise in China's capabilities, and the staggering reliance on Taiwan and South Korea, which grew more conspicuous every year.

Deep in the U.S. government, however, the national security bureaucracy was coming to adopt a different view. This part of the government is paid to be paranoid, so it's no surprise security officials viewed China's tech industry more skeptically and its government more cynically. Many officials worried that China's leverage over the world's critical technology systems was growing. They also presumed China would use its position as the world's key manufacturer of electronics to insert back doors and to spy more effectively, just as the U.S. had done for decades. Pentagon officials devising weapons of the future began to realize how reliant they'd be on semiconductors. Officials focused on telecom infrastructure, meanwhile, worried that U.S. allies were buying less telecom equipment from Europe and the U.S. and more from Chinese firms like ZTE and Huawei.

U.S. intelligence had voiced concerns about Huawei's alleged links to the Chinese government for many years, though it was only in the mid-2010s that the company and its smaller peer, ZTE, started attracting public attention. Both companies sold competing telecom equipment; ZTE was state-owned, while Huawei was private but was alleged by U.S. officials to have close ties with the government. Both companies had spent decades fighting allegations that they'd bribed officials in multiple countries to win contracts. And in 2016, during the final year of the Obama administration, both were accused of violating U.S. sanctions by supplying goods to Iran and North Korea.

The Obama administration considered imposing financial sanctions on ZTE, which would have severed the company's access to the international banking system, but instead opted to punish the company in 2016 by restricting U.S. firms from selling to it. Export controls like this had previously been used mostly against military targets, to stop the transfer of technology to companies supplying components to Iran's missile program, for example. But the Commerce Department had broad authority to prohibit the export of civilian technologies, too. ZTE was highly reliant on American components in its systems—above all, American chips. However, in March 2017, before the threatened restrictions were implemented, the company signed a plea deal with the U.S. government and paid a fine, so the export restrictions were removed before they'd taken force. Hardly anyone understood just how drastic a move it would have been to ban a major Chinese tech company from buying U.S. chips.

ZTE's plea deal was signed just as the Trump administration took office. Trump repeatedly attacked China for "ripping us off," but he had little interest in policy details and none in technology. His focus was on trade and tariffs, where his officials like Peter Navarro and Robert Lighthizer tried and mostly failed to reduce the bilateral trade deficit and slow offshoring. Far from the political limelight, however, on the National Security Council, a handful of discreet officials led by Matt Pottinger, a former journalist and Marine, who eventually rose to become Trump's deputy national security advisor, were transforming America's policy toward China, casting off several decades of technology policy in the process. Rather than tariffs, the China hawks on the NSC were fixated on Beijing's geopolitical agenda and its technological foundation. They thought America's position had weakened dangerously and Washington's inaction was to blame. "This is really important," one Trump appointee reported an Obama official telling him during the presidential transition, regarding China's technological advances, "but there's nothing you can do."

The new administration's China team didn't agree. They concluded, as one senior official put it, "that everything we're competing on in the twenty-first century . . . all of it rests on the cornerstone of semiconductor mastery." Inaction wasn't a viable option, they believed. Nor was "running faster"—which they saw as code for inaction. "It would be great for us to run faster," one NSC official put it, but the strategy didn't work because of China's "enormous leverage in forcing the turnover of technology." The new NSC adopted a much more combative, zero-sum approach to technology policy. From the officials in the Treasury Department's investment screening unit to those managing the Pentagon's supply chains for military systems, key elements of the government began focusing on semiconductors as part of their strategy for dealing with China.

This made the semiconductor industry's leaders deeply uncomfortable. They wanted the government's help but feared Chinese retaliation. The chip industry would happily accept lower taxes or reduced regulation, both of which would make doing business in the U.S. more attractive, but it didn't want to have to change its multinational business model. It didn't help matters that many in Silicon Valley detested Trump. Intel's CEO Brian Krzanich faced a backlash after agreeing to hold a fundraiser for Trump when he was a candidate. Then, after joining an advisory council convened by the White House, Krzanich later resigned from it. Even when industry executives overlooked Trump's domestic policies, his volatility made him a problematic ally. Announcing tariffs via tweet was never a tactic that would impress CEOs.

However, the messages coming from the chip industry weren't any more coherent than the contradictory leaks from the Trump White House. Publicly, semiconductor CEOs and their lobbyists urged the new administration to work with China and encourage it to comply with trade agreements. Privately, they admitted this strategy was hopeless and feared that state-supported Chinese competitors would grab market share at their expense. The entire chip industry depended on sales to China—be it chipmakers like Intel, fabless designers like Qualcomm, or equipment manufacturers like Applied Materials. One U.S. semiconductor executive wryly summed things up to a White House official: "Our fundamental problem is that our number one customer is our number one competitor."

The China hawks on the National Security Council concluded that America's semiconductor industry needed to be saved from itself. Left to the whim of their shareholders and to market forces, chip firms would slowly transfer staff, technology, and intellectual property to China until Silicon Valley was hollowed out. The U.S. needed a stronger export control regime, the China hawks believed. They thought Washington's discussion about export controls had been hijacked by the industry, letting Chinese firms acquire too much advanced chipmaking design and machinery. Administration officials cited the revolving door between the Commerce Department and law firms who worked for the chip industry and lobbied against export controls, though these officials were also among the few people in the government who understood the complexity of semiconductor supply chains. Because of this revolving

door, Trump administration officials believed, regulations allowed too
much technological leakage, weakening America's position relative to
China.

Amid the fire and fury of President Trump's Twitter feed, most
people barely noticed how different parts of the government—from
Congress to the Commerce Department, from the White House to
the Pentagon—were refocusing on semiconductors in ways unseen in
Washington since the late 1980s. Media attention focused on Trump's
"trade war" with Beijing and his tariff hikes, carefully announced to
maximize media attention. Among the many products that Trump
imposed tariffs on were chips, causing some analysts to see semiconductors as mostly a trade issue. Within the government's national security
bureaucracy, though, the president's tariffs and his trade war were seen
as a distraction from the high-stakes technological struggle underway.

In April 2018, as Trump's trade dispute with China escalated, the
U.S. government concluded that ZTE had violated the terms of its
plea agreement by providing false information to U.S. officials. Wilbur
Ross, Trump's commerce secretary, took it "very personally," according
to one aide, since he'd played a role in negotiating the deal with ZTE
the previous year. The Commerce Department began reimposing the
restrictions on U.S. firms' ability to sell to ZTE, a decision that moved
through the bureaucracy "almost without anyone knowing," according
to one participant. When the rules snapped back, ZTE was again cut off
from its ability to buy U.S. semiconductors, among other products. If the
U.S. didn't change policy, the company would careen toward collapse.

Trump himself was more interested in trade than technology, however. He saw the potential strangulation of ZTE simply as leverage over
Xi Jinping. So when the Chinese leader proposed doing a deal, Trump
eagerly accepted the offer, tweeting that he'd find a way to keep ZTE
in business out of concern for the company "losing too many jobs in
China." Soon ZTE agreed to pay another fine in exchange for regaining access to U.S. suppliers. Trump thought he'd gained leverage in
the trade war, though this proved illusory. Washington's China hawks

thought he'd been duped by officials like Treasury Secretary Steven Mnuchin, who repeatedly urged Trump to offer concessions to Beijing. What the ZTE saga showed above all was the extent to which all the world's major tech firms relied on U.S. chips. Semiconductors weren't simply the "cornerstone" of "everything we're competing on," as one administration official had put it. They could also be a devastatingly powerful weapon.

CHAPTER 50

Fujian Jinhua

"Clear computer data," Kenny Wang typed into Google, searching for a program to cover his tracks as he downloaded confidential files from Micron's network. Unsatisfied with Google's results, he tried a different search. "Clear computer use records," he entered. Eventually he found and ran a program called CCleaner, apparently trying to wipe files off his company-supplied HP laptop. This didn't stop investigators from discovering he'd downloaded nine hundred files from his employer, Micron, America's memory chip champion, which he put on a USB drive and uploaded to Google Drive. "Micron Confidential / Do Not Duplicate," the files were labeled. Wang wasn't simply duplicating files: he planned to duplicate Micron's secret recipe for cutting-edge DRAM chips, downloading files detailing Micron's chip layouts, details for how the company made masks for its lithography processes, and test and yield details—secrets that would have taken several years and hundreds of millions of dollars to replicate, Micron estimated.

Three companies dominate the world's market for DRAM chips today, Micron and its two Korean rivals, Samsung and SK Hynix. Taiwanese firms spent billions trying to break into the DRAM business in the 1990s and 2000s but never managed to establish profitable businesses. The DRAM market requires economies of scale, so it's difficult for small producers to be price competitive. Though Taiwan never succeeded in building a sustainable memory chip industry, both Japan and South Korea had focused on DRAM chips when they first entered the chip industry in the 1970s and 1980s. DRAM requires specialized know-how, advanced equipment, and large quantities of capital investment. Advanced equipment can generally be purchased off-the-shelf from the big American, Japanese, and Dutch toolmakers. The know-how is the hard part. When Samsung entered the business in the late 1980s, it licensed technology from Micron, opened an R&D facility in Silicon Valley, and hired dozens of American-trained PhDs. Another, faster, method for acquiring know-how is to poach employees and steal files.

China's Fujian Province is right across the straits from Taiwan. In the harbor of Fujian's historic port city of Xiamen sits the Taiwanese-controlled island of Kinmen, which Mao Zedong's armies repeatedly shelled during the tensest moments of the Cold War. The relationship between Taiwan and Fujian Province is close but not always friendly. Yet when the government of Fujian Province decided to open a DRAM chipmaker called Jinhua and provided it with over $5 billion in government funding, Jinhua wagered that a partnership with Taiwan was its best path to success. Taiwan didn't have any leading memory chip companies, but it did have DRAM facilities, which Micron had purchased in 2013.

Micron wasn't going to provide any help to Jinhua, which it saw as a dangerous competitor. If Jinhua could ever learn to master DRAM technology, the massive government subsidies it received would provide a major competitive advantage, letting it flood the DRAM market with cheap chips, reducing profit margins at Micron, Samsung, and Hynix. The big three DRAM firms had spent decades investing in ultra-specialized technology processes, which not only created the most advanced memory chips on earth, but also had produced a regular cadence of improvements and cost reductions. Their expertise was defended by patents, but even more important was the know-how that only their engineers had.

To compete, Jinhua had to acquire this manufacturing know-how by means fair or foul. There's a long history in the chip industry of acquiring rivals' technology, dating back to the string of allegations about Japanese intellectual property theft in the 1980s. Jinhua's technique, however, was closer to the KGB's Directorate T. First, Jinhua cut a deal with Taiwan's UMC, which fabricated logic chips (not memory chips), whereby UMC would receive around $700 million in exchange for providing expertise in producing DRAM. Licensing agreements are common in the semiconductor industry, but this agreement had a twist. UMC was promising to provide DRAM technology, but it wasn't in the DRAM business. So in September 2015, UMC hired multiple employees from Micron's facility in Taiwan, starting with the president, Steven Chen, who was put in charge of developing UMC's DRAM technology and managing its relationship with Jinhua. The next month, UMC hired a process manager at Micron's Taiwan facility named J. T. Ho. Over the subsequent year, Ho received a series of documents from his former Micron colleague, Kenny Wang, who was still working at the Idaho chipmaker's facility in Taiwan. Eventually, Wang left Micron to move to UMC, bringing nine hundred files uploaded to Google Drive with him.

Taiwanese prosecutors were notified by Micron of the conspiracy and started gathering evidence by tapping Wang's phone. They soon accumulated enough evidence to bring charges against UMC, which had since filed for patents on some of the technology it stole from Micron. When Micron sued UMC and Jinhua for violating its patents, they countersued in China's Fujian Province. A Fujian court ruled that Micron was responsible for violating UMC and Jinhua's patents—patents that had been filed using material stolen from Micron. To "remedy" the situation, Fuzhou Intermediate People's Court banned Micron from selling twenty-six products in China, the company's biggest market.

This was a perfect case study of the state-backed intellectual property theft foreign companies operating in China had long complained of. The Taiwanese naturally understood why the Chinese preferred not to abide by intellectual property rules, of course. When Texas Instruments first arrived in Taiwan in the 1960s, Minister K. T. Li had sneered that "intellectual property rights are how imperialists bully backward countries." Yet Taiwan had concluded it was better to respect intellectual property norms, especially as its companies began developing their own technologies and had their own patents to defend. Many intellectual property experts predicted that China would soon begin stealing less IP as its companies produced more sophisticated goods. However, the evidence for this thesis was mixed. Efforts by the Obama administration to cut a deal with China's spy agencies whereby they agreed to stop providing stolen secrets to Chinese companies lasted only long enough for Americans to forget about the issue, at which point the hacking promptly restarted.

Micron had little reason to expect a fair trial in China. Winning court cases in Taiwan or California meant little when kangaroo courts in Fujian could lock the company out of its biggest market. Around the same time, Veeco, an American producer of semiconductor manufacturing equipment, had launched an intellectual property suit in U.S. courts against a Chinese competitor, AMEC, which countersued in a Fujian provincial court—the same province where Micron's competitor was located. A New York judge issued a preliminary injunction in Veeco's favor. The Fujian court retaliated with a preliminary injunction of its own, banning Veeco from importing machinery to China, a move that occurs in only 0.01 percent of Chinese patent cases, according to research by Berkeley professor Mark Cohen, an expert on Chinese law. Whereas the U.S. court case took months, the Fujian court reached its decision in just nine business days. The ruling itself is still secret.

Micron seemed set to face a similar fate. With Micron's secrets at Jinhua's disposal, some analysts thought it would only be a few years before Jinhua was producing DRAM chips at scale—at which point it wouldn't matter if Micron was let back into the Chinese market, because Jinhua would be producing chips using Micron's technology and selling them at subsidized prices. Had this occurred during the Obama administration, the case would have resulted in stern statements but little else. American CEOs, knowing they couldn't count on serious U.S. government backing, would have tried to cut a deal with Beijing, surrendering their intellectual property in hopes of regaining access to the Chinese market. Jinhua, knowing to expect nothing worse than an angry press release, would have squeezed the company as hard as it could. Other foreign firms would have stayed quiet even though they knew they could be next.

The China hawks on the NSC were determined to change this dynamic. They saw the Micron case as the type of unfair trade that Trump had promised to fix, even though the president himself displayed no particular interest in Micron. Some administration officials advocated imposing financial sanctions on Jinhua, using powers set out in an executive order on cyber espionage signed by President Obama in 2015, though the order hadn't been used against a major Chinese company. After deliberating, the Trump administration decided to use the same tool it had deployed against ZTE, reasoning that it made more sense to address a trade dispute with a trade regulation. Jinhua was cut off from buying U.S. equipment for manufacturing chips.

U.S. companies like Applied Materials, Lam Research, and KLA are part of a small oligopoly of companies that produce irreplaceable machinery, like the tools that deposit microscopically thin layers of materials on silicon wafers or recognize nanometer-scale defects. Without this machinery—much of it still built in the U.S.—it's impossible to produce advanced semiconductors. Only Japan has companies producing some comparable machinery, so if Tokyo and Washington agreed, they could make it impossible for any firm, in any country, to make advanced chips. After detailed consultations with officials at Japan's powerful Ministry of Economics, Trade, and Industry, the Trump administration was confident Tokyo supported a tough move against Jinhua and would ensure Japanese companies didn't undercut American restrictions on the firm. This gave the U.S. a powerful new tool to put out of business any chipmaker, anywhere in the world. Some of the doves in the Trump administration, like Treasury Secretary Mnuchin, were nervous. But Commerce Secretary Wilbur Ross, who had the authority to impose export controls, thought "why the fuck wouldn't we use this?" according to one aide. So after Jinhua paid invoices to the U.S. firms that supplied its crucial chipmaking tools, the U.S. banned their export. Within months, production at Jinhua ground to a halt. China's most advanced DRAM firm was destroyed.

CHAPTER 51

The Assault on Huawei

" I call it the spyway," President Trump explained to the hosts of *Fox & Friends*, one of his favorite TV programs, when asked about Huawei. "We don't want their equipment in the United States because they spy on us. . . . They know everything." It was hardly a revelation that tech infrastructure could be used to pilfer confidential information. After former National Security Agency employee Edward Snowden defected to Russia in 2013 while releasing many of the agency's most closely held secrets, news of American cyber sleuths' capabilities were regularly discussed in the world's newspapers. China's impressive hacking capabilities were also well known after a string of high-profile breaches of ostensibly secret U.S. government data.

Within the Pentagon and the NSC, Huawei was seen less as an espionage challenge—though U.S. officials had little doubt the company would support Chinese spycraft—than as the first battle in a long struggle for technological dominance. Matt Turpin, a Pentagon official who'd worked on the military's new offset strategy, saw Huawei as symptomatic of a broader problem in the U.S. tech industry: Chinese firms "were effectively inside the system with the United States," given that they designed chips with U.S. software, produced them using U.S. machinery, and often plugged them into devices built for American consumers. Given this, it was impossible "for the United States to 'out-innovate'

China and then deny them the fruits of that innovation." Huawei and other Chinese firms were assuming central roles in tech subsectors that the U.S. thought it needed to dominate to retain a technological advantage over China, militarily and strategically. "Huawei became really a proxy for everything we had done wrong with our tech competition with China," another senior Trump administration official put it.

Concern about Huawei wasn't confined to the Trump administration or the United States. Australia had banned Huawei from 5G networks after its security services concluded the risk simply couldn't be mitigated, even if Huawei turned over access to all its software source code and hardware. Australian prime minister Malcolm Turnbull had at first been skeptical of an outright ban. According to Australian journalist Peter Hartcher, Turnbull bought himself a 474-page-book titled *A Comprehensive Guide to 5G Security* to study the topic so that he could ask better questions of his tech experts. Eventually he was convinced he had no choice but to ban the firm. Australia became the first country to formally cut Huawei's equipment from its 5G networks, a decision that was soon followed by Japan, New Zealand, and others.

Not every country had the same threat assessment. Many of China's neighbors were skeptical of the company and unwilling to take risks with network security. In Europe, by contrast, several traditional American allies looked warily at the Trump administration's pressure campaign to convince them to ban Huawei. Some close American allies in Eastern Europe openly banned the company, like Poland, which also in 2019 arrested a former company executive on espionage charges. France also quietly imposed strict restrictions. Other big European countries tried to find a middle ground. Germany, which exports large quantities of cars and machinery to China, was warned by the Chinese ambassador of "consequences" if it banned Huawei. "The Chinese government will not stand idly by," the Chinese diplomat threatened.

Ultimately the Trump administration expected pushback from Germany, which it saw as a free-riding ally on a range of issues. The bigger surprise was Britain, which despite its "special relationship" with the

United States was spurning U.S. requests to ban Huawei from the UK's 5G networks and, instead, buy equipment from alternative suppliers like Sweden's Ericsson or Finland's Nokia. In 2019, the UK government's National Cyber Security Centre concluded the risk of Huawei systems could be managed without a ban.

Why did Australian and British cybersecurity experts differ in their assessment of Huawei risk? There's no evidence of technical disagreements. UK regulators were quite critical of deficiencies in Huawei's cybersecurity practices, for example. The debate was really about whether China should be stopped from playing an ever-larger role in the world's tech infrastructure. Robert Hannigan, former head of the UK's signals intelligence agency, argued that "we should accept that China will be a global tech power in the future and start managing the risk now, rather than pretending the west can sit out China's technological rise." Many Europeans also thought China's technological advance was inevitable and therefore not worth trying to stop.

The United States government didn't agree. The issue with Huawei went far beyond the debate over whether the company helped tap phones or pilfer data. Huawei executives' admission that they'd violated U.S. sanctions on Iran angered many in Washington but was ultimately a sideshow. The real issue was that a company in the People's Republic of China had marched up the technology ladder—from, in the late 1980s, simple phone switches to, by the late 2010s, the most advanced telecom and networking gear. Its annual R&D spending now rivaled American tech giants like Microsoft, Google, and Intel. Of all China's tech firms, it was the most successful exporter, giving it detailed knowledge of foreign markets. It not only produced hardware for cell towers, it also designed cutting-edge smartphone chips. It had become TSMC's second biggest customer, behind only Apple. The pressing question was: Could the United States let a Chinese company like this succeed?

Questions like this made many people in Washington uncomfortable. For a generation, America's elite had welcomed and enabled China's economic rise. The United States had also encouraged technology companies across Asia, providing market access to Japanese firms like Sony during the years of Japan's rapid growth and doing the same for South Korea's Samsung several decades later. Huawei's business model wasn't much different from that of Sony or Samsung when they first won a major position in the world's tech ecosystem. Wasn't a bit more competition a good thing?

On the National Security Council, however, competition with China was now seen primarily in zero-sum terms. These officials interpreted Huawei not as a commercial challenge but as a strategic one. Sony and Samsung were tech firms based in countries that were allied with the U.S. Huawei was a national champion of America's primary geopolitical rival. Viewed through this lens, Huawei's expansion was a threat. Congress wanted a tougher, more combative policy, too. "The United States needs to strangle Huawei," Republican senator Ben Sasse declared in 2020. "Modern wars are fought with semiconductors and we were letting Huawei use our American designs."

The point was less that Huawei was directly supporting China's military than that the company was advancing China's overall level of chip design and microelectronics know-how. The more advanced electronics the country produced, the more cutting-edge chips it would buy, and the more the world's semiconductor ecosystem would rely on China, at the expense of the United States. Moreover, targeting China's highest-profile tech firm would send a message worldwide, warning other countries to prepare to take sides. Hobbling Huawei's rise became a fixation of the administration.

When the Trump administration first decided to turn up its pressure on Huawei, it prohibited the sale of U.S.-made chips to the company. This restriction alone was devastating, given that Intel chips are ubiquitous and many other U.S. companies manufacture all-but-irreplaceable analog chips. Yet after decades of offshoring, far less of the semiconductor production process took place in the United States than previously. For example, Huawei produced the chips that it designed not in the U.S.—which lacked facilities capable of building advanced smartphone processors—but at Taiwan's TSMC. Restricting the export of U.S.-made goods to Huawei would do nothing to stop TSMC from fabricating advanced chips for Huawei.

One might have expected the offshoring of chipmaking to have reduced the U.S. government's ability to restrict access to advanced chip fabrication. It would certainly have been easier to cut off Huawei if all the world's advanced chipmaking was still based on U.S. soil. However, the U.S. still had cards to play. For example, the process of offshoring chip fabrication had coincided with a growing monopolization of chip industry choke points. Nearly every chip in the world uses software from at least one of three U.S.-based companies, Cadence, Synopsys, and Mentor (the latter of which is owned by Germany's Siemens but based in Oregon). Excluding the chips Intel builds in-house, all the most advanced logic chips are fabricated by just two companies, Samsung and TSMC, both located in countries that rely on the U.S. military for their security. Moreover, making advanced processors requires EUV lithography machines produced by just one company, the Netherlands' ASML, which in turn relies on its San Diego subsidiary, Cymer (which it purchased in 2013), to supply the irreplaceable light sources in its EUV lithography tools. It's far easier to control choke points in the chip-making process when so many essential steps require tools, materials, or software produced by just a handful of firms. Many of these choke points remained in American hands. Those that didn't were mostly controlled by close U.S. allies.

Around this time, two academics, Henry Farrell and Abraham Newman, noticed that international political and economic relations were increasingly impacted by what they called "weaponized inter-dependence." Countries were more intwined than ever, they pointed out, but rather than defusing conflicts and encouraging cooperation, interdependence was creating new venues for competition. Networks that knit together nations had become a domain of conflict. In the finan-cial sphere, the U.S. had weaponized other countries' reliance on access to the banking system to punish Iran, for example. These academics worried that the U.S. government's use of trade and capital flows as political weapons threatened globalization and risked dangerous unintended consequences. The Trump administration, by contrast, concluded it had unique power to weaponize semiconductor supply chains.

In May 2020, the administration tightened restrictions on Huawei further. Now, the Commerce Department declared, it would "protect U.S. national security by restricting Huawei's ability to use U.S. technology and software to design and manufacture its semiconductors abroad." The new Commerce Department rules didn't simply stop the sale of U.S.-produced goods to Huawei. They restricted any goods made with U.S.-produced technology from being sold to Huawei, too. In a chip industry full of choke points, this meant almost any chip. TSMC can't fabricate advanced chips for Huawei without using U.S. manufacturing equipment. Huawei can't design chips without U.S.-produced software. Even China's most advanced foundry, SMIC, relies extensively on U.S. tools. Huawei was simply cut off from the world's entire chipmaking infrastructure, except for chips that the U.S. Commerce Department deigned to give it a special license to buy.

The world's chip industry quickly began implementing the U.S. rules. Even though the U.S. was trying to eviscerate its second-largest customer, TSMC's chairman, Mark Liu, promised not only to abide by the letter of the law but also its spirit. "This is something that can be solved not solely through the interpretation of the rules, but also has to do with the intentions of the U.S. government," he told journalists. Since then, Huawei's been forced to divest part of its smartphone business and its server business, since it can't get the necessary chips. China's rollout of its own 5G telecoms network, which was once a high-profile government priority, has been delayed due to chip shortages. After the U.S. restrictions took place, other countries, notably Britain, decided to ban Huawei, reasoning that in the absence of U.S. chips the company would struggle to service its products.

The assault on Huawei was followed by blacklisting multiple other Chinese tech firms. After discussions with the United States, the Netherlands decided not to approve the sale of ASML's EUV machines to Chinese firms. Sugon, the supercomputer company that AMD described in 2017 as a "strategic partner," was blacklisted by the U.S. in 2019. So, too, was Phytium, a company that U.S. officials say has designed chips for supercomputers that were used to test hypersonic missiles, according to a report in the *Washington Post*. Phytium's chips were designed using U.S. software and produced in Taiwan at TSMC. Access to the semiconductor ecosystem of America and its allies enabled Phytium's growth. However, the company's reliance on foreign software and manufacturing left it critically vulnerable to U.S. restrictions.

Ultimately, though, the American assault on China's tech firms has been a limited strike. Many of China's biggest tech companies, like Tencent and Alibaba, still face no specific limits on their purchases of U.S. chips or their ability to have TSMC manufacture their semiconductors. SMIC, China's most advanced producer of logic chips, faces new restrictions on its purchases of advanced chipmaking tools, but it has not been put out of business. Even Huawei is allowed to buy older semiconductors, like those used for connecting to 4G networks.

Nevertheless, it's surprising that China's done nothing to retaliate against the hobbling of its most global tech firm. It has repeatedly threatened to punish U.S. tech firms but never pulled the trigger. Beijing said it was drawing up an "unreliable entity list" of foreign companies that endanger Chinese security, but it doesn't appear to have added any firms to the list. Beijing has evidently calculated that it's better to accept that Huawei will become a second-rate technology player than to hit back against the United States. The U.S., it turns out, has escalation dominance when it comes to severing supply chains. "Weaponized interdependence," one former senior official mused after the strike on Huawei. "It's a beautiful thing."

CHAPTER 52

China's Sputnik Moment?

When the Chinese city of Wuhan locked down on January 23, 2020, amid a tsunami of cases of COVID-19, it faced some of the harshest, longest restrictions of any city at any point in the pandemic. The COVID virus and the disease it caused was still little understood. China's government had suppressed discussion of the virus until it ripped through Wuhan and was spreading across China and the world. The government belatedly shut down travel in and out of Wuhan, imposing checkpoints on the city's perimeter, shuttering businesses, and ordering almost all the city's 10 million people not to leave their apartments until the lockdown ended. Never before had such a massive metropolis simply frozen. Highways were empty, sidewalks desolate, airports and train stations closed. Except for hospitals and grocery stores, almost everything was shut.

Except for one facility, that is. Yangzte Memory Technologies Corporation (YMTC), based in Wuhan, is China's leading producer of NAND memory, a type of chip that's ubiquitous in consumer devices from smartphones to USB memory sticks. There are five companies that make competitive NAND chips today; none are headquartered in China. Many industry experts, however, think that of all types of chips, China's best chance at achieving world-class manufacturing capabilities is in NAND production. Tsinghua Unigroup, the semiconductor slush fund that invested in chip companies worldwide, provided YMTC with at least $24 billion in funding, alongside China's national chip fund and the provincial government.

So great is China's government support for YMTC that even during the COVID lockdown it was allowed to keep working, according to *Nikkei Asia*, a Japanese newspaper with some of the best coverage of China's chip industry. Trains passing through Wuhan carried special passenger cars specifically for YMTC employees, letting them enter Wuhan despite the lockdown. The company was even hiring for Wuhan-based positions in late February and early March 2020, as the rest of the country remained frozen. China's leaders were willing to do almost anything in their fight against the coronavirus, but their effort to build a semiconductor industry took priority.

It's commonly argued that the escalating tech competition with the United States is like a "Sputnik moment" for China's government. The allusion is to the United States' fear after the launch of Sputnik in 1957 that it was falling behind its rival, driving Washington to pour funding into science and technology. China certainly faced a Sputnik-scale shock after the U.S. banned sales of chips to firms like Huawei. Dan Wang, one of the smartest analysts of China's tech policy, has argued that American restrictions have "boosted Beijing's quest for tech dominance" by catalyzing new government policies to support the chip industry. In the absence of America's new export controls, he argues, Made in China 2025 would have ended up like China's previous industrial policy efforts, with the government wasting substantial sums of money. Thanks to U.S. pressure, China's government may provide Chinese chipmakers more support than they'd otherwise have received.

The debate is about whether the U.S. should try to derail China's growing chip ecosystem—thereby spurring an inevitable counterreaction—or whether it's smarter simply to invest at home while hoping China's chip drive peters out. U.S. restrictions have certainly catalyzed a new wave of government support for Chinese chipmakers. Xi Jinping recently appointed his top economic aide, Liu He, to serve as a "chip czar," managing the country's semiconductor efforts. There's no doubt that China's spending billions to subsidize chip firms. Whether this funding produces new technology remains to be seen. For example, the city of Wuhan is home not only to YMTC, China's brightest hope for NAND chip parity, but also to the country's biggest recent semiconductor scam.

The case of Wuhan Hongxin (HSMC) shows the risk of shoveling money into semiconductors without asking enough questions. According to a Chinese media report that's since been removed from the internet, HSMC was founded by a group of scam artists who carried fake business cards that read "TSMC—Vice President" and spread rumors that their relatives were top Communist Party officials. They duped the Wuhan local government into investing in their company, then used the funds to hire as CEO TSMC's former head of R&D. With him on board, they acquired a deep-ultraviolet lithography machine from ASML, then used this feat to raise more funds from investors. But the factory in Wuhan was a shoddily built copy of an old TSMC facility; HSMC was still trying to produce its first chip when the company went bust.

It isn't only provincial experiments that have failed. Tsinghua Unigroup recently ran out of cash after its global acquisition spree and defaulted on some of its bonds. Even Tsinghua CEO Zhao Weiguo's top-level political connections weren't enough to save the firm, though the chip companies it owns will likely survive mostly unscathed. An official from China's government planning agency publicly lamented that the country's chip industry had "no experience, no technology, no talent." This is an overstatement, but it's clear that billions of dollars have been wasted in China on semiconductor projects that are either hopelessly unrealistic or, like HSMC, blatant frauds. If China's Sputnik moment inspires more state-backed semiconductor programs like these, the country won't be on a path to technological independence.

In an industry with such a multinational supply chain, technological independence was always a pipe dream, even for the United States, which remains the world's biggest semiconductor player. For China, which lacks competitive firms in many parts of the supply chain, from machinery to software, technological independence is even more difficult. For complete independence, China would need to acquire cutting-edge design software, design capabilities, advanced materials, and fabrication know-how, among other steps. China will no doubt make progress in some of these spheres, yet some are simply too expensive and too difficult for China to replicate at home.

Consider, for example, what it would take to replicate one of ASML's EUV machines, which have taken nearly three decades to develop and commercialize. EUV machines have multiple components that, on their own, constitute epically complex engineering challenges. Replicating just the laser in an EUV system requires perfectly identifying and assembling 457,329 parts. A single defect could cause debilitating delays or reliability problems. No doubt the Chinese government has deployed some of its best spies to study ASML's production processes. However, even if they've already hacked into the relevant systems and downloaded design specs, machinery this complex can't simply be copied and pasted like a stolen file. Even if a spy were to gain access to specialized information, they'd need a PhD in optics or lasers to understand the science—and even still, they'd lack the three decades of experience accumulated by the engineers who've developed EUV.

Perhaps in a decade China *can* succeed in building its own EUV scanner. If so, the program will cost tens of billions of dollars, but—in a revelation that is bound to be discouraging—when it's ready it will no longer be cutting edge. By that time, ASML will have introduced a new generation tool, called high-aperture EUV, which is scheduled to be ready in the mid-2020s and cost $300 million per machine, twice the cost of the first generation EUV machine. Even if a future Chinese EUV scanner works just as well as ASML's current equipment—hard to imagine, given that the U.S. will try to restrict its ability to access components from other countries—Chinese chipmakers using this hypothetical alternative EUV machine will struggle to produce profitably with it, because by 2030, TSMC, Samsung, and Intel will have already used their own EUV scanners for a decade, during which time, they'll have perfected their use and paid down the cost of these tools. They'll be able to sell chips produced with EUV for far cheaper than a Chinese company using a hypothetical Chinese-built EUV tool.

EUV machines are just one of many tools that are produced via multinational supply chains. Domesticating every part of the supply chain would be impossibly expensive. The global chip industry spends over $100 billion annually on capital expenditures. China would have to replicate this spending in addition to building a base of expertise and facilities that it currently lacks. Establishing a cutting-edge, all-domestic supply chain would take over a decade and cost well over a trillion dollars in that period.

This is why, despite the rhetoric, China's not actually pursuing an all-domestic supply chain. Beijing recognizes this is simply impossible. China would like a non-U.S. supply chain, but because of America's heft in the chip industry and the extraterritorial power of its export regulations, a non-American supply chain is also unrealistic, except perhaps in the distant future. What is plausible is for China to reduce its reliance on the United States in certain spheres and to increase its overall weight in the chip industry, weaning itself off as many choke-point technologies as possible.

One of China's core challenges today is that many chips use either the x86 architecture (for PCs and servers) or the Arm architecture (for mobile devices); x86 is dominated by two U.S. firms, Intel and AMD, while Arm, which licenses other companies to use its architecture, is based in the UK. However, there's now a new instruction set architecture called RISC-V that is open-sourced, so it's available to anyone without a fee. The idea of an open-source architecture appeals to many parts of the chip industry. Anyone who currently must pay Arm for a license would prefer a free alternative. Moreover, the risk of security defects may be lower, because the open nature of an open-source architecture like RISC-V means that more engineers will be able to verify details and identify errors. For the same reason, the pace of innovation may be faster, too. These two factors explain why DARPA has funded a variety of projects related to developing RISC-V. Chinese firms have also embraced RISC-V, because they see it as geopolitically neutral. In 2019, the RISC-V Foundation, which manages the architecture, moved from the U.S. to Switzerland for this reason. Companies like Alibaba are designing processors based on the RISC-V architecture with this in mind.

In addition to working with emerging architectures, China's also focusing on older process technology to build logic chips. Smartphones and data centers require the most cutting-edge chips, but cars and other consumer devices often use older process technology, which is sufficiently powerful and far cheaper. Most of the investment in new fabs in China, including at companies like SMIC, is in production capacity at lagging-edge nodes. SMIC has already shown that China has the workforce to produce competitive lagging-edge logic chips. Even if U.S. export restrictions get tighter, they're unlikely to prohibit the export of decades-old manufacturing equipment. China's also investing heavily in emerging semiconductor materials like silicon carbide and gallium nitride, which are unlikely to displace pure silicon in most chips but will likely play a bigger role in managing the power systems in electric vehicles. Here, too, China probably has the requisite technology, so government subsidies may help it win business on price.

The worry for other countries is that China's slew of subsidies will let it win market share across multiple parts of the supply chain, especially those that don't require the most advanced technologies. Barring severe new restrictions on access to foreign software and machinery, China looks likely to play a much bigger role in producing non-cutting-edge logic chips. In addition, it's pouring money into the materials needed to develop power management chips for electric vehicles. China's YMTC, meanwhile, has a real chance to win a chunk of the NAND memory market. Across the chip industry, estimates suggest that China's share of fabrication will increase from 15 percent at the start of the decade to 24 percent of global capacity by 2030, overtaking Taiwan and South Korea in terms of volume. China will almost certainly still lag technologically.

But if more of the chip industry moves to China, the country will have more leverage in demanding technology transfer. It will become more costly for the U.S. and other countries to impose export restrictions, and China will have a broader pool of workers from which to draw. Almost all of China's chip firms are dependent on government support, so they're oriented toward national goals as much as commercial ones. "Making profits and going public . . . are not the priority" at YMTC, one executive told the *Nikkei Asia* newspaper. Instead, the company's focused on "building the country's own chips and realizing the Chinese dream."

CHAPTER 53

Shortages and Supply Chains

"For too long as a nation, we haven't been making the big, bold investments we need to outpace our global competitors," President Biden declared to a screenful of CEOs. Sitting in the White House under a painting of Teddy Roosevelt, holding aloft a twelve-inch silicon wafer, Biden looked into the Zoom screen and castigated the executives for "falling behind on research and development and manufacturing. . . . We have to step up our game," he told them. Many of the nineteen executives on the screen agreed. To discuss America's response to the chip shortage, Biden invited foreign companies like TSMC alongside U.S. chipmakers like Intel, as well as prominent users of semiconductors who were suffering severe semiconductor shortages. The CEOs of Ford and GM weren't normally invited to high-level meetings about chips, and normally they wouldn't have been interested. But over the course of 2021, as the world's economy and its supply chains convulsed between pandemic-induced disruptions, people around the world began to understand just how much their lives, and often their livelihoods, depended on semiconductors.

In 2020, just as the United States began to impose a chip choke on China, cutting off some of the country's leading tech companies from accessing U.S. chip technology, a second chip choke began asphyxiating parts of the world economy. Certain types of chips became difficult to acquire, especially the types of basic logic chips that are widely used in automobiles. The two chip chokes were partially interrelated. Chinese firms like Huawei had been stockpiling chips since at least 2019, in preparation for potential future U.S. sanctions, while Chinese fabs were buying as much manufacturing equipment as possible in case the U.S. decided to tighten export restrictions on chipmaking tools.

However, Chinese stockpiling explains only part of the COVID-era chip choke. The bigger cause is vast swings in orders for chips after the pandemic began, as companies and consumers adjusted their demand for different goods. PC demand spiked in 2020, as millions of people upgraded their computers to work from home. Data centers' demand for servers grew, too, as more of life shifted online. Car companies at first cut chip orders, expecting car sales to slump. When demand quickly recovered, they found that chipmakers had already reallocated capacity to other customers. According to the American Automotive Policy Council, an industry group, the world's biggest auto companies can use over a thousand chips in each car. If even one chip is missing, the car can't be shipped. Carmakers spent much of 2021 struggling and often failing to acquire semiconductors. These firms are estimated to have produced 7.7 million fewer cars in 2021 than would have been possible had they *not* faced chip shortages, which implies a $210 billion collective revenue loss, according to industry estimates.

The Biden administration and most of the media interpreted the chip shortage as a supply chain problem. The White House commissioned a 250-page report on supply chain vulnerabilities that focused on semiconductors. However, the semiconductor shortage wasn't primarily caused by issues in the chip supply chain. There were some supply disruptions, like COVID lockdowns in Malaysia, which impacted semiconductor packaging operations there. But the world produced more chips in 2021 than ever before—over 1.1 trillion semiconductor devices, according to research firm IC Insights. This was a 13 percent increase compared to 2020. The semiconductor shortage is mostly a story of demand growth rather than supply issues. It's driven by new PCs, 5G phones, AI-enabled data centers—and, ultimately, our insatiable demand for computing power.

Politicians around the world have therefore misdiagnosed the semiconductor supply chain dilemma. The problem isn't that the chip industry's far-flung production processes dealt poorly with COVID and the resulting lockdowns. There are few industries that sailed through the pandemic with so little disruption. Such problems that emerged, notably the shortage of auto chips, are mostly the fault of carmakers' frantic and ill-advised cancelation of chip orders in the early days of the pandemic coupled with their just-in-time manufacturing practices that provide little margin of error. For the car industry, which suffered a several-hundred-billion-dollar hit to revenue, there's plenty of reason to rethink how they've managed their own supply chains. The semiconductor industry, however, had a banner year. Besides a massive earthquake—a low but non-zero probability risk—it's hard to imagine a more severe peacetime shock to supply chains than what the industry has survived since early 2020. The substantial increase in chip production during both 2020 and 2021 is not a sign that multinational supply chains are broken. It's a sign that they've worked.

Nevertheless, governments should think harder about semiconductor supply chains than they used to. The real supply chain lesson of the past few years is not about fragility but about profits and power. Taiwan's extraordinary ascent shows how one company—with a vision and with government financial support—can remake an entire industry. Meanwhile, U.S. restrictions on China's access to chip technology demonstrate just how powerful the chip industry's choke points are. The rise of China's semiconductor industry over the past decade, however, is a reminder that these choke points are not infinitely durable. Countries and governments can often find ways around choke points, though doing so is time-consuming and expensive, sometimes extraordinarily so. Technological shifts can erode the efficacy of choke points, too.

These choke points only work if they're controlled by a couple of companies, and ideally only by one. Although the Biden administration has promised to work "with industry, allies, and partners," the U.S. and its allies aren't completely aligned when it comes to the future of the chip industry. The U.S. wants to reverse its declining share of chip fabrication and retain its dominant position in semiconductor design and machinery. Countries in Europe and Asia, however, would like to grab a bigger share of the high-value chip design market. Taiwan and South Korea, meanwhile, have no plans to surrender their market-leading positions fabricating advanced logic and memory chips. With China viewing expansion of its own fabrication capacity as a national security necessity, there's a limited amount of future chip fabrication business that can be shared between the U.S., Europe, and Asia. If the U.S. wants to increase its market share, some other country's market share must decrease. The U.S. is implicitly hoping to grab market share from one of the other areas with modern chipmaking facilities. Yet outside China, all the world's advanced chip fabs are in countries that are U.S. allies or close friends.

South Korea, however, plans to retain its leading position in making memory chips while trying to expand its role in making logic chips. "Rivalries among semiconductor businesses have now begun to draw in countries," South Korean president Moon Jae-in has noted. "My administration will also work with business as one team so Korea stays a semiconductor powerhouse." The Korean government has poured money into a city called Pyeongtaek, formerly home to a U.S. military base but now the site of a major Samsung facility. All the major chipmaking equipment companies, from Applied Materials to Tokyo Electron, have opened offices in the city. Samsung has said it plans to spend over $100 billion by 2030 on its logic chip business in addition to investing comparable sums in memory chip production. The grandson of Samsung's founder, Lee Jay-yong, was paroled from prison in 2021, where he was serving a sentence for bribery. Korea's Justice Ministry cited "economic factors" in justifying his release, including, media reports suggested, expectations that he will help the company make major semiconductor investment decisions.

Samsung and its smaller Korean rival SK Hynix benefit from the support of the Korean government but are stuck between China and the U.S., with each country trying to cajole South Korea's chip giants to build more manufacturing in their countries. Samsung recently announced plans to expand and upgrade its facility for producing advanced logic chips in Austin, Texas, for example, an investment estimated to cost $17 billion. Both companies face scrutiny from the U.S. over proposals to upgrade their facilities in China, however. U.S. pressure to restrict the transfer of EUV tools to SK Hynix's facility in Wuxi, China, is reportedly delaying its modernization—and presumably imposing a substantial cost on the company.

South Korea isn't the only country where chip companies and the government work as a "team," to use President Moon's phrase. Taiwan's government remains fiercely protective of its chip industry, which it recognizes as its greatest source of leverage on the international stage. Morris Chang, now ostensibly fully retired from TSMC, has served as a trade envoy for Taiwan. His primary interest—and Taiwan's—remains ensuring that TSMC retains its central role in the world's chip industry. The company itself plans to invest over $100 billion between 2022 and 2024 to upgrade its technology and expand chipmaking capacity. Most of this money will be invested in Taiwan, though the company plans to upgrade its facility in Nanjing, China, and to open a new fab in Arizona. Neither of these new fabs will produce the most cutting-edge chips, however, so TSMC's most advanced technology will remain in Taiwan. Chang continues to call for "free trade" in the semiconductor industry, threatening that otherwise "costs will go up, technology development will slow down." Meanwhile, Taiwan's government has repeatedly intervened to support TSMC through such measures as keeping Taiwan's currency undervalued to make Taiwanese exports more competitive.

Europe, Japan, and Singapore are three other regions looking for new semiconductor investments. Some European Union leaders have suggested the continent can "invest massively" and produce 3nm or

2nm chips, putting European fabs near the cutting edge. Given the continent's low market share in advanced logic, this is unlikely. More plausible is that Europe will convince a big foreign chip firm, like Intel, to build a new facility providing a stable source of supply for European automakers. Singapore continues to provide substantial incentives for chipmaking, recently winning a $4 billion investment from U.S.-based GlobalFoundries for a new fab. Japan, meanwhile, is heavily subsidizing TSMC to build a new chipmaking facility in partnership with Sony. Japan has lost much of its chipmaking in the decades since executives like Akio Morita left the scene, but Sony still retains a sizeable and profitable business making semiconductors that can sense images and which are used in the cameras in many consumer devices. Japan's decision to subsidize a new TSMC facility, though, wasn't primarily to help Sony. Japan's government feared that if manufacturing kept shifting offshore, the parts of the supply chain in which Japan retains a strong position, like machine tools and advanced materials, would shift abroad, too.

While Japan could use a new Akio Morita, the United States is in desperate need of a new Andy Grove. America still has an enviable position in the chip industry. Its control over many of the industry's choke points, including software and machinery, is as strong as ever. Companies like Nvidia look likely to play a foundational role in the future of computing trends like artificial intelligence. Moreover, after a decade in which chip startups were out of fashion, in the past few years Silicon Valley has poured money into fabless firms designing new chips, often focused on new architectures that are optimized for artificial intelligence applications.

When it comes to making these chips, however, the U.S. currently lags behind. The primary hope for advanced manufacturing in the United States is Intel. After years of drift, the company named Pat Gelsinger as CEO in 2021. Born in small-town Pennsylvania, Gelsinger started his career at Intel and was mentored by Andy Grove. He eventually left to take on senior roles at two cloud computing companies before he was brought back to turn Intel around. He's set out an ambitious and expensive strategy with three prongs. The first is to regain manufacturing leadership, overtaking Samsung and TSMC. To do this, Gelsinger has cut a deal with ASML to let Intel acquire the first next-generation EUV machine, which is expected to be ready in 2025. If Intel can learn how to use these new tools before rivals, it could provide a technological edge.

The second prong of Gelsinger's strategy is launching a foundry business that will compete directly with Samsung and TSMC, producing chips for fabless firms and helping Intel win more market share. Intel's spending heavily on new facilities in the U.S. and Europe to build capacity that potential future foundry customers will require. However, making the foundry business financially viable will likely require winning some customers who are producing at the technological cutting edge—meaning that Intel's foundry business will only work if the company can reduce its technological lag with Samsung and TSMC. Intel's foundry pivot comes as its market share in data center chips continues to decline, both because of competition from AMD and Nvidia and because cloud computing companies like Amazon Web Services and Google are designing their own chips.

Whether Intel succeeds or fails will depend on whether it can execute Gelsinger's strategy and whether Samsung or TSMC slip up. Moore's Law requires these companies to roll out new technologies every few years, so one or both of Intel's competitors could easily face major delays. Yet Intel's strategy has an uncomfortable third prong: get help from TSMC. Publicly, Intel is encouraging a new wave of chip nationalism and nervousness about reliance on production in Asia. It's trying to extract subsidies from both the U.S. and European governments to build fabs at home. "The world needs a more balanced supply chain," Gelsinger argues. "God decided where the oil reserves are, we get to decide where the fabs are." Yet while Intel tries to sort out its in-house chip fabrication, it is outsourcing production of a growing share of its advanced chip designs to TSMC's most advanced facilities in Taiwan.

As it began to reckon with the concentration of advanced chipmaking in East Asia, the U.S. government convinced both TSMC and Samsung to open new facilities in the U.S., with TSMC planning a new fab in Arizona and Samsung expanding a facility near Austin, Texas. These fabs are partially intended to appease American politicians, though they will also produce chips for defense and other critical infrastructure that the U.S. would prefer to fabricate onshore. However, both companies plan to keep the vast majority of their production capacity—and their most advanced technology—at home. Even promises of subsidies from the U.S. government are unlikely to change this.

Among American national security officials, there is growing discussion about whether to use threats of export controls on chip design software and manufacturing equipment to pressure TSMC to roll out its newest process technologies simultaneously in the U.S. and in Taiwan. Alternatively, TSMC could be pressed to commit that every dollar of capital expenditure in Taiwan will be matched, for example, by a dollar of capital expenditure at one of TSMC's new facilities in Japan, Arizona, or Singapore. Such moves might begin to reduce the world's reliance on chipmaking in Taiwan. But for now, Washington is unwilling to exert the pressure that would be required. The entire world's dependence on Taiwan, therefore, continues to grow.

CHAPTER 54

The Taiwan Dilemma

"Are your customers concerned," one financial analyst asked TSMC chairman Mark Liu, when China from time to time threatens "a war against Taiwan?" CEOs are used to tough questions on quarterly earnings calls, but they're usually about missed profit targets or product launches gone wrong. At the time of this call, July 15, 2021, TSMC's financials looked fine. The company had weathered the sanctioning of its second-largest customer, Huawei, with scarcely any impact on its performance. TSMC's share price was near a record high. The global semiconductor shortage had made its business even more lucrative. For a time in 2021, it was the most valuable publicly traded company in Asia, one of the ten most valuable publicly traded companies in the world.

Yet the more indispensable TSMC has become, the more risk has risen—not to TSMC's financials, but to its facilities. Even investors who for years chose to ignore the severity of the U.S.-China antagonism began looking nervously at the map of TSMC's chip fabs, arrayed along the western coast of the Taiwan Strait. TSMC's chairman insisted that there was no reason for concern. "As to the invasion of China, let me tell you," he declared, "everybody wants to have a peaceful Taiwan Strait." Taipei-born, Berkeley-educated, and Bell Labs–trained, Liu has an impeccable chipmaking record. His skill in assessing the risk of war, however, has yet to be tested. Peace in the Taiwan Strait "is to every country's benefit," he argued, given the world's reliance on "the semiconductor supply chain in Taiwan. No one wants to disrupt it."

The next day, July 16, dozens of People's Liberation Army Type 05 amphibious armored vehicles stormed off the Chinese coast into the ocean. Though they look like tanks, these vehicles are equally capable of driving on beaches as they are of speeding through the water like small boats. They'd be instrumental in any PLA amphibious assault. After motoring into the ocean, dozens of these vehicles approached landing ships stationed offshore, driving from the water up onto the ships, where they prepared for "a long-distance sea-crossing," Chinese state media reported. The landing ships steamed toward their target. Upon arrival, wide doors in the ships' bows swung open and amphibious vehicles streamed off into the water, making their way to the beach and firing their guns as they went.

This time, it was just an exercise. Over the next few days, the PLA launched other drills near the north and south entrances to the Taiwan Strait. "We must train hard under scenarios just like those in real battles, be combat-ready at all times and resolutely safeguard national sovereignty and territorial integrity," China's *Global Times* newspaper quoted one battalion commander as saying. The newspaper pointedly noted that the exercises took place only three hundred kilometers from Pratas Island, a tiny atoll equidistant between Hong Kong and Taiwan and administered by the latter.

There are many ways a war over Taiwan could begin, but some defense planners think a ramped-up dispute over isolated Pratas Island is the most likely. One recent war game organized by American defense experts envisioned Chinese troops landing on the island and seizing the small Taiwanese garrison there without firing a shot. Taiwan and the U.S. would face the difficult choice of starting a war over an irrelevant atoll or establishing a precedent that China can slice off chunks of Taiwanese territory like pieces of soft salami. "Moderate" responses would include stationing large numbers of U.S. troops in Taiwan or launching cyberattacks on China, both of which could easily escalate into a full-blown conflict.

The Pentagon's public reports on Chinese military power have identified multiple ways China could use force against Taiwan. The most straightforward—but most unlikely—is a D-Day style invasion, with hundreds of Chinese ships steaming across the Strait and landing thousands of PLA infantrymen on shore. The history of amphibious invasions is littered with disasters, however, and the Pentagon judges that such an operation would "strain" the PLA's capabilities. China would have little difficulty in knocking out Taiwan's airfields and naval facilities as well as electricity and other critical infrastructure before any assault, but even still, it would be a tough fight.

Other options would be easier for the PLA to implement, in the Pentagon's judgment. A partial air and maritime blockade would be impossible for Taiwan to defeat on its own. Even if the U.S. and Japanese militaries joined Taiwan to try and break the blockade, it would be difficult to do. China has powerful weapons systems arrayed along its shores. A blockade wouldn't need to be perfectly effective to strangle the island's trade. Ending a blockade would require Taiwan and its friends—mainly, the U.S.—to disable hundreds of Chinese military systems sitting on Chinese territory. A blockade-busting operation could easily spiral into a bloody great power war.

Even without a blockade, a Chinese air and missile campaign alone could defang Taiwan's military and shut down the country's economy without placing a single pair of Chinese boots on the ground. In a couple days, absent immediate U.S. and Japanese aid, Chinese air and missile forces could probably disarm key Taiwanese military assets—airfields, radar facilities, communications hubs, and the like—without severely impacting the island's productive capacity.

TSMC's chairman is certainly right that no one wants to "disrupt" the semiconductor supply chains that crisscross the Taiwan Strait. But both Washington and Beijing would like more control over them. The idea that China would simply destroy TSMC's fabs out of spite doesn't make sense, because China would suffer as much as anyone, especially since the U.S. and its friends would still have access to Intel's and Samsung's chip fabs. Nor has it ever been realistic that Chinese forces could invade and straightforwardly seize TSMC's facilities. They'd soon discover that crucial materials and software updates for irreplaceable tools must be acquired from the U.S., Japan, and other countries. Moreover, if China were to invade, it's unlikely to capture all TSMC employees. If China did, it would only take a handful of angry engineers to sabotage the entire operation. The PLA's proven it can seize Himalayan peaks from India on the two countries' disputed border, but grabbing the world's most complex factories, full of explosive gases, dangerous chemicals, and the world's most precise machinery—that's a different matter entirely.

However, it's easy to imagine a way that an accident, like a collision in air or at sea, could spiral into a disastrous war that neither side wants. It's also perfectly reasonable to think China might conclude that military pressure without a full-scale invasion could decisively undermine America's implicit security guarantee and fatally demoralize Taiwan. Beijing knows that Taiwan's defense strategy is to fight long enough for the U.S. and Japan to arrive and help. The island is so small relative to the cross-strait superpower that there's no realistic option besides counting on friends. Imagine if Beijing were to use its navy to impose customs checks on a fraction of the ships sailing in and out of Taipei. How would the U.S. respond? A blockade is an act of war, but no one would want to shoot first. If the U.S. did nothing, the impact on Taiwan's will to fight could be devastating. If China then demanded that TSMC restart chip fabrication for Huawei and other Chinese companies, or even to transfer critical personnel and know-how to the mainland, would Taiwan be able to say no?

Such a series of moves would be risky for Beijing, but they wouldn't be unthinkable. China's ruling party has no higher goal than asserting control over Taiwan. Its leaders constantly promise to do so. The government has passed an "Anti-Secession Law" envisioning the potential use of what it calls "non-peaceful means" in the Taiwan Strait.

It's invested heavily in the type of military systems, like amphibious assault vehicles, needed for a cross-strait invasion. It exercises these capabilities regularly. Analysts uniformly agree that the military balance in the Strait has shifted decisively in China's direction. Long gone are the days, as during the 1996 Taiwan Strait crisis, that the U.S. could simply sail an entire aircraft carrier battlegroup through the Strait to force Beijing to stand down. Now such an operation would be fraught with risk for the U.S. warships. Today Chinese missiles threaten not only U.S. ships around Taiwan but also bases as far away as Guam and Japan. The stronger the PLA gets, the less likely the U.S. is to risk war to defend Taiwan. If China were to try a campaign of limited military pressure on Taiwan, it's more likely than ever that the U.S. might look at the correlation of forces and conclude that pushing back isn't worth the risk.

If China were to succeed in pressuring Taiwan into giving Beijing equal access—or even preferential access—to TSMC's fabs, the U.S. and Japan would surely respond by placing new limits on the export of advanced machinery and materials, which largely come from these two countries and their European allies. But it would take years to replicate Taiwan's chipmaking capacity in other countries, and in the meantime we'd still depend on Taiwan. If so, we'd find ourselves not only reliant on China to assemble our iPhones. Beijing could conceivably gain influence or control over the only fabs with the technological capability and production capacity to churn out the chips we depend on.

Such a scenario would be disastrous for America's economic and geopolitical position. It would be even worse if a war knocked out TSMC's fabs. The world economy and the supply chains that crisscross Asia and the Taiwan Strait are predicated on this precarious peace. Every company that's invested on either side of the Taiwan Strait, from Apple to Huawei to TSMC, is implicitly betting on peace. Trillions of dollars are invested in firms and facilities within easy missile shot of the Taiwan Strait, from Hong Kong to Hsinchu. The world's chip industry, as well as the assembly of all the electronic goods chips enable, depends more on the Taiwan Strait and the South China coast than on any other chunk of the world's territory except Silicon Valley.

Business as usual is not nearly as fraught in California's tech epicenter. Much of Silicon Valley's knowledge could be easily relocated in case of war or earthquake. This was tested during the pandemic, when almost all the region's workers were told to sit at home. Big tech firms' profits even went up. If Facebook's fancy headquarters were to sink into the San Andreas Fault, the company might barely notice.

If TSMC's fabs were to slip into the Chelungpu Fault, whose movement caused Taiwan's last big earthquake in 1999, the reverberations would shake the global economy. It would only take a handful of explosions, deliberate or accidental, to cause comparable damage. Some back-of-the-envelope calculations illustrate what's at stake. Taiwan produces 11 percent of the world's memory chips. More important, it fabricates 37 percent of the world's logic chips. Computers, phones, data centers, and most other electronic devices simply can't work without them, so if Taiwan's fabs were knocked offline, we'd produce 37 percent less computing power during the following year.

The impact on the world economy would be catastrophic. The post-COVID semiconductor shortage was a reminder that chips aren't only needed in phones and computers. Airplanes and autos, microwaves and manufacturing equipment—products of all types would face devastating delays. Around one-third of PC processor production, including chips designed by Apple and AMD, would be knocked offline until new fabs could be built elsewhere. Growth in data center capacity would slow dramatically, especially for servers focused on AI algorithms, which are more reliant on Taiwan-manufactured chips from companies like Nvidia and AMD. Other data infrastructure would be hit harder. New 5G radio units, for example, require chips from several different firms, many of which are made in Taiwan. There'd be an almost complete halt to the rollout of 5G networks.

It would make sense to halt cell phone network upgrades because it would be extremely difficult to buy a new phone, too. Most smartphone processors are fabricated in Taiwan, as are many of the ten or more chips that go into a typical phone. Autos often need hundreds of chips to work, so we'd face delays far more severe than the shortages of 2021. Of course, if a war broke out, we'd need to think about a lot more than chips. China's vast electronics assembly infrastructure could be cut off. We'd have to find other people to screw together whatever phones and computers we had components for.

Yet it would be far easier to find new assembly workers—as difficult as that would be—than to replicate Taiwan's chipmaking facilities. The challenge wouldn't simply be building new fabs. Those facilities would need trained personnel, unless somehow many TSMC staff could be exfiltrated from Taiwan. Even still, new fabs must be stocked with machinery, like tools from ASML and Applied Materials. During the 2021–2022 chip shortage, ASML and Applied Materials both announced they were facing delays in producing machinery because they couldn't acquire enough semiconductors. In case of a Taiwan crisis, they'd face delays in acquiring the chips their machinery requires.

After a disaster in Taiwan, in other words, the total costs would be measured in the trillions. Losing 37 percent of our production of computing power each year could well be more costly than the COVID pandemic and its economically disastrous lockdowns. It would take at least half a decade to rebuild the lost chipmaking capacity. These days, when we look five years out we hope to be building 5G networks and metaverses, but if Taiwan were taken offline we might find ourselves struggling to acquire dishwashers.

Taiwan's president Tsai Ing-wen recently argued in *Foreign Affairs* that the island's chip industry is a "'silicon shield' that allows Taiwan to protect itself and others from aggressive attempts by authoritarian regimes to disrupt global supply chains." That's a highly optimistic way of looking at the situation. The island's chip industry certainly forces the U.S. to take Taiwan's defense more seriously. However, the concentration of semiconductor production in Taiwan also puts the world economy at risk if the "silicon shield" doesn't deter China.

In a 2021 poll, most Taiwanese reported thinking that a war between China and Taiwan was either unlikely (45 percent) or impossible (17 percent). The Russian invasion of Ukraine, however, is a reminder that just because the Taiwan Strait has been mostly peaceful for the past few decades, a war of conquest is far from unthinkable. The Russia-Ukraine War also illustrates the extent to which any large conflict will be determined in part by a country's position in the semiconductor supply chain, which will shape its ability to wield military and economic power.

Russia's chip industry, which lagged behind Silicon Valley since the days of Soviet minister Shokin and the founding of Zelenograd, had decayed since the Cold War ended, as most Russian customers chose to stop buying from domestic chipmakers and outsourced production to TSMC. The only remaining customers were Russia's defense and space industries, which were not big enough buyers of chips to fund advanced chipmaking at home. As a result, even high priority defense projects in Russia struggled to acquire the chips they needed. Russia's equivalent of GPS satellites, for example, have faced wrenching delays due to problems sourcing semiconductors.

Russia's ongoing difficulties with fabricating and acquiring chips explains why the country's drones shot down over Ukraine are full of foreign microelectronics. It also explains why Russia's military continues to rely extensively on non-precision-guided munitions. A recent analysis of Russia's war in Syria found that up to 95 percent of munitions dropped were unguided. The fact that Russia faced shortages of guided cruise missiles within several weeks of attacking Ukraine is also partly due to the sorry state of its semiconductor industry. Meanwhile, Ukraine has received huge stockpiles of guided munitions from the West, such as Javelin anti-tank missiles that rely on over 200 semiconductors each as they home in on enemy tanks.

Russia's dependence on foreign semiconductor technology has given the United States and its allies a powerful point of leverage. After Russia invaded, the U.S. rolled out sweeping restrictions on the sale of certain types of chips across Russia's tech, defense, and telecoms sectors, which was coordinated with partners in Europe, Japan, South Korea, and Taiwan. Key chipmakers from America's Intel to Taiwan's TSMC have now cut off the Kremlin. Russia's manufacturing sector has faced wrenching disruptions, with a substantial portion of Russian auto production knocked offline. Even in sensitive sectors like defense, Russian factories are taking evasive maneuvers such as deploying chips intended for dishwashers into missile systems, according to U.S. intelligence. Russia has little recourse other than to cut its consumption of chips, because its chipmaking capabilities today are even weaker than during the heyday of the space race.

The emerging Cold War between the U.S. and China, however, will be a less lopsided match when it comes to semiconductors, given Beijing's investment in the industry and given that much of the chipmaking capacity America relies on is within easy range of PLA missiles. It would be naïve to assume that what happened in Ukraine couldn't happen in East Asia. Looking at the role of semiconductors in the Russia-Ukraine War, Chinese government analysts have publicly argued that if tensions between the U.S. and China intensify, "we must seize TSMC."

Cold War I had its own standoffs over Taiwan, in 1954 and again in 1958, after Mao Zedong's military barraged Taiwanese-held islands with artillery. Today Taiwan is within range of far more destructive Chinese forces—not only an array of short- and medium-range missiles but also aircraft from the Longtian and Huian airbases on the Chinese side of the Strait, from which it's only a seven-minute flight to Taiwan. Not coincidentally, in 2021, these airbases were upgraded with new bunkers, runway extensions, and missile defenses. A new Taiwan Strait crisis would be far more dangerous than the crises of the 1950s. There'd still be the risk of nuclear war, especially given China's growing atomic arsenal. But rather than a standoff over an impoverished island, this time the battleground would be the beating heart of the digital world. What's worse is that unlike in the 1950s, it's not clear the People's Liberation Army would eventually back down. This time, Beijing might wager that it could well win.

Conclusion

I t was only five days after People's Liberation Army forces began shelling the Taiwanese-held Quemoy Island in 1958 that, amid the sweltering Dallas summer, Jack Kilby demonstrated to his colleagues that all the components of a circuit—transistors, resistors, and capacitors—could be made from semiconductor materials. Four days after that, Jay Lathrop pulled into the Texas Instruments parking lot for the first time. He'd already filed for a patent on the process of making transistors via photolithography but had yet to receive the Army prize that enabled him to buy a new station wagon. Several months earlier, Morris Chang had left his job at a Massachusetts electronics firm and moved to Texas Instruments, earning a reputation for a nearly magical ability to eliminate errors from TI's semiconductor fabrication processes. That same year, Pat Haggerty was named president of Texas Instruments, with the board of directors betting that his vision of building electronics for military systems was a better business than producing the oil exploration instruments that the company had been founded to create. Haggerty had already assembled a talented team of engineers like Weldon Word, who were building the electronics needed for "smart" weapons and accurate sensors.

Texas was on the opposite side of the world from Taiwan, but it wasn't a coincidence that Kilby invented his integrated circuit amid a

U.S.-China crisis. Defense dollars were flowing into electronics firms. The U.S. military was relying on technology to preserve its edge. With Soviet Russia and Communist China building industrial-scale militaries, the U.S. couldn't count on fielding bigger armies or more tanks. It *could* build more transistors, more precise sensors, and more effective communications equipment, all of which would eventually make American weapons far more capable.

Nor was it a coincidence that Morris Chang was seeking work in Texas rather than, say, Tianjin. For an ambitious child of an upper-class family, staying in China risked harassment or even death. Amid Cold War chaos and the disruptions of decolonization that swept the world, the best and the brightest from many countries tried to make their way to the United States. John Bardeen and Walter Brattain invented the first transistor, but it was their Bell Labs colleagues Mohamed Atalla and Dawon Kahng who devised a transistor structure that could be mass-produced. Two of the "traitorous eight" engineers who founded Fairchild Semiconductor with Bob Noyce were born outside the United States. A few years later, a sharp-elbowed Hungarian émigré formerly known as Andras Grof helped Fairchild optimize the use of chemicals in the company's chipmaking processes and set himself on a path to becoming CEO.

At a time when most of the world had never heard of silicon chips, and still fewer understood anything about how they worked, America's centers of semiconductor production were drawing the world's most brilliant minds to Texas, Massachusetts, and above all to California. These engineers and physicists were driven by the belief that miniaturizing transistors could quite literally change the future. They were proven right far beyond their wildest dreams. Visionaries like Gordon Moore and Caltech professor Carver Mead saw decades ahead, but Moore's prediction from 1965 of "home computers" and "personal portable communications equipment" barely begins to describe the centrality of chips in our lives today. The idea that the semiconductor industry would eventually produce more transistors each day than there are cells in the human body was something the founders of Silicon Valley would have found inconceivable.

As the industry's scaled up, and transistors have scaled down, the need for vast, global markets is more important than ever. Today, even the Pentagon's $700 billion budget isn't big enough to afford facilities for building cutting-edge chips for defense purposes on U.S. soil. The Defense Department has dedicated shipyards for billion-dollar submarines and ten-billion-dollar aircraft carriers, but it buys many of the chips it uses from commercial suppliers, often in Taiwan. Even the cost of *designing* a leading-edge chip, which can exceed $100 million, is getting too expensive for the Pentagon. A facility to fabricate the most advanced logic chips costs twice as much as an aircraft carrier but will only be cutting-edge for a couple of years.

The staggering complexity of producing computing power shows that Silicon Valley isn't simply a story of science or engineering. Technology only advances when it finds a market. The history of the semiconductor is also a story of sales, marketing, supply chain management, and cost reduction. Silicon Valley wouldn't exist without the entrepreneurs who built it. Bob Noyce was an MIT-trained physicist, but he made his mark as a businessman, perceiving a vast market for a product that didn't yet exist. Fairchild Semiconductor's ability to "cram more components onto integrated circuits"—as Gordon Moore put it in his famous 1965 article—depended not only on the company's physicists and chemists, but also on hard-driving manufacturing bosses like Charlie Sporck. Pursuing union-free fabs and offering stock options to most employees drove productivity relentlessly higher. Transistors today cost far less than a millionth of their 1958 price thanks to the spirit expressed by the now-forgotten Fairchild employee who wrote on his exit survey when leaving the company: "I . . . WANT . . . TO . . . GET . . . RICH."

On reflection, it's too simple to say that the chip made the modern world, because our society and our politics have structured how chips were researched, designed, produced, assembled, and used. For example, DARPA, the Pentagon's R&D unit, has literally shaped the

semiconductor by funding crucial research into the 3D transistor structures, called FinFETs, used in the most advanced logic chips. And
in the future China's deluge of subsidies will profoundly reshape the
semiconductor supply chain, whether China achieves its goal of semiconductor supremacy or not.

There's no guarantee, of course, that chips will remain as important
as they've been in the past. Our demand for computing power is unlikely
ever to diminish, but we *could* run out of supply. Gordon Moore's famous
law is only a prediction, not a fact of physics. Industry luminaries from
Nvidia CEO Jensen Huang to former Stanford president and Alphabet
chairman John Hennessy have declared Moore's Law dead. At some
point, the laws of physics will make it impossible to shrink transistors
further. Even before then, it could become too costly to manufacture
them. The rate of cost declines has already significantly slowed. The
tools needed to make ever-smaller chips are staggeringly expensive,
none more so than the EUV lithography machines that cost more than
$100 million each.

The end of Moore's Law would be devastating for the semiconductor
industry—and for the world. We produce more transistors each year
only because it's economically viable to do so. This isn't the first time,
though, that Moore's Law has been declared near dead. In 1988, Erich
Bloch, an esteemed expert at IBM and later head of the National Science Foundation, declared that Moore's Law would stop working when
transistors shrank to a quarter of a micron—a barrier that the industry
bashed through a decade later. Gordon Moore worried in a 2003 presentation that "business as usual will certainly bump up against barriers
in the next decade or so," but all these potential barriers were overcome.
At the time, Moore thought a 3D transistor structure was a "radical
idea," but less than two decades later, we've already produced trillions of
these 3D FinFET transistors. Carver Mead, the Caltech professor who
coined the phrase "Moore's Law," shocked the world's semiconductor
scientists with his prediction half a century ago that chips might eventually contain 100 million transistors per square centimeter. Today, the

most advanced fabs can squeeze a hundred times as many transistors on a chip than even Mead thought possible.

The durability of Moore's Law, in other words, has surprised even the person who it's named after and the person who coined it. It may well surprise today's pessimists, too. Jim Keller, the star semiconductor designer who's widely credited for transformative work on chips at Apple, Tesla, AMD, and Intel, has said he sees a clear path toward a fifty times increase in the density with which transistors can be packed on chips. First, he argues, existing fin-shaped transistors can be printed thinner to allow three times as many to be packed together. Next, fin-shaped transistors will be replaced by new tube-shaped transistors, often called "gate-all-around." These are wire-shaped tubes that let an electric field be applied from all directions—top, sides, and bottom—providing better control of the "switch" to cope with challenges as transistors shrink. These tiny wires will double the density at which transistors can be packed, Keller argues. Stacking these wires on top of each other can increase density eight times further, he predicts. This adds up to a roughly fifty times increase in the number of transistors that can fit on a chip. "We're not running out of atoms," Keller has said. "We know how to print single layers of atoms."

For all the talk of Moore's Law ending, there's more money than ever before flowing into the chip industry. Startups designing chips optimized for AI algorithms have raised billions of dollars in the past few years, each hoping that they can become the next Nvidia. Big tech firms—Google, Amazon, Microsoft, Apple, Facebook, Alibaba, and others—are now pouring money into designing their own chips. There's clearly no deficit of innovation.

The best argument in favor of the thesis that Moore's Law is ending is that all this new activity in chips for specific purposes, or even for individual companies, is displacing the improvements in "general-purpose" computing that Intel's regular cadence of ever-more-powerful microprocessors provided for the past half century. Neil Thompson and Svenja Spanuth, two researchers, have gone so far as to argue that we're seeing a "decline of computers as a general purpose technology." They think the future of computing will be divided between "'fast lane' applications that get powerful customized chips and 'slow lane' applications that get stuck using general-purpose chips whose progress fades."

It's undeniable that the microprocessor, the workhorse of modern computing, is being partially displaced by chips made for specific purposes. What's less clear is whether this is a problem. Nvidia's GPUs are not general purpose like an Intel microprocessor, in the sense that they're designed specifically for graphics and, increasingly, AI. However, Nvidia and other companies offering chips that are optimized for AI have made artificial intelligence far cheaper to implement, and therefore more widely accessible. AI has become a lot more "general purpose" today than was conceivable a decade ago, largely thanks to new, more powerful chips.

The recent trend of big tech firms like Amazon and Google designing their own chips marks another change from recent decades. Both Amazon and Google entered the chip design business to improve the efficiency of the servers that run their publicly available clouds. Anyone can access Google's TPU chips on Google's cloud for a fee. The pessimistic view is to see this as a bifurcation of computing into a "slow lane" and a "fast lane." What's surprising though, is how easy it is for almost anyone to access the fast lane by buying an Nvidia chip or by renting access to an AI-optimized cloud.

Moreover, it's easier than ever before to combine different types of chips. In the past, a device would often have a single processor chip. Now it might have multiple processors, some focused on general operations, with others optimized to manage specific features like a camera. This is possible because new packaging technologies make it easier to connect chips efficiently, letting companies easily swap certain chips in or out of a device as processing requirements or cost considerations change. Big chipmakers are now putting more thought than ever before into the systems in which their chips will operate. So the important question isn't whether we're finally reaching the limits of Moore's Law as Gordon Moore initially defined it—exponential increase in the number of transistors per chip—but whether we've reached a peak in the amount of computing power a chip can cost-effectively produce. Many thousands of engineers and many billions of dollars are betting not.

Back in December 1958—the same year that saw Morris Chang, Pat Haggerty, Weldon Word, Jay Lathrop, and Jack Kilby all assembled at Texas Instruments—an electronics conference took place in a wintry Washington, D.C. Attending that day were Chang, Gordon Moore, and Bob Noyce, who all went out for beers and then, in the day's waning hours, meandered back to their hotel, young and excited, singing amid the snowdrifts. No one they passed in the street would have guessed these were three future titans of technology. Yet they've left an enduring imprint not only on billions of silicon wafers but on all our lives. The chips they invented and the industry they built provide the hidden circuitry that's structured our history and will shape our future.

Acknowledgments

F abricating a cutting-edge chip involves hundreds of process steps and a supply chain that stretches across multiple countries. Writing this book was only slightly less complex than making a chip. I'm grateful to the many people, in many countries, who have helped along the way.

For making archival material available, especially amid the restrictions of the pandemic, I thank the librarians and archivists at the Library of Congress, Washington, D.C.; Southern Methodist University; Stanford University; the Hoover Institution; the Archive of the Russian Academy of Sciences; and Academica Sinica in Taiwan.

I am equally grateful for the opportunity to have conducted well over one hundred interviews with semiconductor experts from industry, academia, and government. Several dozen interview subjects asked not to be named in the book so that they could speak freely about their work. I would, however, like to publicly thank the following individuals for sharing insights or helping to arrange interviews: Bob Adams, Richard Anderson, Susie Armstrong, Jeff Arnold, David Attwood, Vivek Bakshi, Jon Bathgate, Peter Bealo, Doug Bettinger, Michael Bruck, Ralph Calvin, Gordon Campbell, Walter Cardwell, John Carruthers, Rick Cassidy, Anand Chandrasekher, Morris Chang, Shang-yi Chiang, Bryan Clark, Lynn Conway, Barry Couture, Andrea Cuomo, Aart de

Geus, Seth Davis, Anirudh Devgan, Steve Director, Greg Dunn, Mark Durcan, John East, Kenneth Flamm, Igor Fomenkov, Gene Frantz, Adi Fuchs, Mike Geselowitz, Lance Glasser, Jay Goldberg, Peter Gordon, John Gowdy, Doug Grouse, Chuck Gwyn, Rene Haas, Wesley Hallman, David Hanke, Bill Heye, Chris Hill, David Hodges, Sander Hofman, Tristan Holtam, Eric Hosler, Gene Irisari, Nina Kao, John Kibarian, Valery Kotkin, Michael Kramer, Lev Lapkis, Steve Leibiger, Chris Mack, Chris Malachowsky, Dave Markle, Christopher McGuire, Marshall McMurran, Carver Mead, Bruno Murari, Bob Nease, Daniel Nenni, Jim Neroda, Ron Norris, Ted Odell, Sergei Osokin, Ward Parkison, Jim Partridge, Malcolm Penn, William Perry, Pasquale Pistorio, Mary Anne Potter, Stacy Rasgon, Griff Resor, Wally Rhines, Dave Robertson, Steve Roemerman, Aldo Romano, Jeanne Roussel, Rob Rutenbar, Zain Saidin, Alberto Sangiovanni-Vincentelli, Robin Saxby, Brian Shirley, Peter Simone, Marko Slusarczuk, Randy Steck, Sergey Sudjin, Will Swope, John Taylor, Bill Tobey, Roger Van Art, Dick Van Atta, Gil Varnell, Michael von Borstel, Stephen Welby, Lloyd Whitman, Pat Windham, Alan Wolff, Stefan Wurm, Tony Yen, Ross Young, Victor Zhirnov, and Annie Zhou. None of them, of course, are responsible for any conclusions I've drawn.

Ajit Manocha, president and CEO of SEMI, provided a very helpful set of introductions. John Neuffer, Jimmy Goodrich, and Meghan Biery of the Semiconductor Industry Association helped me understand their perspective on the industry. Terry Daly, an industry veteran, was extraordinarily generous with his time, and I'm grateful for his guidance. Bob Loynd and Craig Keast at MIT's Lincoln Labs were kind enough to give me a tour of their microelectronics facility. I also benefitted from guidance through FinFETs, high-k materials, and many other details of the science underlying semiconductors by a technical reviewer in the industry who wishes to remain anonymous.

My thinking about the intersection of chips and politics was shaped by a fascinating series of conversations with Danny Crichton and Jordan Schneider. Jordan and Dong Yan read the manuscript and helped me sharpen its arguments. Kevin Xu and his indispensable newsletter provided some crucial anecdotes about Morris Chang that I otherwise would have missed. A set of conversations with Sahil Mahtani, Philip Saunders, and their team crystalized my thinking about China's chip challenges.

Portions of this research were presented at International Security Studies at Yale University. I'm grateful to Paul Kennedy and Arne Westad for the opportunity. I also benefitted greatly from the opportunity to present early stage research at the Naval War College and thank Rebecca Lissner for the invitation. In addition, the Hoover Institution's history workshop and the American Enterprise Institute provided forums for tough questions that honed my argument.

This book drew heavily on existing research and journalism about the origins of Silicon Valley and on the history of computing. I've learned much from the scholars and journalists who have previously examined different angles of this topic and whose work is cited in the notes. I am especially thankful to Leslie Berlin, Geoffrey Cain, Doug Fuller, Slava Gerovitch, Paul Gillespie, Philip Hanson, James Larson, David Laws, Wen-Yee Lee, Willy Shih, Denis Fred Simon, Paul Snell, David Stumpf, David Talbot, Zachary Wasserman, and Debby Wu for sharing their research and expertise with me. George Leopold has been a helpful guide to the contemporary chip and electronics industry. Jose Moura was generous with introductions to his colleagues at an early stage of this project. Murray Scott was a frequent source of ideas and encouragement.

I thank Danny Gottfried, Jacob Clemente, Gertie Robinson, Ben Cooper, Claus Soong, Wei-Ting Chen, Mindy Tu, Freddy Lin, Will Baumgartner, Soyoung Oh, Miina Matsuyama, Matyas Kisiday, Zoe Huang, Chihiro Aita, and Sara Ashbaugh for help collecting and translating sources. Ashley Theis has been enormously helpful across the board. Support from the Smith Richardson Foundation and the Sloan Foundation made this research possible.

My colleagues and students at the Fletcher School have provided a sounding board for many of the ideas in this book, in particular Dan

Drezner's 2019 workshop on "weaponized independence." At FPRI, Rollie Flynn, Maia Otarashvili, and Aaron Stein supported this research from its earliest stages. Kori Schake, Dany Pletka, and Hal Brands helped make the American Enterprise Institute an intellectual home as I put the finishing touches on the manuscript. My colleagues at Greenmantle have provided a stimulating environment for thinking about the intersection of technology, finance, macroeconomics, and politics. I'm grateful to Niall Ferguson for his early enthusiasm about this project; Pierpaolo Barbieri for a valuable set of introductions; Alice Han for helping me understand Chinese tech policy; and Stephanie Petrella for her incisive criticism in the project's initial stages.

Working with Rick Horgan and the entire Scribner team has been a pleasure. Without Toby Mundy's early confidence in this book, it wouldn't have gotten off the ground. Jon Hillman made an early introduction that set this project rolling.

Finally, and most important, my family has been invariably supportive throughout this project. My parents have been tough critics of each chapter. Lucy and Vlad have been the best babysitters anyone could ask for. Liya, Anton, and Evie have tolerated this book interrupting mornings, evenings, weekends, vacations, and parental leaves alike. I dedicate this book to them.

Notes

Introduction

xvii **On board the USS _Mustin_:** "USS Mustin Transits the Taiwan Strait," _Navy Press Releases_, August 19, 2020, https://www.navy.mil/Press-Office/Press-Releases /display-pressreleases/Article/2317449/uss-mustin-transits-the-taiwan -strait/#images-3; Sam LaGrone, "Destroyer USS Mustin Transits Taiwan Strait Following Operations with Japanese Warship," _USNI News_, August 18, 2020, https://news.usni.org/2020/08/18/destroyer-uss-mustin-transits-taiwan -strait-following-operations-with-japanese-warship.

xviii **"reunification-by-force":** "China Says Latest US Navy Sailing Near Taiwan 'Extremely Dangerous,'" _Straits Times_, August 20, 2020, https://www.straits times.com/asia/east-asia/china-says-latest-us-navy-sailing-near-taiwan-extremely -dangerous; Liu Xuanzun, "PLA Holds Concentrated Military Drills to Deter Taiwan Secessionists, US," _Global Times_, August 23, 2020, https://www.global times.cn/page/202008/1198593.shtml.

xix **chip choke:** This phrase was coined by Murray Scott, whose _Zen on Tech_ newsletter shaped my thinking about the geopolitics of semiconductors.

xx **a quarter of the chip industry's revenue:** Antonio Varas, Raj Varadarajan, Jimmy Goodrich, and Falan Yinug, "Strengthening the Global Semiconductor Supply Chain in an Uncertain Era," _Semiconductor Industry Association_, April 2021, exhibit 2, https://www.semiconductors.org/wp-content/uploads/2021/05/BCG -x-SIA-Strengthening-the-Global-Semiconductor-Value-Chain-April-2021_1 .pdf; Phones are 26 percent of semiconductor sales by dollar value.

xx **It buys most off-the-shelf:** "iPhone 12 and 12 Pro Teardown," _IFixit_, October 20, 2020, https://www.ifixit.com/Teardown/iPhone+12+and+12+Pro+ Teardown/137669.

xx **most expensive factory in human history:** "A Look Inside the Factory Around Which the Modern World Turns," _Economist_, December 21, 2019.

xxi   **sold over 100 million:** Angelique Chatman, "Apple iPhone 12 Has Reached 100 Million Sales, Analyst Says," CNET, June 30, 2021; Omar Sohail, "Apple A14 Bionic Gets Highlighted with 11.8 Billion Transistors," *WCCFTech*, September 15, 2020.

xxi   **wasn't 11.8 billion, but 4:** Isy Haas, Jay Last, Lionel Kattner, and Bob Norman moderated by David Laws, "Oral History of Panel on the Development and Promotion of Fairchild Micrologic Integrated Circuits," Computer History Museum, October 6, 2007, https://archive.computerhistory.org/resources/access/text/2013/05/102658200-05-01-acc.pdf; interview with David Laws, 2022.

xxi   **two cents per bit:** Gordon E. Moore, "Cramming More Components onto Integrated Circuits," *Electronics* 38, No. 8 (April 19, 1965), https://newsroom.intel.com/wp-content/uploads/sites/11/2018/05/moores-law-electronics.pdf; Intel 1103 data from "Memory Lane," *Nature Electronics* 1 (June 13, 2018), https://www.nature.com/articles/s41928-018-0098-9.

xxiii **a third of the new computing power we use each year:** Per Semiconductor Industry Association data, 37 percent of logic chips were produced in Taiwan in 2019; Varas et al., "Strengthening the Global Semiconductor Supply Chain in an Uncertain Era."

xxiii **almost all the world's most advanced processor chips:** Varas et al., "Strengthening the Global Semiconductor Supply Chain in an Uncertain Era," p. 35.

xxiv   **General Motors had to shut factories:** Mark Fulthorpe and Phil Amsrud, "Global Light Vehicle Production Impacts Now Expected Well into 2022," *IHS Market*, August 19, 2021, https://ihsmarkit.com/research-analysis/global-light-vehicle-production-impacts-now-expected-well-into.html.

xxv   **44 percent of the world's memory chips:** Varas et al., "Strengthening the Global Semiconductor Supply Chain in an Uncertain Era."

xxvi   **security clearance:** Interview with Morris Chang, 2022.

CHAPTER 1 From Steel to Silicon

3   **a studious young engineer:** Details on Morita's life are from Akio Morita, *Made in Japan: Akio Morita and Sony* (HarperCollins, 1987).

3   **Morris Chang's childhood:** Morris C. M. Chang, *The Autobiography of Morris C. M. Chang* (Commonwealth Publishing, 2018). Thanks to Mindy Tu for help with translation.

4   **Andy Grove lived through the same typhoon of steel:** Andrew Grove, *Swimming Across* (Warner Books, 2002), p. 52.

5   **ritual suicide:** John Nathan, *Sony: A Private Life* (Houghton Mifflin, 2001), p. 16.

5   **leisurely teenaged life:** Chang, *Autobiography of Morris C. M. Chang*.

5   **heat-seeking missiles:** Morita, *Made in Japan*, p. 1.

6   **human "computers":** David Alan Grier, *When Computers Were Human* (Princeton University Press, 2005), ch. 13; Mathematical Tables Project, *Table of Reciprocals of the Integers from 100,000 through 200,009* (Columbia University Press, 1943).

7 **within one thousand feet of their target:** Robert P. Patterson, *The United States Strategic Bombing Survey: Summary Report* (United States Department of War, 1945), p. 15, in *The United States Strategic Bombing Surveys* (Air University Press, 1987), https://www.airuniversity.af.edu/Portals/10/AUPress/Books/B_0020 _SPANGRUD_STRATEGIC_BOMBING_SURVEYS.pdf.

7 **"debugging":** T. R. Reid, *The Chip* (Random House, 2001), p. 11.

7 **eighteen thousand tubes:** Derek Cheung and Eric Brach, *Conquering the Electron: The Geniuses, Visionaries, Egomaniacs, and Scoundrels Who Built Our Electronic Age* (Roman & Littlefield, 2011), p. 173.

CHAPTER 2 The Switch

9 **William Shockley had long assumed:** Joel Shurkin, *Broken Genius: The Rise and Fall of William Shockley, Creator of the Electronic Age* (Macmillan, 2006) is the best account of Shockley. See also Michael Riordan and Lillian Hoddeson, *Crystal Fire: The Birth of the Information Age* (Norton, 1997).

9 **he could actually *see* electrons:** Gino Del Guercio and Ira Flatow, "Transistorized!" PBS, 1999, https://www.pbs.org/transistor/tv/script1.html.

10 **"solid state valve":** Riordan and Hoddeson, *Crystal Fire*, esp. pp. 112–114.

11 **surging across the germanium:** This account of the transistor draws heavily on Riordan and Hoddeson, *Crystal Fire*, and Cheung and Brach, *Conquering the Electron*.

11 **Shockley had designed a switch:** Cheung and Brach, *Conquering the Electron*, pp. 206–207.

12 **replace human brains:** Riordan and Hoddeson, *Crystal Fire*, p. 165; "SCIENCE 1948: Little Brain Cell," *Time*, 1948, http://content.time.com/time/subscriber /article/0,33009,952095,00.html.

CHAPTER 3 Noyce, Kilby, and the Integrated Circuit

13 **in the *Wall Street Journal*, too:** Cheung and Brach, *Conquering the Electron*, p. 228.

13 **$25,000:** Ibid., p. 214.

14 **Jack Kilby . . . spent:** Interview with Ralph Calvin, 2021; Jay W. Lathrop, an oral history conducted in 1996 by David Morton, IEEE History Center, Piscataway, NJ, USA.

14 **licensed the technology from AT&T:** Jack Kilby interview by Arthur L. Norberg, Charles Babbage Institute, June 21, 1984, pp. 11–19, https://conservancy.umn .edu/bitstream/handle/11299/r107410/oh074jk.pdf?sequence=1&isAllowed=y.

14 **track enemy submarines:** Caleb III Pirtle, *Engineering the World: Stories from the First 75 Years of Texas Instruments* (Southern Methodist University Press, 2005), p. 29.

15 **on the same piece of semiconductor material:** David Brock and David Laws, "The Early History of Microcircuitry," *IEEE Annals of the History of Computing* 34, No. 1 (January 2012), https://ieeexplore.ieee.org/document/6109206; T. R. Reid, *The Chip* (Random House, 2001).

15 **Fairchild Semiconductor:** Shurkin, *Broken Genius*, p. 173; "Gordon Moore," PBS, 1999, https://www.pbs.org/transistor/album1/moore/index.html; other important books on Fairchild include Arnold Thackray, David C. Brock, and Rachel Jones, *Moore's Law: The Life of Gordon Moore, Silicon Valley's Quiet Revolutionary* (Basic, 2015), and Leslie Berlin, *The Man Behind the Microchip: Robert Noyce and the Invention of Silicon Valley* (Oxford University Press, 2005).

16 **Noyce realized Hoerni's "planar method":** "1959: Practical Monolithic Integrated Circuit Concept Patented," Computer History Museum, https://www.computerhistory.org/siliconengine/practical-monolithic-integrated-circuit-concept-patented/; Christophe Lecuyer and David Brock, *Makers of the Microchip* (MIT Press, 2010); Robert N. Noyce, Semiconductor Device-and-Lead Structure, USA, 2981877, filed Jul 30, 1959 and issued Apr 25, 1961, https://patentimages.storage.googleapis.com/e1/73/1e/7404cd5ad6325c/US2981877.pdf; Michael Riordan, "The Silicon Dioxide Solution," *IEEE Spectrum*, December 1, 2007, https://spectrum.ieee.org/the-silicon-dioxide-solution; Berlin, *The Man Behind the Microchip*, pp. 53–81.

17 **fifty times as much to make:** Berlin, *The Man Behind the Microchip*, p. 112.

CHAPTER 4 Liftoff

19 **"Russ 'Moon' Circling Globe":** "Satellite Reported Seen over S.F.," *San Francisco Chronicle*, October 5, 1957, p. 1.

19 **the Soviet space program caused a crisis of confidence:** Robert Divine, *The Sputnik Challenge* (Oxford, 1993). My thinking on the impact of the Cold War on American science was shaped by Margaret O'Mara, *Cities of Knowledge: Cold War Science and the Search for the Next Silicon Valley* (Princeton University Press, 2015); Audra J. Wolfe, *Competing with the Soviets: Science, Technology, and the State in Cold War America* (Johns Hopkins University Press, 2013); and Steve Blank, "Secret History of Silicon Valley," Lecture at the Computer History Museum, November 20, 2008, https://www.youtube.com/watch?v=ZTC_RxWN_xo.

20 **consume more electricity:** Eldon C. Hall, *Journey to the Moon: The History of the Apollo Guidance Computer* (American Institute of Aeronautics, 1996), pp. xxi, 2; Paul Cerruzi, "The Other Side of Moore's Law: The Apollo Guidance Computer, the Integrated Circuit, and the Microelectronics Revolution, 1962–1975," in R. Lanius and H. McCurdy, *NASA Spaceflight* (Palgrave Macmillan, 2018).

20 **"see if they are real":** Hall, *Journey to the Moon*, p. 80.

20 **a computer using Noyce's integrated circuits:** Hall, *Journey to the Moon*, pp. xxi, 2, 4, 19, 80, 82; Tom Wolfe, "The Tinkerings of Robert Noyce," *Esquire*, December 1983.

21 **$21 million:** Robert N. Noyce, "Integrated Circuits in Military Equipment," *Institute of Electrical and Electronics Engineers Spectrum*, June 1964; Christophe Lecuyer, "Silicon for Industry: Component Design, Mass Production, and the Move to Commercial Markets at Fairchild Semiconductor, 1960–1967," *History and Technology* 16 (1999): 183; Michael Riordan, "The Silicon Dioxide

Solution," *IEEE Spectrum*, December 1, 2007, https://spectrum.ieee.org/the
-silicon-dioxide-solution.

22 **discounted to $15:** Hall, *Journey to the Moon*, p. 83.

22 **selling electronic systems to the military:** Charles Phipps, "The Early History
of ICs at Texas Instruments: A Personal View," *IEEE Annals of the History of
Computing* 34, No. 1 (January 2012): 37–47.

22 **every piece of electronics the U.S. military used:** Norman J. Asher and Leland
D. Strom, "The Role of the Department of Defense in the Development of Integrated Circuits," *Institute for Defense Analyses*, May 1, 1977, p. 54.

22 **"like a messiah":** Interview with Bill Heye, 2021; Interview with Morris Chang,
2022.

22 **Air Force began looking for a new computer:** Patrick E. Haggerty, "Strategies,
Tactics, and Research," *Research Management* 9, No. 3 (May 1966): 152–153.

22 **Mylar tape:** Marshall William McMurran, *Achieving Accuracy: A Legacy of
Computers and Missiles* (Xlibris US, 2008), p. 281.

22 **"There was really not much of a choice":** Interviews with Bob Nease, Marshall
McMurran, and Steve Roemerman, 2021; David K. Stumpf, *Minuteman: A Technical
History of the Missile That Defined American Nuclear Warfare* (University of Arkansas
Press, 2020), p. 214; Patrick E. Haggerty, "Strategies, Tactics, and Research," *Research
Management* 9, No. 3 (May 1966): 152–153; see also Bob Nease and D. C. Hendrick-
son, *A Brief History of Minuteman Guidance and Control* (Rockwell Autonetics
Defense Electronics, 1995); McMurran, *Achieving Accuracy*, ch. 12. I am grateful to
David Stumpf for sharing Nease and Henderson's paper with me.

22 **20 percent of all integrated circuits sold:** Asher and Strom, "The Role of the
Department of Defense in the Development of Integrated Circuits," p. 83; Hall,
Journey to the Moon, p. 19; "Minuteman Is Top Semiconductor User," *Aviation
Week & Space Technology*, July 26, 1965, p. 83.

CHAPTER 5 Mortars and Mass Production

23 **Jay Lathrop pulled into:** Correspondence with Jay Lathrop, 2021; Interview
with Walter Cardwell, 2021; Interview with John Gowdy, 2021; Jay Lathrop and
James R. Nall, Semiconductor Construction, USA, 2890395A, filed October
31, 1957, and issued June 9, 1959, https://patentimages.storage.googleapis.com
/e2/4d/4b/8d90caa48db31b/US2890395.pdf; Jay Lathrop, "The Diamond Ordi-
nance Fuze Laboratory's Photolithographic Approach to Microcircuits," *IEEE
Annals of the History of Computing* 35, No. 1 (2013): 48-55.

25 **Jack Kilby spent each Saturday pacing:** Correspondence with Jay Lathrop,
2021; Interview with Mary Anne Potter, 2021.

25 **Mary Anne Potter spent months:** Interview with Mary Anne Potter, 2021; Mary
Anne Potter, "Oral History," *Transistor Museum*, September 2001, http://www
.semiconductormuseum.com/Transistors/TexasInstruments/OralHistories/Potter
/Potter_Page2.htm.

25 **Morris Chang arrived at TI in 1958:** Chang, *Autobiography of Morris Chang*;
"Stanford Engineering Hero Lecture: Morris Chang in Conversation with President

John L. Hennessy," Stanford Online, YouTube Video, April 25, 2014, https://www.youtube.com/watch?v=wEh3ZgbvBrE.

26 **tossed out:** Oral History of Morris Chang, interviewed by Alan Patterson, Computer History Museum, August 24, 2007; Interview with Morris Chang, 2022.

27 **"If you hadn't ever been chewed out by Morris":** Interviews with Bill Heye and Gil Varnell, 2021.

27 **the yield on his production line:** Oral History of Morris Chang, interviewed by Alan Patterson, Computer History Museum, August 24, 2007.

27 **Executives from IBM:** Tekla S. Perry, "Morris Chang: Foundry Father," *Institute of Electrical and Electronics Engineers Spectrum*, April 19, 2011, https://spectrum.ieee.org/at-work/tech-careers/morris-chang-foundry-father.

27 **"Unless we could make it work":** David Laws, "A Company of Legend: The Legacy of Fairchild Semiconductor," *IEEE Annals of the History of Computing* 32, No. 1 (January 2010): 64.

27 **"It was love at first sight":** Charles E. Sporck and Richard Molay, *Spinoff: A Personal History of the Industry That Changed the World* (Saranac Lake Publishing, 2001), pp. 71–72; Christophe Lecuyer, "Silicon for Industry": 45.

CHAPTER 6 "I...WANT...TO...GET...RICH"

29 **torpedoes to telemetry:** Asher and Strom, "The Role of the Department of Defense in the Development of Integrated Circuits," p. 74.

29 **use "over 95% of the circuits":** Robert Noyce, "Integrated Circuits in Military Equipment," *IEEE Spectrum* (June 1964): 71.

29 **"not often career officers":** Thomas Heinrich, "Cold War Armory: Military Contracting in Silicon Valley," *Enterprise & Society* 3, No. 2 (June 2002): 269; Lecuyer, "Silicon for Industry": 186.

30 **a Zenith hearing aid:** Reid, *The Chip*, p. 151.

30 **"Venturing is venturing":** Dirk Hanson, *The New Alchemists: Silicon Valley and the Microelectronics Revolution* (Avon Books, 1983), p. 93.

30 **Lockheed was far ahead:** US Government Armed Services Technical Information Agency, *Survey of Microminiaturization of Electronic Equipment*, P. V. Horton and T. D. Smith, AD269 300, Arlington, VA: Air Force Ballistic Missile Division Air Research Development Command, United States Air Force, 1961, pp. 23, 37, 39, https://apps.dtic.mil/sti/citations/AD0269300.

31 **came to be known as Moore's Law:** Moore, "Cramming More Computers onto Integrated Circuits."

31 **"means good business":** Asher and Strom, "The Role of the Department of Defense in the Development of Integrated Circuits," p. 73; Herbert Kleiman, *The Integrated Circuit: A Case Study of Product Innovation in the Electronics Industry* (George Washington University Press, 1966), p. 57.

31 **Fairchild even sold products below manufacturing cost:** Lecuyer, "Silicon for Industry": esp. 189, 194, 222; Kleiman, *The Integrated Circuit*, p. 212; Ernest Braun and Stuart Macdonald, *Revolution in Miniature: The History and Impact of Semiconductor Electronics* (Cambridge University Press, 1982), p. 114.

32 **Fairchild chips served 80 percent:** Asher and Strom, "The Role of the Department of Defense in the Development of Integrated Circuits," p. 64; Berlin, *The Man Behind the Microchip*, p. 138; Lecuyer, "Silicon for Industry": 180, 188.

32 **Noyce's price cuts:** "Oral History of Charlie Sporck," Computer History Museum, YouTube Video, March 2, 2017, 1:11:48, https://www.youtube.com/watch?v=du MUvoKP-pk; Asher and Strom, "The Role of the Department of Defense in the Development of Integrated Circuits," p. 73; Berlin, *The Man Behind the Microchip*, p. 138.

32 **"creeping socialism":** Berlin, *The Man Behind the Microchip*, p. 120.

32 **"I . . . WANT . . . TO . . . GET . . . RICH":** Michael Malone, *The Intel Trinity* (Michael Collins, 2014), p. 31.

CHAPTER 7 Soviet Silicon Valley

35 **an unexpected visitor arrived in Palo Alto:** Y. Nosov, "*Tranzistor—Nashe Vse. K Istorii Velikogo Otkrytiya*," *Elektronika*, 2008, https://www.electronics.ru /journal/article/363; A. F. Trutko, IREX Papers, Library of Congress, Washington, D.C.; for "Crothers Memorial Hall," see the Stanford 1960 Yearbook.

36 **A CIA report in 1959 found:** CIA, "Production of Semiconductor Devices in the USSR," CIA/*RR*, November 1959, 59-44.

36 **For an ambitious young engineer like Yuri Osokin:** Interviews with Lev Lapkis, Valery Kotkin, Sergei Osokin, and Sergey Sudjin, 2021; on Soviet study of US publications: N. S. Simonov, *Nesostoyavshayasya Informatsionnaya Revolyutsiya* (Universitet Dmitriya Pozharskogo, 2013), pp. 206–207; "Automate the Boss' Office," *Business Week*, April 1956, p. 59; A. A. Vasenkov, "*Nekotorye Sobytiya iz Istorii Mikroelekroniki*," *Virtualnyi Kompyuternyi Muzei*, 2010, https:// computer-museum.ru/books/vasenkov/vasenkov_3-1.htm; B. Malashevich, "*Pervie Integralnie Skhemi*," *Virtualnyi Kompyuternyi Muzei*, 2008, https://www .computer-museum.ru/histekb/integral_1.htm.

37 **whenever Osokin put down his guitar:** Interviews with Lev Lapkis, Valery Kotkin, and Sergey Sudjin.

37 **"the size of a cigarette box":** A. A. Shokin, *Ocherki Istorii Rossiiskoi Elektroniki*, v. 6 (Tehnosfera, 2014), p. 520.

37 **Joel Barr was the son of:** In the Soviet Union, Sarant went by the name Philip Staros, while Barr was known as Joseph Berg; details of their work draws heavily from Steven T. Usdin, *Engineering Communism* (Yale University Press, 2005).

38 **Barr and Sarant had dreamt up their own version in a Moscow suburb:** Usdin, *Engineering Communism*, p. 175; Simonov, *Nesostoyavshayasya Informatsionnaya Revolyutsiya*, p. 212. There's some debate among Russian microelectronics experts about the scale of Barr and Sarant's impact. They didn't single-handedly create the Soviet computer industry, but they clearly played an important role.

38 **On May 4, 1962:** Usdin, *Engineering Communism*, pp. 203–209.

39 **"It is our future":** Shokin, *Ocherki Istorii Rossiiskoi Elektroniki*, v. 6, pp. 522–523, 531.

CHAPTER 8 "Copy It"

41 **"Copy it":** Simonov, *Nesostoyavshayasya Informatsionnaya Revolyutsiya*, p. 210; see also A. A. Vasenkov, *"Nekotorye Sobytiya iz Istorii Mikroelekroniki," Virtualnyi Kompyuternyi Muzei*, 2010, https://computer-museum.ru/books /vasenkov/vasenkov_3-1.htm; Boris Malin file, IREX Papers, Library of Congress, Washington, D.C; Shokin, *Ocherki Istorii Rossiiskoi Elektroniki* v. 6, p. 543.

41 **Soviet exchange students . . . reported learning little:** B. Malashevich, *"Pervie Integralnie Shemi," Virtualnyi Kompyuternyi Muzei*, 2008, https://www .computer-museum.ru/histekb/integral_1.htm; Simonov, *Nesostoyavshayasya Informatsionnaya Revolyutsiya*, p. 65; Oral History of Yury R. Nosov, interviewed by Rosemary Remackle, Computer History Museum, May 17, 2012, pp. 22–23.

42 **lagged in nearly every type of advanced manufacturing:** Ronald Amann et al., *The Technological Level of Soviet Industry* (Yale University Press, 1977).

43 **some chipmaking machinery using inches:** A. A. Vasenkov, *"Nekotorye Sobytiya iz Istorii Mikroelekroniki," Virtualnyi Kompyuternyi Muzei*, 2010, https:// computer-museum.ru/books/vasenkov/vasenkov_3-1.htm; B. V. Malin, *"Sozdanie Pervoi Otechestvennoi Mikroshemy," Virtualnyi Kompyuternyi Muzei*, 2000, https://www.computer-museum.ru/technlgy/su_chip.htm.

44 **unable to speak about his invention:** Interview with Sergei Osokin, 2021.

CHAPTER 9 The Transistor Salesman

45 **Ikeda behaved like a "transistor salesman":** This account of Ikeda's visit derives from Japanese sources translated by Miina Matsuyama; see Nick Kapur, *Japan at the Crossroads After Anpo* (Harvard University Press, 2018), p. 84; Shiota Ushio, *Tokyo Wa Moetaka* (Kodansha, 1988); Shintaro Ikeda, "The Ikeda Administration's Diplomacy Toward Europe and the 'Three-Pillar' Theory," *Hiroshima Journal of International Studies* 13 (2007); Kawamura Kazuhiko, *Recollections of Postwar Japan, S25* (History Study Group, 2020).

46 **"a strong Japan is a better risk":** Office of the Historian, U.S. Department of State, "National Security Council Report," in David W. Mabon, ed., *Foreign Relations of the United States, 1955–1957, Japan, Volume XXIII, Part 1* (United States Government Printing Office, 1991), https://history.state.gov/historicaldocuments /frus1955-57v23p1/d28; Office of the Historian, U.S. Department of State, "No. 588 Note by the Executive Secretary (Lay) to the National Security Council," in David W. Mabon and Harriet D. Schwar, eds., *Foreign Relations of the United States, 1952–1954, China and Japan, Volume XIV, Part 2* (United States Government Printing Office, 1985), https://history.state.gov/historicaldocuments /frus1952-54v14p2/d588.

46 **the U.S. government supported Japan's rebirth:** Office of the Historian, U.S. Department of State, "National Security Council Report."

46 **called him into his office with interesting news:** Bob Johnstone, *We Were Burning: Japanese Entrepreneurs and the Forging of the Electronic Age* (Basic

Books, 1999), p. 16; Makoto Kikuchi, an oral history conducted in 1994 by William Aspray, IEEE History Center, Piscataway, NJ, USA.

46 **"my heart would start to pound"**: Makoto Kikuchi, "How a Physicist Fell in Love with Silicon in the Early Years of Japanese R&D," in H. R. Huff, H. Tsuya, and U. Gosele, eds., *Silicon Materials Science and Technology*, v. 1 (The Electrochemical Society, Inc., 1998), p. 126; Makoto Kikuchi, an oral history conducted in 1994 by William Aspray, IEEE History Center, Piscataway, NJ, USA; Johnstone, *We Were Burning*, p. 15.

46 **"I've never seen so many flashbulbs"**: Vicki Daitch and Lillian Hoddeson, *True Genius: The Life and Science of John Bardeen: The Only Winner of Two Nobel Prizes in Physics* (Joseph Henry Press, 2002), pp. 173–174.

47 **It seemed "miraculous"**: Nathan, *Sony*, p. 13; Morita, *Made in Japan*, pp. 70–71.

47 *This country seems to have everything*: Morita, *Made in Japan*, p. 1.

48 **"inexcusably outrageous"**: Hyungsub Choi, "Manufacturing Knowledge in Transit: Technical Practice, Organizational Change, and the Rise of the Semiconductor Industry in the United States and Japan, 1948–1960," PhD dissertation, Johns Hopkins University, 2007, p. 113; Johnstone, *We Were Burning*, p. xv.

48 **"The public does not know what is possible"**: Simon Christopher Partner, "Manufacturing Desire: The Japanese Electrical Goods Industry in the 1950s," PhD dissertation, Columbia University, 1997, p. 296; Andrew Pollack, "Akio Morita, Co-Founder of Sony and Japanese Business Leader, Dies at 78," *New York Times*, October 4, 1999.

48 **Texas Instruments had tried to market transistor radios**: Pirtle, *Engineering the World*, pp. 73–74; Robert J. Simcoe, "The Revolution in Your Pocket," *American Heritage* 20, No. 2 (Fall 2004).

48 **handing over 4.5 percent**: John E. Tilton, *International Diffusion of Technology: The Case of Semiconductors* (Brookings Institution, 1971), pp. 57, 141, 148; "Leo Esaki Facts," The Nobel Foundation, https://www.nobelprize.org/prizes/physics/1973/esaki/facts/.

49 **TI "would have been the Sony of computer electronics"**: Johnstone, *We Were Burning*, ch. 1 and pp. 40–41.

49 **$60 billion**: Kenneth Flamm, "Internationalization in the Semiconductor Industry," in Joseph Grunwald and Kenneth Flamm, eds., *The Global Factory: Foreign Assembly in International Trade* (Brookings Institution, 1985), p. 70; Bundo Yamada, "Internationalization Strategies of Japanese Electronics Companies: Implications for Asian Newly Industrializing Economies (NIEs)," OECD Development Centre, October 1990, https://www.oecd.org/japan/33750058.pdf.

49 **appealed to the U.S. government for help**: Choi, *Manufacturing Knowledge in Transit*, pp. 191–192.

49 **"Japan is a keystone"**: "Marketing and Export: Status of Electronics Business," *Electronics*, May 27, 1960, p. 95.

50 **"A people with their history"**: Henry Kissinger, "Memorandum of Conversation, Washington, April 10, 1973, 11:13 a.m.–12:18 p.m.," in Bradley Lynn Coleman,

David Goldman, and David Nickles, eds., *Foreign Relations of the United States, 1969–1976, Volume E–12, Documents on East and Southeast Asia, 1973–1976* (Government Printing Office, 2010), https://history.state.gov/historicaldocuments/frus1969-76ve12/d293.

50 **"We will cover for you"**: Interview with Bill Heye, 2021; interview with Morris Chang, 2022; J. Fred Bucy, *Dodging Elephants: The Autobiography of J. Fred Bucy* (Dog Ear Publishing, 2014), pp. 92–93.

50 **ahead of schedule:** Johnstone, *We Were Burning*, p. 364.

CHAPTER 10 **"Transistor Girls"**

51 *Transistor Girls*: Paul Daniels, *The Transistor Girls* (Stag, 1964).

51 **Sporck was fixated on efficiency:** Eugene J. Flath interview by David C. Brock, Science History Institute, February 28, 2007.

52 *To hell with this*: Oral History of Charlie Sporck, Computer History Museum; Sporck and Molay, *Spinoff: A Personal History of the Industry That Changed the World.*

53 **maximizing their productivity:** Andrew Pollack, "In the Trenches of the Chip Wars, a Struggle for Survival," *New York Times*, July 2, 1989; Sporck and Molay, *Spinoff*, p. 63; Oral History of Charlie Sporck, Computer History Museum.

53 **staffed their assembly lines with women:** Glenna Matthew, *Silicon Valley, Women, and the California Dream: Gender, Class, and Opportunity in the Twentieth Century* (Stanford University Press, 2002), ch. 1–3.

53 **another step that at the time could only be done by hand:** Sporck and Molay, *Spinoff*, pp. 87–88.

54 **soon on a plane:** Sporck and Molay, *Spinoff*, pp. 91–93; William F. Finan, *Matching Japan in Quality: How the Leading U.S. Semiconductor Firms Caught Up with the Best in Japan* (MIT Japan Program, 1993), p. 61; Julius Blank interview by David C. Brock, Science History Institute, March 20, 2006, p. 10; Oral History of Julius Blank, interviewed by Craig Addison, Computer History Museum, January 25, 2008.

54 **"willing to tolerate monotonous work":** John Henderson, *The Globalisation of High Technology Production* (Routledge, 1989), p. 110; Sporck and Molay, *Spinoff*, p. 94; Harry Sello Oral History interview by Craig Addison, SEMI, April 2, 2004.

54 **prohibitively expensive in California:** Sporck and Molay, *Spinoff*, p. 95; Oral History of Charlie Sporck, Computer History Museum.

54 **only a dime:** William F. Finan, "The International Transfer of Semiconductor Technology Through U.S.-Based Firms," NBER Working Paper no. 118, December 1975, pp. 61–62.

54 **"pretty much outlawed":** Craig Addison, Oral History Interview with Clements E. Pausa, June 17, 2004.

55 **"We never had any union problems in the Orient":** Oral History of Charlie Sporck, Computer History Museum; see also the extensive discussion of unionization, wage negotiations, and International Labor Organization regulations in

Computer History Museum, "Fairchild Oral History Panel: Manufacturing and Support Services," October 5, 2007.

CHAPTER 11 Precision Strike

57 **halfway on the flight:** Interview with Bill Heye, 2021.

57 **eight hundred thousand tons:** Samuel J. Cox, "H-017-2: Rolling Thunder—A Short Overview," Naval History and Heritage Command, March 27, 2018, https://www.history.navy.mil/about-us/leadership/director/directors-corner/h-grams/h-gram-017/h-017-2.html#:~:text=These%20U.S.%20strikes%20dropped%20864%2C000,years%20of%20World%20War%20II.

58 **only four examples:** Barry Watts, *Six Decades of Guided Munitions and Battle Networks: Progress and Prospects* (Center for Strategic and Budgetary Assessments, 2007), p. 133.

58 **the rest simply missed:** US Government Naval Air Systems Command, "Report of the Air-to-Air Missile System Capability Review July–November 1968," AD-A955-143, Naval History and Heritage Command, April 23, 2021, https://www.history.navy.mil/research/histories/naval-aviation-history/ault-report.html; Watts, *Six Decades of Guided Munitions*, p. 140.

58 **within 420 feet of their target:** James E. Hickey, *Precision-Guided Munitions and Human Suffering in War* (Routledge, 2016), p. 98.

58 **TI already produced the necessary components:** Interview with Steve Roemerman, 2021; Paul G. Gillespie, "Precision Guided Munitions: Constructing a Bomb More Potent Than the A-Bomb," PhD dissertation, Lehigh University, 2002.

59 **"cheap and familiar":** Interview with Steve Roemerman, 2021.

59 **priced like an inexpensive family sedan:** Interview with Steve Roemerman, 2021.

60 **Could Texas Instruments do anything to help?:** "Obituary of Colonel Joseph Davis Jr.," *Northwest Florida Daily News*, August 24–26, 2014; Gillespie, "Precision Guided Munitions," pp. 117–118; Walter J. Boyne, "Breaking the Dragon's Jaw," *Air Force Magazine*, August 2011, pp. 58–60, https://www.airforcemag.com/PDF/MagazineArchive/Documents/2011/August%202011/0811jaw.pdf; Vernon Loeb, "Bursts of Brilliance," *Washington Post*, December 15, 2002.

60 **Word started with a standard-issue bomb:** Gillespie, "Precision Guided Munitions," p. 116.

60 **a tool of precision destruction:** Ibid., pp. 125, 172.

60 **"automated fire control":** William Beecher, "Automated Warfare Is Foreseen by Westmoreland After Vietnam," *New York Times*, October 14, 1969. Defense theorists, however, had already realized that precision munitions would transform warfare; see James F. Digby, *Precision-Guided Munitions: Capabilities and Consequences*, RAND Paper P-5257, June 1974, and *The Technology of Precision Guidance: Changing Weapon Priorities, New Risks, New Opportunities*, RAND Paper P-5537, November 1975.

CHAPTER 12 Supply Chain Statecraft

63 **"bars and dancing girls":** "Taiwan's Development of Semiconductors Was Not Smooth Sailing," tr. Claus Soong, *Storm Media*, June 5, 2019, https://www.storm.mg/article/1358975?mode=whole.000.

63 **son of a Dallas police officer:** "Mark Shepherd Jr. Obituary," *Dallas Morning News*, February 6–8, 2009; Ashlee Vance, "Mark Shepherd, a Force in Electronics, Dies at 86," *New York Times*, February 9, 2009.

63 **"bully less-advanced countries":** "Taiwan's Development of Semiconductors was not Smooth Sailing"; Interview with Morris Chang, 2022.

64 **the U.S. cut economic aid:** David W. Chang, "U.S. Aid and Economic Progress in Taiwan," *Asian Survey* 5, No. 3 (March 1965): 156; Nick Cullather, "'Fuel for the Good Dragon': The United States and Industrial Policy in Taiwan, 1950–1960," *Diplomatic History* 20, No. 1 (Winter 1996): 1.

64 **officials like K. T. Li:** Wolfgang Saxon, "Li Kwoh-ting, 91, of Taiwan Dies; Led Effort to Transform Economy," *New York Times*, June 2, 2001.

65 **Two of Chang's PhD classmates:** "Taiwan's Development of Semiconductors was not Smooth Sailing."

65 **shipped its billionth unit:** L. Sophia Wang, *K.T. LI and the Taiwan Experience* (National Tsing Hua University Press, 2006), p. 216; "TI Taiwan Chronology," in *Far East Briefing Book*, Texas Instruments Papers, Southern Methodist University Library, October 18, 1989.

65 **"sop up unemployment":** Henry Kissinger, "Memorandum of Conversation, Washington, April 10, 1973, 11:13 a.m.–12:18 p.m.," in Bradley Lynn Coleman, David Goldman, and David Nickles, eds., *Foreign Relations of the United States, 1969–1976, Volume E–12, Documents on East and Southeast Asia, 1973–1976* (Government Printing Office, 2010), https://history.state.gov/historicaldocuments/frus1969-76ve12/d293; Linda Lim and Pang Eng Fong, *Trade, Employment and Industrialisation in Singapore* (International Labour Office, 1986), p. 156.

65 **employed tens of thousands of workers:** Joseph Grunwald and Kenneth Flamm, *The Global Factory: Foreign Assembly in International Trade* (Brookings Institution Press, 1994), p. 100.

66 **well-paid electronics assembly jobs:** Kenneth Flamm, "Internationalization in the Semiconductor Industry," in Grunwald and Flamm, *The Global Factory*, p. 110; Lim and Pang Eng Fong, *Trade, Employment and Industrialisation in Singapore*, p. 156; *Hong Kong Annual Digest of Statistics* (Census and Statistics Department, 1984), table 3.12, https://www.censtatd.gov.hk/en/data/stat_report/product/B1010003/att/B10100031984AN84E0100.pdf; G. T. Harris and Tai Shzee Yew, "Unemployment Trends in Peninsular Malaysia During the 1970s," *ASEAN Economic Bulletin* 2, No. 2 (November 1985): 118–132.

66 **"TI will stay and continue to grow in Taiwan":** *Meeting with Prime Minister Li, Taipei, September 23, 1977,* and *Reception/Buffett—Taipei. September 23, 1977. Mark Shepherd Remarks,* in Mark Shepherd Papers, Correspondence, Reports, Speeches, 1977, Southern Methodist University Library, folder 90-69; Associated

Press, "Mark Shepherd Jr.; led Texas Instruments," *Boston Globe*, February 9, 2009.

CHAPTER 13 Intel's Revolutionaries

67 **"Founders Leave Fairchild":** Marge Scandling, "2 of Founders Leave Fairchild; Form Own Electronics Firm," *Palo Alto Times*, August 2, 1968.

68 **magnetic cores couldn't keep up:** Lucien V. Auletta, Herbert J. Hallstead, and Denis J. Sullivan, "Ferrite Core Planes and Arrays: IBM's Manufacturing Evolution," *IEEE Transactions on Magnetics* 5, No. 4 (December 1969); John Markoff, "IBM's Robert H. Dennard and the Chip That Changed the World," IBM, November 7, 2019, https://www.ibm.com/blogs/think/2019/11/ibms-robert-h -dennard-and-the-chip-that-changed-the-world/.

69 **Hoff's background in computer architectures:** Emma Neiman, "A Look at Stanford Computer Science, Part I: Past and Present," *Stanford Daily*, April 15, 2015; "Interview with Marcian E. Hoff, Jr., 1995 March 03," Stanford Libraries, March 3, 1995, https://exhibits.stanford.edu/silicongenesis/catalog/jj158jn5943.

70 **no one was building memory chips more powerful than Intel's:** Robert N. Noyce and Marcian E. Hoff, "A History of Microprocessor Development at Intel," *IEEE Micro* 1, No. 1 (February 1981); Ted Hoff and Stan Mazor interview by David Laws, Computer History Museum, September 20, 2006; "Ted Hoff: The Birth of the Microprocessor and Beyond," *Stanford Engineering*, November 2006.

70 **set off a revolution in computing:** Sarah Fallon, "The Secret History of the First Microprocessor," *Wired*, December 23, 2020; Ken Shirriff, "The Surprising Story of the First Microprocessors," *IEEE Spectrum*, August 30, 2016.

70 **"This is going to change the world":** Berlin, *The Man Behind the Microchip*, p. 205; Gordon Moore, "On Microprocessors," *IEEE*, 1976; Ross Knox Bassett, *To the Digital Age* (Johns Hopkins University Press, 2002), p. 281; Malone, *The Intel Trinity*, pp. 177–178; Gene Bylinsky, "How Intel Won Its Bet on Memory Chips," *Fortune*, November 1973; Fallon, "The Secret History of the First Microprocessor."

70 **pulled out a sock:** Interview with Carver Mead, 2021.

71 **"coming out of our ears":** Carver Mead, "Computers That Put the Power Where It Belongs," *Engineering and Science* XXXVI, No. 4 (February 1972).

71 **"We are really the revolutionaries in the world today":** Gene Bylinsky, "How Intel Won Its Bet on Memory Chips."

CHAPTER 14 The Pentagon's Offset Strategy

74 **one of the country's top experts on military affairs:** William Perry interview by Russell Riley, University of Virginia's The Miller Center, February 21, 2006; William J. Perry, *My Journey at the Nuclear Brink* (Stanford Security Studies, 2015), ch. 1–2.

74 **bought chips from his singing partner:** Interview with William Perry, 2021; Zachary Wasserman, "Inventing Startup Capitalism," PhD dissertation, Yale University, 2015.

74 **machine tools factory:** Andrew Krepinevich and Barry Watts, *The Last Warrior: Andrew Marshall and the Shaping of Modern American Defense Strategy* (Basic Books, 2015), pp. 4, 9, 95.

75 **"substantial and durable lead" in computers:** A. W. Marshall, "Long-Term Competition with the Soviets: A Framework for Strategic Analysis," Rand Corporation, R-862-PR, April 1972, https://www.rand.org/pubs/reports/R862.html.

75 **$30 to $50 billion:** Testimony of William Perry, Senate Committee on Armed Services, Department of Defense, Authorization for Appropriations for FY 79, Part 8: Research and Development, 96th United States Congress, 1979, pp. 5506–5937; Kenneth P. Werrell, *The Evolution of the Cruise Missile* (Air University Press, 1985), p. 180.

76 **distinguish a whale from a submarine:** Richard H. Van Atta, Sidney Reed, and Seymour J. Deitchman, DARPA *Technical Accomplishments Volume II* (Institute for Defense Analyses, 1991), p. "12-2."

76 **New systems like the Tomahawk:** Werrell, *Evolution of the Cruise Missile*, p. 136.

76 **"Assault Breaker":** Van Atta et al., DARPA *Technical Accomplishments Volume II*, pp. 5–10.

77 **"'smart' weapons at all levels":** Interview with Steve Roemerman, 2021; William J. Perry interview by Alfred Goldberg, Office of the Secretary of Defense, January 9, 1981.

77 **"bells and whistles":** Fred Kaplan, "Cruise Missiles: Wonder Weapon or Dud?" *High Technology*, February 1983; James Fallows, *National Defense* (Random House, 1981), p. 55; William Perry, "Fallows' Fallacies: A Review Essay," *International Security* 6, No. 4 (Spring 1982): 179.

77 **"Luddites":** William Perry interview by Russell Riley, University of Virginia's The Miller Center, February 21, 2006.

CHAPTER 15 **"That Competition Is Tough"**

81 **"my life has been hell":** Interview with Richard Anderson, 2021; Michael Malone, *Bill and Dave: How Hewlett and Packard Built the World's Greatest Company* (Portfolio Hardcover, 2006); "Market Conditions and International Trade in Semiconductors," Field Hearing Before the Subcommittee on Trade of the Committee of Ways and Means, House of Representatives, 96th Congress, April 28, 1980.

82 **"click, click":** Michael Malone, *The Big Score* (Stripe Press, 2021), p. 248; Jorge Contreras, Laura Handley, and Terrence Yang, "Breaking New Ground in the Law of Copyright," *Harvard Law Journal of Technology* 3 (Spring 1990).

82 **ten times as bad:** Rosen Electronics Newsletter, March 31, 1980.

83 **"long tail":** Malone, *The Intel Trinity*, p. 284; Fred Warshofsky, *Chip War: The Battle for the World of Tomorrow* (Scribner, 1989), p. 101.

83 **five of the company's cutting-edge integrated circuits:** *TPS-L2: User Manual* (Sony Corporation, 1981), p. 24.

83 **385 million:** "Vol. 20: Walkman Finds Its Way into the Global Vocabulary," Sony, https://www.sony.com/en/SonyInfo/CorporateInfo/History/capsule/20/.

84 **"that competition is tough":** Oral History of Charlie Sporck, Computer History Museum.

CHAPTER 16 "At War with Japan"

85 **"I can't walk away from a fight":** Mark Simon, "Jerry Sanders/Silicon Valley's Tough Guy," *San Francisco Chronicle*, October 4, 2001; Thomas Skornia, *A Case Study in Realizing the American Dream: Sanders and Advanced Micro Devices: The First Fifteen Years, 1969–1984* (1984), https://archive.computerhistory.org /resources/access/text/2019/01/102721657-05-01-acc.pdf.

85 **"Knock 'em down, fight 'em, kill 'em":** Oral History of Charlie Sporck, Computer History Museum.

86 **"an economic war":** Michael S. Malone, "Tokyo, Calif," *New York Times*, November 1, 1981; Oral History of Charlie Sporck, Computer History Museum.

86 **Hitachi's employees were arrested:** Thomas C. Hayes, "American Posts Bail as Details of Operation by F.B.I. Unfold," *New York Times*, June 25, 1982.

87 **quieter submarines:** Wende A. Wrubel, "The Toshiba-Kongsberg Incident: Shortcomings of Cocom, and Recommendations for Increased Effectiveness of Export Controls to the East Bloc," *American University International Law Review* 4, No. 1 (2011).

87 **dirty dealing:** Stuart Auerbach, "CIA Says Toshiba Sold More to Soviet Bloc," *Washington Post*, March 15, 1988.

88 **low market share in Japan:** Michael E. Porter and Mariko Sakakibara, "Competition in Japan," *Journal of Economic Perspectives* 18, No. 1 (Winter 2004): 36; *The Effect of Government Targeting on World Semiconductor Competition* (Semiconductor Industry Association, 1983), pp. 69–74.

88 **half the budget:** Kiyonari Sakakibara, "From Imitation to Innovation: The Very Large Scale Integrated (VLSI) Semiconductor Project in Japan," Working Paper, MIT Sloan School of Management, October 1983, https://dspace.mit.edu /handle/1721.1/47985.

88 **"18 percent on a good day":** Reid, *The Chip*, p. 224.

88 **driven them to bankruptcy:** *The Effect of Government Targeting on World Semiconductor Competition*, p. 67.

89 **paid lower rates to borrow:** Jeffrey A. Frankel, "Japanese Finance in the 1980s: A Survey," National Bureau of Economic Research, 1991; data on household savings, household consumption, and bank lending as percent of GDP from data .worldbank.org.

89 **1.7 percent of the global DRAM market:** P. R. Morris, *A History of the World Semiconductor Industry* (Institute of Electrical Engineers, 1990), p. 104; Robert Burgelman and Andrew S. Grove, *Strategy Is Destiny: How Strategy-Making Shapes a Company's Future* (Free Press, 2002), p. 35.

89 **happy to foot the bill:** Scott Callan, "Japan, Disincorporated: Competition and Conflict, Success and Failure in Japanese High-Technology Consortia," PhD dissertation, Stanford University, 1993, p. 188, Table 7.14; Clair Brown and Greg Linden, *Chips and Change: How Crisis Reshapes the Semiconductor Industry* (MIT Press, 2009).

CHAPTER 17 "Shipping Junk"

91 **"hottest high-technology corporations":** Clayton Jones, "Computerized Laser Swiftly Carves Circuits for Microchips," *Christian Science Monitor*, March 10, 1981; David E. Sanger, "Big Worries Over Small GCA," *New York Times*, January 19, 1987.

91 **Bob Noyce driving up and down:** Berlin, *The Man Behind the Microchip*, pp. 94, 119. Thanks to Chris Mack for pointing me to this.

92 **Perkin Elmer's scanner:** Interview with Chris Mack, 2021; interview with Dave Markle, 2021; Perkin Elmer, "Micralign Projection Mask Alignment System," The Chip History Center, https://www.chiphistory.org/154-perkin-elmer-micralign -projection-mask-alignment-system; Daniel P. Burbank, "The Near Impossibility of Making a Microchip," *Invention and Technology* (Fall 1999); Alexis C. Madrigal, "TOP SECRET: Your Briefing on the CIA's Cold-War Spy Satellite, 'Big Bird,'" *Atlantic*, December 29, 2011; Chris Mack, "Milestones in Optical Lithography Tool Suppliers," http://www.lithoguru.com/scientist/litho_history /milestones_tools.pdf.

92 **photographs of the Soviet Union:** James E. Gallagher interview by Craig Addison, SEMI, March 9, 2005; Arthur W. Zafiropoulo interview by Craig Addison, SEMI, May 25, 2006; Geophysics Corporation of America, "About Our Corporation Members," *Bulletin American Meteorological Society*, December 12, 1962; Jones, "Computerized Laser Swiftly Carves Circuits for Microchips."

93 **Morris Chang walked up:** Interview with Griff Resor, 2021; "Griff Resor on Photolithography," Semi-History, YouTube video, January 30, 2009, 2:30, https:// www.youtube.com/watch?v=OKfdHZCEfmY.

93 **GCA introduced its first stepper:** "Griff Resor on Photolithography," Semi-History, YouTube video, January 30, 2009, 2:30, https://www.youtube.com /watch?v=OKfdHZCEfmY; Chris Mack, "Milestones in Optical Lithography Tool Suppliers," http://www.lithoguru.com/scientist/litho_history/milestones_tools .pdf; "GCA Burlington Division Shipment History of All 4800 DSW's as of September 1980," p. 1, in the possession of the author.

93 **stock price surged:** Sales data from Rebecca Marta Henderson, "The Failure of Established Firms in the Face of Technical Change," PhD dissertation, Harvard University, 1988, p. 217; Jones, "Computerized Laser Swiftly Carves Circuits for Microchips."

93 **"drunken sailor":** Interviews with Peter Bealo, Ross Young, and Bill Tobey, 2021; James E. Gallagher interview by Craig Addison, SEMI, March 9, 2005.

94 **"We had Milt":** Interviews with Bill Tobey, Jim Neroda, and Peter Bealo, 2021; Ross Young, *Silicon Sumo* (Semiconductor Services, 1994), p. 279; Charles N. Pieczulewski, "Benchmarking Semiconductor Lithography Equipment Development & Sourcing Practices Among Leading Edge Manufacturers," Master's thesis, MIT, 1995, p. 54.

94 **"customers got fed up":** Interviews with Griff Resor, Bill Tobey, Jim Neroda, and Peter Bealo, 2021; Young, *Silicon Sumo*, p. 279.

94 **thunderstorm rolling through:** Interview with Griff Resor, 2021.

95 **"paper entrepreneurialism":** Robert Reich, *The Next American Frontier* (Crown, 1983), p. 159.

95 **"arrogant" and "not responsive":** Interview with Gil Varnell, 2021; Rebecca Marta Henderson, "The Failure of Established Firms in the Face of Technical Change," p. 225; U.S. Department of Commerce, Bureau of Export Administration, Office of Strategic Industries and Economic Security, Strategic Analysis Division, *National Security Assessment of the U.S. Semiconductor Wafer Processing Industry Equipment* (1991), pp. 4–10.

95 **ten times that duration:** Henderson, "The Failure of Established Firms in the Face of Technical Change," pp. 220–222, 227; interview with former AMD executive, 2021.

96 **no plan to turn things around:** Interviews with Pete Bealo and Bill Tobey, 2021; Henderson, "The Failure of Established Firms in the Face of Technical Change," pp. 222–225; Jay Stowsky, "The Weakest Link: Semiconductor Production Equipment, Linkages, and the Limits to International Trade," working paper, University of California, Berkeley, September 1987, p. 2.

96 **Everyone could breathe a bit easier:** Arthur W. Zafiropoulo interview by Craig Addison, SEMI, May 25, 2006; interviews with Peter Bealo and Jim Neroda, 2021.

CHAPTER 18 The Crude Oil of the 1980s

97 **under a sloping, pagoda-style roof:** Skornia, *Sanders and Advanced Micro Devices*, p. 138; Daryl Savage, "Palo Alto: Ming's Restaurant to Close Dec. 28," Palo Alto Online, December 18, 2014, https://www.paloaltoonline.com/news/2014/12/18/mings-restaurant-to-close-dec-28.

97 **"crude oil of the 1980s":** Arthur L. Robinson, "Perilous Times for U.S. Microcircuit Makers," *Science* 208, No. 4444 (May 9, 1980): 582; Skornia, *Sanders and Advanced Micro Devices*, p. 140.

98 **"Saudi Arabia of semiconductors":** Marvin J. Wolf, *The Japanese Conspiracy: The Plot to Dominate Industry Worldwide* (New English Library, 1984), p. 83.

99 **"simply something we can't lose":** David E. Sanger, "Big Worries Over Small GCA," *New York Times*, January 19, 1987.

99 **"Silicon Valley cowboys":** Interview with Richard Van Atta, 2021.

100 **The Pentagon's task force:** Defense Science Board, *Report on Defense Semiconductor Dependency—February 1987*, pp. 1–2.

101 **"you're in nowheresville":** Oral History of Charlie Sporck, Computer History Museum.

CHAPTER 19 Death Spiral

103 **"We're in a death spiral":** Berlin, *The Man Behind the Microchip*, p. 264.

103 **over 90 percent:** Richard Langlois and Edward Steinmueller, "Strategy and Circumstance," working paper, University of Connecticut, 1999, p. 1166.

104 **Potato chips:** Clyde V. Prestowitz, Jr., "Beyond Laissez Faire," *Foreign Policy*, No. 87 (Summer 1992): 71; email exchange with Michael Boskin, 2021; though this quote is repeated in many articles, I've found no evidence he actually said this.

104 **testified to Congress:** Berlin, *The Man Behind the Microchip*, p. 262; John G. Rauch, "The Realities of Our Times," *Fordham Intellectual Property, Media and Entertainment Law Journal* 3, No. 2 (1993): 412.

105 **DRAM sales into Japan barely budged:** Wolf, *The Japanese Conspiracy*, pp. 5, 91; interview with Alan Wolff, 2021; Berlin, *The Man Behind the Microchip*, p. 270.

105 **Higher prices actually benefitted Japan's producers:** Doug Irwin, "Trade Politics and the Semiconductor Industry," NBER working paper W4745, May 1994.

105 **created a consortium:** Young, *Silicon Sumo*, pp. 262–263.

106 **one employee estimated:** Ibid., pp. 268–269; interview with Intel employee seconded to Sematech, 2021; Larry D. Browning and Judy C. Shetler, *Sematech: Saving the U.S. Semiconductor Industry* (Texas A&M Press, 2000).

106 **Sematech organized seminars:** Interview with Intel employee seconded to Sematech, 2021.

107 **"half the problem":** Robert Noyce, testifying before a Congressional committee, November 8, 1989; Peter N. Dunn, "GCA: A Lesson in Industrial Policy," *Solid State Technology* 36, No. 2 (December 1993); Young, *Silicon Sumo*, pp. 270–276.

107 **"You're done":** Interview with Peter Simone, 2021.

107 **he decided that day to buy:** Interview with Peter Simone, 2021.

108 **"They were ahead of their time":** Interview with Tony Yen, 2021; interview with Peter Simone, 2021; Young, *Silicon Sumo*, pp. 262, 285.

108 **switch its allegiance from Nikon:** Young, *Silicon Sumo*, p. 286.

108 **nothing could be done:** Berlin, *The Man Behind the Microchip*, p. 304; Young, *Silicon Sumo*, pp. 294–295; Jonathan Weber, "Chip Making Pioneer GCA Corp. Closes Factory: Technology: $60 Million in Government Funds Has Failed to Restore Massachusetts Firm to Financial Health," *Los Angeles Times*, May 22, 1993.

CHAPTER 20 The Japan That Can Say No

109 **Akio Morita began to detect:** Morita, *Made in Japan*, pp. 73, 110–120, 134.

110 **ten meals a day:** Nathan, *Sony*, p. 73.

110 **Japan's system simply worked better:** Morita, *Made in Japan*, pp. 193, 199, 205.

111 *Season of the Sun*: Ann Sherif, "The Aesthetics of Speed and the Illogicality of Politics: Ishihara Shintaro's Literary Debut," *Japan Forum* 17, No. 2 (2005): 185–211.

111 **"economically we can overcome":** Wolf, *The Japanese Conspiracy*, p. 16.

112 **"Japan has become a very important country":** Akio Morita and Shintaro Ishihara, *The Japan That Can Say No* (Konbusha Publishing Ltd., 1996).

113 **"giant version of Denmark":** Samuel Huntington, "Why International Primacy Matters," *International Security* (January 2009): 75–76.

113 **"going absolutely bananas":** Steven L. Herman, "Bootleg Translation of Japanese Book Hot Item in Congress," Associated Press, November 11, 1989.

113 **"I don't feel U.S. readers understand":** James Flanigan, "U.S. Bashing Book by Sony's Chief Costs Him Credibility," *Los Angeles Times*, October 11, 1989.

113 **"High Tech Is Foreign Policy":** Harold Brown, "The United States and Japan: High Tech Is Foreign Policy," *SAIS Review* 9, No. 2 (Fall 1989).

114 **the CIA tasked:** Central Intelligence Agency, "East Asia's Economic Potential for the 1990s: A Speculative Essay," CREST Database, 1987.

CHAPTER 21 The Potato Chip King

117 **"Mr. Spud":** Interview with Micron employee, 2021; George Anders, "At Potato Empire, an Heir Peels Away Years of Tradition," *Wall Street Journal*, October 7, 2004; Laurence Zuckerman, "From Mr. Spud to Mr. Chips; The Potato Tycoon Who Is the Force Behind Micron," *New York Times*, February 8, 1996; Andrew E. Serwer, "The Simplot Saga: How America's French Fry King Made Billions More in Semiconductors," *Fortune*, February 12, 2012.

119 **So they turned to Mr. Spud:** Interview with Ward Parkinson, 2021; Luc Olivier Bauer and E. Marshall Wilder, *Microchip Revolution* (Independently published, 2020), pp. 279–280.

119 **a local greasy spoon:** Interview with Elmer's staff member, 2021; interview with Ward Parkinson, 2021.

119 **pour in millions more:** Donald Woutat, "Maverick Chip Maker Shifts Stance: Micron Backs Protectionism After Launching Price War," *Los Angeles Times*, December 16, 1985; Peter Burrows, "Micron's Comeback Kid," *Business Week*, June 14, 1997.

119 **losses and layoffs:** David E. Sanger, "Prospects Appear Grim for U.S. Chip Makers," *New York Times*, October 29, 1985.

120 **they embraced their Idaho outsider image:** David Staats, "How an Executive's Hair Dryer Saved the Memory Chips—Tales of Micron's 40 Years," *Idaho Statesman*, July 21, 2021.

120 **"a self-defeating strategy":** Woutat, "Maverick Chip Maker Shifts Stance."

120 **"the law says they can't do that":** David E. Sanger, "Japan Chip 'Dumping' Is Found," *New York Times*, August 3, 1985.

121 **"by far the least expensive to produce":** Interviews with Ward Parkinson, Brian Shirley, and Mark Durcan, 2021; Woutat, "Maverick Chip Maker Shifts Stance."

121 **"hadn't been written in a paper before":** Interviews with Brian Shirley and Mark Durcan, 2021; Yoshitaka Okada, "Decline of the Japanese Semiconductor Industry," *Development of Japanese Semiconductor Industry* (January 2006): 41; Bauer and Wilder, *The Microchip Revolution*, pp. 301–302.

121 **cut salaries for the remainder:** Bauer and Wilder, *The Microchip Revolution*, pp. 286, 302.

122 **"Memory chips is a brutal, brutal business":** Interviews with Mark Durcan, Ward Parkinson, and Brian Shirley, 2021.

CHAPTER 22 Disrupting Intel

123 **"I'm a busy man"**: James Allworth, "Intel's Disruption Is Now Complete," *Medium*, November 11, 2020, https://jamesallworth.medium.com/intels-disruption -is-now-complete-d4fa771f0f2c.

123 **"butt-kicking Hungarian"**: Craig R. Barrett, interviews by Arnold Thackray and David C. Brock at Santa Clara, California, December 14, 2005 and March 23, 2006 (Philadelphia: Chemical Heritage Foundation, Oral History Transcript 0324).

124 **worried he'd missed news:** Andrew S. Grove, *Only the Paranoid Survive: How to Exploit the Crisis Points That Challenge Every Company* (Currency Press, 1999), pp. 117–118.

124 **like one of the cabins on the Ferris wheel:** Grove, *Only the Paranoid Survive*, pp. 88–90; Robert A. Burgelman, "Fading Memories: A Process Theory of Strategic Business Exist in Dynamic Environments," *Administrative Science Quarterly* 39, No. 1 (March 1994): 41.

124 **Intel had won a small contract with IBM:** Gerry Parker, "Intel's IBM PC Design Win," *Gerry Parker's Word Press Blog*, July 20, 2014, https://gerrythetravelhund .wordpress.com/tag/ibm-pc/; Jimmy Maher, "The Complete History of the IBM PC, Part One: The Deal of the Century," *ars TECHNICA*, June 30, 2017, https:// arstechnica.com/gadgets/2017/06/ibm-pc-history-part-1/.

124 **IBM announced the launch of its personal computer:** "The Birth of the IBM PC," IBM Debut Reference Room, https://www.ibm.com/ibm/history/exhibits /pc25/pc25_birth.html; "IBM Personal Computer Launch," Waldorf Astoria, January 23, 2019.

124 **mind-boggling:** Craig R. Barrett, interviews by Arnold Thackray and David C. Brock at Santa Clara, California, December 14, 2005 and March 23, 2006.

125 **"bickering and arguments":** Grove, *Only the Paranoid Survive*, pp. 88–92.

125 **"constructive confrontation":** Elizabeth Corcoran, "Intel CEO Andy Grove Steps Aside," *Washington Post*, March 27, 1998; interview with former Intel employee, 2021.

125 **"the control part":** Christophe Lecuyer, "Confronting the Japanese Challenge: The Revival of Manufacturing at Intel," *Business History Review* (July 2019); Berlin, *The Man Behind the Microchip*, p. 180.

126 **"This is how you are supposed to do it":** Lecuyer, "Confronting the Japanese Challenge," pp. 363–364; Craig R. Barrett, interviews by Arnold Thackray and David C. Brock at Santa Clara, California, December 14, 2005 and March 23, 2006. Richard S. Tedlow, *Andy Grove: The Life and Times of an American Business Icon* (Penguin, 2007), p. 203.

126 **more like a finely tuned machine:** Lecuyer, "Confronting the Japanese Challenge," pp. 363, 364, 369, 370; Craig R. Barrett, interviews by Arnold Thackray and David C. Brock at Santa Clara, California, December 14, 2005 and March 23, 2006. pp. 65, 79.

126 **sold more units than IBM itself:** Therese Poletti, "Crucial Mistakes: IBM's Stumbles Opened Door for Microsoft, Intel," *Chicago Tribune*, August 13, 2001.

CHAPTER 23 "My Enemy's Enemy": The Rise of Korea

129 **"big, strong, and eternal":** Geoffrey Cain, *Samsung Rising* (Currency Press, 2020), p. 33.

130 **drove it around the occupied capital:** Cain, *Samsung Rising*, pp. 33–41.

130 **"Serving the nation through business":** Dong-Sung Cho and John A. Mathews, *Tiger Technology* (Cambridge University Press, 2007), pp. 105–106; Cain, *Samsung Rising*, pp. 40, 41, 46; on Lee's wealth, "Half a Century of Rise and Fall of the Korean Chaebol in Terms of Income and Stock Price," Yohap News Agency, November 7, 2006, https://www.yna.co.kr/view/AKR20110708154800008.

130 **struggled to make money:** Si-on Park, *Like Lee Byung-chul*, p. 71; Cho and Mathews, *Tiger Technology*, p. 112; Daniel Nenni and Don Dingee, *Mobile Unleashed* (Semi Wiki, 2015); Kim Dong-Won and Stuart W. Leslie, "Winning Markets or Winning Nobel Prizes? KAIST and the Challenges of Late Industrialization," *Osiris* 13 (1998): 167–170; Donald L. Benedict, KunMo Chung, Franklin A. Long, Thomas L. Martin, and Frederick E. Terman, "Survey Report on the Establishment of the Korea Advanced Institute of Science," prepared for US Agency for International Development, December 1970, http://large.stanford.edu/history/kaist/docs/terman/summary/. On Samsung's early difficulties, see Hankook semiconductor; eg. Samsung Newsroom, "Semiconductor Will Be My Last Business," *Samsung*, March 30, 2010, https://news.samsung.com /kr/91.

131 **"can't be replicated by mere observation":** Park Si-on, *Like Lee Byung-chul*, pp. 399, 436.

131 **at least $100 million:** Myung Oh and James F. Larson, *Digital Development in Korea: Building an Information Society* (Routledge, 2011), p. 54; Park Si-on, *Like Lee Byung-chul*, p. 386; Cho and Mathews, *Tiger Technology*, pp. 105, 119, 125; Lee Jae-goo, "Why Should We Do the Semiconductor Industry," tr. Soyoung Oh, *ZDNET Korea*, Mar 15, 1983, https://zdnet.co.kr /view/?no=20110328005714.

132 **the result would be "deadly":** Tedlow, *Andy Grove*, p. 218; Robert W. Crandall and Kenneth Flamm, *Changing the Rules* (Brookings Institution Press, 1989), p. 315; Susan Chira, "Korea's Chip Makers Race to Catch Up," *New York Times*, July 15, 1985; "Company News: Intel Chip Pact," *New York Times*, June 26, 1987.

132 **trade tension helped Korean companies, too:** Richard E. Baldwin, "The Impact of the 1986 US-Japan Semiconductor Agreement," *Japan and the World Economy* 6, No. 2 (June 1994): 136–137; Douglas A. Irwin, "Trade Policies and the Semiconductor Industry," in Anne O. Krueger, ed., *The Political Economy of American Trade Policy* (University of Chicago Press, 1994), pp. 46–47.

133 **"my enemy's enemy is my friend":** Linsu Kim, "Imitation to Innovation: The Dynamics of Korea's Technological Learning," Columbia University East Asian Center, 1997, p. 89, cites the example of Zyrtek transferring advanced production knowledge for a $2.1 million fee; interview with Ward Parkinson, 2021; Andrew Pollack, "U.S.-Korea Chip Ties Grow," *New York Times*, July 15, 1985.

CHAPTER 24 "This Is the Future"

136 **Faggin had created a chip:** Federico Faggin, "The Making of the First Microprocessor," IEEE, 2009; Federico Faggin, *Silicon* (Waterline, 2021), esp. ch. 3.

136 **was puzzling over this dilemma:** B. Hoeneisen and C. A. Mead, "Fundamental Limitations in Microelectronics—I. MOS Technology," *Solid State Electronics* 15, No. 7 (July 1972), https://authors.library.caltech.edu/54798/.

136 **a brilliant computer scientist:** Interview with Lynn Conway, 2021, where she surprised me by wanting to discuss the nuances of John Gaddis, *The Landscape of History* (Oxford University Press, 2004).

136 **"stealth mode":** Dianne Lynch, "Wired Women: Engineer Lynn Conway's Secret," ABC News, January 7, 2006.

137 **bizarrely backward:** Interview with Lynn Conway, 2021.

137 **"you write your own":** "Lambda Magazine Lights the Way for VLSI Design," IEEE Silicon Valley History Videos, YouTube Video, July 27, 2015, 00:01:40, https://www.youtube.com/watch?v=DEYbQiXvbnc; "History of VLSI – C. Mead – 2/1/2011," California Institute of Technology, YouTube Video, May 29, 2018, https://www.youtube.com/watch?v=okZBhJ-KvaY.

137 **The Gutenberg moment had arrived:** "1981 *Electronics* AWARD FOR ACHIEVEMENT," University of Michigan, https://ai.eecs.umich.edu/people /conway/Awards/Electronics/ElectAchiev.html; Interviews with Lynn Conway and Carver Mead, 2021.

137 **ample supply of chip designers:** Van Atta et al., DARPA *Technical Accomplishments: An Historical Review of Selected DARPA Projects II*, February 1990, AD-A239 925, p. 17-5.

137 **Helping companies and professors keep Moore's Law alive:** Interview with Paul Losleben, 2021; Van Atta et al., DARPA *Technical Accomplishments*, p. 17-1.

138 **founded and built by alumni:** Interviews with David Hodges, Steve Director, Aart de Geus, Alberto Sangiovanni-Vincentelli, and Rob Rutenbar; "1984 Annual Report," Semiconductor Research Corporation, 1984, https://www.src.org/src /story/timeline.

138 **how information can be stored and communicated:** Irwin Jacobs interview by David Morton, IEEE History Center, October 29, 1999.

139 **"This is the future":** Daniel J. Costello, Jr., and David Forney, Jr., "Channel Coding: The Road to Channel Capacity," Proceedings of the IEEE 95, No. 6 (June 2007); O. Aftab, P. Cheung, A. Kim, S. Thakkar, and N. Yeddanapudi, "Information Theory and the Digital Age," 6.933 Project History, MIT, https://web.mit .edu/6.933/www/Fall2001/Shannon2.pdf; David Forney Jr. interview by Andrew Goldstein, Center for the History of Electrical Engineering, May 10, 1995; Daniel Nenni, "A Detailed History of Qualcomm," *SemiWiki*, March 19, 2018, https:// semiwiki.com/general/7353-a-detailed-history-of-qualcomm/.

CHAPTER 25 The KGB's Directorate T

141 **stay in Moscow and get drunk:** Details of Vetrov's life draw heavily from Sergei Kostin and Eric Raynaud, *Farewell: The Greatest Spy Story of the Twentieth Century* (Amazon Crossing, 2011).

141 **"improve its ability to produce integrated circuits":** CIA, "The Technology Acquisition Efforts of the Soviet Intelligence Services," June 18, 1982, p. 15, https://www.cia.gov/readingroom/docs/DOC_0000261337.pdf; Philip Hanson, *Soviet Industrial Espionage* (Royal Institute of International Affairs, 1987).

142 **died after "falling":** Sergey Chertoprud, *Naucho-Tekhnicheskaia Razvedka* (Olma Press, 2002), p. 283; Daniela Iacono, "A British Banker Who Plunged to His Death," United Press International, May 15, 1984; Michael S. Malone, "Going Underground in Silicon Valley," *New York Times*, May 30, 1982.

142 **shut down a Soviet research unit:** Jay Tuck, *High-Tech Espionage* (St. Martin's Press, 1986), p. 107; Simonov, *Nesostoyavshayasya Informatsionnaya Revolyutsiya*, p. 34.

142 **via shell companies:** Edgar Ulsamer, "Moscow's Technology Parasites," *Air Force Magazine*, December 1, 1984.

143 **doping, packaging, and testing chips:** Central Intelligence Agency, "Soviet Acquisition of Militarily Significant Western Technology: An Update," September 1985, p. 25, http://insidethecoldwar.org/sites/default/files/documents/CIA%20Report%20on%20Soviet%20Acquisition%20of%20Militarily%20Significant%20Western%20Technology%20September%201985.pdf.

143 **connected with the French intelligence services:** Kostin and Raynaud, *Farewell*.

144 **how much the Soviets stole:** Hanson, *Soviet Industrial Espionage*; Central Intelligence Agency, "Soviet Acquisition of Militarily Significant Western Technology: An Update"; Kostin and Raynaud, *Farewell*; Thierry Wolton, *Le KGB en France* (Club Express, 1986).

144 **always half a decade behind:** Central Intelligence Agency, "Soviet Computer Technology: Little Prospect of Catching Up," National Security Archive, March 1985, p. 4, https://nsarchive.gwu.edu/document/22579-document-02 -central-intelligence-agency-soviet; Bruce B. Weyrauch, "Operation Exodus," *Computer/Law Journal* 7, No. 2 (Fall 1986); Hanson, *Soviet Industrial Espionage*; Jon Zonderman, "Policing High-Tech Exports," *New York Times*, November 27, 1983.

CHAPTER 26 "Weapons of Mass Destruction": The Impact of the Offset

145 **"weapons of mass destruction":** Dale Roy Herspring, *The Soviet High Command, 1967–1989* (Princeton University Press, 2016), p. 175.

145 **"asking for it":** Christopher Andrew and Oleg Gordievsky, "1983 Downing of KAL Flight Showed Soviets Lacked Skill of the Fictional 007," *Los Angeles Times*, November 11, 1990.

146 **had a clear advantage:** Brian A Davenport, "The Ogarkov Ouster," *Journal of Strategic Studies* 14, No. 2 (1991): 133; CIA and Defense Department, "US and Soviet Strategic Forces: Joint Net Assessment," Secretary of Defense, November 14, 1983, https://nsarchive2.gwu.edu/NSAEBB/NSAEBB428/docs/1.US%20 and%20Soviet%20Strategic%20Forces%20Joint%20Net%20Assessment.pdf.

146 **"military-technical revolution":** Center for Naval Analyses, *Marshal Ogarkov on Modern War: 1977–1985*, AD-A176 138, p. 27; Dima P. Adamsky, "Through the Looking Glass: The Soviet Military-Technical Revolution and the American Revolution in Military Affairs," *Journal of Strategic Studies* 31, No. 2 (2008).

146 **Perry's "offset strategy" was working:** An excellent overview of the technologies of the offset, all of which rely fundamentally on semiconductors, is in David Burbach, Brendan Rittenhouse Green, and Benjamin Friedman, "The Technology of the Revolution in Military Affairs," in Harvey Sapolsky, Benjamin Friedman, and Brendan Green, eds., *U.S. Military Innovation Since the Cold War: Creation Without Destruction* (Routledge, 2012), pp. 14–42; CIA, "Soviet Defense Industry: Coping with the Military-Technological Challenge," CIA Historical Review Program, July 1987, p. 17, https://www.cia.gov/readingroom/docs /DOC_0000499526.pdf; Adamsky, "Through the Looking Glass," p. 260.

146 **the Soviets' first missile guidance computer using integrated circuits:** Anatoly Krivonosov, "Khartron: Computers for Rocket Guidance Systems," in Boris Malinovsky, "History of Computer Science and Technology in Ukraine," tr. Slava Gerovitch, *Computing in the Soviet Space Program*, December 16, 2002, https://web.mit.edu/slava/space/essays/essay-krivonosov.htm; Donald MacKenzie, "The Soviet Union and Strategic Missile Guidance," *International Security* 13, No. 2 (Fall 1988); Georgii Priss interview by Slava Gerovitch, *Computing in the Soviet Space Program*, May 23, 2002, https://web.mit.edu/slava/space/interview /interview-priss.htm#q3.

147 **calculated their own path to the target:** MacKenzie, "The Soviet Union and Strategic Missile Guidance," pp. 30–32, 35.

147 **destroyed 98 percent of Soviet ICBMs:** MacKenzie, "The Soviet Union and Strategic Missile Guidance," p. 52, citing a CEP of .06 nautical miles; Pavel Podvig, "The Window of Opportunity That Wasn't: Soviet Military Buildup in the 1970s," *International Security* (Summer 2008): 129, cites a CEP of 0.35–0.43 kilometers. There are other variables on which missiles could be compared, including the size and number of warheads they carry and the speed at which they can be launched or retargeted. But the basic trend of America's accuracy advantage holds; the 98 percent figure is from John G. Hines, Ellis M. Mishulovich, and John F. Shull, *Soviet Intentions, 1965–1985*, Vol. 2 (BDM Federal, Inc., 1995), pp. 46, 90. Note that this 98 percent likely substantially overstated U.S. capabilities, but is nevertheless evidence of Soviet fears. Cf. Brendan R. Green and Austin Long, "The MAD Who Wasn't There: Soviet Reactions to Late Cold War Nuclear Balance," *Security Studies* 26, No. 4 (July 7, 2017).

148 **track Soviet subs:** Owen R. Cote, Jr., "The Third Battle: Innovation in the U.S. Navy's Silent Cold War Struggle with Soviet Submarines," Newport Papers, Naval War College, 2003; Joel S. Wit, "Advances in Antisubmarine Warfare," *Scientific*

American 244, No. 2 (February 1981): 31–41; D. L. Slotnick, "The Conception and Development of Parallel Processors: A Personal Memoir," *Annals of the History of Computing* 4, No. 1 (January–March 1982); Van Atta et al., DARPA *Technical Accomplishments II*; Christopher A. Ford and David A. Rosenberg, "The Naval Intelligence Underpinnings of Reagan's Maritime Strategy," *Journal of Strategic Studies* 28, No. 2 (April 2005): 398; John G. Hines, Ellis M. Mishulovich, and John F. Shull, *Soviet Intentions 1965–1985*, Vol. 1 (BDM Federal, Inc., 1995), p. 75; Green and Long, "The MAD Who Wasn't There," pp. 607, 639. There were also substantial problems with reliability of Soviet SSBN missiles in the 1980s; see Steven J. Zaloga, *The Kremlin's Nuclear Sword: The Rise and Fall of Russia's Strategic Nuclear Forces 1945–2000* (Smithsonian Books, 2014), p. 188.

148 **"substantially inferior in strategic weapons":** Green and Long, "The MAD Who Wasn't There," p. 617.

148 **the very survival of the Soviet state:** Danilevich quoted in Hines, Mishulovich, and Shull, *Soviet Intentions 1965–1985*, Vol. 1, p. 57; Dale R. Herspring, "Nikolay Ogarkov and the Scientific-Technical Revolution in Soviet Military Affairs," *Comparative Strategy* 6, No. 1 (1987); Mary C. Fitzgerald, "Soviet Views on Future War: The Impact of New Technologies," *Defense Analysis* 7, Nos. 2-3 (1991). Soviet officials expressed deep concern over the survivability of command and control and communications systems; see Hines, Mishulovich, and Shull, *Soviet Intentions 1965–1985*, Vol. 1, p. 90; Marshal Vasili Petrov, quoted in 1983 as perceiving a NATO plan to "create and make use of the potential for a 'disarming' first [conventional] strike," in Thomas M. Nichols, *The Sacred Cause: Civil-Military Conflict over Soviet National Security, 1917–1992* (NCROL, 1993), p. 117; Mary C. Fitzgerald, "Marshal Ogarkov on the Modern Theater Operation," *Naval War College Review* 39, No. 4 (1986); Mary C. Fitzgerald, "Marshal Ogarkov and the New Revolution in Soviet Military Affairs," *Defense Analysis* 3, No. 1 (1987).

148 **"more discipline":** Mikhail Gorbachev, *"Zasedanie Politbyuro Tsk Kpss 30 Iiulia Goda,"* in *Sobranie Sochinenii*, Book 9 (Ves' Mir, 2008), pp. 339–343. I've translated liberally here.

148 **Osokin was removed:** Interview with Sergei Osokin, 2021.

149 **eight times as much on capital investment:** Simonov, *Nesostoyavshayasya Informatsionnaya Revolutsiya*, p. 70; Seymour Goodman and William K. McHenry, "The Soviet Computer Industry: A Tale of Two Sectors," *Communications of the ACM* (January 1991): 32.

149 **lacked an international supply chain:** V. V. Zhurkin, *"Ispolzovanie Ssha Noveishhikh Dostizhenii Nauki i Tekhniki v Sfere Vneshnei Politiki,"* Academy of Sciences Archive, August 7, 1987.

149 **East German chip output:** Charles S. Maier, *Dissolution* (Princeton University Press, 1999), pp. 74–75.

CHAPTER 27 War Hero

151 **Norman Schwarzkopf:** Robert D. McFadden, "Gen. H. Norman Schwarzkopf, U.S. Commander in Gulf War, Dies at 78," *New York Times*, December 27, 2012.

151 **The Persian Gulf War had begun:** Rick Aktinson, *Crusade: The Untold Story of the Persian Gulf War* (Mariner Books, 1994), pp. 35–37.

152 **U.S. airstrikes sought to decapitate:** "The Theater's Opening Act," *Washington Post*, 1998; Aktinson, *Crusade*, p. 37.

152 **The Paveway laser-guided bombs:** Details on Paveway electronics from interview with Steve Roemerman, 2021.

152 **thirteen times:** Stephen P. Rosen, "The Impact of the Office of Net Assessment on the American Military in the Matter of the Revolution of Military Affairs," *Journal of Strategic Studies* 33, No. 4 (2010): 480.

153 **"ten thousand Americans":** Interview with Steve Roemerman, 2021.

154 **"High-tech works":** Bobby R. Inman, Joseph S. Nye Jr., William J. Perry, and Roger K. Smith, "Lessons from the Gulf War," *Washington Quarterly* 15, No. 1 (1992): 68; Benjamin S. Lambeth, *Desert Storm and Its Meaning* (RAND Corporation, 1992).

154 **"War Hero Status":** William J. Broad, "War in the Gulf: High Tech; War Hero Status Possible for the Computer Chip," *New York Times*, January 21, 1991; Barry D. Watts, *Six Decades of Guided Munitions and Battle Networks: Progress and Prospects* (Center for Strategic and Budgetary Assessments, 2007), p. 146; interview with Steve Roemerman.

154 **Iraq's speedy surrender:** Mary C. Fitzgerald, "The Soviet Military and the New 'Technological Operation' in the Gulf," *Naval War College Review* 44, No. 4 (Fall 1991): 16–43, https://www.jstor.org/stable/44638558; Stuart Kaufman, "Lessons from the 1991 Gulf War and Military Doctrine," *Journal of Slavic Military Studies* 6, No. 3 (1993); Graham E. Fuller, "Moscow and the Gulf War," *Foreign Affairs* (Summer 1991); Gilberto Villahermosa, "Desert Storm: The Soviet View," Foreign Military Studies Office, May 25, 2005, p. 4.

CHAPTER 28 "The Cold War Is Over and You Have Won"

156 **government-backed overinvestment:** Michael Pettis, *The Great Rebalancing* (Princeton University Press, 2013).

156 **Samsung undercut Japanese rivals:** Yoshitaka Okada, "Decline of the Japanese Semiconductor Industry," in Yoshitaka Okada, ed., *Struggles for Survival* (Springer, 2006), p. 72.

156 **"you can't sleep at night":** Marie Anchordoguy, *Reprogramming Japan* (Cornell University Press, 2005), p. 192.

156 **the company failed to cut investment:** Sumio Saruyama and Peng Xu, *Excess Capacity and the Difficulty of Exit: Evidence from Japan's Electronics Industry* (Springer Singapore, 2021); "Determination Drove the Development of the CCD 'Electric Eye,'" Sony, https://www.sony.com/en/SonyInfo/CorporateInfo/History/SonyHistory/2-11.html.

157 **this new type of memory chip:** Kenji Hall, "Fujio Masuoka: Thanks for the Memory," *Bloomberg*, April 3, 2006; Falan Yinung, "The Rise of the Flash Memory Market: Its Impact on Firm Behavior and Global Semiconductor Trade Patterns," *Journal of International Commerce and Economics* (July 2007).

157 **20 percent by 1998:** Andrew Pollack, "U.S. Chips' Gain Is Japan's Loss," *New York Times*, January 3, 1991; Okada, "Decline of the Japanese Semiconductor Industry," p. 41; "Trends in the Semiconductor Industry," Semiconductor History Museum of Japan, https://www.shmj.or.jp/english/trends/trd90s.html.

157 **support Iraq's neighbors:** Japan Ministry of Foreign Affairs, "How the Gulf Crisis Began and Ended," in *Diplomatic Bluebook 1991*, https://www.mofa.go.jp /policy/other/bluebook/1991/1991-2-1.htm; Japan Ministry of Foreign Affairs, "Japan's Response to the Gulf Crisis," in *Diplomatic Bluebook 1991*, https://www .mofa.go.jp/policy/other/bluebook/1991/1991-2-2.htm; Kent E. Calder, "The United States, Japan, and the Gulf Region," The Sasakawa Peace Foundation, August 2015, p. 31; T. R. Reid, "Japan's New Frustration," *Washington Post*, March 17, 1991.

158 **"Let's not wrangle over who won it":** "G-Day: Soviet President Gorbachev Visits Stanford Business School," Stanford Graduate School of Business, September 1990, https://www.gsb.stanford.edu/experience/news-history/history/g-day -soviet-president-gorbachev-visits-stanford-business-school; David Remnick, "In U.S., Gorbachev Tried to Sell a Dream," *Washington Post*, June 6, 1990.

159 **"has a computer from age 5":** Gelb first recounted this story in 1992; I quote from his 2011 article on the topic; Leslie H. Gelb, "Foreign Affairs; Who Won the Cold War?" *New York Times*, August 20, 1992; Leslie H. Gelb, "The Forgotten Cold War: 20 Years Later, Myths About U.S. Victory Persist," *Daily Beast*, July 14, 2017.

159 **Happy Meal toys:** Interview with Peter Gordon, 2021.

CHAPTER 29 "We Want a Semiconductor Industry in Taiwan"

163 **"how much money you need":** Wang, *K.T. Li and the Taiwan Experience*, p. 217; Oral History of Morris Chang, taken by Alan Patterson, August 24, 2007, Computer History Museum.

164 **the company's capabilities lagged:** Tekla S. Perry, "Morris Chang: Foundry Father," *IEEE Spectrum*, April 19, 2011; "Stanford Engineering Hero Lecture: Morris Chang in conversation with President John L. Hennessy," Stanford Online, YouTube Video, April 25, 2004, around minute 36, https://www.youtube.com/watch?v=wE h3ZgbvBrE.

164 **economic "warfare":** "TI Board Visit to Taiwan 1978," Texas Instruments Special Collection, 90-69 TI Board Visit to Taiwan, DeGolyer Library, Southern Methodist University.

165 **"put out to pasture":** Oral History of Morris Chang, Computer History Museum.

165 **"a strange place to me":** "Morris Chang's Last Speech," tr. Kevin Xu, *Interconnected Newsletter*, September 12, 2021, https://interconnected.blog/morris-changs -last-speech; on turning down a job offer, see L. Sophia Wang, ed., *K. T. Li Oral History* (2nd edition, 2001), pp. 239–40, with thanks to Mindy Tu for translating; "Stanford Engineering Hero Lecture: Morris Chang in conversation with President John L. Hennessy," around minute 34, https://www.youtube.com/watch?v=wE h3ZgbvBrE. On Chang's Texan identity: Interview with Morris Chang, 2022.

166 **wide leeway:** Oral History of Morris Chang, Computer History Museum.

166 **"a wealth of applications":** "1976 Morris Chang Planning Doc," Texas Instruments Special Collection, Fred Bucy Papers, DeGolyer Library, Southern Methodist University.

167 **already been percolating in Taiwan:** Chintay Shih interview by Ling-Fei Lin, Computer History Museum, February 21, 2011; National Research Council, "Appendix A3: Taiwan's Industrial Technology Research Institute," in *21st Century Manufacturing* (The National Academies Press, 2013); Oral History of Morris Chang, Computer History Museum.

167 **"This isn't one of them":** Douglas B. Fuller, "Globalization for Nation Building: Industrial Policy for High-Technology Products in Taiwan," working paper, Massachusetts Institute of Technology, 2002.

167 **27.5 percent stake:** Rene Raaijmakers, *ASML's Architects* (Techwatch Books, 2018), ch. 57. On Philips' transfer of IP, see John A. Mathews, "A Silicon Valley of the East," *California Management Review* (1997): 36; Daniel Nenni, "A Brief History of TSMC," *SemiWiki*, August 2, 2012.

167 **a project of the Taiwanese state:** "Stanford Engineering Hero Lecture: Morris Chang in conversation with President John L. Hennessy"; Donald Brooks interview by Rob Walker, Stanford University Libraries, February 8, 2000, 1:45, https://exhibits.stanford.edu/silicongenesis/catalog/cj789gh7170.

167 **deep ties with the U.S. chip industry:** "TSMC Announces Resignation of Don Brooks," *EE Times*, March 7, 1997; Donald Brooks interview by Rob Walker, 1:44; "1995 Annual Report," Taiwan Semiconductor Manufacturing, Ltd, 1995; on educational links, see Douglas B. Fuller, "The Increasing Irrelevance of Industrial Policy in Taiwan, 2016–2020," in Gunter Schubert and Chun-Yi Lee, eds., *Taiwan During the First Administration of Tsai Ing-wen: Navigating Stormy Waters* (Routledge, 2020), p. 15.

168 **benefitted Taiwan and Silicon Valley:** AnnaLee Saxenian, *Regional Advantage: Culture and Competition in Silicon Valley and Route 128* (Harvard University Press, 1994); AnnaLee Saxenian, *The New Argonauts: Regional Advantage in a Global Economy* (Harvard University Press, 2006).

CHAPTER 30 "All People Must Make Semiconductors"

172 **the same storage capacity:** Jonathan Pollack, "The Chinese Electronics Industry in Transition," Rand Corporation, N-2306, May 1985; David Dorman, "The Military Imperative in Chinese Economic Reform: The Politics of Electronics, 1949–1999," PhD dissertation, University of Maryland, College Park, 2002; on the 1KB DRAM, see Richard Baum, "DOS ex Machina," in Denis Fred Simon and Merle Goldman, eds., *Science and Technology in Post-Mao China* (Harvard University Asia Center, 1989), p. 357.

172 **Chinese engineers forged their first integrated circuit:** Yiwei Zhu, *Essays on China's IC Industry Development*, tr. Zoe Huang (2006), pp. 140–144.

173 **"after a few years study":** National Research Council, "Solid State Physics in the People's Republic of China: A Trip Report of the American Solid State Physics Delegation," 1976, p. 89.

173 **"earth-shaking mass movement":** "Shanghai Workers Vigorously Develop Electronics Industry," October 9, 1969, translation of *Renmin Ribao* article in *Survey of the Chinese Mainland Press*, No. 4520, October 21, 1969, pp. 11–13.

173 **socialist utopia in China:** Denis Fred Simon and Detlef Rehn, *Technological Innovation in China: The Case of Shanghai Semiconductor Industry* (Ballinger Publishing Company, 1988), pp. 47, 50; Lowell Dittmer, "Death and Transfiguration," *Journal of Asian Studies* 40, No. 3 (May 1981): 463.

174 **"all people must make semiconductors":** Lan You Hang, "The Construction of Commercial Electron Microscopes in China," *Advances in Imaging and Electron Physics* 96 (1996): 821; Sungho Rho, Keun Lee, and Seong Hee Kim, "Limited Catch Up in China's Semiconductor Industry: A Sectoral Innovation System Perspective," *Millennial Asia* (August 19, 2015): 159.

174 **"So much is being wasted":** Hua Guafeng, September 26, 1975, quoted in Roderick MacFarquhar and Michael Schoenhals, *Mao's Last Revolution* (Belknap Press, 2008), pp. 400–401.

175 **"self-glorification":** National Research Council, "Solid State Physics in the People's Republic of China," p. 151.

175 **political minders:** Hoddeson and Daitch, *True Genius*, p. 277.

175 **fifteen hundred computers:** Baum, "DOS ex Machina," pp. 347–348; National Research Council, "Solid State Physics in the People's Republic of China," pp. 52–53.

176 **weapons systems, consumer electronics, and computers:** Simon and Rehn, *Technological Innovation in China*, pp. 15, 59, 66; Baum, "DOS ex Machina," pp. 347–348.

176 **"'the third machine exported'":** Simon and Rehn, *Technological Innovation in China*, pp. 17, 27, 48.

CHAPTER 31 **"Sharing God's Love with the Chinese"**

177 **"share God's love with the Chinese":** Evelyn Iritani, "China's Next Challenge: Mastering the Microchip," *Los Angeles Times*, October 22, 2002.

177 **including a church:** Andrew Ross, *Fast Boat to China* (Vintage Books, 2007), p. 250.

177 **13 percent by 2010:** Antonio Varas, Raj Varadarajan, Jimmy Goodrich, and Falan Yinug, "Government Incentives and US Competitiveness in Semiconductor Manufacturing," Boston Consulting Group and Semiconductor Industry Association (September 2020), p. 7.

178 **Chartered Semiconductor:** John A. Matthews, "A Silicon Valley of the East," *California Management Review* (1997).

178 **like a game of chicken:** Interview with Samsung executive, 2021.

178 **Samsung had the capital to keep investing:** On credit subsidies, see S. Ran Kim, "The Korean System of Innovation and the Semiconductor Industry," *Industrial and Corporate Change* 7, No. 2 (June 1, 1998): 297–298.

179 **stuffing suitcases:** Interview with China technology analyst, 2021.

179 **running TI's facilities around the world:** Peter Clarke, "ST Process Technology Is Base for Chang's Next Chinese Foundry," tr. Claus Soong, *EE News Analog*,

February 24, 2020; "Business Figures Weekly: the Father of Chinese Semiconductors—Richard Chang," CCTV, YouTube Video, April 29, 2010, https://www.youtube.com/watch?v=NVHAyrGRM2E; http://magazine.sina.com/bg/southern peopleweekly/2009045/2009-12-09/ba80442.html; https://www.coolloud.org.tw/node/6695.

179 **Most of the early results:** Douglas B. Fuller, *Paper Tigers, Hidden Dragons* (Oxford University Press, 2016), pp. 122–126; John VerWey, "Chinese Semiconductor Industrial Policy: Past and Present," *United States International Trade Commission Journal of International Commerce and Economics* (July 2019): 11.

179 **sweet financial deal:** This is the judgment of Doug Fuller, a leading expert on China's chip industry, in *Paper Tigers, Hidden Dragons*, p. 122.

179 **a "wafer fab located in China":** Fuller, *Paper Tigers, Hidden Dragons*, p. 125; Yin Li, "From Classic Failures to Global Competitors: Business Organization and Economic Development in the Chinese Semiconductor Industry," Master's thesis, University of Massachusetts, Lowell, pp. 32–33.

180 **Taiwanese plastics dynasty:** Lee Chyen Yee and David Lin, "Hua Hong NEC, Grace Close to Merger," Reuters, December 1, 2011.

180 **Neil Bush:** "China's Shanghai Grace Semiconductor Breaks Ground on New Fab, Report Says," *EE Times*, November 20, 2000; Warren Vieth and Lianne Hart, "Bush's Brother Has Contract to Help Chinese Chip Maker," *Los Angeles Times*, November 27, 2003.

180 **struggled to acquire customers:** Ming-chin Monique Chu, *The East Asian Computer Chip War* (Routledge, 2013), pp. 212–213; "Fast-Track Success of Jiang Zemin's Eldest Son, Jiang Mianheng, Questioned by Chinese Academics for Years," *South China Morning Post*, January 9, 2015. On the difficulties of Grace, see Fuller, *Paper Tigers, Hidden Dragons*, ch. 5; Michael S. Chase, Kevin L. Pollpeter, and James C. Mulvenon, "Shanghaied: The Economic and Political Implications for the Flow of Information Technology and Investment Across the Taiwan Strait (Technical Report)," RAND Corporation, July 26, 2004, pp. 127–135.

180 **Goldman Sachs, Motorola, and Toshiba:** "Richard Chang: Taiwan's Silicon Invasion," *Bloomberg Businessweek*, December 9, 2002; Ross, *Fast Boat to China*, p. 250.

180 **half of SMIC's startup capital:** Chase et al., "Shanghaied," p. 149.

180 **four hundred from Taiwan:** "Richard Chang and His SMIC Team," *Cheers Magazine*, April 1, 2000, https://www.cheers.com.tw/article/article.action?id=5053843.

181 **foreign-trained workforce:** Fuller, *Paper Tigers, Hidden Dragons*, pp. 132, 134–135; VerWey, "Chinese Semiconductor Industrial Policy," pp. 11–12; Yin Li, "From Classic Failures to Global Competitors," pp. 45–48; Er Hao Lu, *The Developmental Model of China's Semiconductor Industry, 2000–2005* (Zhongguo bandaoti chanye fazhan moshi), Doctoral dissertation, National Chengchi University, Taipei, Taiwan, 2008, pp. 33–35, with thanks to Claus Soong for translating; Ross, *Fast Boat to China*, p. 248.

181 **reduced sales tax:** Yin-Yin Chen, "The Political Economy of the Development of the Semiconductor Industry in Shanghai,1956–2006," Thesis, National Taiwan University, 2007, pp. 71–72; Lu, *The Developmental Model of China's*

Semiconductor Industry, pp. 75–77. Thanks to Claus Soong for translating these sources.

181 **near the cutting edge:** Yin Li, "From Classic Failures to Global Competitors," pp. 45–48.

181 **on track to become a top-notch foundry:** Fuller, *Paper Tigers, Hidden Dragons*, pp. 132, 136; "Semiconductor Manufacturing International Corporation Announces Proposed Dual Listing on SEHK and NYSE," SMIC, March 7, 2004, https://www.smics.com/en/site/news_read/4212; "Chip maker SMIC falls on debut," CNN, Mar 18, 2004.

CHAPTER 32 Lithography Wars

184 **He gave Carruthers $200 million:** Interview with John Carruthers, 2021; this chapter benefitted from interviews with Vivek Bakshi, Chris Mack, Chuck Gwyn, David Attwood, Frits van Houts, John Taylor, John Carruthers, Bill Siegle, Stefan Wurm, Tony Yen, Shang-yi Chiang, and other lithography experts who asked not to be named, none of whom are responsible for the conclusions.

185 **"lithography wars":** Mark L. Schattenburg, "History of the 'Three Beams' Conference, the Birth of the Information and the Era of Lithography Wars," https://eipbn.org/2020/wp-content/uploads/2015/01/EIPBN_history.pdf.

185 **joined voluntarily:** Peter Van Den Hurk, "Farewell to a 'Big Family of Top Class People,'" ASML, April 23, 2021, https://www.asml.com/en/news/stories/2021/frits-van-hout-retires-from-asml.

185 **"no facilities and no money":** Interview with Frits van Hout, 2021.

186 **competitors in Japan:** Rene Raiijmakers, "Technology Ownership Is No Birthright," *Bits & Chips*, June 24, 2021.

186 **forming a partnership:** Interview with Fritz van Hout, 2021; "Lithography Wars (Middle): How Did TSMC's Fire Save the Lithography Giant ASML?" *iNews*, February 5, 2022, https://inf.news/en/news/5620365e89323be681610733c6a32d22.html.

186 **"unipolar moment":** Charles Krauthammer, "The Unipolar Moment," *Foreign Affairs*, September 18, 1990.

187 **"borderless world":** Kenichi Ohmae, "Managing in a Borderless World," *Harvard Business Review* (May–June 1989).

187 **made a profit every year:** According to Bloomberg data.

187 **"95 percent gorilla":** Interview with John Taylor, 2021.

187 **ASML was the only lithography firm left:** Chuck Gwyn and Stefan Wurm, "EUV LLC: A Historical Perspective," in Bakshi, ed., EUV *Lithography* (SPIE, 2008); interviews with John Carruthers and John Taylor, 2021.

188 **hardly anyone in Washington was concerned:** Interviews with Kenneth Flamm and Richard Van Atta, 2021.

188 **jobs, not geopolitics:** David Lammers, "U.S. Gives Ok to ASML on EUV," *EE Times*, February 24, 1999; this media report cites a deal with the U.S. government whereby ASML promised to produce a portion of its machines in the U.S. I was unable to verify the existence of such a promise via interviews with U.S. officials

or ASML, though multiple former officials said the deal sounded plausible and that it could have been informal rather than formal. ASML today produces a portion of each EUV tool in a manufacturing facility in Connecticut so appears to be upholding its side of the deal, if in fact it made such a promise.

188 **government's decision to let this arrangement proceed:** None of my interview subjects thought that foreign policy considerations were crucial to this decision, and many said they could not recall any discussion of the topic.

188 **"all of the U.S. government's EUV technology":** Don Clark and Glenn Simpson, "Opponents of SVG Sale to Dutch Worry About Foreign Competition," *Wall Street Journal*, April 26, 2001; interview with lithography industry expert, 2021; interview with Dick Van Atta, 2021; interview with former Commerce Department official, 2021.

189 **EUV didn't make the list:** Clark and Simpson, "Opponents of SVG Sale to Dutch Worry About Foreign Competition."

189 **America, Japan, Slovenia, and Greece:** Interview with John Taylor, 2021.

CHAPTER 33 The Innovator's Dilemma

191 **"Intel is ready":** "First Intel Mac (10 Jan 2006)," all about Steve Jobs.com, YouTube Video, September 18, 2009, https://www.youtube.com/watch?v=cp49T mmtmf8.

192 **wore ties more often:** Interview with veteran Intel executive, 2021.

192 **milking Intel's de facto monopoly on x86 chips:** Alexis C. Madrigal, "Paul Otellini's Intel: Can the Company That Built the Future Survive It?" *Atlantic*, May 16, 2013; interviews with four former Intel executives, 2021.

192 **the moat, defending the castle, was x86:** Interview with Michael Bruck, 2021.

193 **won a near monopoly:** Kurt Shuler, "Semiconductor Slowdown? Invest!" *Semiconductor Engineering*, January 26, 2012.

193 **"the only chance we've got":** Interview with Robin Saxby, 2021; "Sir Robin Saxby: The ARM Architecture Was Invented Inside Acorn Computers," Anu Partha, YouTube Video, June 1, 2017, https://www.youtube.com/watch?v=jx UT3wE5Kwg; Don Dingee and Daniel Nenni, *Mobile Unleashed: The Origin and Evolution of ARM Processors in Our Devices* (SemiWiki LLC, 2015), esp. p. 42; "Alumnus Receives Top Honour from Institute of Electrical and Electronics Engineers (IEEE)," University of Liverpool, May 17, 2019.

194 **Zoom-esque video conferencing:** Interview with former Intel executive, 2021.

195 **mobile devices seemed like a wild gamble:** Interview with Ted Odell, 2020, and Will Swope, 2021.

195 **"the volume was 100× what anyone thought":** Alexis C. Madrigal, "Paul Otellini's Intel."

196 **Intel never found a way to win a foothold in mobile:** Joel Hruska, "How Intel Lost the Mobile Market, Part 2: The Rise and Neglect of Atom," *Extreme Tech*, December 3, 2020; Joel Hruska, "How Intel Lost $10 Billion and the Mobile Market," *Extreme Tech*, December 3, 2020; Mark Lipacis et al., "Semiconductors: The 4th Tectonic Shift in Computing: To a Parallel Processing / IoT Model," *Jeffries*

Research Note, July 10, 2017; conversations with Michael Bruck and Will Swope helped crystalize this point; Varas et al., "Strengthening the Global Semiconductor Supply Chain in an Uncertain Area."

196 **"didn't want to take the margin hit":** Interview with former Intel executive, 2021.

CHAPTER 34 Running Faster?

198 **"fight to win":** Andy Grove, "Andy Grove: How America Can Create Jobs," *Businessweek*, July 1, 2010.

199 **"I doubt they will ever catch up":** Ibid.

199 **a billion transistors on each chip:** Jon Stokes, "Two Billion-Transistor Beasts: POWER7 and Niagara 3," *Ars Technica*, February 8, 2010.

199 **controlled around three-quarters of the market:** Wally Rhines, "Competitive Dynamics in the Electronic Design Automation Industry," *SemiWiki*, August 23, 2019.

200 **an earthquake measuring 7.3:** Mark Veverka, "Taiwan Quake Sends a Wakeup Call, But Effects May Be Short Lived," *Barron's*, September 27, 1999.

200 **the fifth took even longer:** Jonathan Moore, "Fast Chips, Faster Cleanup," *BusinessWeek*, October 11, 1999.

200 **disruptions were limited:** Baker Li, Dow Jones Newswires, "Shortage in Parts Appears to Fade Following Earthquake in Taiwan," *Wall Street Journal*, November 9, 1999.

200 **five since 1900:** Interview with fabless company executive, 2021; "20 Largest Earthquakes in the World," USGS, https://www.usgs.gov/natural-hazards /earthquake-hazards/science/20-largest-earthquakes-world?qt-science _center_objects=0#qt-science_center_objects.

201 **"responsible stakeholder":** Robert Zoellick speech, September 21, 2005, "Whither China? From Membership to Responsibility," National Committee on U.S. China Relations.

201 **"exceedingly small":** Adam Segal, "Practical Engagement: Drawing a Fine Line for U.S.-China Trade," *Washington Quarterly* 27, No. 3 (January 7, 2010): 162.

201 **"validated end-user":** "SMIC Attains Validated End-User Status for U.S. Government," SMIC, October 19, 2007, https://www.smics.com/en/site/news _read/4294.

201 **"running faster" than rivals:** The best history of the emergence of this consensus is Hugo Meijer, *Trading with the Enemy* (Oxford University Press, 2016).

202 **No one was listening:** Van Atta et al., "Globalization and the US Semiconductor Industry," Institute for Defense Analyses, November 20, 2007, pp. 2–3.

CHAPTER 35 "Real Men Have Fabs"

205 **could end up killing you:** Craig Addison, *Silicon Shield* (Fusion PR, 2001), p. 77.

205 **flamboyant and successful salesman:** Peter J. Schuyten, "The Metamorphosis of a Salesman," *New York Times*, February 25, 1979.

206 **180 nanometers:** Varas et al., "Strengthening the Global Semiconductor Supply Chain in an Uncertain Era," p. 18.

206 **requiring a quarter the capital investment:** Ibid., p. 17.

206 **the biggest analog chipmakers:** Peter Clarke, "Top Ten Analog Chip Makers in 2020," *eeNews*, June 3, 2021.

207 **these four companies controlled around 85 percent:** Joonkyu Kang, "A Study of the DRAM Industry," Master's thesis, Massachusetts Institute of Technology, 2010, p. 13.

207 **Elpida struggled to survive:** Hiroko Tabuchi, "In Japan, Bankruptcy for a Builder of PC Chips," *New York Times*, February 27, 2012.

207 **Government subsidies in countries like Singapore:** Varas et al., "Strengthening the Global Semiconductor Supply Chain in an Uncertain Era," p. 18.

207 **supplies 35 percent of the market:** Ken Koyanagi, "SK-Intel NAND Deal Points to Wider Shake-Up of Chip Sector," *Nikkei Asia*, October 23, 2020; "Samsung Electronics Adds NAND Flash Memory Line in Pyeongtaek," *Pulse*, June 1, 2020.

208 **"Now hear me and hear me well":** John East, "Real Men Have Fabs. Jerry Sanders, TJ Rodgers, and AMD," *SemiWiki*, July 29, 2019.

CHAPTER 36 The Fabless Revolution

209 **"wasn't a real semiconductor company":** Paul McLellan, "A Brief History of Chips and Technologies," *SemiWiki*, March 19, 2013, https://semiwiki.com /eda/2152-a-brief-history-of-chips-and-technologies/; Interview with Gordon Campbell, 2021.

210 **Nvidia, had its humble beginnings:** Interview with Chris Malachowsky, 2021.

210 **as a child:** Steve Henn, "Tech Pioneer Channels Hard Lessons into Silicon Valley Success," NPR, February 20, 2012, https://www.npr.org/sections /alltechconsidered/2012/02/20/147162496/tech-pioneer-channels-hard-lessons -into-silicon-valley-success.

210 **the future of graphics:** "Jen-Hsun Huang," StanfordOnline, YouTube Video, June 23, 2011, https://www.youtube.com/watch?v=Xn1EsFe7snQ.

211 **spent lavishly on this software effort:** Ian Buck, "The Evolution of GPUs for General Purpose Computing," September 20–23, 2010, https://www.nvidia.com /content/GTC-2010/pdfs/2275_GTC2010.pdf; Don Clark, "Why a 24-Year-Old Chipmaker Is One of Tech's Hot Prospects," *New York Times*, September 1, 2017; Pradeep Gupta, "CUDA Refresher: Reviewing the Origins of GPU Computing," Nvidia, April 23, 2020, https://developer.nvidia.com/blog/cuda-refresher -reviewing-the-origins-of-gpu-computing/.

211 **discovered a vast new market for parallel processing:** Ben Thompson, "Apple to Build Own GPU, the Evolution of GPUs, Apple and the General-Purpose GPU," *Stratechery Newsletter*, April 12, 2017; Ben Thompson, "Nvidia's Integration Dreams," Stratechery Newsletter, September 15, 2020.

212 **impossible to make a cell phone without them:** Hsiao-Wen Wang, "TSMC Takes on Samsung," *CommonWealth*, May 9, 2013; Timothy B. Lee, "How

Qualcomm Shook Down the Cell Phone Industry for Almost 20 years," *Ars Technica*, May 30, 2019.

212 **tens of millions of lines of code:** Interview with Susie Armstrong, 2021.

213 **hasn't fabricated any chips:** Daniel Nenni, "A Detailed History of Qualcomm," *SemiWiki*, March 9, 2018; Joel West, "Before Qualcomm: Linkabit and the Origins of San Diego's Telecom Industry," *Journal of San Diego History*, https://sandiegohistory.org/journal/v55-1/pdf/v55-1west.pdf.

213 **focus on their core strengths in managing spectrum and in semiconductor design:** Interview with two Qualcomm executives, 2021.

CHAPTER 37 Morris Chang's Grand Alliance

216 **the company announced it was dividing its chip design and fabrication businesses:** Michael Kanellos, "End of Era as AMD's Sanders Steps Aside," CNET, April 24, 2002; Peter Bright, "AMD Completes Exit from Chip Manufacturing Biz," *Wired*, March 5, 2012.

218 **Even TSMC was worried:** Interview with Shang-yi Chiang, 2021.

218 **already had around half of the world's foundry market:** Mark LaPedus, "Will GlobalFoundries Succeed or Fail?" *EE Times*, September 21, 2010, https://www.eetimes.com/will-globalfoundries-succeed-or-fail/.

218 **a chance to distinguish itself from its large rival:** Claire Sung and Jessie Shen, "TSMC 40nm Yield Issues Resurface, CEO Promises Fix by Year-End," *Digitimes*, October 30, 2009; Mark LaPedus, "TSMC Confirms 40-nm Yield Issues, Gives Predictions," *EE Times*, April 30, 2009.

218 **felt like an elevator:** Interview with Rick Cassidy, 2022.

219 **whatever the cost:** Russell Flannery, "Ageless and Peerless in an Era of Fabless," *Forbes*, December 9, 2012; Hsiao-Wen Wang, "TSMC Takes on Samsung," *CommonWealth*, May 9, 2013.

220 **coalescing around TSMC:** Wang, "TSMC Takes on Samsung."

220 **"There was stagnation":** Flannery, "Ageless and Peerless in an Era of Fabless."

220 **retook direct control:** Lisa Wang, "TSMC Reshuffle Stuns Analysts," *Taipei Times*, June 12, 2009; Yin-chuen Wu and Jimmy Hsiung, "I'm Willing to Start from Scratch," *CommonWealth*, June 18, 2009.

220 **"too much capacity":** Robin Kwong, "Too Much Capacity Better Than Too Little for TSMC," *Financial Times*, June 24, 2010.

220 **"We're just at the start":** Flannery, "Ageless and Peerless in an Era of Fabless."

CHAPTER 38 Apple Silicon

221 **"What is software?":** Dag Spicer, "Steve Jobs: From Garage to World's Most Valuable Company," Computer History Museum, December 2, 2011; I was directed to this by Steve Cheney, "1980: Steve Jobs on Hardware and Software Convergence," *Steve Cheney—Technology, Business, and Strategy*, August 18, 2013.

221 **The revolutionary new phone had many other chips:** For details from these iPhone 1 teardowns, see Jonathan Zdziarski, "Chapter 2. Understanding

the iPhone," O'Reilly, https://www.oreilly.com/library/view/iphone-forensics /9780596153588/ch02.html; "iPhone 1st Generation Teardown," *IFIXIT*, June 29, 2007.

222 **the new iPad and the iPhone 4:** Bryan Gardiner, "Four Reasons Apple Bought PA Semi," *Wired*, April 23, 2000; Brad Stone, Adam Satariano, and Gwen Ackerman, "The Most Important Apple Executive You've Never Heard Of," *Bloomberg*, February 18, 2016.

222 **why Apple's products work so smoothly:** Ben Thompson, "Apple's Shifting Differentiation," *Stratechery*, November 11, 2020; Andrei Frumusanu, "Apple Announces the Apple Silicon M1: Ditching x86—What to Expect, Based on A14," *AnandTech*, November 10, 2020.

222 **60 percent of all the world's profits:** Harald Bauer, Felix Grawert, and Sebastian Schink, "Semiconductors for Wireless Communications: Growth Engine of the Industry," McKinsey & Company (Autumn 2012): Exhibit 2.

222 **assembly line workers in China:** Harrison Jacobs, "Inside 'iPhone City,' the Massive Chinese Factory Town Where Half of the World's iPhones Are Produced," *Business Insider*, May 7, 2018.

223 **Vietnam and India, too:** Yu Nakamura, "Foxconn Set to Make iPhone 12 in India, Shifting from China," *Nikkei Asia*, March 11, 2021.

CHAPTER 39 EUV

225 **invested $4 billion in ASML in 2012:** Dylan McGrath, "Intel Again Cuts Stake in ASML," *EE Times*, October 12, 2018.

225 **"solving an impossible problem":** Interview with John Taylor, 2021.

227 **sucking heat out of the laser system:** Interview with two Trumpf executives, 2021.

227 **millions of times a second:** "TRUMPF Laser Amplifier," Trumpf, https://www .trumpf.com/en_US/products/laser/euv-drive-laser/.

228 **457,329 component parts:** Interview with two Trumpf executives, 2021; Mark Lourie, "II-VI Incorporated Expands Manufacturing Capacity of Diamond Windows for TRUMPF High Power CO2 Lasers in EUV Lithography," GlobeNewswire, December 19, 2018, https://www.globenewswire .com/news-release/2018/12/19/1669962/11543/en/II-VI-Incorporated -Expands-Manufacturing-Capacity-of-Diamond-Windows-for-TRUMPF -High-Power-CO2-Lasers-in-EUV-Lithography.html.

228 **Researchers in Lawrence Livermore National Lab:** C. Montcalm, "Multilayer Reflective Coatings for Extreme-Ultraviolet Lithography," Department of Energy Office of Scientific and Technical Information, March 10, 1998, https://www.osti .gov/servlets/purl/310916.

228 **hit a golf ball as far away as the moon:** "Interview with Dr. Peter Kurz: 'Hitting a Golf Ball on the Moon,'" *World of Photonics*, https://world-of-photonics.com /en/newsroom/photonics-industry-portal/photonics-interview/dr-peter-kuerz/; "ZEISS—Breaking New Ground for the Microchips of Tomorrow," ZEISS Group, YouTube Video, August 2, 2019, https://www.youtube.com/watch?v=XeDCrlxBtTw.

228 **"like a machine":** "Responsible Supply Chain: Setting the Bar Higher for the High-Tech Industry," ASML, https://www.asml.com/en/company/sustainability /responsible-supply-chain; interview with Frits van Houts, 2021.

229 **$1 billion it paid Zeiss:** "Press Release: ZEISS and ASML Strengthen Partnership for Next Generation of EUV Lithography Due in Early 2020s," ASML, November 3, 2016, https://www.asml.com/en/news/press-releases/2016/zeiss -and-asml-strengthen-partnership-for-next-generation-of-euv-lithography.

229 **"If you don't behave":** Interview with executive at ASML supplier, 2021.

229 **thirty thousand hours:** Igor Fomenkov et al., "Light Sources for High-Volume Manufacturing EUV Lithography: Technology, Performance, and Power Scaling," *Advanced Optical Technologies* 6, Issue 3-4 (June 8, 2017).

229 **Printing an "x":** This description of computational lithography draws on Jim Keller, "Moore's Law Is Not Dead," UC Berkeley EECS Events, YouTube Video, September 18, 2019, https://www.youtube.com/watch?v=oIG9ztQw2Gc.

230 **critical pieces of U.S.-produced equipment:** "Trumpf Consolidates EUV Lithography Supply Chain with Access Laser Deal," Optics.org, October 4, 2017, https://optics.org/news/8/10/6.

CHAPTER 40 **"There Is No Plan B"**

232 **"There is no Plan B":** Anthony Yen, "Developing EUV Lithography for High Volume Manufacturing—A Personal Journey," *IEEE Technical Briefs*, https:// www.ieee.org/ns/periodicals/EDS/EDS-APRIL-2021-HTML-V2/InnerFiles /LandPage.html.

232 **"their spouse does not complain":** Interview with Shang-yi Chiang, 2021.

233 **spared no expense in testing and improving EUV tools:** Lisa Wang, "TSMC Stalwart Takes SMIC Role," *Taipei Times*, December 22, 2016; Jimmy Hsiung, "Shang-yi Chiang: Rallying the Troops," *CommonWealth*, December 5, 2007; interviews with Shang-yi Chiang and Tony Yen, 2021.

233 **bought Chartered Semiconductor:** Timothy Prickett Morgan, "AMD's Global-Foundries Consumes Chartered Semi Rival," *Register*, January 14, 2010.

233 **an upside-down pyramid:** Interview with former IBM executive, 2021.

233 **selling their chip division:** Interviews with two semiconductor executives, 2021.

233 **10 percent of the foundry marketplace:** "Apple Drove Entire Foundry Sales Increase at TSMC in 2015," *IC Insights*, April 26, 2016.

233 **700,000:** "Samsung, TSMC Remain Tops in Available Wafer Fab Capacity," *IC Insights*, January 6, 2016. This number calculates wafers-per-month as 200mm wafers. At the time the industry's cutting edge was shifting to 300mm wafers, which could accommodate roughly twice as many chips per wafer. Wafer-per-month calculations on a 300mm wafer basis are therefore lower.

234 **license its 14nm process from Samsung:** Peter Bright, "AMD Completes Exit from Chip Manufacturing Biz," *Wired*, March 5, 2012.

234 **The EUV program was being canceled:** Interviews with three former Global-Foundries executives, one of whom focused on EUV, 2021; on R&D spending, see

GlobalFoundries' IPO prospectus, Security and Exchange Commission, October 4, 2021, p. 81, https://www.sec.gov/Archives/edgar/data/0001709048/00011931 2521290644/d192411df1.htm. See also Mark Gilbert, "Q4 Hiring Remains Strong Outlook for Q1 2019," *SemiWiki*, November 4, 2018, https://semiwiki.com/semicon ductor-manufacturers/globalfoundries/7749-globalfoundries-pivot-explained/q.

CHAPTER 41 How Intel Forgot Innovation

236 **more chance to hone its process:** Nick Flaherty, "Top Five Chip Makers Dominate Global Wafer Capacity," *eeNews*, February 11, 2021.

237 **can stretch into the millions of dollars:** Or Sharir, Barak Peleg, and Yoav Shoham, "The Cost of Training NLP Models: A Concise Overview," *AI21 Labs*, April 2020.

238 **America's most valuable semiconductor company:** Wallace Witkowski, "Nvidia Surpasses Intel as Largest U.S. Chip Maker by Market Cap," *Market-Watch*, July 8, 2020.

239 **prices for more powerful TPUs:** "Cloud TPU Pricing," Google Cloud, https://cloud.google.com/tpu/pricing; prices as of November 5, 2021.

239 **"I've been basically running our foundry business":** Chris Nuttall, "Chip Off the Old Block Takes Helm at Intel," *Financial Times*, May 2, 2013.

239 **little internal support:** Interview with former Intel foundry executive, 2021.

239 **shuttered after just several years:** Dylan McGrath, "Intel Confirmed as Foundry for Second FPGA Startup," *EE Times*, February 21, 2012.

240 **done little to explain what went wrong:** Joel Hruska, "Intel Acknowledges It Was 'Too Aggressive' with Its 10nm Plans," *Extreme Tech*, July 18, 2019.

240 **delayed adoption of EUV tools:** Interview with Pat Gelsinger, *Bloomberg*, January 19, 2021, https://www.bloomberg.com/news/videos/2022-01-19/intel-ceo-gelsinger-on-year-ahead-for-global-business-video.

240 **installed at TSMC:** Ian Cutress, "TSMC: We Have 50% of All EUV Installations, 60% Wafer Capacity," *AnandTech*, August 27, 2020.

CHAPTER 42 Made in China

243 **"without informatization, there is no modernization":** Rogier Creemers, ed., "Central Leading Group for Internet Security and Informatization Established," *China Copyright and Media*, March 1, 2014, https://chinacopyrightandmedia.wordpress.com/2014/03/01/central-leading-group-for-internet-security-and-informatization-established/.

243 **"undertake real political reform":** Evan Osnos, "Xi's American Journey," *New Yorker*, February 15, 2012.

243 **many thousands of censors:** Katie Hunt and CY Xu, "China Employs 2 Million to Police Internet,'" CNN, October 7, 2013.

244 **"global village":** Rogier Creemers, ed., Xi Jinping, "Speech at the Work Conference for Cybersecurity and Informatization," *China Copyright and Media*, April 19, 2016, https://chinacopyrightandmedia.wordpress.com/2016/04/19

/speech-at-the-work-conference-for-cybersecurity-and-informatization/, translation adjusted.

245 **"the 'vital gate' of the supply chain":** Ibid.

245 **"paired with Intel chips":** Ibid.

245 **most computers in China:** Almost all CPU chips in PCs are designed by America's Intel or AMD, though both firms manufacture their chips in other countries.

245 **more money importing semiconductors than oil:** See U.N. Comtrade data for integrated circuits (8542) and petroleum (2709).

245 **surveillance technology:** Drew Harwell and Eva Dou, "Huawei Tested AI Software That Could Recognize Uighur Minorities and Alert Police, Report Says," *Washington Post*, December 8, 2020.

245 **rely on chips from American companies:** Paul Mozur and Don Clark, "China's Surveillance State Sucks Up Data. U.S. Tech Is Key to Sorting It," *New York Times*, November 22, 2020.

246 **K. T. Li:** Oral History of Morris Chang, Computer History Museum.

CHAPTER 43 "Call Forth the Assault"

247 **"No one will emerge as a winner in a trade war":** Anna Bruce-Lockhart, "Top Quotes by China President Xi Jinping at Davos 2017," World Economic Forum, January 17, 2017, https://www.weforum.org/agenda/2017/01/chinas-xi-jinping-at-davos-2017-top-quotes/.

247 **"protection will lead to great prosperity and strength":** "Full Text: 2017 Donald Trump Inauguration Speech Transcript," *Politico*, January 20, 2017.

247 **"Xi sounding rather more presidential":** Ian Bremmer, "Xi sounding rather more presidential than US president-elect. #Davos," Twitter, January 17, 2017, https://twitter.com/ianbremmer/status/821304485226119169.

247 **"Robust Defence of Globalisation":** Jamil Anderlini, Wang Feng, and Tom Mitchell, "Xi Jinping Delivers Robust Defence of Globalisation at Davos," *Financial Times*, January 17, 2017; Xi Jinping, "Full Text of Xi Jinping Keynote at the World Economic Forum," CGTN, January 17, 2017, https://america.cgtn.com/2017/01/17/full-text-of-xi-jinping-keynote-at-the-world-economic-forum.

247 **"Hope for Globalization":** Max Ehrenfreund, "World Leaders Find Hope for Globalization in Davos Amid Populist Revolt," *Washington Post*, January 17, 2017.

248 **"The international community is looking to China":** Isaac Stone Fish, "A Communist Party Man at Davos," *Atlantic*, January 18, 2017.

248 **"storm the passes":** http://politics.people.com.cn/n1/2016/0420/c1001-28291806.html; Creemers, ed., Xi Jinping, "Speech at the Work Conference for Cybersecurity and Informatization."

248 **government officials who preferred the status quo:** On Xi's impotence versus the status quo, see Daniel H. Rosen, "China's Economic Reckoning," *Foreign Affairs*, July–August 2021.

249 **"The scale of investment has risen rapidly":** China's State Council report, "Outline for Promoting the Development of the National Integrated Circuit Industry," http://www.csia.net.cn/Article/ShowInfo.asp?InfoID=88343.

249 **data aggregated by scholars at Georgetown University's:** Saif M. Khan, Alexander Mann, and Dahlia Peterson, "The Semiconductor Supply Chain: Assessing National Competitiveness," Center for Security and Emerging Technology, January 2021, p. 8, https://cset.georgetown.edu/wp-content/uploads/The-Semiconductor-Supply-Chain-Issue-Brief.pdf.

250 **leaving China reliant on Nvidia and AMD:** Saif M. Khan and Alexander Mann, "AI Chips: What They Are and Why They Matter," Center for Security and Emerging Technology, April 2020, pp. 29–31, https://cset.georgetown.edu/publication/ai-chips-what-they-are-and-why-they-matter/.

250 **30 percent by 2025:** "China Forecast to Fall Far Short of Its 'Made in China 2025' Goals for ICs," *IC Insights*, January 6, 2021, https://www.icinsights.com/news/bulletins/China-Forecast-To-Fall-Far-Short-Of-Its-Made-In-China-2025-Goals-For-ICs/.

250 **private-sector investors were displaced:** "Dr. Zixue Zhou Appointed as Chairman of SMIC," press release, SMIC, March 6, 2015, http://www.smics.com/en/site/news_read/4539; Doug Fuller, *Paper Tigers, Hidden Dragons* (Oxford University Press, 2016) charts the early stages of the increase in government influence.

251 **small facilities spread across the country:** Interview with former CEO of a Chinese foundry, 2021; Fuller, *Paper Tigers, Hidden Dragons*.

251 **"'Let's lose money'":** Interview with European semiconductor executive, 2020.

251 **Key "investors" in the fund:** Barry Naughton, *Rise of China's Industrial Policy, 1978 to 2020* (Academic Network of Latin America and the Caribbean on China, 2021), p. 114.

251 **a new "venture capital" model:** Arthur Kroeber, "The Venture Capitalist State," *GaveKal Dragonomics*, March 2021.

251 **Only a government could take such a gamble:** Dieter Ernest, *From Catching Up to Forging Ahead: China's Policies for Semiconductors* (East West Center, 2015), p 19.

252 **reduce the share of foreign chips:** Luffy Liu, "Countdown: How Close Is China to 40% Chip Self-Sufficiency?" *EE Times*, April 11, 2019.

253 **the "red supply chain":** https://www.cw.com.tw/article/5053334; https://www.twse.com.tw/ch/products/publication/download/0003000156.pdf. Thanks to Wei-Ting Chen for help translating these documents.

CHAPTER 44 Technology Transfer

255 **"a great opportunity":** David Wolf, "Why Buy the Hardware When China Is Getting the IP for Free?" *Foreign Policy*, April 24, 2015.

255 **collaborating with American cyber sleuths:** IBM denied giving the National Security Agency any client data; Claire Cain Miller, "Revelations of N.S.A. Spying Cost U.S. Tech Companies," *New York Times*, March 21, 2014; Sam Gustin, "IBM: We Haven't Given the NSA Any Client Data," *Time*, March 14, 2014.

255 **"a very significant economic set of reforms":** Matthew Miller, "IBM's CEO Visits China for Trust-Building Talks with Govt Leaders: Sources," Reuters, February 12, 2014.

255 **meeting with top Chinese officials:** See July 2014 meeting with Beijing mayor, IBM News, "Today, #IBM CEO Ginni Rometty met with Beijing Mayor Wang Anshun at the Beijing Convention Center in #China.[PHOTO]," Twitter, July 9, 2014, https://mobile.twitter.com/ibmnews/status/486873143911669760; 2016 meeting with Li Keqiang, "Ginni Rometty of IBM Meets Chinese Premier Li Keqiang," *Forbes*, October 22, 2016.

256 **a report by the Reuters:** Miller, "IBM's CEO Visits China for Trust-Building Talks with Govt Leaders: Sources."

256 **"enhancing cooperation in integrated circuit":** "Chinese Vice Premier Meets IBM President," English.People.CN, November 13, 2014, http://en.people .cn/n/2014/1113/c90883-8808371.html.

256 **little server market share:** Timothy Prickett Morgan, "X86 Servers Dominate the Datacenter—for Now," *Next Platform*, June 4, 2015.

257 **"create a new and vibrant ecosystem":** Paul Mozur, "IBM Venture with China Stirs Concerns," *New York Times*, April 19, 2015.

257 **"huge security risks":** Ibid.

257 **a key source of Qualcomm's revenue:** "China Deal Squeezes Royalty Cuts from Qualcomm," *EE Times*, February 10, 2015.

257 **Huaxintong didn't have a track record:** Chen Qingqing, "Qualcomm's Failed JV Reveals Poor Chipset Strategy Amid Rising Competition: Insiders," *Global Times*, April 22, 2019; Aaron Tilley, Wayne Ma, and Juro Osawa, "Qualcomm's China Venture Shows Risks of Beijing's Tech Ambition," *Information*, April 3, 2019; Li Tao, "Qualcomm Said to End Chip Partnership with Local Government in China's Rural Guizhou Province," *South China Morning Post*, April 19, 2019.

258 **included Phytium:** "Server and Cloud Leaders Collaborate to Create China-Based Green Computing Consortium," *Arm*, April 15, 2016, https://www.arm.com /company/news/2016/04/server-and-cloud-leaders-collaborate-to-create -china-based-green-computing-consortium.

258 **work for Phytium:** See "Wei Li," LinkedIn, https://www.linkedin.com/in/ wei-li-8b0490b/?originalSubdomain=cn; Ellen Nakashima and Gerry Shih, "China Builds Advanced Weapons Systems Using American Chip Technology," *Washington Post*, April 9, 2021.

258 **"world-class":** "AMD and Nantong Fujitsu Microelectronics Co., Ltd. Close on Semiconductor Assembly and Test Joint Venture," AMD, April 29, 2016,

258 **Chinese firms and government bodies:** One of the investors in this joint venture with AMD is the Chinese Academy of Sciences, part of the Chinese state; see Ian Cutress and Wendell Wilson, "Testing a Chinese x86 CPU: A Deep Dive into Zen-Based Hygon Dhyana Processors," *AnandTech*, February 27, 2020.

258 **"know anything about microprocessors, or semiconductors, or China":** Interview with chip industry insider, 2021.

258 **ended up not depending on the money:** Interview with Stacy Rasgon, 2021.

259 **simply tweaking AMD designs:** Interviews with one industry insider and one former U.S. official, 2021; Don Clark, "AMD to License Chip Technology to China Chip Venture," *Wall Street Journal*, April 21, 2016; Usman Pirzada, "No, AMD Did Not Sell the Keys to the x86 Kingdom—Here's How the Chinese Joint

Venture Works," *Wccftech*, June 29, 2019; Cutress and Wilson, "Testing a Chinese x86 CPU"; Stewart Randall, "Did AMD Really Give Away 'Keys to the Kingdom'?" *TechNode*, July 10, 2019.

259 **The *Wall Street Journal* reported:** Kate O'Keeffe and Brian Spegele, "How a Big U.S. Chip Maker Gave China the 'Keys to the Kingdom,'" *Wall Street Journal*, June 27, 2019.

259 **raise eyebrows in Washington:** "AMD EPYC Momentum Grows with Datacenter Commitments from Tencent and JD.com, New Product Details from Sugon and Lenovo," press release, AMD, August 23, 2017, https://ir.amd.com/news -events/press-releases/detail/788/amd-epyc-momentum-grows-with-datacenter -commitments-from; interview with former U.S. official, 2021.

259 **"nuclear weapons and hypersonic weapons":** Craig Timberg and Ellen Nakashima, "Supercomputing Is Latest Front in U.S.-China High-Tech Battle," *Washington Post*, June 21, 2019; Industry and Security Bureau, "Addition of Entities to the Entity List and Revision of an Entry on the Entity List," Federal Register, June 24, 2019, https://www.federalregister.gov/documents /2019/06/24/2019-13245/addition-of-entities-to-the-entity-list-and-revision -of-an-entry-on-the-entity-list; Michael Kan, "US Tries to Thwart China's Work on Exascale Supercomputer by Blocking Exports," *PC Mag*, April 8, 2021.

259 **advertised its links to the Chinese military:** "Statement of Elsa Kania," in "Hearing on Technology, Trade, and Military-Civil Fusion: China's Pursuit of Artificial Intelligence, New Materials, and New Energy," U.S.-China Economic and Security Review Commission, June 7, 2019, p. 69, https://www.uscc.gov /sites/default/files/2019-10/June%207,%202019%20Hearing%20Transcript .pdf.

259 **wasn't sure how Sugon acquired the chips:** Anton Shilov, "Chinese Server Maker Sugon Has Its Own Radeon Instinct MI50 Compute Cards (Updated)," *Tom's Hardware*, October 15, 2020, https://www.tomshardware.com/news/chinese -server-maker-sugon-has-its-own-radeon-instinct-mi50-compute-cards. An AMD representative did not respond to my request for information about its relationship with Sugon.

260 **vulnerable to political pressure from Beijing:** Alexandra Alper and Greg Roumeliotis, "Exclusive: U.S. Clears SoftBank's $2.25 Billion Investment in GM-Backed Cruise," Reuters, July 5, 2019; Dan Primack, "SoftBank's CFIUS Workaround," *Axios*, November 29, 2018; Heather Somerville, "SoftBank Picking Its Battles with U.S. National Security Committee," Reuters, April 11, 2019.

260 **only $775 million:** Cheng Ting-Fang, Lauly Li, and Michelle Chan, "How SoftBank's Sale of Arm China Sowed the Seeds of Discord," *Nikkei Asia*, June 16, 2020; "Inside the Battle for Arm China," *Financial Times*, June 26, 2020.

260 **one Arm executive told *Nikkei Asia*:** Cheng Ting-Fang and Debby Wu, "ARM in China Joint Venture to Help Foster 'Secure' Chip Technology," *Nikkei Asia*, May 30, 2017.

CHAPTER 45 "Mergers Are Bound to Happen"

263 **celebrated as a chip billionaire:** Nobutaka Hirooka, "Inside Tsinghua Unigroup, a Key Player in China's Chip Strategy," *Nikkei Asia*, November 12, 2020; "University's Deal Spree Exposes Zhao as Chip Billionaire," *China Daily*, March 25, 2015.

263 **a path toward a billion-dollar fortune:** Hirooka, "Inside Tsinghua Unigroup"; Yue Wang, "Meet Tsinghua's Zhao Weiguo, the Man Spearheading China's Chip Ambition," *Forbes*, July 29, 2015.

264 **"personal friend":** Kenji Kawase, "Was Tsinghua Unigroup's Bond Default a Surprise?" *Nikkei Asia*, December 4, 2020; Eva Dou, "China's Biggest Chip Maker's Possible Tie-Up with H-P Values Unit at Up to $5 Billion," *Wall Street Journal*, April 15, 2015; Wang, "Meet Tsinghua's Zhao Weiguo"; Yue Wang, "Tsinghua Spearheads China's Chip Drive," *Nikkei Asia*, July 29, 2015.

264 **college roommate of Xi Jinping:** Dieter Ernst, "China's Bold Strategy for Semiconductors—Zero-Sum Game or Catalyst for Cooperation?" East-West Center, September 2016; Willy Wo-Lap Lam, "Members of the Xi Jinping Clique Revealed," The Jamestown Foundation, February 7, 2014; Chen Xi stepped down as Tsinghua University president at the end of 2008.

264 **"All our deals are market-oriented":** Wang, "Meet Tsinghua's Zhao Weiguo."

264 **"Maybe you'll catch a deer":** Dou, "China's Biggest Chip Maker's Possible Tie-Up with H-P Values Unit at Up to $5 Billion."

264 **the sums Zhao spent:** Zijing Wu and Jonathan Browning, "China University Deal Spree Exposes Zhao as Chip Billionaire," *Bloomberg*, March 23, 2015.

265 **"enormous synergies":** Saabira Chaudhuri, "Spreadtrum Communications Agrees to $1.78 Billion Takeover," *Wall Street Journal*, July 12, 2013.

265 **Zhao cut a deal with Intel:** "Intel and Tsinghua Unigroup Collaborate to Accelerate Development and Adoption of Intel-Based Mobile Devices," news release, Intel Newsroom, September 25, 2014, https://newsroom.intel.com/news-releases /intel-and-tsinghua-unigroup-collaborate-to-accelerate-development-and -adoption-of-intel-based-mobile-devices/#gs.7y1hjm.

265 **"national priority":** Eva Dou and Wayne Ma, "Intel Invests $1.5 Billion for State in Chinese Chip Maker," *Wall Street Journal*, September 26, 2014; Cheng Ting-Fang, "Intel's 5G Modem Alliance with Beijing-Backed Chipmaker Ends," *Nikkei Asia*, February 26, 2019.

265 **take $24 billion instead:** Paul McLellan, "Memory in China: XMC," *Cadence*, April 15, 2016, https://community.cadence.com/cadence_blogs_8/b/breakfast -bytes/posts/china-memory-2; "China's Tsinghua Unigroup to Build $30 Billion Nanjing Chip Plant," Reuters, January 19, 2017; Eva Dou, "Tsinghua Unigroup Acquires Control of XMC in Chinese-Chip Deal," *Wall Street Journal*, July 26, 2016.

265 **real estate and online gambling:** Josh Horwitz, "Analysis: China's Would-Be Chip Darling Tsinghua Unigroup Bedevilled by Debt and Bad Bets," Reuters, January 19, 2021.

265　**announced plans to invest:** Dou, "China's Biggest Chip Maker's Possible Tie-Up with H-P Values Unit at Up to $5 Billion."

266　**hired several leading Taiwanese semiconductor executives:** Josephine Lien and Jessie Shen, "Former UMC CEO to Join Tsinghua Unigroup," *Digitimes Asia*, January 10, 2017; Matthew Fulco, "Taiwan Chipmakers Eye China Market," *Taiwan Business Topics*, February 8, 2017, https://topics.amcham.com.tw/2017/02/taiwan-chipmakers-eye-china-market/.

266　**pursued stakes and joint ventures:** Debby Wu and Cheng Ting-Fang, "Tsinghua Unigroup-SPIL Deal Axed on Policy Worries," *Nikkei Asia*, April 28, 2016.

266　**buying the island's crown jewels:** Peter Clarke, "China's Tsinghua Interested in MediaTek," *EE News*, November 3, 2015.

266　**suggested China should ban imports of Taiwanese chips:** Simon Mundy, "Taiwan's Chipmakers Push for China Thaw," *Financial Times*, December 6, 2015; Zou Chi, TNL Media Group, November 3, 2015, https://www.thenewslens.com/article/30138.

266　**"if the price is right":** Cheng Ting-Fang, "Chipmaker Would Sell Stake to China 'If the Price Is Right,'" *Nikkei Asia*, November 7, 2015.

266　**"it will not be that easy to protect intellectual property":** J. R. Wu, "Chinese Investors Should Not Get Board Seats on Taiwan Chip Firms—TSMC Chief," Reuters, June 7, 2016.

267　**"join hands and raise the status":** J. R. Wu, "Taiwan's Mediatek Says Open to Cooperation with China in Chip Sector," Reuters, November 2, 2015.

267　**"You cannot escape from this issue":** Ben Bland and Simon Mundy, "Taiwan Considers Lifting China Semiconductor Ban," *Financial Times*, November 22, 2015.

267　**floated the idea of buying Micron:** Eva Dou and Don Clark, "State-Owned Chinese Chip Maker Tsinghua Unigroup Makes $23 Billion Bid for Micron," *Wall Street Journal*, July 14, 2015.

267　**the U.S. government's security concerns:** Interviews with two former senior officials, 2021.

267　**extending a $3.7 billion offer:** Eva Dou and Don Clark, "Arm of China-Controlled Tsinghua to Buy 15% Stake in Western Digital," *Wall Street Journal*, September 30, 2015.

267　**"This is purely a financial investment":** Eva Dou and Robert McMillan, "China's Tsinghua Unigroup Buys Small Stake in U.S. Chip Maker Lattice," *Wall Street Journal*, April 14, 2016.

267　**weeks after the investment was publicized:** Ed Lin, "China Inc. Retreats from Lattice Semiconductor," *Barron's*, October 7, 2016.

267　**discreetly funded by the Chinese government:** Liana Baker, Koh Gui Qing, and Julie Zhu, "Chinese Government Money Backs Buyout Firm's Deal for U.S. Chipmaker," Reuters, November 28, 2016. China Reform Holding, an investment fund owned by the Chinese government, is a key investor in Canyon Bridge; see Junko Yoshida, "Does China Have Imagination? *EE Times*, April 14, 2020.

267　**simultaneously bought Imagination:** Nick Fletcher, "Imagination Technologies Jumps 13% as Chinese Firm Takes 3% Stake," *Guardian*, May 9, 2016.

268 **so that Washington didn't block it, too:** "Canyon Bridge Confident Imagination Deal Satisfies UK Government," *Financial Times*, September 25, 2017; Turner et al., "Canyon Bridge Is Said to Ready Imagination Bid Minus U.S. Unit," *Bloomberg*, September 7, 2017.

268 **restructure the board of directors:** Nic Fides, "Chinese Move to Take Control of Imagination Technologies Stalls," *Financial Times*, April 7, 2020.

268 **insider trading:** "USA v. Chow," https://www.corporatedefensedisputes.com/wp-content/uploads/sites/19/2021/04/United-States-v.-Chow-2d-Cir.-Apr.-6-2021.pdf; "United States of America v. Benjamin Chow," https://www.justice.gov/usao-sdny/press-release/file/1007536/download; Jennifer Bennett, "Canyon Bridge Founder's Insider Trading Conviction Upheld," *Bloomberg Law*, April 6, 2021.

268 **"bound to happen":** Wang, "Meet Tsinghua's Zhao Weiguo."

268 **received new "investment":** Sijia Jang, "China's Tsinghua Unigroup Signs Financing Deal for Up to 150 Bln Yuan," Reuters, March 28, 2017.

CHAPTER 46 The Rise of Huawei

269 **ties between Huawei and the Chinese state:** Chairman Mike Rogers and Ranking Member C. A. Dutch Ruppersberger, "Investigative Report on the U.S. National Security Issues Posed by Chinese Telecommunications Companies Huawei and ZTE," Permanent Select Committee on Intelligence, U.S. House of Representatives, October 8, 2012, https://republicans-intelligence.house.gov/sites/intelligence.house.gov/files/documents/huawei-zte%20investigative%20report%20(final).pdf, pp. 11–25.

271 **synthetic fiber:** William Kirby et al., "Huawei: A Global Tech Giant in the Crossfire of a Digital Cold War," Harvard Business School Case N-1-320-089, p. 2.

271 **building switching equipment:** Kirby et al., "Huawei"; Jeff Black, Allen Wan, and Zhu Lin, "Xi Jinping's Tech Wonderland Runs into Headwinds," *Bloomberg*, September 29, 2020.

271 **copied directly:** Scott Thurm, "Huawei Admits Copying Code from Cisco in Router Software," *Wall Street Journal*, March 24, 2003.

272 **the country's spy agencies believe:** Tom Blackwell, "Exclusive: Did Huawei Bring Down Nortel? Corporate Espionage, Theft, and the Parallel Rise and Fall of Two Telecom Giants," *National Post*, February 20, 2020.

272 **$15 billion annual R&D budget:** Nathaniel Ahrens, "China's Competitiveness," Center for Strategic and International Studies, February 2013, https://csis-website-prod.s3.amazonaws.com/s3fs-public/legacy_files/files/publication/130215_competitiveness_Huawei_casestudy_Web.pdf.

272 **tour the U.S.:** Tian Tao and Wu Chunbo, *The Huawei Story* (Sage Publications Pvt. Ltd., 2016), p. 53.

272 **"they felt they were a hundred years behind":** Interview with former IBM consultant and later Huawei employee, 2021.

273 **"Sacrifice is a soldier's highest cause":** Raymond Zhong, "Huawei's 'Wolf Culture' Helped It Grow, and Got It into Trouble," *New York Times*, December 18, 2018.

273 **studied Stalingrad:** "Stanford Engineering Hero Lecture: Morris Chang in Conversation with President John L. Hennessy," Stanford Online, YouTube Video, April 25, 2014, https://www.youtube.com/watch?v=wEh3ZgbvBrE.

273 **$75 billion:** Chuin-Wei Yap, "State Support Helped Fuel Huawei's Global Rise," *Wall Street Journal*, December 25, 2019.

273 **top Chinese officials:** Ahrens, "China's Competitiveness."

274 **"Democrat or Republican":** Tao and Chunbo, *The Huawei Story*, p. 58; Mike Rogers and Dutch Ruppersberger, "Investigative Report on the U.S. National Security Issues Posed by Chinese Telecommunications Companies Huawei and ZTE," U.S. House of Representatives, October 8, 2012, https://stacks.stanford.edu/file/druid:rm226yb7473/Huawei-ZTE%20Investigative%20Report%20(FINAL).pdf.

275 **designing as many as possible in-house:** Interview with former IBM consultant and Huawei employee, 2021.

275 **TSMC's second-largest customer:** Cheng Ting-Fang and Lauly Li, "TSMC Halts New Huawei Orders After US Tightens Restrictions," *Nikkei Asia*, May 18, 2020.

CHAPTER 47 The 5G Future

277 **switching gear the size of a closet:** Interview with Ken Hunkler, 2021.

278 **more precision while using less power:** Interview with Dave Robertson, 2021.

280 **"resemble a smartphone":** Spencer Chin, "Teardown Reveals the Tesla S Resembles a Smartphone," *Power Electronics*, October 28, 2014.

280 **high-quality and competitively priced:** Ray Le Maistre, "BT's McRae: Huawei Is 'the Only True 5G Supplier Right Now,'" *Light Reading*, November 21, 2018.

280 **one study of Huawei's radio units:** Norio Matsumoto and Naoki Watanabe, "Huawei's Base Station Teardown Shows Dependence on US-Made Parts," *Nikkei Asia*, October 12, 2020.

CHAPTER 48 The Next Offset

283 **"psychological nuclear attack":** Liu Zhen, "China-US Rivalry: How the Gulf War Sparked Beijing's Military Revolution," *South China Morning Post*, January 18, 2021; see also Harlan W. Jencks, "Chinese Evaluations of 'Desert Storm': Implications for PRC Security," *Journal of East Asian Affairs* 6, No. 2 (Summer/Fall 1992): 447–477.

284 **"China could surpass the United States":** "Final Report," National Security Commission on Artificial Intelligence, p. 25.

284 **"AI weapons":** Elsa B. Kania, "'AI Weapons' in China's Military Innovation," Global China, Brookings Institution, April 2020.

285 **a "triad":** Ben Buchanan, "The AI Triad and What It Means for National Security Strategy," Center for Security and Emerging Technology, August 2020.

285 **China doesn't have any built-in advantages in gathering data:** Matt Sheehan, "Much Ado About Data: How America and China Stack Up," MacroPolo, July 16, 2019, https://macropolo.org/ai-data-us-china/?rp=e.

286 **59 percent of the world's top AI researchers:** "The Global AI Talent Tracker," MacroPolo, https://macropolo.org/digital-projects/the-global-ai-talent-tracker/.

286 **95 percent of GPUs:** "White Paper on China's Computing Power Development Index," tr. Jeffrey Ding, China Academy of Information and Communications Technology, September 2021, https://docs.google.com/document/d/1Mq5vpZQe7n rKgkYJA2-yZNV1Eo8swh_w36TUEzFWIWs/edit#, original Chinese source: http://www.caict.ac.cn/kxyj/qwfb/bps/202109/t20210918_390058.htm.

286 **researchers at Georgetown University:** Ryan Fedasiuk, Jennifer Melot, and Ben Murphy, "Harnessed Lightning: How the Chinese Military Is Adopting Artificial Intelligence," CSET, October 2021, https://cset.georgetown.edu/publication /harnessed-lightning/, esp. fn 84; on civil military fusion, see Elsa B. Kania and Lorand Laskai, "Myths and Realities of China's Military-Civil Fusion Strategy," Center for a New American Security, January 28, 2021.

287 **a decisive technological advantage:** Gian Gentile, Michael Shurkin, Alexandra T. Evans, Michelle Grise, Mark Hvizda, and Rebecca Jensen, "A History of the Third Offset, 2014–2018," Rand Corporation, 2021; "Remarks by Deputy Secretary Work on Third Offset Strategy," U.S. Department of Defense, April 28, 2016.

288 **"computers distributed across the battlespace":** "DARPA Tiles Together a Vision of Mosaic Warfare," Defense Advanced Research Projects Agency, https:// www.darpa.mil/work-with-us/darpa-tiles-together-a-vision-of-mosiac-warfare.

288 **"human-machine teaming":** "Designing Agile Human-Machine Teams," Defense Advanced Research Projects Agency, November 28, 2016, https://www.darpa .mil/program/2016-11-28.

288 **The Russian government also reportedly obstructs GPS signals:** Roger N. McDermott, "Russia's Electronic Warfare Capabilities to 2025," International Centre for Defence and Security, September 2017; "Study Maps 'Extensive Russian GPS Spoofing,'" BBC News, April 2, 2019.

288 **alternative navigation systems:** "Adaptable Navigation Systems (ANS) (Archived)," Defense Advanced Research Projects Agency, https://www.darpa .mil/program/adaptable-navigation-systems.

289 **a military's ability to see and to communicate:** Bryan Clark and Dan Patt, "The US Needs a Strategy to Secure Microelectronics—Not Just Funding," Hudson Institute, March 15, 2021.

289 **Electronics Resurgence Initiative:** "DARPA Electronics Resurgence Initiative," Defense Advanced Research Projects Agency, June 28, 2021, https://www.darpa .mil/work-with-us/electronics-resurgence-initiative.

289 **transistor structures:** On FinFET, see Tekla S. Perry, "How the Father of FinFETs Helped Save Moore's Law," *IEEE Spectrum*, April 21, 2020.

289 **10–15 percent:** Norman J. Asher and Leland D. Strom, "The Role of the Department of Defense in the Development of Integrated Circuits," *Institute for Defense Analyses*, May 1977, p. 74.

289 **several hundred million dollars:** Ed Sperling, "How Much Will That Chip Cost?" *Semiconductor Engineering*, March 27, 2014.

290 **Spectre and Meltdown:** Cade Metz and Nicole Perlroth, "Researchers Discover Two Major Flaws in the World's Computers," *New York Times*, January 3, 2018.

290 **before notifying the U.S. government:** Robert McMillan and Liza Lin, "Intel Warned Chinese Companies of Chip Flaws Before U.S. Government," *Wall Street Journal*, January 28, 2018.

290 **"zero trust":** Serge Leef, "Supply Chain Hardware Integrity for Electronics Defense (SHIELD) (Archived)," Defense Advanced Research Projects Agency, https://www.darpa.mil/program/supply-chain-hardware-integrity-for-electronics -defense#:~:text=The%20goal%20of%20DARPA's%20SHIELD,consuming%20 to%20be%20cost%20effective; "A DARPA Approach to Trusted Microelectronics," https://www.darpa.mil/attachments/ATrustthroughTechnologyApproach _FINAL.PDF.

291 **now betting the future:** "Remarks by Deputy Secretary Work on Third Offset Strategy."

291 **"in the car with us":** Interview with former U.S. official, 2021; Gian Gentile, Michael Shurkin, Alexandra T. Evans, Michelle Grise, Mark Hvizda, and Rebecca Jensen, "A History of the Third Offset, 2014–2018."

CHAPTER 49 "Everything We're Competing On"

295 **"palpable sense of fear":** Interview with former senior U.S. official, 2021.

296 **"going to bury us":** Ibid.

296 **didn't see chips as an important issue:** Ibid.

296 **Pritzker gave a high-profile address:** "U.S. Secretary of Commerce Penny Pritzker Delivers Major Policy Address on Semiconductors at Center for Strategic and International Studies," speech by Penny Pritzker, U.S. Department of Commerce, November 2, 2016.

297 **issued a report:** "Ensuring Long-Term U.S. Leadership in Semiconductors," report to the president, President's Council of Advisors on Science and Technology, January 2017.

299 **spent decades fighting allegations:** Mike Rogers and Dutch Ruppersberger, "Investigative Report on the U.S. National Security Issues Posed by Chinese Telecommunications Companies Huawei and ZTE," U.S. House of Representatives, October 8, 2012; Kenji Kawase, "ZTE's Less-Known Roots: Chinese Tech Company Falls from Grace," *Nikkei Asia*, April 27, 2018; Nick McKenzie and Angus Grigg, "China's ZTE Was Built to Spy and Bribe, Court Documents Allege," *Sydney Morning Herald*, May 31, 2018; Nick McKenzie and Angus Grigg, "Corrupt Chinese Company on Telstra Shortlist," *Sydney Morning Herald*, May 13, 2018; "ZTE Tops 2006 International CDMA Market," CIOL Bureau, https:// web.archive.org/web/20070927230100/http://www.ciol.com/ciol-techportal /Content/Mobility/News/2007/20703081355.asp.

299 **accused of violating:** Juro Osawa and Eva Dou, "U.S. to Place Trade Restrictions on China's ZTE," *Wall Street Journal*, March 7, 2016; Paul Mozur, "U.S. Subpoenas Huawei Over Its Dealings in Iran and North Korea," *New York Times*, June 2, 2016.

299 **opted to punish the company:** Interviews with two Obama administration officials, 2021; Osawa and Dou, "U.S. to Place Trade Restrictions on China's ZTE."

299 **before they'd taken force:** Industry and Security Bureau, "Removal of Certain Persons from the Entity List; Addition of a Person to the Entity List; and EAR Conforming Change," Federal Register, March 29, 2017, https://www.federalregister .gov/documents/2017/03/29/2017-06227/removal-of-certain-persons-from -the-entity-list-addition-of-a-person-to-the-entity-list-and-ear; Brian Heater, "ZTE Pleads Guilty to Violating Iran Sanctions, Agrees to $892 Million Fine," *TechCrunch*, March 7, 2017.

299 **Trump repeatedly attacked China for "ripping us off":** Veronica Stracqualursi, "10 Times Trump Attacked China and Its Trade Relations with the US," ABC News, November 9, 2017.

300 **"there's nothing you can do":** Interviews with four former senior officials, 2021.

300 **"everything we're competing on in the twenty-first century":** Interview with former senior official, 2021.

300 **the government began focusing on semiconductors:** Ibid.

301 **Krzanich faced a backlash:** Lucinda Shen, "Donald Trump's Tweets Triggered Intel CEO's Exit from Business Council," *Fortune*, November 9, 2017; Dawn Chmielewski and Ina Fried, "Intel's CEO Planned, Then Scrapped, a Donald Trump Fundraiser," CNBC, June 1, 2016.

301 **"our number one competitor":** Interview with former senior administration official, 2021.

302 **too much technological leakage:** Interview with three former senior officials, 2021.

302 **mostly a trade issue:** Chad Bown, Euijin Jung, and Zhiyao Lu, "Trump, China, and Tariffs: From Soybeans to Semiconductors," *Vox EU*, June 19, 2018.

302 **violated the terms of its plea agreement:** Steve Stecklow, Karen Freifeld, and Sijia Jiang, "U.S. Ban on Sales to China's ZTE Opens Fresh Front as Tensions Escalate," Reuters, April 16, 2018.

302 **"almost without anyone knowing":** Interview with senior administration official, 2021.

302 **"losing too many jobs in China":** Dan Strumpf and John D. McKinnon, "Trump Extends Lifeline to Sanctioned Tech Company ZTE," *Wall Street Journal*, May 13, 2018; Scott Horsley and Scott Neuman, "President Trump Puts 'America First' on Hold to Save Chinese Jobs," NPR, May 14, 2018.

CHAPTER 50 Fujian Jinhua

305 **"Clear computer data":** This account is drawn from "United States of America v. United Microelectronics Corporation, et al., Defendant(s)," United States District Court for the Northern District of California, September 27, 2018, https://www .justice.gov/opa/press-release/file/1107251/download and "MICRON TECHNOLOGY, INC.'S COMPLAINT." UMC pled guilty to these charges as part of a settlement with the U.S. government. The UMC employees in question were convicted on criminal charges, fined, and sentenced to prison by a Taiwanese court; Office of Public Affairs, "Taiwan Company Pleads Guilty to Trade Secret Theft in Criminal Case Involving PRC State-Owned Company," U.S. Department

of Justice, October 28, 2020, https://www.justice.gov/opa/pr/taiwan-company
-pleads-guilty-trade-secret-theft-criminal-case-involving-prc-state-owned.

306 **over $5 billion:** Chuin-Wei Yap and Yoko Kubota, "U.S. Ban Threatens Beijing's
Ambitions as Tech Power," *Wall Street Journal*, October 30, 2018.

307 **receive around $700 million:** Chuin-Wei Yap, "Micron Barred from Selling
Some Products in China," *Wall Street Journal*, July 4, 2018.

307 **wasn't in the DRAM business:** In its defense in the Fujian Jinhua case, UMC
emphasized its prior memory chip expertise, but its 2016 Annual Report stated
emphatically that "we . . . do not intend to enter the DRAM industry." See UMC
Form 20-F, filed with the U.S. Securities and Exchanges Commission, 2016, p. 27.

307 **nine hundred files:** Paul Mozur, "Inside a Heist of American Chip Designs, as
China Bids for Tech Power," *New York Times*, June 22, 2018.

307 **tapping Wang's phone:** Ibid.

307 **banned Micron from selling:** Yap, "Micron Barred from Selling Some Products
in China."

308 **"bully backward countries":** https://www.storm.mg/article/1358975?
mode=whole, tr. Wei-Ting Chen.

308 **promptly restarted:** David E. Sanger and Steven Lee Meyers, "After a Hiatus,
China Accelerates Cyberspying Efforts to Obtain U.S. Technology," *New York
Times*, November 29, 2018.

308 **still secret:** Advanced Micro-Fabrication Equipment Inc., "AMEC Wins Injunction in Patent Infringement Dispute Involving Veeco Instruments (Shanghai)
Co. Ltd.," *PR Newswire*, December 8, 2017, https://www.prnewswire.com/news
-releases/amec-wins-injunction-in-patent-infringement-dispute-involving-veeco
-instruments-shanghai-co-ltd-300569295.html; Mark Cohen, "Semiconductor
Patent Litigation Part 2: Nationalism, Transparency and Rule of Law," *China
IPR*, July 4, 2018, https://chinaipr.com/2018/07/04/semiconductor-patent
-litigation-part-2-nationalism-transparency-and-rule-of-law/; "Veeco Instruments Inc., Plaintiff, against SGL Carbon, LLC, and SGL Group SE, Defendants,"
United States District Court Eastern District of New York, https://chinaipr2.files
.wordpress.com/2018/07/uscourts-nyed-1_17-cv-02217-0.pdf.

309 **advocated imposing financial sanctions:** Kate O'Keeffe, "U.S. Adopts New Battle
Plan to Fight China's Theft of Trade Secrets," *Wall Street Journal*, November 12,
2018.

309 **the Trump administration was confident Tokyo supported a tough move:**
Interviews with five government officials in Washington and Tokyo, 2019–2021.

310 **"why the fuck wouldn't we use this?":** Interview with former senior official,
2021.

310 **ground to a halt:** James Politi, Emily Feng, and Kathrin Hille, "US Targets China
Chipmaker over Security Concerns," *Financial Times*, October 30, 2018.

CHAPTER 51 The Assault on Huawei

311 **"They know everything":** Dan Strumpf and Katy Stech Ferek, "U.S. Tightens
Restrictions on Huawei's Access to Chips," *Wall Street Journal*, August 17, 2020.

312 **"deny them the fruits"**: Turpin quoted in Elizabeth C. Economy, *The World According to China* (Wiley, 2021).

312 **"a proxy for everything we had done wrong"**: Interview with two senior Trump administration officials, 2021.

312 **Turnbull bought himself a 474-page-book**: Peter Hartcher, *Red Zone: China's Challenge and Australia's Future* (Black Inc., 2021), pp. 18–19.

312 **arrested a former company executive**: Alicja Ptak and Justyna Pawlak, "Polish Trial Begins in Huawei-Linked China Espionage Case," Reuters, June 1, 2021.

312 **quietly imposed strict restrictions**: Mathieu Rosemain and Gwenaelle Barzic, "Exclusive: French Limits on Huawei 5G Equipment Amount to De Facto Ban by 2028," Reuters, July 22, 2020.

312 **"consequences"**: Katrin Bennhold and Jack Ewing, "In Huawei Battle, China Threatens Germany 'Where It Hurts': Automakers," *New York Times*, January 16, 2020.

313 **deficiencies in Huawei's cybersecurity practices**: Gordon Corera, "Huawei 'Failed to Improve UK Security Standards,'" BBC News, October 1, 2020.

313 **"China will be a global tech power"**: Robert Hannigan, "Blanket Bans on Chinese Tech Companies like Huawei Make No Sense," *Financial Times*, February 12, 2019.

313 **violated U.S. sanctions on Iran**: Shayna Jacobs and Amanda Coletta, "Meng Wanzhou Can Return to China, Admits Helping Huawei Conceal Dealings in Iran," *Washington Post*, September 24, 2021.

314 **"strangle Huawei"**: James Politi and Kiran Stacey, "US Escalates China Tensions with Tighter Huawei Controls," *Financial Times*, May 15, 2020.

315 **"weaponized interdependence"**: Henry Farrell and Abraham L. Newman, "Weaponized Interdependence: How Global Economic Networks Shape State Coercion," *International Security* 44, No. 1 (2019): 42–79.

316 **tightened restrictions on Huawei further**: "Commerce Addresses Huawei's Efforts to Undermine Entity List, Restricts Products Designed and Produced with U.S. Technologies," U.S. Department of Commerce, May 15, 2020, https:/2017-2021 .commerce.gov/news/press-releases/2020/05/commerce-addresses-huaweis -efforts-undermine-entity-list-restricts.html.

316 **also its spirit**: Kathrin Hille and Kiran Stacey, "TSMC Falls into Line with US Export Controls on Huawei," *Financial Times*, June 9, 2020.

316 **Huawei's been forced to divest**: "Huawei Said to Sell Key Server Division Due to U.S. Blacklisting," *Bloomberg*, November 2, 2021.

316 **can't get the necessary chips**: Craig S. Smith, "How the Huawei Fight Is Changing the Face of 5G," *IEEE Spectrum*, September 29, 2021.

316 **delayed due to chip shortages**: Lauly Li and Kenji Kawase, "Huawei and ZTE Slow Down China 5G Rollout as US Curbs Start to Bite," *Nikkei Asia*, August 19, 2020.

317 **ASML's EUV machines to Chinese firms**: Alexandra Alper, Toby Sterling, and Stephen Nellis, "Trump Administration Pressed Dutch Hard to Cancel China Chip-Equipment Sale: Sources," Reuters, January 6, 2020.

317 **Sugon**: Industry and Security Bureau, "Addition of Entities to the Entity List and Revision of an Entry on the Entity List," Federal Register, June 24, 2019,

https://www.federalregister.gov/documents/2019/06/24/2019-13245/addition
-of-entities-to-the-entity-list-and-revision-of-an-entry-on-the-entity-list.

317 **Phytium:** Ellen Nakashima and Gerry Shih, "China Builds Advanced Weapons Systems Using American Chip Technology," *Washington Post*, April 9, 2021.

318 **"unreliable entity list":** Zhong Shan, "MOFCOM Order No. 4 of 2020 on Provisions on the Unreliable Entity List," Order of the Ministry of Commerce of the People's Republic of China, September 19, 2020, http://english.mofcom.gov .cn/article/policyrelease/questions/202009/20200903002580.shtml.

318 **"a beautiful thing":** Interview with former senior US official, 2021.

CHAPTER 52 China's Sputnik Moment?

320 **as the rest of the country remained frozen:** Cheng Ting-Fang and Lauly Li, "How China's Chip Industry Defied the Coronavirus Lockdown," *Nikkei Asia*, March 18, 2020.

320 **"boosted Beijing's quest for tech dominance":** Dan Wang, "China's Sputnik Moment?" *Foreign Affairs*, July 29, 2021.

320 **"chip czar":** "Xi Jinping Picks Top Lieutenant to Lead China's Chip Battle Against U.S.," *Bloomberg*, June 16, 2021.

321 **spending billions to subsidize:** News headlines that suggest China's ready to spend as much as $1.4 trillion to subsidize technology shouldn't be taken seriously. Beijing has approved industrial "guidance funds" with a nominal value of around $1.5 trillion, mostly to be raised and spent by local authorities. These aren't solely focused on technology, however; official guidelines allow these funds to be spent not only on "strategic emerging industries" but also infrastructure and social housing. So, like many investment projects in China, there's a good chance a portion of this money ends up simply subsidizing yet more real estate development rather than supporting semiconductors. Tianlei Huang, "Government-Guided Funds in China: Financing Vehicles for State Industrial Policy," *PIIE*, June 17, 2019, https://www.piie.com/blogs/china-economic-watch/government-guided -funds-china-financing-vehicles-state-industrial-policy; Tang Ziyi and Xue Xiaoli, "Four Things to Know About China's $670 Billion Government Guidance Funds," *Caixin Global*, February 25, 2020.

321 **"no experience, no technology, no talent":** HSMC investigation by Qiu Xiaofen and Su Jianxun, Yang Xuan, ed., tr. Alexander Boyd, in Jordan Schneider, "Billion Dollar Heist: How Scammers Rode China's Chip Boom to Riches," *ChinaTalk*, March 30, 2021, https://chinatalk.substack.com/p/billion-dollar-heist -how-scammers; Luo Guoping and Mo Yelin, "Wuhan's Troubled $18.5 Billion Chipmaking Project Isn't as Special as Local Officials Claimed," *Caixin Global*, September 4, 2020.

322 **cost $300 million per machine:** Toby Sterling, "Intel Orders ASML System for Well Over $340 mln in Quest for Chipmaking Edge," Reuters, January 19, 2022.

324 **moved from the U.S. to Switzerland:** David Manners, "RISC-V Foundation Moves to Switzerland," *Electronics Weekly*, November 26, 2019.

324 **government subsidies may help it win business:** Dylan Patel, "China Has Built the World's Most Expensive Silicon Carbide Fab, but Numbers Don't Add Up," *SemiAnalysis*, September 30, 2021, https://semianalysis.com/china-has-built -the-worlds-most-expensive-silicon-carbide-fab-but-numbers-dont-add-up/.

324 **estimates suggest that China's share of fabrication will increase:** Varas et al., "Government Incentives and US Competitiveness in Semiconductor Manu- facturing."

325 **"realizing the Chinese dream":** Cheng Ting-Fang and Lauly Li, "How China's Chip Industry Defied the Coronavirus Lockdown," *Nikkei Asia*, March 18, 2020.

CHAPTER 53 **Shortages and Supply Chains**

327 **"We have to step up our game":** "Remarks by President Biden at a Virtual CEO Summit on Semiconductor and Supply Chain Resilience," The White House, April 12, 2021; Alex Fang and Yifan Yu, "US to Lead World Again, Biden Tells CEOs at Semiconductor Summit," *Nikkei Asia*, April 13, 2021.

328 **$210 billion:** AAPC Submission to the BIS Commerce Department Semicon- ductor Supply Chain Review, April 5, 2021; Michael Wayland, "Chip Shortage Expected to Cost Auto Industry $210 Billion in Revenue in 2021," CNBC, Sep- tember 23, 2021.

328 **13 percent increase:** "Semiconductor Units Forecast to Exceed 1 Trillion Devices Again in 2021," *IC Insights*, April 7, 2021, https://www.icinsights.com /news/bulletins/Semiconductor-Units-Forecast-To-Exceed-1-Trillion-Devices -Again-In-2021/.

330 **"with industry, allies, and partners":** "Fact Sheet: Biden-Harris Adminis- tration Announces Supply Chain Disruptions Task Force," June 8, 2021, https:// www.whitehouse.gov/briefing-room/statements-releases/2021/06/08/fact-sheet -biden-harris-administration-announces-supply-chain-disruptions-task-force -to-address-short-term-supply-chain-discontinuities/.

330 **"work with business as one team":** Kotaro Hosokawa, "Samsung Turns South Korea Garrison City into Chipmaking Boom Town," *Nikkei Asia*, June 20, 2021.

330 **"economic factors":** Jiyoung Sohn, "Samsung to Invest $205 Billion in Chip, Biotech Expansion," *Wall Street Journal*, August 24, 2021; Song Jung-a and Edward White, "South Korean PM Backs Early Return to Work for Paroled Sam- sung Chief Lee Jae-yong," *Financial Times*, August 30, 2021.

331 **restrict the transfer of EUV tools:** Stephen Nellis, Joyce Lee, and Toby Sterling, "Exclusive: U.S.-China Tech War Clouds SK Hynix's Plans for a Key Chip Factory," Reuters, November 17, 2021.

331 **make Taiwanese exports more competitive:** Brad W. Setser, "Shadow FX Intervention in Taiwan: Solving a 100+ Billion Dollar Enigma (Part 1)," Council on Foreign Relations, October 3, 2019.

331 **European Union leaders have suggested:** "Speech by Commissioner Thierry Breton at Hannover Messe Digital Days," European Commission, July 15, 2020.

332 **in partnership with Sony:** Cheng Ting-Fang and Lauly Li, "TSMC Says It Will Build First Japan Chip Plant with Sony," *Nikkei Asia*, November 9, 2021.

333   **"we get to decide where the fabs are"**: Christiaan Hetzner, "Intel CEO Says 'Big, Honkin' Fab' Planned for Europe Will Be World's Most Advanced," *Fortune,* September 10, 2021; Leo Kelion, "Intel Chief Pat Gelsinger: Too Many Chips Made in Asia," BBC News, March 24, 2021.

CHAPTER 54   The Taiwan Dilemma

335   **"Are your customers concerned"**: "Edited Transcript: 2330.TW - Q2 2021 Taiwan Semiconductor Manufacturing Co Ltd Earnings Call," *Refinitiv,* July 15, 2021, https://investor.tsmc.com/english/encrypt/files/encrypt_file /reports/2021-10/44ec4960f6771366a2b992ace4ae47566d7206a6/TSMC%20 2Q21%20transcript.pdf.

336   **firing their guns as they went:** Liu Xuanzun, "PLA Holds Beach Assault Drills After US Military Aircraft's Taiwan Island Landing," *Global Times,* July 18, 2021.

336   **"resolutely safeguard national sovereignty":** Liu Xuanzun, "PLA Holds Drills in All Major Chinese Sea Areas Amid Consecutive US Military Provocations," *Global Times,* July 20, 2021.

336   **pieces of soft salami:** Chris Dougherty, Jennie Matuschak, and Ripley Hunter, "The Poison Frog Strategy," Center for a New American Security, October 26, 2021.

337   **tough fight:** "Military and Security Developments Involving the People's Republic of China," Annual Report to Congress, Office of the Secretary of Defense, 2020, p. 114.

337   **systems sitting on Chinese territory:** Lonnie Henley, "PLA Operational Concepts and Centers of Gravity in a Taiwan Conflict," testimony before the U.S.-China Economic and Security Review Commission Hearing on Cross-Strait Deterrence, February 18, 2021.

338   **"non-peaceful means":** Michael J. Green, "What Is the U.S. 'One China' Policy, and Why Does it Matter?" Center for Strategic and International Studies, January 13, 2017.

341   **couldn't acquire enough semiconductors:** Debby Wu, "Chip Linchpin ASML Joins Carmakers Warning of Vicious Cycle," *Bloomberg,* January 19, 2022.

341   **Tsai Ing-wen recently argued:** Tsai Ing-wen, "Taiwan and the Fight for Democracy," *Foreign Affairs,* November–December 2021.

342   **most Taiwanese reported thinking:** Sherry Hsiao, "Most Say Cross-Strait War Unlikely: Poll," *Taipei Times,* October 21, 2020.

342   **wrenching delays due to problems sourcing semiconductors:** Ivan Cheberko, "Kosmicheskii Mashtab Importozameshcheniia," *Vedomosti,* September 27, 2020.

342   **full of foreign microelectronics:** Jack Watling and Nick Reynolds, "Operation Z: The Death Throes of an Imperial Delusion," Royal United Services Institute, April 22, 2022, pp. 10–12.

342   **up to 95 percent of Russian munitions:** Michael Simpson et al., "Road to Damascus: The Russian Air Campaign in Syria," Rand Corporation, RR-A1170-1, 2022, p. 80.

342   **over 200 semiconductors each:** Rebecca Shabad, "Biden Emphasizes the Need to Keep Arming Ukraine in Tour of Alabama Weapons Plant," CNBC, May 3, 2022.

343 **cut off the Kremlin:** Sebastian Moss, "Intel and AMD Halt Chip Sales to Russia, TSMC Joins in on Sanctions," Data Center Dynamics, February 28, 2022, https://www.datacenterdynamics.com/en/news/intel-and-amd-halt-chip-sales-to-russia-tsmc-joins-in-on-sanctions/.

343 **chips intended for dishwashers:** Jeanne Whalen, "Sanctions Forcing Russia to Use Appliance Parts in Military Gear," *Washington Post*, May 11, 2022.

343 **"we must seize TSMC":** "Top Economist Urges China to Seize TSMC if US Ramps Up Sanctions," *Bloomberg News*, June 7, 2022.

343 **in 2021 these airbases were upgraded:** Keoni Everington, "China Expands Its 2 Air Force Bases Closest to Taiwan," *Taiwan News*, March 8, 2021; Minnie Chan, "Upgrades for Chinese Military Airbases Facing Taiwan Hint at War Plans," *South China Morning Post*, October 15, 2021; "Major Construction Underway at Three of China's Airbases Closest to Taiwan," *Drive*, October 13, 2021.

Conclusion

345 **made from semiconductor materials:** Jack Kilby, "Invention of the Integrated Circuit," *IEEE Transactions on Electron Devices* 23, No. 7 (July 1976): 650.

345 **engineers like Weldon Word:** Paul G. Gillespie, "Precision Guided Munitions: Constructing a Bomb More Potent Than the A-Bomb," PhD dissertation, Lehigh University, p. 115. Word appears to have started work at TI in 1953, according to his posthumously available LinkedIn page. I was unable to confirm this.

346 **"home computers":** Gordon E. Moore, "Cramming More Components onto Integrated Circuits," *Electronics* 38, No. 8 (April 19, 1965).

346 **than there are cells in the human body:** Dan Hutcheson, "Graphic: Transistor Production Has Reached Astronomical Scales," *IEEE Spectrum*, April 2, 2015.

347 **"I . . . WANT . . . TO . . . GET . . . RICH":** Michael Malone, *The Intel Trinity* (Michael Collins, 2014), p. 31.

348 **declared Moore's Law dead:** John Hennessy, "The End of Moore's Law and Faster General-Purpose Processors, and a New Path Forward," National Science Foundation, CISE Distinguished Lecture, November 22, 2019, https://www.nsf.gov/events/event_summ.jsp?cntn_id=299531&org=NSF.

348 **bashed through a decade later:** Andrey Ovsyannikov, "Update from Intel: Insights into Intel Innovations for HPC and AI," Intel, September 26, 2019, https://www2.cisl.ucar.edu/sites/default/files/Ovsyannikov%20-%20MC9%20-%20Presentation%20Slides.pdf.

348 **"radical idea":** Gordon E. Moore, "No Exponential Is Forever: But 'Forever' Can Be Delayed!" IEEE International Solid-State Circuits Conference, 2003.

349 **a hundred times as many transistors:** Hoeneisen and Mead, "Fundamental Limitations on Microelectronics," pp. 819–829; Scotten Jones, "TSMC and Samsung 5nm Comparison," *SemiWiki*, May 3, 2019, https://semiwiki.com/semiconductor-manufacturers/samsung-foundry/8157-tsmc-and-samsung-5nm-comparison/.

349 **a clear path toward a fifty times increase in the density:** "Jim Keller: Moore's Law Is Not Dead," UC Berkeley EECS Events, YouTube Video, September 18, 2019, 22:00, https://www.youtube.com/watch?v=oIG9ztQw2Gc.

350   **"slow lane":** Neil C. Thompson and Svenja Spanuth, "The Decline of Computers as a General Purpose Technology: Why Deep Learning and the End of Moore's Law Are Fragmenting Computing," working paper, MIT, November 2018, https://ide.mit.edu/wp-content/uploads/2018/11/SSRN-id3287769.pdf.

350   **combine different types of chips:** "Heterogeneous Compute: The Paradigm Shift No One Is Talking About," *Fabricated Knowledge*, February 19, 2020, https://www.fabricatedknowledge.com/p/heterogeneous-compute-the-paradigm.

351   **singing amid the snowdrifts:** Kevin Xu, "Morris Chang's Last Speech," *Interconnected*, September 12, 2021, https://interconnected.blog/morris-changs-last-speech/.

Index